COUNTRIES, REGIONAL STUDIES, TRADING BLOCKS, UNIONS, WORLD ORGANIZATIONS

HEALTH, VIOLENCE, ENVIRONMENT AND HUMAN DEVELOPMENT IN DEVELOPING COUNTRIES

COUNTRIES, REGIONAL STUDIES, TRADING BLOCKS, UNIONS, WORLD ORGANIZATIONS

Additional books in this series can be found on Nova's website under the Series tab.

Additional e-books in this series can be found on Nova's website under the e-book tab.

COUNTRIES, REGIONAL STUDIES, TRADING BLOCKS, UNIONS, WORLD ORGANIZATIONS

HEALTH, VIOLENCE, ENVIRONMENT AND HUMAN DEVELOPMENT IN DEVELOPING COUNTRIES

ALEXANDER COTTE POVEDA
AND
CLARA INÉS PARDO MARTÍNEZ
EDITORS

nova publishers
New York

For permission to use material from this book please contact us:
Telephone 631-231-7269; Fax 631-231-8175
Web Site: http://www.novapublishers.com

Library of Congress Cataloging-in-Publication Data

Health, violence, environment and human development in developing countries / editors,
Alexander Cotte Poveda and Clara Inis Pardo Martinez.
pages cm
Includes index.
ISBN 978-1-62948-038-1 (hardcover)
1. Sustainable development--Developing countries. 2. Environmental health--Developing countries. 3. Violence--Economic aspects--Developing countries. I. Poveda, Alexander Cotte. II. Inis Pardo Martinez, Clara.
HC59.72.E5H425 2013
320.609172'4--dc23

2013033665

Published by Nova Science Publishers, Inc. † New York

CONTENTS

PREFACE

Currently, developing countries seek to maintain a sustained long-term growth as a key issue for increasing the welfare of their populations. Topics such as health, violence and the environment are decisive factors for strengthening human development and achieving sustainable development in these countries that have a variety of resources but also have problems with corruption and governance. It is for this reason that this book, which focuses on health, violence, environment and human development from the different perspectives of these countries, is integral for furthering a well-founded discussion of this topic.

Achieving human development and greater sustainability in developing countries requires improvements to the health systems and increase in environmentally friendly production, while controlling violence and urbanisation problems. These objectives can be facilitated through policy and government initiatives as well as empowerment and innovation strategies developed by communities. This book combines different scientific approaches for enhancing our understanding of human development by analysing health, violence and the environment in several developing countries. This text will be essential reading for anyone that is interested in strengthening human development in developing countries and formulating new strategies for improving health and sustainability development, while decreasing violence and urbanisation problems.

The book is organised as follows. Cutolo and Giatti discuss environmental health from an inequities approach in the Metropolitan Region of São Paulo, Brazil. In Chapter 2, Wartchow and Daronco demonstrate the importance of municipal sanitation plans to achieve millennial developmental goals in a Brazilian context.

The following two chapters focus on health and development in Nigeria. Idowu's analysis of geographic information systems may be a solution for public health problems. In Chapter 4, Ogujiuba and Omoju discuss health poverty traps and their main implications for economic development.

Chapters 5, 6, 7, 8, and 9 relate, in different ways, to human development in Colombia. In Chapter 5, Cotte explains crime and violence from different econometric approaches. In Chapter 6, Correa discusses the importance of water for decreasing poverty in the Colombian Orinoquia region. In Chapter 7, Carmona and Ocampo evaluate the environmental performance of Bus Rapid Transit and its contribution to public policy in Bogotá. In Chapter 8, Pardo describes the effects of urbanisation and suburbanisation on health in the Bogotá region. In Chapter 9, Cotte evaluates violence and social aspects in cities.

Chapters 10 and 11 demonstrate the elements of sustainable development in Peruvian regions. In Chapter 10, Rodriguez applies dynamic systems to analyse river basins, while in Chapter 11, Martinez-Valderrama, Martinez-Vicente and Rodriguez evaluate the economic, ecological and social aspects of the Libertad region of Peru using dynamic systems.

Human and sustainable development demands new strategies, solutions, and policy-making approaches. This book discusses a wide spectrum of studies on how to achieve ambitious policy goals for addressing human development, health and violence in developing countries, from analysing how different strategies can be designed and improved to contributing to the development and economic growth in these countries.

About the Editors

Clara Ines Pardo Martinez

Clara has 10 years professional experience working as professor in several Colombian Universities, as consultant different private and public sectors in topics related to HSEQ management systems with the International standards ISO 9001, ISO 14001 and OHSAS 18001, energy management systems and clean production (this includes the design, development, implementation and audit of the management system, development of training in management systems) and as researcher in the Wuppertal Institute (with research focus on energy efficiency in the manufacturing industries using econometric analysis with the following software Eviews, Stata, SPSS and EMS). She joined the Energy and Climate Studies program in February 2011 as a researcher in the field of energy efficiency in the industrial sector.

Alexander Cotte Poveda

ALEXANDER COTTE POVEDA is professor of Development Economics, Economic Theory and Economic Growth at La Salle University in Bogotá Colombia. He has published numerous articles in refereed journals, among them the Journal Oxford Development Studies; Journal of International Development; Socio-Economic Planning Sciences; Journal Peace Economics, Peace Science and Public Policy; Journal Quality and Quantity; Journal Energy Systems and Journal Social Indicators Research. He is member Editorial Board of the Emerging Markets Case Studies. Most of his current research is in the field of political economy, Development Politics, Economic and Violence, Poverty, Inequality, Economic Growth, Energy and Human Capital.

Scientific Committee

In: Health, Violence, Environment and Human Development … ISBN: 978-1-62948-038-1
Editors: A. Cotte Poveda and C. I. Pardo Martínez

Chapter 1

A Different Look at Environmental Health: Social and Environmental Inequities in the Metropolitan Region of São Paulo, Brazil

***Silvana Audrá Cutolo*[*] *and Leandro Luiz Giatti*[†]**
Departamento de Saúde Ambiental, Universidade de São Paulo,
São Paulo (SP), Brazil

Abstract

The concentration of large populations in metropolitan areas is a great matter of interest in the field of public health, especially in developing countries. Although the metropolization process is considered a worldwide phenomenon, this trend is accentuated in low and medium income countries considered as emerging countries of Asia, Africa and Latin America. In the process of metropolization, irreversible impacts were observed on the natural environment, including with respect to pressures on environmental services. In this chapter, the Metropolitan Region of São Paulo in São Paulo (Brazil) is the object of study focused on the analysis of the occupation of watershed protection areas, which provide environmental services and social inequalities, which may be relevant in the context of violence, reflected as a matter of public and environmental health. We used data from Brazilian public institutions, allowing verifying the relations between inequalities in socioeconomic and environmental health of the Metropolitan Region of São Paulo (MRSP), state of São Paulo, Brazil. We applied a critical analysis to contextualize the 39 municipalities' components of the MRSP with about 20 million inhabitants. The city of São Paulo has a forceful representation as headquarters of the metropolis, with 11.253.503 inhabitants in 2010 with GDP of R$ 389 billion and GDP / capita of R$ 35,271.9 in 2009.As for this economic indicator, we note that the inequality is large, ranging from the highest in the city of Barueri with the lowest R$ 99,595.7 in Francisco Morato with R$ 5,492.6 in 2009. However, the environmental and health inequalities are presented in forms of spatialization with the economic disparities. Thus, under the condition of relevant environmental services providers, we focus the discussion on distinct patterns of inequalities that occur in municipalities with a significant portion

[*] cutolosa@usp.br.
[†] lgiatti@usp.br.

of the watershed protection area, providing water to the city of São Paulo. In this condition, exploring the aspect of violence as an important indicator of public health, we observed an increase in the rate of homicides in Mairiporã with 49.9 in 2001 to 53.1 per 100,000 inhabitants in 2009 and Juquitiba with 36.7 in 2001 to 68.2 per 100,000 inhabitants in 2009, while Francisco Morato (45.9 in 2001 to 21.6 per 100,000 inhabitants in 2009) and Taboão Serra (84.6 in 2001 to 19.4 per 100,000 inhabitants in 2009). The urban segregation and social exclusion can be considered as some of the factors associated with increased violence. Concluding Remarks, the watershed areas in MRSP can be considered the most fragile areas by the presence of remnants of green areas, are providers of ecosystem services and suppliers of water to metropolis, and where overlapping social inequities as the areas of greatest violence and environmental degradation. It can be inferred that the environmental and social problems such as violence and inequities in watershed areas can be compounded with the possible exacerbation of climate phenomena.

Keywords: Public Health, Metropolitan Region of São Paulo, violence, watershed protection area

1. Introduction

The concentration of large populations in metropolitan areas is a matter of great interest in the field of public health, especially in developing countries. Although the metropolization process is considered a worldwide phenomenon, this trend is accentuated in low and medium income countries considered as emerging countries of Asia, Africa and Latin America. Among the 49 largest cities in the world in 1890, 42 were in the called First World, while seven were in the Third World. Among the 50 largest cities in the world in 2000, 11 were in the First World and the other in developing or emerging countries. This trend increases, especially with the late urbanization of countries in Asia and Africa, notably China and India. In 2025 it is estimated that Asia will have 10 to 11 cities with over 20 million inhabitants (Maricato, 2011; Davis, 2006).

According to estimates of the United Nations (2007), the urban world population should continue to grow faster than the growth of world population. As a consequence, the world's urban population today of 3,5 billion (50.6%), should reach 4,9 billion (59.7%) in 2030 and 6,4 billion (69.6%) in 2050. In Latin America, the situation is even more alarming, with 79.4% of the population now living in urban areas, with the prospect of increasing to 88.7% by 2050. This means that 682,551 people from 769,229 million people expected for the year 2050 will be living in urban areas in this region. However, despite the alarming figures, according to ECLAC - Economic Commission for Latin America and the Caribbean, the economy of Latin America and the Caribbean is around 6% of the world´s Gross Domestic Product (GDP) and the share in the global exports of countries reaches 20% (Philippi Jr and Coutinho, 2011). Urban development in Latin America and the Caribbean, by contrast, is characterized by intense urbanization in major cities, although the future trend of the urban population increase is directed to smaller cities. In Latin America about 14% of the urban population lives in megacities, Sao Paulo and Mexico City are among the five most populated cities in the world (Philippi Jr and Coutinho, 2011). In 2000, a fifth of the urban population lived in cities of five million or more, usually in the capital (Philippi Jr e Coutinho, 2011; UNITED NATIONS/HABITAT, 2008).

The expansion of the metropolitan regions and peripheries can be caused both by the arrival of new migrants and by the sub-urbanization of the middle class out of the central city (Cohen, 2006). In Latin America, the largest cities like Mexico City, Buenos Aires, Santiago and São Paulo have had dramatic expansion of economic activities and urban population into regional metropolitan peripheries and beyond the suburbs (Iglesias et al., 2007).

A significant part of the population lives in squatter settlements as slums and dwellings which are often built in hazardous areas as riverbanks, mountain slopes and areas of watershed protection (Tucci, 2010). Several authors have attempted to the effects of metropolitan expansion on natural environmental areas with illegal occupation of nature reserves, degradation of watershed, lack of infrastructure in sanitation, increasing the risk of areas supply with chemical and organic pollution, contamination of rivers by industrial and diffuse loads from household sewage, floods generated by the urban poor use of space and the inadequate management of urban drainage, and, finally, the lack of collection and waste disposal (Giatti and Cutolo, 2012).

Rapid urbanization in developing countries, transforming troubled midsize cities in the other metropolises or megacities, consequently making the high vulnerability of urban populations, particularly those that live in squatter settlements, informal and marginal (IPCC, 2012). The impact of urbanization in developing countries in the natural environment has become in an irreversible due to the chaotic and disorganized (Iglesias et al., 2007). According to IPCC (2012), socioeconomic development interacts with natural climate variations and human-caused climate change to influence disaster risk (Figure 1). Impacts from weather and climate events depend on: 1) Disaster risk with nature and severity of event - the likelihood of severe alterations in the normal functioning of a community or society due to weather or climate events interacting with vulnerable social conditions; 2) Vulnerability (The concept of vulnerability can be understood as the state of a system exposed to risks, conditioned by socio-cultural and biophysical factors at different temporal and spatial scales combined with their capacity to respond (INCLINE, 2013)) as the predisposition of a person or group to be adversely affected; and 3) Exposure as the presence of people; livelihoods; environmental services and resources; infrastructure; or economic, social, or cultural assets in places that could be adversely affected.

Millions of people with low adaptive capacity increases as: malnutrition with implications for child growth and development; deaths, disease and injury due to heat waves, floods, storms, fires and droughts; diarrhoeal diseases; and frequency of cardiorespiratory diseases. In many countries around the world, communities are differentially exposed and vulnerable based on inequalities expressed through levels of wealth and education, disability and health status. Patterns of informal settlements as slums or favelas and occupation of marginal areas on urbanization process have influenced observed trends in exposure and vulnerability to climate extremes (IPCC, 2012).

There is evidence that extreme events are associated with anthropogenic influences such as carbon emissions and increase gas into the atmosphere. In the process of urbanization, there is an increase in temperature associated with the sources of atmospheric emissions, reduction of green areas, assisting in the formation of heat islands, with heavy rainfall events and extreme with flooding and landslides in tropical countries and common in Latin America, which has complex river basin systems and mountainous terrain (Rubin and Rossing, 2012).

Pollution effects may also play a significant role in controlling precipitation in large urban areas primarily through the radiation balance with a cooling effect at the surface due to scattering of solar radiation by aerosols. This effect reduces the sensible heat flux at the surface and thus has a potentially negative impact on precipitation (Dias et al., 2012).

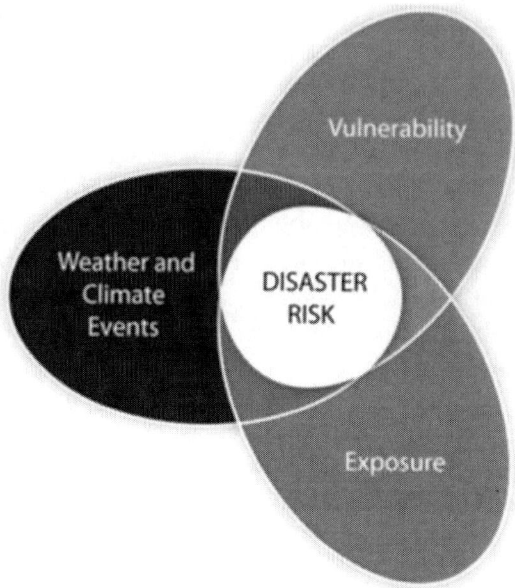

Source: IPCC, 2012.

Figure 1. Climate events, exposure and vulnerability.

Climate change may have many other indirect negative effects as some authors argue about the relation of elevated temperatures with aggressive behaviors or reactions that can increase violence and violent crimes (Anderson, 2001; Backer et al., 2002; Larrick et al., 2011). In this sense although the urban heat islands have been more concentrated in the central areas of the MRSP, the peripheral sprawl typically concentrating poverty and lack of infrastructure and social services (Santos, 2009) could be viewed as a potential factor in association with the climate variability leading to worse scenarios of urban violence. This could be relevant especially in the context of the municipalities with large areas under watershed protection.

In the case of water resources for urban purposes, including water supply, wastewater and stormwater, climate variability can be considered as a risk, especially in relation to changes in the hydrological cycle. It is likely that the frequency of heavy precipitation or the proportion of total heavy precipitation will increase in particular in tropical countries and will change in fluvial floods and in local flooding in some watersheds (IPCC, 2012). Besides the evidences about climate changes, natural ecosystems are being changed faster, often seriously degraded in terms of the ecosystem services they provide for humans and their activities (Likens, 2001).

Water is widely regarded as the most essential of the natural resources, yet freshwater systems are directly threatened by human activities and stand to be further affected by anthropogenic climate change. Water systems are transformed through widespread land cover change, urbanization, industrialization and engineering schemes like reservoirs, irrigation and interbasins transfers that maximize human access to water. The benefits of water provision to economic productivity are often accompanied by impairment to ecosystems and biodiversity, with potentially serious but unquantified costs (Vörösmarty et al., 2010).

Migration of the rural population to urban centres has resulted in towns and cities expanding rapidly. The increasing concentration of populations in urban areas and the growth of large cities place a strain on existing public services and, together with prevailing economic realities, result in chaotic conditions in many towns and cities throughout the developing world. According to a study by WHO and UNICEF, the number of urban residents without access to improved water sources in fact rose from 113 million in 1990 (5% of the total urban population) to 173 million in 2000 (6% of the total urban population). Water supply to cities is crucial not only for the survival of its inhabitants but also to maintain a healthy level of economic development. Awareness of what happens when there is a lack of water is all too apparent in many third world cities, where poor living conditions and limited access to adequate water and sanitation significantly increase the health burden on the urban poor, who often constitute the very labour source that generates the cities' wealth (Kala et al., 2008).

In developing countries, cities were growing in extent and spreading without planning and control, creating metropolitan areas or mega-cities. In Brazilian such urban centres, there are irregular areas of occupation as watershed protection areas were occupied by squatter settlements, where fragmentation of Atlantic Forest remnants can be observed, and also degradation of water quality and population explosion with high social vulnerability, which can be described as social exclusion. According to Salgado de Snyder et al. (2011):

> "Social exclusion refers to the systematic denial for certain social groups of the resources and recognition that could facilitate their full participation in the society. These processes operate along and interact across four dimensions—cultural, economic, political, and social—and at different levels including individuals, groups, households, communities, countries, and global regions. These processes result in a continuum of inclusion/exclusion and contribute to unequal access to resources, capabilities, and rights required for human development, valued recognition, involvement and engagement, social proximity, decision making, material well-being, living within environmental limits, and resisting the hazards of environmental change".

2. Objective and Method

In this chapter, the Metropolitan Region of São Paulo in São Paulo State (Brazil) is the object of study focused on the analysis of the urban occupation of watershed protection areas, which provide environmental services associated with social inequalities. Our hypothesis in this study is that aspects of the multidisciplinary vulnerability can be explored besides a direct causality, being possible to find interrelationship between socio-economic, environmental and health indicators in complex scenarios with consideration of possible climatic change consequences. In this sense we aim at verifying asymmetries between metropolitan municipalities regarding socioeconomic conditions and the provisioning of environmental services such as water supply, as much as focusing violence as a public health indicator, capable of association with environmental factors such as heat and occupation of urban areas of watershed protection.

Our arguments and discussions embrace a wider view of the driving forces, situations and effects concerning to the relationships between social, economic and environmental conditions and vulnerable population in a metropolitan region. In order to make possible the necessary dialectic within such different information, the study was conducted exploring secondary data and indicators provided by some Brazilian public institutes. The main sources were provided by IBGE - Brazilian Institute of Geography and Statistics, and by the DATASUS – the Ministry of Health's Information Department's database.

In order to analyse the socio-economic and demographic processes which affect the region, the environment and human health, we have applied the DPSEEA matrix (Driving Forces – Pressures – State – Exposure – Effects - Action) proposed by the World Health Organization - WHO (Corvalán et al., 2000). The main advantage of this model over other indicator models of sustainability is the possibility to consider in depth the environmental exposure of human beings in different socio-environmental situations and the effect of this on health.

With this framework, exploring interrelationship between data from different sectors (i.e. demographic, economic, mortality rates, watershed protection area) is possible and allows showing a panorama of conditions and trends making possible environmental health studies, even aggregating indirect effects of the socio-environmental problems. In the developing countries the interpersonal violence causes of morbidity and mortality can be attributed with a burden of 16% to environmental factors (Prüss-Üstün and Corvalán, 2006), like urban planning, urban design. In this context the urban heating acting as a physic environmental factor can be understood as one more component to the complex and precarious living conditions in the periphery municipalities of the RMSP, which joined with irregular occupation, poverty and lack of infrastructure and social services lead to a singular scenario of vulnerability.

3. Characterization of Metropolitan Region of São Paulo, State of São Paulo, Brazil

The climate of Brazil comprises a wide range of weather conditions across a large area and varied topography, but most of the country is tropical. Brazil has six major climatic subtypes: equatorial, tropical, semiarid, highland tropical, temperate, and subtropical.

In Brazil, the natural water resource is extremely abundant, distributed in 8,511,928 km^2 as watershed and extensive coastline. However the availability and distribution of those goods are quite irregular, with the existence of rivers such as the Amazon, as opposed to scarcity of the northeast region. Moreover, the southern and southeastern of Brazil have rivers with serious pollution problems of domestic and industrial sources (Tundisi et al., 2008).

The surface water resources in Brazil represent 50% of total resources in South America and 11% of global resources, totaling 168,870 m^3/s. The Brazilian Amazon represents 71.1% of the total flow generated in Brazil and therefore 36.6% of the total generated in South America and 8,0% at the global level. Considering the total flow of the Amazon river throughout Brazil, the proportion is 81.1% of the national total. Considering this volume, the total freshwater flowing from Brazil represents 77,0% of total South America and 17,0% at the global level (Tucci 2010).

The Brazilian population increased significantly between 1940 and 1970 due to a decline in the mortality rate, even though the birth rate has also experienced a slight decline in the period. In the 1940s the rate of annual population growth was 2.4%, rising to 3.0% in 1950 and remaining at 2.9% in 1960, with the life expectancy rising from 44 to 54 years and to 72.6 years in 2007. The rate of population growth has declined since 1960, from 3.04% per year between 1950-1960 to 1.05% in 2008, with the perspective of falling to a negative value of -0.29% by 2050, thus completing the demographic transition.

However, there is population growth in urban areas and suburbs transformed into urban, mega-cities or metropolitan areas, due to internal migration and overseas to Brazil in search of better living conditions as a result of growth Brazil's economic. The largest metropolitan areas in Brazil are São Paulo, Rio de Janeiro and Belo Horizonte, all in the Southeast, with 19.5, 11.5 and 5.1 million respectively. From the 1960s to the 1990s, the city of São Paulo experienced a territorial growth of 40%, resulting in the removal of 31% of the vegetative cover. Forests were replaced with inadequately planned roads that cut into the deep valleys and hillsides, and many slums were built (Meyer et al., 2004).

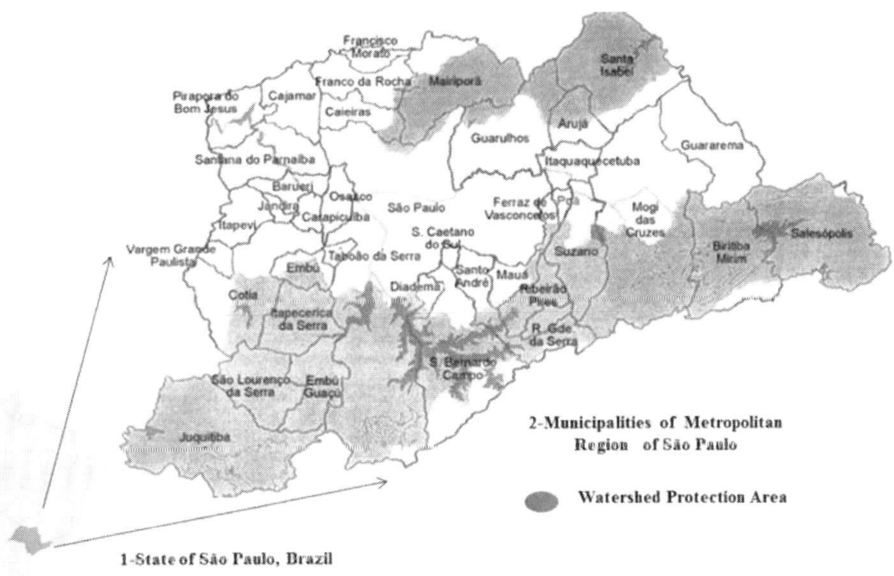

Source: http://sigam.ambiente.sp.gov.br.

Figure 2. Metropolitan Region of São Paulo with 39 municipalities in State of São Paulo, Brazil. Note: the municipalities in highlighted are Watershed Protection Area.

The topography and proximity to the sea (about 70 km) are factors that influence the climate of the metropolitan area. The cold weather is coming from the Atlantic Ocean and reaches the southern escarpment MRSP. The relief above 760 m altitude causes a considerable drop in temperatures, especially at night. Therefore, the climate of the Metropolitan Region of São Paulo is considered subtropical with cool winters and dry, and humid summers and storms floods and landslides. The presence of areas of Atlantic forest, proximity to the coast and humidity are factors that create different microclimates in the municipalities of MRSP.

The MRSP, similar to other large Brazilian and Latin America urban centres, has grown dramatically since the 1950s. This has been accompanied by a multifarious process of peripheralization, where poverty is particularly widespread, leading to an urban fabric that is extremely unequal in spatial terms and where essential public services have not kept up with the speed with which the metropolitan area has been expanding or with the needs of its population (Santos, 2009).

Nowadays, urbanized area corresponds to 2209 km². Between 1962 and 2002, the urban area of 874 km² passed to 2209 km². The Metropolitan Region of São Paulo, also known as Greater São Paulo, gathers 39 municipalities of the state of São Paulo in intense process of conurbation, with their municipalities forming one continuous urban sprawl. MRSP comprises 39 municipalities in an area of 7947 Km^2 with a population around 19.6 million inhabitants, the largest population concentration in Brazil (EMPLASA, 2011) as shown in Figure 2. São Paulo is the sixth largest city of the planet and its metropolitan area is the fourth largest agglomeration in the world.

3.1. Gross Domestic Product (GDP) and Monthly Income per Capita up of MRSP

The GDP was R$ 613.1 billion in 2009, that is, approximately 18.9% of the Brazilian national GDP (PARLAMENTO METROPOLITANO, 2012), representing the largest concentration of wealth in the country. The region is an important national and international financial centre and a hub for service provision in the areas of tourism, leisure, health and education, as well as for industrial activities (EMPLASA, 2011). The central city is São Paulo which concentrates 11.2 million inhabitants (IBGE, 2010), besides having the biggest population this municipality exert a strong force under the metropolitan conurbation, its GDP was R$ 389,3 billion in 2009 (IBGE, 2011), being the highest municipal GDP in Brazil.

As the municipality of São Paulo concentrates wealth it also occurs to some of the municipalities which are contiguous to this centrality. Such situation is possible to analyze in the territory of the MRSP through the Figure 3, where municipalities with lower percentages of low income households are centralized, on the other hand higher municipalities with higher percentages of low income households are typically distributed in the periphery. In this figure we adopted the percentage of households with monthly income per capita up to 1/2 Brazilian minimum wage, this category of low income is similar to each person in certain household living with up to US$ 4,88 per day, by applying monetary values of January 1st, 2010.

3.2. Watershed Protection Area and Homicide Rate in the MRSP

The accelerated economic development of the last decades is reflected in the demography of the region, the demands for environmental services and pressure on the various ecosystems. Between 2000 and 2010 the population in the MRSP grew by 10.1% whilst the demand for the public provision of drinking water grew by 14.2%.

Figure 3 shows the municipalities of MRSP distributed over the sub-watersheds in the territory, meanwhile Table 1 brings the percentage of each municipality under watershed protected area, population, water demand per capita, homicides rate as an indicator of health.

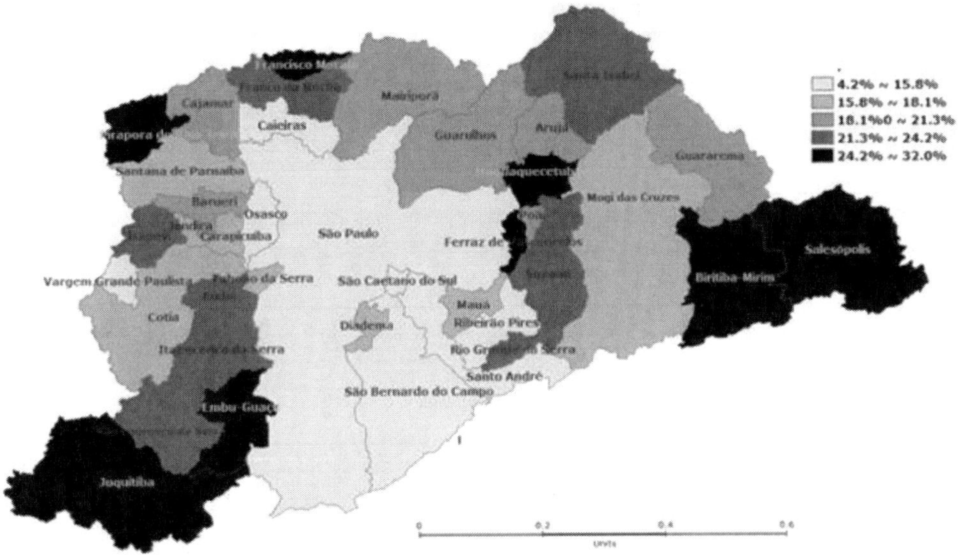

Source: IBGE, 2010.

Figure 3. Metropolitan Region of São Paulo Households with Monthly Income per capita up to 1/2 Brazilian minimum wage (%) – 2010.

Table 1. Values of the number of inhabitants, water demand per capita, percent of municipalities in areas of watershed protection and homicide rate in the MRSP

Municipalities	Inhabitants[1]	Water Demand[2] Liter per capita/day	Percent of Municipal area in Watershed Protection Area[2]	Homicides Rates/100000 Inhabitants[3]
ALTO TIETÊ-BILLINGS				
Diadema	386.089	135,28	22	26.4
Guararema	25.844	WI	WI	37.1
Ribeirão Pires	113.068	137,87	100	28.3
Rio Grande da Serra	43.974	122,96	100	31.2
Santo André	676.407	167,71	54	24
São Bernardo do Campo	765.463	160,09	53	14.4
TIETÊ-CABECEIRAS				
Arujá	74.905	144,48	51	7.4
Biritiba Mirim	28.575	111,73	89	WI
Ferraz de Vasconcelos	168.306	105,98	40	12.3
Guarulhos	1.221.979	122,75	30	14.0
Itaquaquecetuba	321.770	103,57	WI	41.5
Mogi da Cruzes	387.779	118,77	49	14.4
Poá	106.013	114,97	6	8.9
Salesópolis	15.635	114,78	98	12.5
Santa Isabel	50.453	WI	82	12.8
Suzano	262.480	WI	72	21.8
COTIA-GUARAPIRANGA				
Cotia	201.150	149,19	65	17.6

Municipalities	Inhabitants[1]	Water Demand[2] Liter per capita/day	Percent of Municipal area in Watershed Protection Area2	Homicides Rates/100000 Inhabitants[3]
Embu das Artes	240.230	117,41	59	29.8
Embu-Guaçu	62.769	127,07	100	17.7
Itapecerica da Serra	152.614	122,69	100	36.4
Juquitiba	28.737	WI	100	68.2
São Lourenço da Serra	13.973	178,09	100	10.9
Vargem Grande Paulista	42.997	WI	WI	11.2
JUQUERI-CANTAREIRA				
Caieiras	86.529	112,48	20	14.7
Cajamar	64.114	121,32	WI	31.4
Francisco Morato	154.472	101,52	WI	21.6
Franco da Rocha	131.604	119,38	5	22.1
PENHA-PINHEIROS				
Mairiporã	80.956	92,52	80	53.1
Mauá	417.064	118,07	19	28.3
São Caetano do Sul	149.263	254,45	WI	5.3
São Paulo	11.253.503	168,78	36	11.2
Taboão da Serra	244.528	125,56	WI	19.4
PINHEIROS-PIRAPORA				
Barueri	240.749	165,53	WI	14.8
Carapicuiba	369.584	124,34	WI	21.9
Itapevi	200.769	106,71	WI	19.4
Jandira	108.344	109,46	100	25
Osasco	666.740	167,53	WI	24.5
Pirapora do Bom Jesus	15.733	130,73	WI	25.,5
Santana do Parnaíba	108.813	212,38	WI	4.4

Notes: WI-without information; in highlighted is the municipalities in Watershed Protection Area in percentage as Figure 1.

Source:

[1]IBGE, 2010;

[2]http://sigam.ambiente.sp.gov.br; [3]DATASUS (2009); Information System of Mortality (Vieira et al., 2012).

The map below shows the location of the sub-basins the MRSP as Alto Tietê-Billings, Tietê-Cabeceiras, Cotia-Guarapiranga, Juqueri-Cantareira, Penha-Pinheiros, Pinheiros-Pirapora (Figure 4).

Overall, the Watershed Protection Areas (WPAs) represents 54% of the MRSP territory, distributed within 25 municipalities (Figure 1) which are undergoing into rapid population growth and with environmental and social degradation, where more than 2 million live people in risk areas as slums or squatter settlements. The total area of MRSP is divided into six sub-basin as showed in Figure 3, that provide water for many purposes, but the principal rivers are very polluted with industrial, agrochemicals and domestic sewage (Cunha et al., 2011). The river Tietê is a tributary of the Paraná River and runs through the MRSP, considered as a headwaters area for the production of water as one environmental service. However, non-point and point charge of domestic sewage, industrial and agricultural is high (Cunha et al., 2011).

Despite showing rainfall ranging from 1,400 mm per year the MRSP is considered with the most complex and critical watersheds in Brazil with regard to environmental management, mainly because of: changes in hydrological and hydraulic regimes; the high demand of water for multiples uses in the metropolis; and the urban density and water pollution which lead to a low availability of water per capita, with rates comparable to areas in Northeast Brazil under higher scarcity of water resources.

Figure 4. Sub-water basins Alto Tietê-Billings, Tietê-Cabeceiras, Cotia-Guarapiranga, Juqueri-Cantareira, Penha-Pinheiros, Pinheiros-Pirapora in Metropolitan Region of São Paulo.

The urban area of the main basin covers around 37% of the territory and despite the sharp decline in population growth rates, this is not reflected in containing the spread of urban sprawl. The expulsion of the low-income population to the periphery of cities contributes to increased environmental degradation, particularly in the areas of watershed protection and flood plains. Nowadays, the demand for water is basically distributed in three main uses, and 68.8 m^3/s are for urban use, 4.8 m^3/s for industrial, 3.6m^3/s for irrigation. Nowadays, the water availability of RMSP corresponds to 200 m^3 per capita/year. With increasing population, cities are increasing the water requirements into concentrated areas.

Changes to global and regional climates are projected to influence both the total amount and variation of water throughout the globe (Jenerette and Larsen, 2006). In addition, the watersheds require investments to maintain and improve water supplies in MRs. In fact, water quality is the result of urban occupation with a significant proportion of the population living in slums or favelas, occupying areas of risk such as flooded lands, steep hillsides, riparian areas and watershed protection, due to the absence of legal instruments and political planning for the occupation of urban land (Cutolo et al., 2012; Tucci, 2010). We should emphasize that MR of São Paulo removes large volumes of water from the Piracicaba-Capivari-Jundiaí watershed systems located in MR of Campinas, also in São Paulo State, increasing the conflict in a system in collapse.

The violence observed in day-to-day has become a topic of discussion in society as in the media. Nowadays, social inequality is one of the main factors that interfere directly in the violence, considered as a public health problem (Vieira et al., 2012). The demographic explosion in the sub-basins of the MRSP has been accompanied by environmental degradation and social exclusion, which may be associated with violence and homicides. According to the World Health Organization (WHO, 2012), every year there are approximately 530,000 homicides throughout the world, 90% of which occur in low- and middle-income countries (LMIC). For every death, there are numerous non-fatal injuries, and there are estimated to be over 16 million cases of non-fatal violence-related injuries severe enough to require medical attention. Violence is becoming a growing cause of morbidity and mortality in the epideimologic transition of developing countries. Evidence from high-income countries (HIC) and low- and middle-income countries (LMIC) shows strong relationships between levels of violence and potentially modifiable factors such as economic inequality; access to firearms; access to and harmful use of alcohol; and poor monitoring and parental supervision of children (WHO, 2012).

In Brazil, about 52,260 people died in 2010 due to external causes as a result of aggression. In the Metropolitan Region of São In 2001 there were 11,214 registered deaths for violence and 3,535 deaths in 2009 with a decrease of 7,679 deaths (Vieira et al., 2012). Exploring the aspect of violence as an important indicator of public health, there is an increase in the rate of homicides in Mairiporã with 49.9 in 2001 to 53.1 per 100,000 inhabitants in 2009 and Juquitiba with 36.7 in 2001 to 68.2 per 100,000 inhabitants in 2009, while Francisco Morato (45.9 in 2001 to 21.6 per 100,000 inhabitants in 2009) and Taboão Serra (84.6 in 2001 to 19.4 per 100,000 inhabitants in 2009), also with watershed areas, obtained a reduction of this rate, respectively. Despite having seen one general decrease in mortality rates by violence, this fraction of external causes is still a great problem for public health in municipalities in metropolitan areas of developing countries.

According to the data in Table 1, in 2009 the municipalities with the highest percentage in watershed areas had the highest homicide rates as Guararema, Ribeirão Pires and Rio Grande da Serra in the sub-basin of Alto Tietê-Billings; Itaquaquecetuba in sub-basin of Tietê-Cabeceiras; Itapecerica and Juquitiba in sub-basin of Cotia–Guarapiranga; Mairiporã in sub-basin of Penha-Pinheiros and Jandira in sub-basin of Pinheiros-Pirapora. It may also be noted that among the municipalities with water demand per capita per day, not all are water providers, but are consumers of water, as an example Barueri in sub-basin of Pinheiros-Pirapora, São Caetano do Sul and São Paulo in sub-basin of Penha-Pinheiros; Itaquaquecetuba and Guarulhos in sub-basin of Tietê-Cabeceira in MRSP.

The WHO model, known as DPSEEA (Driving Force-Pressure-State-Exposure-Effect-Action), allowed a comprehensive and integrated understanding of how the driving forces of development processes result in "pressures" on the environment. In our analysis we assumed the GDP per capita as an indicator of driving force linked to the economic development which is centralized in the metropolis. As the main pressure considered in this study we choose the conflict of certain municipality as being provider of water. In terms of environmental state we considered the water demand per capita which also can be linked to a pressure. Indeed, applying this model such indicator as the water demand per capita can be viewed in more than one category of the matrix.

As the spatial conflict and the asymmetric identified are in relation to the center and to the periphery, we choose to incorporate the health indicator violence, as an effect, because the relation of this health problem is direct associated to peripherization, especially in the fast urbanization in developing countries.

Thus, with the application of the methodology DPSEEA in this study, we observed that the irregular settlement of areas of watershed protection for a population with socioeconomic profile, considered as a population excluded, may be associated with worse rates of homicides, exacerbating the risk exposure and making the local population more vulnerable and have the effect of the loss of ecosystem services and providers of public water supply.

CONCLUSION

In the context of MRSP, the watershed areas can be considered the most fragile areas by the presence of remnants of green areas. The municipalities with significant area under watershed protection are providers of ecosystem services and suppliers of water to metropolis, and suffer the overlapping of social inequities as the have areas of greatest violence and environmental degradation. It can be inferred that the environmental and social problems such as violence and inequities in watershed areas can be compounded with the possible exacerbation of climate phenomena, and that is a challenge for public policy intersectoral and interdisciplinary, with a view to public health.

Although violence has not often been associated as an environmental health problem, it is possible to point out that a comprehensive analysis of socio-economic, environmental and health indicators can offer the possibility to understand that the municipalities most affected in terms of exclusion social and environmental injustice, are also the providers of environmental services. In this sense, the morbidity and mortality caused by violence should be seen as interconnected to the socio-environmental context, especially considering the history and prospects for climate variability associated with climate change, since higher temperatures may exacerbate critical situations for determinants such public health problems.

ACKNOWLEDGMENTS

Fundação de Amparo à Pesquisa do Estado de São Paulo - FAPESP - Process: 2010/20899-0 of the research" Indicators of environmental sustainability and health for the Metropolitan Region of São Paulo - An ecosystem approach to study at different holarchic levels"; CNPq – Produtividade em Pesquisa – Process: 306489/2012-0 of the research "Water resources management, vulnerability and adaptability in water availability in metropolitan areas in Brazil".

REFERENCES

Baptista S.R. Metropolitan land-change science: A framework for research on tropical and subtropical forest recovery in city-regions. *Land Use Policy* 27 (2010) 139–147.

Borsdorf A, Hidalgo R, Sánchez R. A new model of urban development in Latin America: The gated communities and fenced cities in the metropolitan areas of Santiago de Chile and Valparaíso. *Cities,* 24 (5): 365–378. 2007.

Brazil. Fundo Monetário Internacional (FMI). Página visitada em 17 de abril de 2012.

Cunha, D. G.F.; Grull, D., Damato, M.; Blum, J. R. C.; Eiger, S.; Lutti, J. E. I.; Mancuso, P.C.S . Contiguous urban rivers should not be necessarily submitted to the same management plan: the case of Tietê and Pinheiros Rivers (São Paulo-Brazil). Anais da Academia Brasileira de Ciências (Impresso), v. 83, p. 1465-1479, 2011.

Davis M. Planet of slums. *New Perspectives Quarterly,* 23 (2): 6-11, 2006.

Freitas S R., Hawbaker TJ., Metzger JP. Effects of roads, topography, and land use on forest cover dynamics in the Brazilian Atlantic Forest. *Forest Ecology and Management* 259 (2010) 410–417.

Hotez, P.J.; Bottazzi, M.E.; Franco-Paredes, C.; Ault, S.K., Periago, M.R. The neglected tropical diseases of Latin America and the Caribbean: a review of disease burden and distribution and a roadmap for control and elimination. *PLoS Negl. trop. Dis.,* 2008, 2, e300.

IBGE. População residente por situação, sexo e grupos de idade. PNAD, Brasil: IBGE, 2008.

IBGE. Estimativa Populacional 2012. Estimativa Populacional 2012. Instituto Brasileiro de Geografia e Estatística (IBGE) (01 de julho de 2012). *Página visitada em 09 de dezembro* de 2012.

Jenerette G.D., Larsen L. 2006. A global perspective on changing sustainable urban water supplies. Global and Planetary Change 50: 202–211 doi:10.1016/j.gloplacha.2006.01.004

Maricato E. Metrópoles desgovernadas. *Estudos Avançados,* 25 (71): 7-22, 2011 http://dx.doi.org/10.1590/S0103-40142011000100002.

Prüss-Üstün, A, Corvalán, C. Preventing disease through healthy environments – Towards na estimate of the environmental burden of disease. Geneva: World Health Organization. 2006.

Ribeiro MC ,Metzger JP, Martensen AC, Ponzoni FJ, Hirota M.M. The Brazilian Atlantic Forest: How much is left, and how is the remaining forest distributed? Implications for conservation. *Biological Conservation* 142 (2009) 1141–1153.

Tucci, C.E.M.. Integrated urban water management in the humid tropic. In: UNESCO Taylor and Francis. (Org.). Integrated urban water management: *humid tropics.,* 2010.

Tundisi JG, Matsumura-Tundisi T, Tundisi JEM. (2008). Reservoirs and human well being: new challenges for evaluating impacts and benefits in the neotropics. *Braz. J. Biol.,* 68(4, Suppl.): 1133-1135, 2008.

Vieira BFS, Costa FNSM, Pereira LPS et al. Aspectos da Violência na Região Metropolitana de São Paulo. Fundap: Observatório de Saúde da Região Metropolitana de São Paulo. 2012. 93p.

Vörösmarty C. J., McIntyre P. B., Gessner M. O, Dudgeon D., Prusevich A., Green P., Glidden S., Bunn S. E., Sullivan C. A., Liermann C. Reidy, Davies P. M. Global threats to human water security and river biodiversity. *Nature,* (467): 555-561, 2010.

Walker R. The scale of forest transition: Amazonia and the Atlantic forests of Brazil. *Applied Geography* 32 (2012): 12-20.

World Health Organization (WHO). Violence prevention alliance global campaign for violence prevention: plan of action for 2012-2020. Global Campaign for Violence Prevention. Geneva, Switzerland, 2012 (http://www.who.int/violence_injury), accessed 03 April, 2012.

In: Health, Violence, Environment and Human Development ... ISBN: 978-1-62948-038-1
Editors: A. Cotte Poveda and C. I. Pardo Martínez

Chapter 2

MUNICIPAL SANITATION PLANS IN BRAZIL AS A TOOL FOR PLANNING AND COOPERATION TO ADDRESSING THE MILLENNIUM DEVELOPMENT GOALS

***Dieter Wartchow*[*,1] *and Giuliano Crauss Daronco*[†2]**
[1] Instituto de Pesquisas Hidráulicas, UFRGS,
Porto Alegre-RS, Brazil
[2] Companhia Riograndense de Saneamento (Corsan),
Santa Rosa-RS, Brazil

ABSTRACT

The paper presents a methodology of participatory strategic planning, developed for the preparation of Basic Sanitation Plans (PMSB). The PMSB aims to qualify the planning and management of sanitation services, priority projects and actions. According to basic sanitation policy in Brazil driven by Brazilian Federal Law 11,445, January, 2007, the preparation of PMSB is mandatory and is the responsibility of municipalities. The dismantling of the structures of planning and management of sanitation services at the municipal level, due to the authoritarian imposition of a model for the provision of water services and sewage, proposed by the National Sanitation Plan (PLANASA) in the 1970s, and increasing urbanization, meant that cities grew without proper sanitation infrastructure. The absence of an integrated PMSB reflects the lack of safe water in rural areas and low rates of coverage of collection and treatment of sewage, are the cause of the formation of risk areas and environmental contamination due to the irregular disposal of waste solids. The study bases itself on a successful experience developed in Santa Rosa-RS, where institutional arrangements for the joint and shared management, as well as participatory sanitation services were developed. The methodology goes beyond the preparation of the PMSB. This empowers the municipal manager, as well as integrates the action of citizens with municipal parliament users. The long term planning for

* dieterw@iph.ufrgs.br.
† giulianodaronco@gmail.com.

integrating actions and programs, especially democratize information, opening pathways to participation councils and citizens in decision-making. The participatory and representative democracy are not opposed and together contribute to its strengthening. Investments are being made in the implementation of a new system of water supply and sewage and prioritizing the use of resources is through a Shared Municipal Fund Management. Analyzing the process of drafting the PMSB, it was concluded that the information has a strategic character to encourage the participation of public management and citizen users in different stages, from diagnosis, through the prioritization of actions and the supervision and control of effective realization of what was planned. The democratization of information will allow the public manager and citizens the knowledge necessary to the fulfillment of their rights, but also to meet their duties. The case study shows that the PMSB is a tool for planning and managing constantly changing that requires intense participation to be effective.

Keywords: Basic Sanitation, Strategic Planning, Cooperation, Associated Management

1. Introduction

One of the United Nations (UN) Millennium Development Goals (MDGs) is to halve the number of people living without clean drinking water by the year 2014. Endeavoring to reach this goal, the UN, led by the UN Secretary-General's Advisory Board on Water and Sanitation (UNSGAB), launched the Hashimoto Action Plan at the 4th World Water Forum in Mexico City in March 2006. The Hashimoto Action Plan envisions actions to improve the performance and quality of water and sewage services with the cooperation of water and sanitation service providers organized through a worldwide alliance called the Global Water Operators' Partnerships Alliance (GWOPA). GWOPA's principles are as follows: (a) social inclusion; (b) non-profit cooperation where the benefits are mutual (everyone wins); (c) constructing examples of good management to promote best practices and training; (d) encouraging global cooperation; (e) encouraging the construction of a sustainable sanitation management model; and (f) building a culture of solidarity. Addressing concerns regarding the MDGs, the plan also recommends, for basic sanitation, that national governments formulate policies, strategies, and plans that have been tailored to economic, social, and environmental conditions (UN-HABITAT, 2007).

One example of this issue's political dimension is the growing recognition that the water crisis is associated with a crisis of governance. The term governance is considered ambiguous in relation to water and sanitation. The crisis associated to sanitation, is an expression of the production and reproduction of structural social inequalities of both a qualitative and quantitative nature. There are justice and equality problems (the poor pay more for water that they do not have), governance problems (mismanagement or management focused either commercially or on profitability), and problems with the inclusion of citizens in the decision-making process.

Through the development of a methodology for participatory strategic planning for the development of Basic Sanitation Plans (PMSB), this study aim to find ways to empower citizens and public managers to improve the management of sanitation services, making projects and actions prioritizing sustainability in its environmental context, political, economic and social. The cities need public policies that democratize access to public resources and put the desires of a community above individuals or corporations, motivating them to participate and take control of society over the state.

Both, the Brazilian Federal Law 11.445 (BRAZIL, 2007) that provides for a National Policy for Basic Sanitation and the Decree 7217/2010, that regulates the aforementioned law, point to the necessity of the creation of Municipal Basic Sanitation Plans. Municipal Sanitation Plans in Brazil is an obligation and a tool for planning and cooperation to addressing higher quality in sanitation services. The lack of planning leaves to corruption and diseases.

The Brazilian National Basic Sanitation Plan (PLANSAB) projects that in 20 years Brazil will have public policies more stable, with better relationship between the Union, States and Municipalities. With strategic planning and sanitation with government commitment to allocate financial resources to finance the infrastructure, especially in deficit areas as sewer, drainage and solid waste, it will be possible to build up a relatively optimistic scenario, with democratic public management and social accountability.

Therefore, this theme aims to encourage and demonstrate that cooperation for the management of water supply and sanitation services in the light of the National State can be Pathways to democratize access and financial resources, human and technological resources to promote sustainable development, access to safe water and sewer infrastructure for all.

The methodology applied in the case study differs from others of the same kind whose PMSB are prepared by third parties with an interest in providing services in the area of water supply and sanitation. It is characterized by the intense participation of the population and training for municipal officials to decision making. The resulting educational process is permanent and is continually renewed.

The contributions of the study are related to the know-how of making sanitation, applying step by step procedures to establish, monitor and organize scenarios and projects. The developed model permit to break the paradigm of the inefficiency of the public sector in the management of sanitation. Also, it includes the correct application of public resources available in federal government programs, avoiding unnecessary works, waste of public money and directing actions towards the priorities in a participatory manner.

The structure of this chapter consists of a review of the purposes of the national policy for sanitation, which leads to its goals. After the explanation of the planning methodology adopted for the development of PMSB, the study presents the results, actions and proposals. Before concluding, the study addresses aspects related to the participatory process used.

2. Literature Review

According to the data from the National Household Sample Survey – PNAD (2007), cited by BRASIL (2009-b), the coverage rates of water, sanitation, and wastewater treatment services are very disparate, if urban areas and rural areas are regionally considered. While water coverage rates in Brazil in the year 2007 stood at 93.09% in urban areas, this rate reached only 62.80% in urban areas in the Northern region. In rural areas, only 28.22% of permanent households had access to a water supply network, usually operated by the own users in form from small water associations. Water coverage is understood as the connection to a water supply system, which the quality suggests safe conditions for human consumption.

The rate of sewage collection in Brazil, which was 59.46% in urban areas and 5.50% in rural areas, signals a serious sanitary and environmental problem. These rates compel us to turn to the National Basic Sanitation Plan (PLANSAB), based on Law 11.445 of January 5, 2007 (BRASIL, 2007). The PLANSAB, drafted, debated and constructed by experts and coordinated by HELLER (2012), awaiting its publication and its implementation. From the national to the local level, we need to develop Municipal Sanitation Plans (PMSB).

Under the Federal Law 11.445 (BRAZIL,2007) that provides the National Policy for Basic Sanitation, and by the Decree 7217 of 21 June 2010 (BRASIL,2010-a) that regulates the afore mentioned law, the creation of Municipal Basic Sanitation Plans is also a condition to access Federal Government programs, which are funded with affordable resources from the Federal Budget (OGU). These plans should be developed with consideration for water supply, sanitation, solid waste, and storm drainage issues in an integrated, interdisciplinary manner, and with broad citizen participation.

To avert the fragmentary implementation of public resources, and to avoid or prevent that works be unable to meet goals and the aimed results, municipalities are recommended to develop a strategic tool: the Municipal Basic Sanitation Plan (PMSB). If there is no plan, there will be no affordable public resources, no effective management, no civil works, no safe water or sewage system, or even no infrastructural works in the areas of solid waste management and storm drainage systems. Therefore, sustainable development, health, and quality of life in cities and rural areas, as well as the efforts to reach the Millennium Development Goals (MDGs), will remain a distant aspiration at the local level.

A clear demonstration that health and sanitation interact with each other can be found in Article 23, paragraph 3, of Decree No. 7217/2010 in which the holder of the services when formulating public sanitation policy should adopt parameters to ensure essential service to public health and, among others, should call the Single Health System (SUS), as described below:

> "... § 3. - The Single Health System - SUS, with their departments of social control and guidance, could participate in the formulation of the policy and execution of basic sanitation through the sanitation plans"

The role of sanitation is to interpose barriers between man, the causative agent of diseases, and the environment, in a preventive way.

The sanitation is seen as part of other social problems, such as universal access for all to safe water. Although it has been two decades of delay, the goal of sanitation policy is to move forward together with other social policies, such as urban and regional development, housing, poverty alleviation, environmental protection and economic sustainability.

Although it does not represent a Sanitation Policy for Brazil, the Federal Law 11.445/2007 has the merit of creating the foundation for the establishment of policy and guidelines that must be followed in the process of regulating the sector, putting the question on a multidisciplinary way and integrating the various federal agencies. Moreover, creates an appropriate legal environment to secure permanent financing and investment in the sector; it just need the will to realization.

According to BRAZIL (2007) the Law No. 11.225/2007, in its Article 11, only guarantees conditions for the validity of contracts for the rendering of public sanitation if a basic sanitation plans exist. The holders of public sanitation are those who may delegate the organization, regulation, supervision and provision of services pursuant to Article 241 of the Federal Constitution and Law No. 11.107, of April 6 2005 (BRAZIL, 2005), Law of Public Grants. It is also of the holder of the services the responsibility of formulating policies for sanitation, and for that they need to develop sanitation plans.

The definition of who is the holder of basic sanitation in Brazil remains under discussion in the Supreme Court (STF), due to a political dispute of who will rule the "business public water": the municipalities or states. In a democracy and a federation, to ensure access to a universal right, rather than a dispute in court, should shatter paradigms through cooperation, solidarity and sharing of responsibilities.

So has the Decree 7.217/2010, in Article 24, paragraph 1, as reproduced below:

> "... § 1 The planning of public sanitation meet the principle of solidarity among members of the Federation and can be develop through federal cooperation."

For the authors, the owner is the municipality, where sanitation starts and where the problem is established when the services are not provided with the required quality. Therefore, being the municipality the holder of sanitation services, the city manager assume the responsible for law enforcement when the sewers pollute water sources, for losses when floods, for deficiencies in the provision of water services or for poor collection and disposal of solid waste.

The forms of provision of basic sanitation services are provided in Article 38 of Decree 7.217/2010, which content is transcribed below:

> "Section ... 38. The owner may provide the sanitation services:
>
> I - directly through its direct administration or local authority, public corporation or mixed capital company that integrates its indirect administration, provided that hire third in the scheme of Law No. 8666 of June 21, 1993, to certain activities;
>
> II - so hired:
>
> (a) indirectly, through a concession or permission, always preceded by public bidding in competition mode, in the scheme of Law No. 8987 of February 13, 1995, or
>
> (b) under joint management of public services by contract program authorized by contract of public consortium or by agreement of cooperation between federal entities in the scheme of Law No. 11.107, of April 6, 2005; .... "

3. Methods and Strategic Proposal

The PMSB in the municipality of Santa Rosa-RS, located in southern Brazil, was designed according to the principles and guidelines laid out in Federal Law No. 11.445 of January 5, 2007, which was regulated by the Decree No. 7127 of June 21, 2010, who establishes the country's National Policy for Basic Sanitation.

The development of the PMSB of the city of Santa Rosa-RS followed the steps outlined in Figure 1 (us built) that were adapted from the methodology proposed in the Guide for the Elaboration of Sanitation Plans of the Federal Ministry of Cities (BRAZIL, 2006). The PMSB's contents seek to meet the Recommended Resolution No. 75 of July 2009 from the Council of Cities, an agency integrating the activities of the Ministry of Cities (BRAZIL, 2009).

In Figure 1 we highlight advances of the management proposed in PMSB, such as Associated Management Services for Water Supply (SAA) and Sewage Services (SES), the creation of a Municipal Fund for Shared Management (FMGC), the creation of a Department as an instance for monitoring the management of PMSB and for the developing of projects and the formation of an Advisory Board for the exercise of social control.

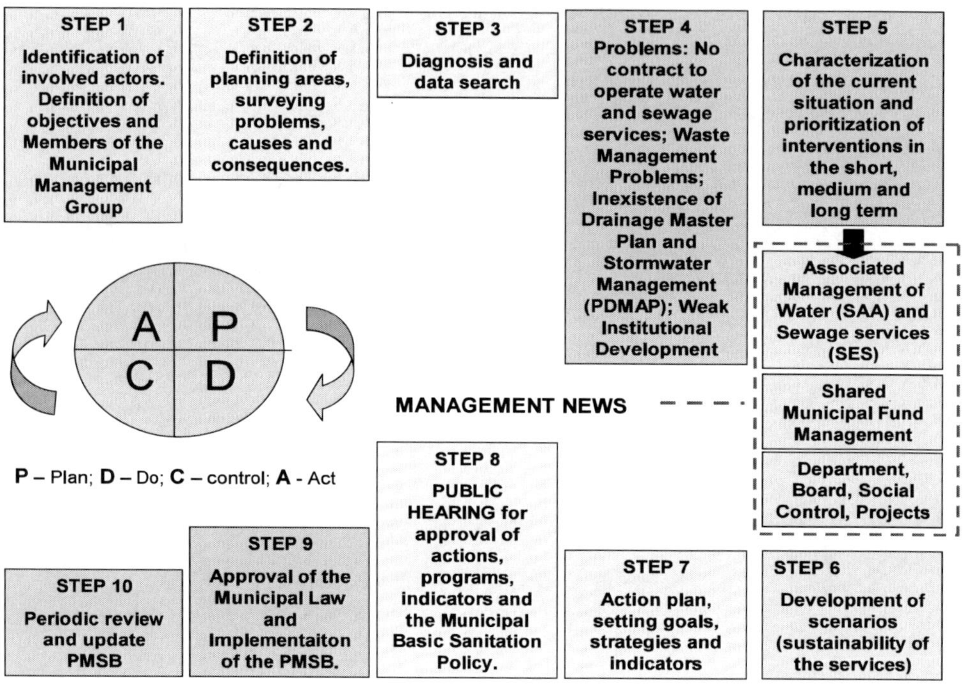

Figure 1. Steps undertaken in the construction of the PMSB of the city of Santa Rosa/RS.

It is up to the municipality, as the head of basic sanitation services, to prepare the Basic Sanitation Plan, with a view to formulating basic local public sanitation policies. The management should be effective and democratic, soliciting the participation of the general population in the formulation, implementation, and monitoring of urban development plans, programs, and projects.

Considering this institutional and legal scenario, and based on a diagnosis made in the area of basic sanitation, the municipality of Santa Rosa-RS, located in southern Brazil, understood the importance of developing their PMSB. This PMSB integrate the Participatory Master Plan for the Sustainable Municipal Development of Santa Rosa and into the policy guidelines in the area of housing, environment, and water resources, among others.

To achieve the MDGs and the goals of Law 11.445 of January 5, 2007, the municipality of Santa Rosa-RS opted to make progress in the search for a new institutional arrangement. In the pursuit of cooperation between public entities, the following issues were considered: (a) an integration between related areas; (b) the duty of federal entities to form a national policy for basic sanitation; (c) the respect for municipal (local) autonomy; (d) a public management with quality and social control; and (e) the financial sustainability of basic sanitation services (water, sewage, solid waste, storm drainage).

To provide water supply and sanitation services in the urban and rural areas, the municipality of Santa Rosa-RS preferred the associated management model. Associated management is one of the forms given in the Law nº 11.445/2007 for the provision of services by a public entity, which was constituted by a public consortium or a public basic sanitation company. In this case, a program contract was signed with the Riograndense Sanitation Company (CORSAN), a public company, wherein targets were established for the expansion of the water supply and sanitation system in the areas of resources, quality standards, regulation, and social control, among others.

The PMSB had the support of the Federal University of Rio Grande do Sul (UFRGS) through the Institute of Hydraulic Research (IPH), which promoted training and advisory boards of municipal employees and assisted in the drafting process. The PMSB was structured with the aim of universalizing basic sanitation services. Whose goals include: (a) the access to potable drinking water; (b) the access of households to the wastewater treatment network; (c) the development of an Integrated Solid Waste Plan, according to the guidelines of the National Solid Waste Policy, advocated by Federal Law No. 12.305 of August 2, 2010 (BRAZIL, 2010-b). In the drainage area the goals are the elimination of high-risk areas in flooding zones and the planning of storm drainage infrastructure, including the use of low impacts technologies.

The PMSB had a planning horizon of 20 years starting from the year 2010. In the regulation procedures are recommended periodic reviews every four years.

The Basic Sanitation Policy proposed in the PMSB seeks to integrate basic sanitation policy within urban development policies and land use policies, in accordance with the guidelines and instruments defined in the Master Plan of the city of Santa Rosa-RS.

The interdisciplinarity between the National Policy, the National Water Resources Policy, and the National Solid Waste Policy, was also an object of evaluation during the PMSB's construction.

The economic scenarios for the provision of water supply and sewage services and for the provision of urban cleaning services and the treatment and disposal of solid waste, were based on encouraging the use of appropriate technologies, on the capacity of users to pay this services, and on the adoption of gradual and progressive solutions.

With the commitment to develop the PMSB, the municipality held the first PMSB public hearing on February 23, 2009 at the city council, wherein the diagnosis of basic sanitation areas (water supply, sewage and sanitation, urban solid wastes, and storm drainage) was presented. In compliance with current legislation, the municipality held a public hearing on May 5, 2010, wherein the proposal and program of works and actions that aimed at providing water supply and sanitation services in the municipality of Santa Rosa-RS were presented and approved.

Improving the management and sustainability of the provision of services is a matter of concern in the PMSB's development. The suggested programs relate the aspects of engineering, economics, planning, institutional and organizational development, law, communications and information technology, environmental management, social participation and control, among others. For example, despite the absence of the Turvo/Santa Rosa/Santo Cristo Rivers Watershed Plan, the PMSB will seek to include elements within its guidelines that constitute a discussion on the framework to be proposed by the Committee for Watershed Management, the future plan for watershed, and water uses.

The PMSB situates possible emergencies that may require preventive and corrective actions, as well as encourages a joint or cooperative action on the part of civil defense institutions, which usually participate in these critical events. The principles adopted for the issue of emergencies refer firstly to precaution, then to prevention, and finally, to corrective action and humanitarian support.

The various meetings and hearings conducted during the plan's preparation aimed to democratize the population's wide access to information and propositions for the PMSB. The PMSB pretend to transform the fragmented relationship and cooperation from the different councils into an integrated and related action, as well as to foster a culture of participation to complement the regulation.

4. Achieving Results and Targets

The results achieved after the development of the PMSB of Santa Rosa - RS and the approval of the municipal sanitation policy are significant. However, considering the goal of the PMSB to promote a continuous process of quality improvement, more instances need to be developed to encourage social participation and to democratize the access to information. After all, who use the infrastructure and pays for it are the citizens.

The presentation of results is structured based on some points observed during the development of the sanitation plan. Following the methodology used in preparing the PMSB (Figure 1), will be listed some recommended actions to achieve the goals and the emergency scenarios to formulate the emergency plan. Moreover, for areas of water supply and sanitation, this work will be presented some indicators that highlight the dialogue between diagnosis, indicators and actions.

One of the most significant results in the development of PMSB was the participation of municipal administrators and population, which led to an understanding of the importance of sanitation to the city and its citizens and to the economy and the environment.

4.1. Basic Sanitation Diagnosis

The water supply services (SAA) and the sewage services (SES) in the urban area of Santa Rosa-RS, are provided by the Riograndense Sanitation Company (CORSAN), while in rural areas, they are provided by the municipality. The management is associated, and the program contract signed between the Municipality and CORSAN is the regulatory instrument. Table 1 lists the assessment of the indicator and the proposed action.

An analysis of the SAA's operational data, suggests some technical-operational measures that should be transformed into actions that aim to ensure the provision of water supply services in an efficient, skilled, and universal manner. The major problems associated with the SAA are verified in the capture of water from the manantial during extreme weather conditions (high rainfall), high water losses, the need to search for efficiency in energy consumption, in ensuring an expansion in water production to meet future demand and to improve the quality of water supplied to the population.

In the diagnosis, the existence of 60 localities, typified as rural settlements that were served by simplified water systems, was noted, benefiting 1,884 households (3.4 people per household = 6,405 people). In the mapped locations, 154 households without water were identified.

Table 1. Relationship – Indicator /Assessment / Proposed Action

INDICATOR	ASSESSMENT	PROPOSED ACTION
AG012 - Macro-metered volume of water [1,000 m³/year]	Insufficient	Undertake sectorization and macro-metering in the short term
AG004 - Number of active micro-metered water connections [connection]	Insufficient micro-metering according to adjustment form (TAC) signed with the Justice (MP)	Provide all economies with hydrometers in the short term
AG025 - Rural population served by water supply [inhabitant]	Survey shows 1,884 households without access to disinfected water and 154 households without access to the general network	Undertake program to increase access to water networks in rural areas and settlements
AG028 - Total electricity consumption in water systems [1,000 kWh/year]	Not available	Demand managed, integrated flow between US and CORSAN's Technical Director
FN034 – Expenses with debt service amortization [R$/year]	Data difficult to read	Request this information when CORSAN provides their annual accounts to the Municipality
G10m - Number of locations served by water supply [location]	Lack of database and system of data registration.	Adjust procedure in the Secretariat responsible for water supply in rural areas and settlements

Source: Indicator posted in www.snis.gov.br.

Table 2. Sewage disposal methods in Santa Rosa

DISPOSAL METHOD	HOUSEHOLDS		%	POPULATION
	2000	2010		Inhabitants
Total	19,223	23.156	100.0%	69.587
General sewage or rainwater network	5,165	5.948	25,69%	17.875
Septic tank	1,326	3.154	13,62%	9.437
Rudimentary cesspits	11,079	12.308	53,15%	36.828
River, lake, or ocean	1,266	1.278	5,52%	3.824
Another outlet	101	150	0,65%	449
No bathroom only toilet	286	326	1,41%	975
No bathroom no toilet		37	0,16%	111

Source: National Survey of Basic Sanitation (IBGE, 2011)

Table 2 presents the forms of household sewage and wastewater disposal according to the IBGE (IBGE, 2011). It can be observed that more than half of the sewage generated is being disposed in rudimentary cesspits, and only 26.9% of households have a general sewage network, this being either a type of unitary water separator or a utilitarian rainwater network in which wastewater is disposed.

The data contained in the Water and Sewage Services Diagnosis (BRAZIL, 2009 b) suggests that compared to the information and indicators relative to the SAA, there is a low rate of sewage connections. The low sewage collection resulting in a sewage rate of 20.45%, is referring the water consumption, or 14.48%, referring to the number of active water connections. This percentage equals a total population of 8,614 inhabitants served by sanitation (Indicator ES001 – SNIS [BRAZIL, 2009 b]).

Seasonal water scarcity, the deficient sewage and waste management and excess rainfall, resulting respectively in shortages in the rural areas and flooding in the municipality's urban area, transform the management of basic sanitation into an environmental challenge in times of climate change.

The PMSB of Santa Rosa / RS (SANTA ROSA, 2011) contain the diagnostic of solid waste management and drainage and rainwater management, however it will not be detailed in this chapter.

4.2. Key Actions and Proposals

The proposed actions and projects presented in the PMSB are the result of a process of analysis and consultation undertaken during numerous meetings, hearings and seminars, as well as analyses of their viability in the short term (C), medium term (M), and long term (L). In all actions, citizen participation was of great importance, as the desired results depend on it as well.

By means of the associated management for the provision of water supply and sanitation services, the creation of a Municipal Fund for Shared Management (FMGC) was established in the Program Contract. Financial resources were used during the first year of operation to fund and facilitate various activities and projects toward achieving MDG 7 Target 10 and, complementarily, Targets 9 and 11. Beginning with the FMGC, it was possible in the year 2010 to make investments enabling the extension of water networks for rural communities, the acquisition of equipment, and the increase in oversight and planning in the area of water resources and basic sanitation, among others.

An educational work plan is in progress, in accordance with the commitments made in the Program Contract by the water supply and sanitation services provider (CORSAN) and the city of Santa Rosa-RS. Other plans include the construction of a new water treatment plant and improvements in the water system and the expansion of the wastewater treatment plant and the sewage collection network, totaling an investment of R$ 31,048,000.00, with own resources from CORSAN and the Federal Budget (OGU).

It is important to emphasize that the goals, targets, and indicators associated with ensuring environmental sustainability are related to the proposed actions and projects as well as the performance indicators set out in the PMSB. The proportion of households without access to the main sewage network is emphasized, which makes this goal one of the most important.

Therefore, a project's worth and results derive from the combination of knowledge (learning to use water and sort waste), competence (achieving efficiency in supply and use), and technology (use of ever more efficient equipment). These aspects are related to the PMSB and the ability to find financial resources for basic sanitation without the need for intermediaries or corporate favors. In this context, the Law 11.445/2007 (Basic Sanitation Law) could contribute significantly because, among other things, it associates a policy of continuous funding with both the development and the essential existence of a Municipal Basic Sanitation Plan (PMSB).

The actions proposed in the PMSB/Santa Rosa clearly dialogue with a vision from the local to the global, as well as between related sectors and areas. Many proposed actions interface with MDG 7 Target 9: "Integrate the principles of sustainable development into country policies and programs, and reverse the loss of environmental resources."

Having preferred the model of associated management through the program contract with CORSAN, intense work can be done on MDG 7 Target 10, which aims to halve the proportion of people without sustainable access to drinking water and basic sanitation by 2015. The control of the quality of drinking water for human consumption and the universalization of water supply in rural areas, as well as amplifying the coverage of the sewage system, including the treatment of secondary wastewater, will bring, in the short term, results that signify the achievement of Target 10.

Target 11 aims to achieve by 2020 a significant improvement in the lives of slum dwellers, the indicator of which is the proportion of households relocated from risk areas. This target will also be met complementarily by the PMSB since this plan provides for flooding and emergency situations.

The main guidelines outlining the proposed actions and scenarios related to the Water Supply System (SAA) were as follows: (a) the implementation of a program to reduce water losses; (b) the preservation of the natural spring area; (c) reevaluation of the Tariff Plan; (d) implementation of specific funding mechanisms to ensure the water supply of rural or dispersed settlements; (e) creation of a professional training program for the technical management of water supply systems; and (f) launch of a public awareness campaign on issues of quality, rationalization of water use, and the timely payment of bills.

Table 3 presents in addition to the actions set out and agreed to in the Program Contract signed between the Municipality and CORSAN, a summary of actions that extend to rural areas, and for the protection of water resources.

The proposed actions and scenarios for the Sanitary System (SES) are oriented on the following guidelines: (a) expansion of sanitary collection networks; (b) adoption of technologies capable of meeting the effluent discharge standard recommended by environmental laws; (c) foresee implementation in stages adequate to the social demand and technical conditions; (d) demonstration of the need for a reassessment of the Tariff Plan for sanitation service fees; and (e) launch of a public awareness campaign on the issues of health and pollution of water bodies and sewage connections.

Table 4 presents projects and civil works complementary to the program of actions to implement the sewage system under the Program Contract signed between the Municipality and CORSAN.

In the first stage of SES's expansion, which will go on until the year 2015, approximately 40% (26,278 inhabitants) of the estimated population in the municipality's urban area will be served. In Stage 2 of implementation, SES aims to serve 80% of the urban population projected for the year 2024.

Table 3. Summary of proposed actions for water supply

ACTION
Undertake the SAA actions planned in the Program Contract
Assess and develop the Municipal Program of natural water conservation on rural properties (rainwater harvesting)
Implement system of training, monitoring, and quality control of water distributed in the municipality's rural area. In conjunction with Sanitary Vigilance (VIGISUS)
Undertake improvements in the water supply systems in rural areas and settlements
Ask CORSAN about a project for substituting water networks in public roads that are slated to be paved and contemplated for the rainwater drainage project. Georeference water leakage
Provide all economies with hydrometering by the end of 2010
Encourage the formation of associations, organize and operate water supply systems in rural areas or settlements
Utilize energy conservation and efficiency technologies
Sectorize the SAA and install macro-meters
Register wells and natural springs, aiming for their granting and monitoring

Table 4. Summary of proposed actions for sewage

ACTION
Address the problem of Public Civil Action against CORSAN/Municipality
Emergency Sewage Project in Vila NOVA
Implementation of the COHAB Morada do Sol sewage treatment system in response to the lawsuit
With CORSAN, deliberate the planning of projects to implement sewage systems on roadways slated to be paved and on sidewalks, in order to avoid generalized interference on public roads
Utilize energy conservation and efficiency technologies (CORSAN and PM)
For the implementation of Stages II and III of the SES, match projects with the demands and priorities established in municipal planning
Implement the actions, civil works, and expansions in the SES according to the Program Contract
Adopt development guidelines used by CORSAN (www.corsan.gov.br)

Table 5. Proposals for activities and projects for the area of solid waste

ACTION
Process 291 08108/Internal PM ref. LI – FEPAM – 014968-567/08-8 for the recuperation of Degraded Area RSD with use
Implement the Integrated Management Program for Civil Construction and Demolition Waste (PGIRCC)
Support and training for the formation of associations or cooperatives of Waste collectors
Develop a project for a Sorting Center to receive and sort selectively collected waste
Develop a project to incentivize industries willing to absorb recycled raw material
Planning for the construction of Voluntary Waste Disposal Stations
Study to evaluate a new system to collect and transport organic waste (containerization of solid organic waste and selective collection). Project to design the construction of a Composting Plant
Design a study for the associated management by way of public consortium for the disposal of selective collection rejects and solid waste

From the study of the different scenarios for the management of solid waste in Santa Rosa, following the guidelines established by the National Solid Waste Policy (BRAZIL, 2010-b), the city intends to seek associated management by way of public consortium. Table 5 presents the proposed actions and projects for the area of solid waste.

Table 6 presents actions for the area of storm drainage in the municipality.

Table 6. Proposed actions for storm drainage

ACTION
Develop Master Plan for Storm Drainage
In areas at risk for flooding, plan a resettlement program for at-risk households
Plan a reserve of areas along stream banks in the urban zone within the city's Urban Planning
Develop planning and projects for the implementation of non-structural measures such as zoning, resettlement of occupants in areas at risk for flooding, implementation of a forecasting and warning system for floods, specific legislation, etc.
Encourage and regulate the adoption of low-impact measures aiming to partially control rainwater at the source in municipal legislature
Program to restore vegetation along stream banks
Implement and adopt measures of structural control of floods in urban planning and the urban mobility program, such as the adoption of high capacity storm drains, permeable or geometrically configured gutters, infiltration devices, and damping and containment basins.

4.3. Participatory Process in the Development of the PMSB

The municipal executive power, the municipal legislature, civil and military entities, non-governmental organizations, residential and neighborhood associations, and citizens of the municipality all were involved in building the PMSB of Santa Rosa-RS.

Aiming to assess sensitivity and to take advantage of the presence of different public participants in the PMSB preparation process, communication channels were opened through debates and public hearings, public consultations (opinion poll), and the municipal ombudsman. One of the ombudsman's duties is to attend to people who report sanitation problems or suggest improvements, among other things.

The information in written, spoken, or televised means of communication played an important role in the evaluation of basic sanitation services provided by CORSAN, and related problems. When analysing a problem's cause and effect, both the opportunity and necessity for a project or action aimed at improving the quality of basic sanitation infrastructure as well as provision of these basic services, should be taken into account.

A Management Council and an Advisory Board were formed for the monitoring and participatory construction of the PMSB. The latter consist primarily of municipal ministers and delegates from the Participatory Budget.

Santa Rosa has, among others, actual participatory agencies such as the Municipal Councils, the Participatory Budget, the "City Hall is here with us" Program, and the Environmental Education Programs, which, in different ways, consult with the public on issues and priorities.

Throughout the process of the PMSB's construction, a multidisciplinary and intersectoral approach to the topic of basic sanitation was sought as well as proposals and actions focused on creating a community awareness for a development process that is economically viable, socially just, and environmentally sustainable.

The Santa Rosa PMSB is a rich initiative for the understanding of a new theoretical and practical framework aimed at a harmonious coexistence of the community with its own environment. This continuous process of improving all instruments of power and collectively deciding on a better future for all, may be considered a democratic act.

Along with the participation of ministers, councilors, and representative bodies, there is also social control exercised by public policy councils. Public policy councils, such as the Social Control Municipal Council, the Participatory Budget Council, and the Sanitation Council, among others, are examples of exercising citizenship that open the space for popular participation in public management. In this manner, the councils can carry out oversight, mobilization, deliberation, or consulting functions according to the circumstances.

The councils' oversight function presupposes the monitoring and control of acts performed by those who are governing. The mobilizing function refers to encouraging popular participation in public management and the contributions toward the formulation and dissemination of information strategies on public policy for the general population. The deliberation function is the ability of the councils to decide on the strategies used in public policy.

From the participation emerged the educational "Management and Environmental Quality" program. The goal of the "Management and Environmental Quality" program is to rate the environmental management in Santa Rosa, taking the population of the municipality's urban and rural areas as its target beneficiary. It has outlined the following actions for environment and sanitation: (a) fencing off Permanent Preservation Areas; (b) qualification for Selective Garbage Collection; (c) implementing appropriate bins for garbage collection; (d) awareness campaigns; (e) reforestation; and (f) revitalization of Santa Rosa's green areas. These initiatives are related to MDG 7 Target 9.

On the occasion of the First Hearing, a questionnaire was administered to gauge the participants' sensitivity to issues related to the area of basic sanitation. The same survey was administered in other entities, locations, and meetings, totaling 684 participants. At the First PMSB Public Hearing, it was resolved to establish an ombudsman who will receive a large amount of information and complaints, making it an important tool for the exercise of citizenship and social control.

The priorities relative to basic sanitation services, which were raised in a survey of public opinion, are given in Figure 2. Note that these are directly related to MDG 7 Target 10 and complementary to Targets 9 and 11.

On August 6, 2010, the seminar presentation of the municipal plan for Participatory Basic Sanitation was held at the Municipal Council, resulting in the adoption of the PMSB and the presentation of actions and goals in the area of sanitation. The seminar highlighted the importance of thinking about the community in terms of the city's sanitation, as well as the need to implement school programs that are aimed at using the theme of sanitation in transverse ways, in order to transmit information to new generations. This opportunity was taken to share the information that the sanitation plan is part of a continuous and ongoing process, which will be followed in the city of Santa Rosa.

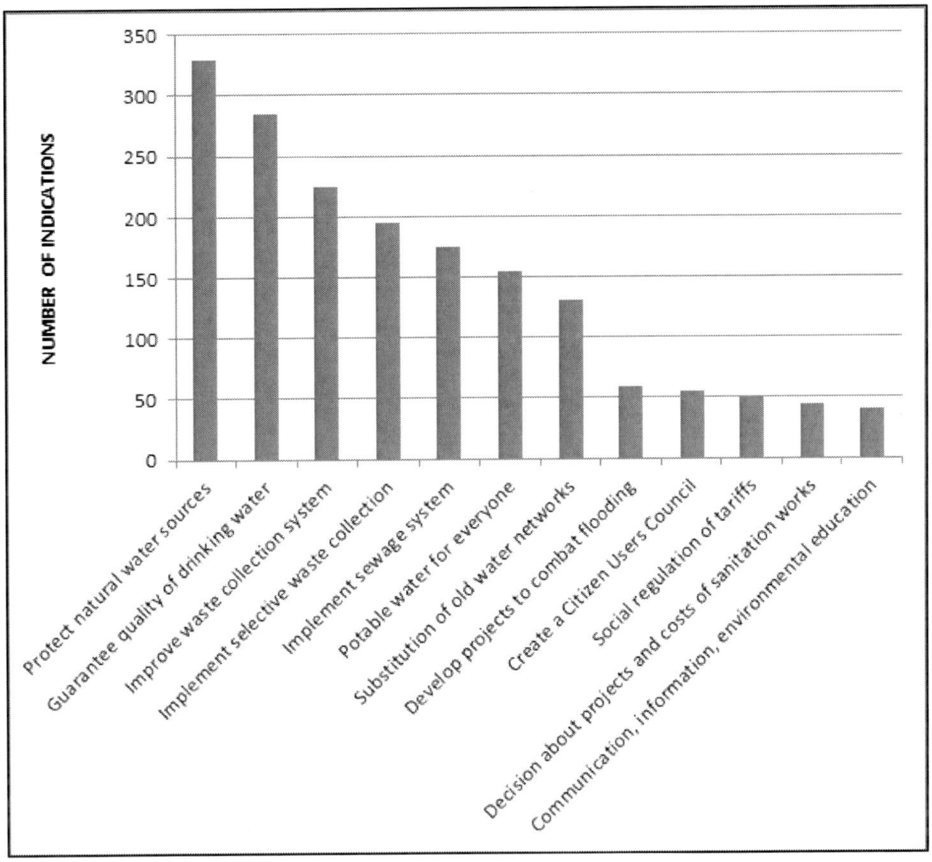

Figure 2. Priorities resulting from the poll - Total of 684 questionnaires (Santa Rosa, 2010).

Conclusion

The Santa Rosa-RS PMSB and its applied strategic methodology can be adopted in Brazil and other countries as an effective tool for planning and cooperative quality management in the area of basic sanitation. The procedures that guide and show ways to improve indicators of basic sanitation should consider local and regional differences as well as the technological, economic, environmental, social, cultural, and educational uniqueness existing in the area of basic sanitation.

The basic sanitation plan, or any specific plan can be developed through technical or financial support provided by other entities of the Federation, by the service provider or by universities or scientific research, ensured the participation of communities, movements and civil society organizations.

The Santa Rosa-RS PMSB is directed to transform the citizens' rights to their city and to well done sanitation services, into a reality, ensuring that each residence, from the urban area to the rural area, receives treated water, and each area has a sewage collection system. Additionally, it ensures that the Integrated Solid Waste Management Program can meet legislative principles and implement sustainable storm drainage conditions, that is, through low-impact technologies.

The report from this successful experience of cooperation in the public sphere signals its potential, especially when there is difficulty in accessing sanitation by the population with the lowest income, as they are concentrated in the remote rural areas and the urban peripheries of cities.

Environmental, financial, political, and social sustainability was sought in planning actions, programs, and targets for basic sanitation. The actions integrate policies and programs, and aim, through their interface, to foster institutional cooperation at the municipal and regional levels as well as between the managing federal entities in the area of basic sanitation.

In this new institutional arrangement proposed for Santa Rosa, through associated management, the Municipal Fund for Shared Management (FMGC) was created, of which short-term results permit the municipality to move closer to its goals in reaching MDG 7 Target 10 and the objectives of Law 11,445/2007. The FMGC is a way for democratization and social control, to make financial data transparent for sustainability in the provision of these essential services, to prioritize the application of tariffs and resources, and to help combat corruption, the latter of which is a major global issue.

With the FMGC, it is possible to bring safe water to rural areas in the municipality of Santa Rosa-RS and meet MDG 7 Target 10, approaching the universalization of access to safe water. In the area of sanitation, results from civic works under construction will approach the indicators of MDG 7 Target 10. However, the technological know-how for sanitation and the high costs for users make connections to the sanitary sewage system difficult, thereby forestalling the achievement of the goals of FMGC.

In addition, MDG 7 Targets 9 and 11 integrate with the PMSB, if one considers the actions that combine housing policy with the removal of hazardous areas, the remediation of waste disposal, the restoration of riparian forests, and sewage treatment, among others.

The knowledge about the PMSB of Santa Rosa-RS lead us to make some recommendations and suggestions, as follow: (a) the training of municipal employees for planning and management activities; (b) the universal access to information in order to promote education and involvement of the citizens in the sustainability and quality of sanitation services; and (c) the development of a info-program to enable data storage, monitoring and management of the PMSB.

References

Brasil (2005). Lei nº 11.107. Dispõe sobre normas gerais de contratação de consórcios públicos e dá outras providências. *Casa Civil.* Brasília-DF. Publicado no DOU de 07/04/2005.

Brasil (2006). Guia Para a Elaboração de Planos Municipais de Saneamento Básico. Ministério das Cidades, Brasília-DF. Acesso: www.mcidades.gov.br, em 14/02/2013.

Brasil. (2007). Lei nº 11.445. Estabelece diretrizes nacionais para o saneamento básico; altera as Leis nº 6.766, de 19/12/1979, 8.036, de 11/05/1990, 8.666, de 21/06/1993, 8.987, de

13/02/1995; revoga a Lei nº 6.528, de 11/05/1978; e dá outras providências. Brasil, Brasília-DF, publicado no DOU de 08/01/2007 e retificado no DOU de 11/01/2007.

Brasil (2009). Resolução Recomendada nº 75. Ministério das Cidades. Conselho das Cidades. Brasília-DF, 02/07/2009, publicada no DOU de 05/10/09 seção 01 nº 190 pág. 51.

Brasil (2009 a). Gasto Público em Saneamento Básico – Relatório de aplicações de 2008. MCidades, SNSA. Brasília-DF, 88p.

Brasil (2009 b). Sistema Nacional de Informações sobre Saneamento: diagnóstico dos serviços de água e esgotos 2007. Brasília: MCIDADES; SNSA, 2009.

Brasil (2010-a). Decreto nº 7.217. Regulamenta a Lei nº 11.445, de 5 de janeiro de 2007, que estabelece diretrizes nacionais para o saneamento básico, e dá outras providências. Casa Civil. Brasília – DF. Publicado no DOU – Edição Extra 22/06/2010.

Brasil. (2010-b). Lei nº 12.305. Institui a Política Nacional de Resíduos Sólidos; altera a Lei nº 9.605, de 12/02/1988; e dá outras providências. Brasil, Brasília-DF, publicado no DOU de 04/08/2010.

IBGE (2011). Censo Demográfico 2010. Available at: <http://www.ibge.gov.br/home/estatistica/populacao/default_censo_2000.shtm>. Accessed on 12/09/2012.

Heller, L. (2012). Plano Nacional de Saneamento Básico (PLANSAB). XII Volumes, Mcidades, Brasilia-DF. Available at www.mcidades.gov.br. Accessed on: 14/02/2013.

PNUD (2010). Desenvolvimento Humano e IDH. Available at: <http://www.pnud.org.br/idh/>. Accessed on: 02/02/2010.

Santa Rosa (2011). Plano Municipal de Saneamento Básico Participativo do Município de Santa Rosa – RS. Projeto de extensão universitária Ufrgs-Faurgs-Município Santa Rosa. Volumes I a VIII.

UN-HABITAT (2007). Framework for Global Water Operators Partnerships Alliance. Nairobi, Kenya, Aug. 2007, 16p.

In: Health, Violence, Environment and Human Development ... ISBN: 978-1-62948-038-1
Editors: A. Cotte Poveda and C. I. Pardo Martínez

Chapter 3

GEOGRAPHICAL INFORMATION SYSTEM: SOLUTION TO NIGERIA'S PUBLIC HEALTH CHALLENGES

*Adebayo Peter Idowu**
Department of Computer Science and Engineering,
Obafemi Awolowo University, Ile-Ife, Nigeria

ABSTRACT

Geographical Information System (GIS) has emerged as an important tool in all human endeavors and most especially in Public Health (PH). It is mostly used by the epidemiologists for disease visualization, exploration, interpretation, monitoring, surveillance, modeling and spatial relationship. Also, GIS is being used to find the relationship between a particular disease, environmental factors and the spread of disease over a particular time in a particular location. In this chapter, GIS, GIS components and GIS in PH were discussed. The reviews of the existing GIS applications in PH were done, so as to know the state of art of GIS in PH and limitations of existing GIS applications. Some current researches in PH in GIS were reviewed in order to identify any ongoing research that is addressing some of the limitations in the existing GIS applications. The chapter also discussed the future trend of GIS in PH. Finally, the chapter recommends the use of GIS to Nigeria's PH sector, because the Nation is characterized with different types of epidemics such as malaria, tuberculosis, HIV/AIDS, fever, cholera among others. As a result, it is expected that GIS will assist in addressing most of the challenges in PH.

Keywords: Public Health, Geographical Information System, Web services.

* Email:paidowu@oauife.edu.ng.

1. INTRODUCTION

The advent of Information Technology has changed almost everything we do in life and has led to Geographical Information System (GIS). GIS is an exciting technology which has become common part of everyday life. It is an information system which deals with geographical or spatial data for the purpose of decision making. An information system itself is a "system whose ultimate goal is to store and manage information as opposed to control systems, which are designed to control physical processes, and manage information largely" (Land, 2004). According to Harris (2003), an information system is a well-coordinated collection of resources that gather and transform data into information products and services that help the enterprise perform its designed functions (Harris, 2003). Information system is a collection of people, machines, data, processes and procedure for collection and distribution of information (Hirschheim, et al. 1995). There are two different ways in which information systems can be viewed which are; computer based (technical way) and non computer based (social way). In this chapter, information systems are referred to in their computer based form.

Moreover, GIS is a specialized information system which deals with geographically referenced data. GIS is a multi-disciplinary field which comprises of areas such as computing, geography, surveying, operation research, mathematics, civil engineering, environmental sciences, statistics, image processing and remote sensing. GIS is often called geographic informatics or geoinformatics or geomatics. Often times, authors defined GIS according to the function it performs in their field. GIS is defined as a computer based information system that combines people, hardware and software to capture, model, store, retrieve, share, process, and manipulate, analyze and present geospatial (geographically referenced) data for the purpose of decision making (Worboys & Duckham, 2004).

GIS consists of spatial information (which is typically the point/line and longitude/latitude of a location), and an interface which join them together in order to create a visualization facility for spatial query and analysis. GIS allows users to select different layers of information to construct a map. The map may include rivers, lakes, roads, motorways, population, and boundaries. GIS often functions as a decision support system because it aids in data analysis, and may give new insights to stakeholders and help in their decision making. It is a powerful tool that enhances the measurement, monitoring, mapping and modelling of geographic data.

GIS is usually considered as a relevant tool in the planning and evaluation of health care system. Its potentials have been deployed in applications areas such (i) monitoring and analysis of spatial changes in health status, (ii) spatial epidemiology, and (iii) health care facilities accessibility and utilization (Murad, 2005). As a powerful automated system for the capture, storage, retrieval, analysis, and display of spatial data; easy spatial data access and dissemination; spatial data exploration; spatial data analysis modeling; and geo-visualization is possible (Peng & Tsou, 2003). The system has been in development for more than 20 years, thus recent software has made it substantially easier to use for those outside the field. The system offers new and expanding opportunities both for the study of the way diseases spread, and how to control them. When used minimally, a spatial perspective on disease is often allowed; but if used to its optimum level (as tools for analysis and decision making), it becomes a new information management vehicle with a rich potential for public health and epidemiology management (Clarke, et al. 1996).

The rationale for this article is that, there is only little information (research) existing regarding the use of GIS application in mitigating Nigerian's PH challenges. The case mentioned in the work of Clarkeet al. (1996) in Kwara State, Nigeria, where a temporal analysis of Landsat Thematic Mapper (LTM) satellite data was used to test the significance of the guinea worm eradication program based on changes in agricultural production (Ahearn , 1996), is a case in point.This is against the backdrop that Nigeria is alleged to be with a population of around 145 million. Thus, with a population growth rate of 2.4%, Nigeria is the most populous country in Africa as well as the 8th most populous country in world. Despite this, Nigeria's health indicators have stagnated or even worsened during the past decade, with life expectancy being as low as 44 years (Gustafsson-Wright, & Van-der-Gaag , 2008). As a result this article seeks to suggest GIS as a solution to the many challenges being faced by the PH sector in Nigeria. It is expected that this article will be useful in solving the problem of the dearth of information regarding the adoption of GIS as a panacea in Nigeria's PH sector among other things.

Furthermore, this chapter discusses GIS components in order to know what makes up a GIS and the relationship between GIS and PH. This chapter also reviews the existing applications of GIS in PH, so as to know the state of art of GIS in PH, and its limitations, and thus appraise the use of web services for PH GIS. It reviews the current research trend in order to know if there is any ongoing research that is addressing some of the limitations highlighted in the existing GIS applications. The chapter reviews future research in PH GIS with the benefits of GIS in PH. Also a review of the case study, the challenges encountered and how GIS could be used as solution was discussed.

This chapter is structured as follows: introduction is the first section, follow by literature and in the literature section, GIS in Public Health, existing GIS Applications in Public Health, current research trends in Public Health GIS, ,and benefits of GIS in Public Health were discussed. Also, in the GIS in Public Health section, the chapter deals with GIS web services, distributed Public Health GIS, and mobile agent based Public Health GIS. In addition, this chapter discusses the application of GIS as Solution to Public Health in Nigeria, under this section it describes Public Health in Nigeria with its challenges and explains how GIS can be used to address these challenges.

2. Literature Review

2.1. GIS Components

GIS can be grouped into four major components namely; users, computer system (software and hardware), procedure and data. Moreover, GIS users, who are often referred to as GIS personnel are key to the power of GIS. Users are the ones that actually develop and make use of GIS. Users can include people from different fields such as PH, surveying, computing and so on. The users of GIS are categorised into three groups: viewers, GIS specialist and general users. Viewers are the largest class of users and they are the ones that use it for reference purposes.

GIS specialists are the people that develop GIS and make it function. They provide support for other users. General users are the people that use it for decision making; some of them are government representatives, businessmen, politicians, engineers, and so on. Among all other GIS users, GIS specialists are central because other GIS users depend on them.

The computer system as one of the components of GIS comprises of software and hardware. While the software is often made up of a GIS package, an operating system and so on; the hardware includes technical tools needed for GIS such as the main computer, a visual display unit, scanner and digitizers. As well, data as a GIS component is very important in that the reliability of any GIS's analysis is determined by its consistency. In any GIS data, the sources of data, their method of data collection, date of update, accuracy of the data (in terms of their attribute and positional features), relationships between the data and also the completeness of the data are very important (Worboys & Duckham, 2004). The fourth component, procedure constitutes the methods and algorithms, often applied to the data component to obtain the answers to the questions posed.

2.2. GIS and Public Health

a. GIS Technology in Public Health

GIS is a technology which has been around for many years. 1854 marked the beginning of research on how to use mapping in PH when a major cholera outbreak in London claimed the lives of almost six hundred people. Water problem was identified as the cause of this outbreak in London by Dr John Snow a British physician.He mapped the affected areas (ESRI, 1999), and this became the foundation of GIS research in PH. As a result, Dr Snow was named as the founding father of GIS in epidemiology (Laymon, 1999).

PH deals with the relationship between the environment and the health of people living in the environment. It deals with where people live and the diseases associated with them in the environment. The health of people in an environment is defined as the social, physical and well being of the people in an environment. GIS in Public Health (PH)Hh can simply be referred to as PH GIS, and it is the collection, storage, analysis, modelling, querying and display of spatially referenced health or disease data. It has also been identified as a system that provides opportunities for connecting people; their health and well being with their physical and social environment (Cromely & Mclafferty, 2002).

One of the first major uses of computer based GIS can be traced to 1964 when the Canadian Geographic Information System (CGIS) started. After CGIS began, several other organisations came up, among which is the Environmental Systems Research Institute Incorporated (ESRI) that further researched and developed large GIS applications (Ramirez et al., 2004). One of such application is the Esri software, which is a GIS mapping software that helps to understand and visualize data, even at the click of a button. A summary of other GIS applications is in table 1 below. GIS is becoming popular among health care providers and it is increasingly been used in many areas of health care such as research, health education, epidemiology, and planning (Scholten and Lepper,1991).

Apart from GIS being a useful technology in PH and especially in epidemiology; it is also being used for several other areas in PH, among which are: To help in the understanding of disease diffusion and distribution as shown in Figure 1 below (Public Health Agency of Canada,2013); to detect the correlation between disease and causal environmental factors such as climate, temperatures, precipitation, population and so on that influence diseases (Hakre et al., 2004); to provide opportunities for connecting people, health and well being with their physical and social environment (Scholten and Lepper , 1991); to locate patient and health care facilities; to provide care services; to provide spatial patter and temporal trends of diseases (Pillay, 2007) and for the mapping of population at risk of diseases (Reinhardt et al., 2007).

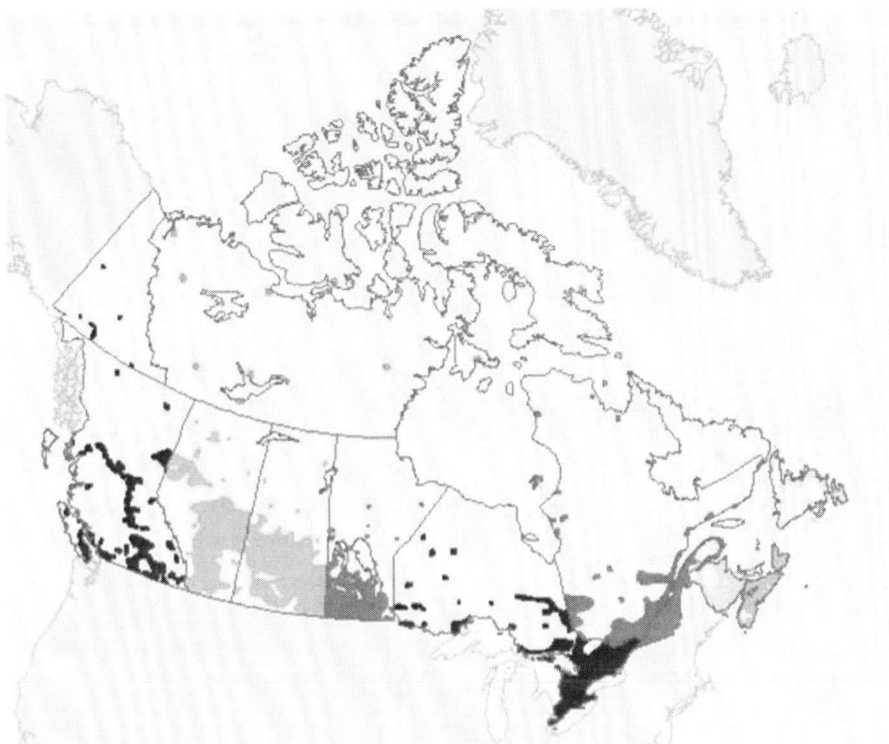

Source: Public Health Agency of Canada (2013).

Figure 1. Showing the distribution and diffusion of disease.

b. Existing GIS Applications in Public Health

GIS is being used widely in epidemiology which is a branch of PH. GIS has been used widely for disease surveillance and mapping (Colak & Yomralioglu, 2005), disease monitoring Gupta & Shriram, 2004), immunization evaluation (Vyas & Kalsaria, 2007), epidemic outbreak monitoring (Mutitanon et al., 2007), clinical medicine (Garb et al., 2007) and disease prediction Shukla & Goel, 2007). In California, GIS was used to predict areas of high risk for child pedestrian-motor vehicle collision injuries (Lightsone et al., 2001). Also, in Wisconsin, Rhode Island and Baltimore, GIS has been used to analyse the spread and distribution of Lyme disease. The system was used to identify areas with highest human risk for Lyme disease and determine correlation between the disease and vegetation type (Kitron &Kazmierczak, 1997; Glass et al., 1995). GIS was also used to analyze the relationship between malaria and the environmental factors in Belize (Hakre et al., 2004).

Table 1. Comparison of Selected Open Source GIS Applications in Public Health

Application	Use in PH	Geographic Data Support	Data-base	Compatibility with other GIS Software	Operation System	Ownership/ Developers	Cost	Limitations
Health-Mapper	Analysis of disease outbreaks:Malaria, HIV/AIDS, Guinea Worm, Onchocer-ciasis, Polio	Shapefiles (Importa-tion and Modifi-cation)	Excel, Access Dbase, CSV	ESRI ArcView MapInfor DevInfor	Windows (98/NT/2000/MeXP)	WHO/ UNICEF	Free	* Stand-alone * Limited statistical capacity * Runs only on desktop
Epi info/ EpiMap	PH analyses of diseases: Malaria, Cancer, Guinea worm	Shapefiles (Impor-tation and Modifi-cation)	Excel, Access Dbase, SQL, CSV, XML	ESRI ArcView	Windows (98/NT/2000/MeXP)	Center for disease Control/WHO	Free	* Stand-alone * Lack Statistical spatial data analysis * Runs only on desktop
SaTScan	Spatial analysis of diseases(Cancer, Leukemia, Lym-phoma, Fever)	No Shapefile Support expect (Text file, Parameter Files)	ASCII, & Dbase, CSV	Not compatible with ESRI ArcView	Windows 98, ME, 2000, XP and Vista	Martin Kulldriff & Information management Services Inc, NCI	Free	* Stand-alone * Lack visualization of Map * Runs only on desktop
SAGA	Use for examining trends in the pattern of ill health in the region and used for editing any spatial data			Kosmo	Available for windows, Linux and FreeBSD, and cross plathform	Dept. for Physical Geography, Göttingen (Germany), SAGA User Group Association	Free	*Desktop
Quan-tum GIS (QGIS)	Data viewing, editing, and analysis capabilities	Shapefile		ESRI, except its newer geodatabase format	Mac OS X, Linux, UNIX, and Microsoft Windows.	QGIS Development Team	Free	
GRASS GIS	Handling raster, topological vector, image processing, and graphic data.	Shapefile		Quantum GIS (QGIS)	Mac OS X, Microsoft Windows, Linux and cross platform	USA Govt.	Free	

GIS has been used too, to enhance understanding of West Nile virus bird and mapping of diseases such as cardiovascular disease, cancer and injury surveillance in Canada (Shuai et al., 2006; PH Agency of Canada, 2005).

GIS was also used for mapping the National health scheme's (NHS) performance rating report, as well as the interactive map of Sexually transmitted diseases (STDs) diagnosis by the Primary care trust (PCT) in London (Boulos, 2003; Boulos, 2005). GIS is being used for the detection of meningococcal disease outbreaks in order to provide stakeholders with the access and timely information on meningococcal infections in Germany (Reinhardt, 2007).

In Africa, GIS was used to explore the spatial correlation between ages related malaria infection among children in Gambia and the amount of seasonal environmental greenness as measured using the normalized difference vegetation index derived from satellite images at different points in time (Thomson,1999). It was also used to know the degree of malaria transmission in Kenya (Omumbo, 1998) and to determine areas with low and high level exposures to Plasmodium falciparum so as to know areas that is likely to have severe cases.

Apart from the above use of GIS applications, there is a number of different open source GIS software used in PH; these GIS software are developed by some countries of the world, and have established a network of resources and expertise in GIS development for PH. The development of these GIS applications for PH is often funded by United Nations (UN), World Health Organisation (WHO), United States Agency for International Development (USAID), and PH Agency of Canada (PHAC) among others. The GIS developed was purposely for health mapping, disease elimination, disease surveillance and as well as for system monitoring (World Health Organisation, 2005; PH Agency of Canada, 2005). Below is an overview of some open source GIS health mapping applications.

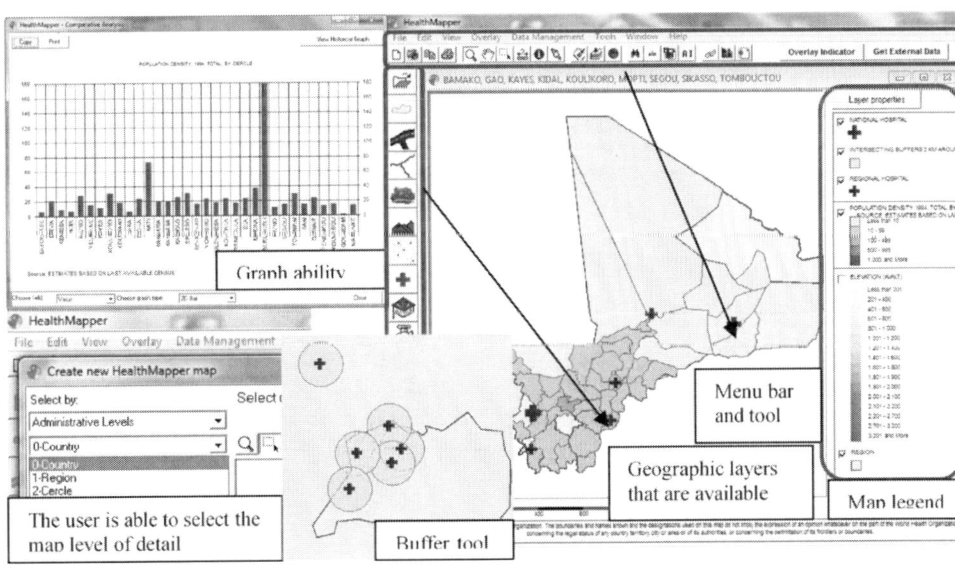

Source: ww.who.int/health_mapping.

Figure 2. Showing the Mapping interface of HealthMapper.

Health Mapper (HM) was developed as a joint GIS programme between the WHO and United Nations International Children's Fund (UNICEF). The programme was initiated in

1993 to provide GIS support for monitoring and the management of the Guinea Worm especially in developing nations. In 1995 it was expanded to cover other diseases such as leprosy, malaria, and HIV/AIDS. The Figure 2 below shows a mapping interface of the Healthmapper, being used for creating interactive maps for easy visualization of data. Some of its key features include its ability to generates thematic maps, measure distance (zoom in and out), allow importation of other files types, enable compatibility with shape- files, Microsoft Access, CSV?, Excel, and Dbase, and logistic regression and Kaplan-Meier survival analysis.

In addition HM has been successfully used in PH to monitor diseases and interventions with time; to detect relationship and correlation between diseases and environmental factors; to determine distribution of disease geographically; to assess resources allocation such as health facility, water supply, and schools, and to support planning and target interventions in disease ravaged areas. Basically, the Operating system Requirements to implement the HM are: Windows 98, Windows NT, 2000, Me and XP. One major advantage with HM, apart from it being open source, is that it is Free and easily downloadable from WHO's website. However, some of its Limitations is that It is usually implemented as a stand-alone software running on desktop alone. As such it is not a web based system and thus this makes it difficult for stakeholders to access anywhere and anytime the need arises. Also, as stand-alone software, it does not support web services, which is the recent trend in GIS; and Its statistical capacities are very limited.

Epiinfo/EpiMap (Ef/EM) is a GIS program developed by the US Centre for Disease Control, and World Health Organisation (WHO) for PH officers and researchers. It was built to provide an inexpensive user-friendly tool for health data management and analysis, as well as display information in form of maps as shown in Figure 3 below. Epiinfor/EpiMap is currently being used in over 180 countries of the world.

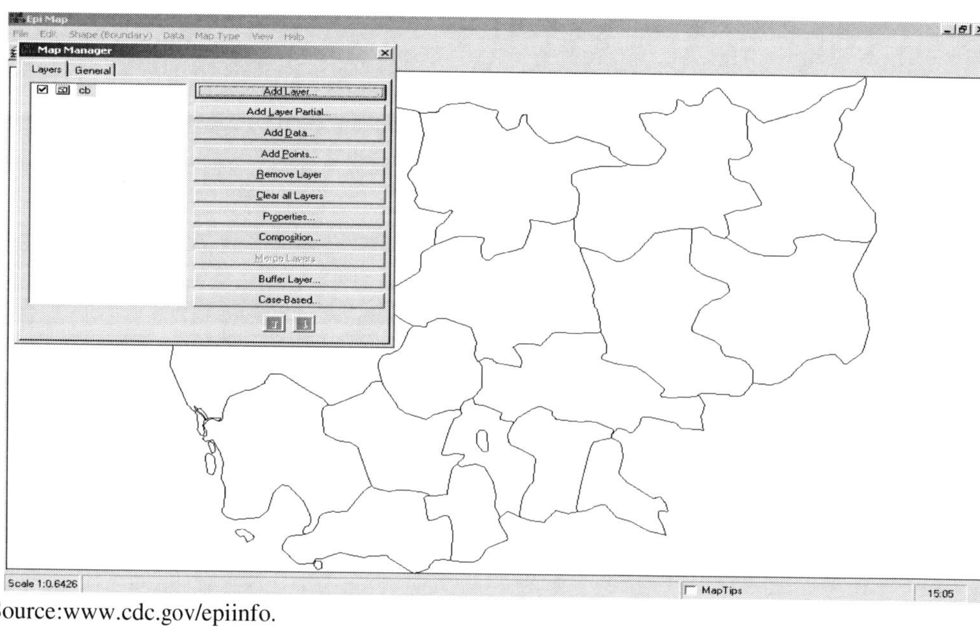

Source:www.cdc.gov/epiinfo.

Figure 3. Showing the display of Information in map form.

Moreover, some of the Key features of Ef/EM are that; it allows import of other files types, it is Arcview compatible, which allows modification and addition of modules, it is compatible with shapefiles, Microsft Access, SQL, Excel, Dbase and XML, and it also supports logistic regression as well as Kaplan-Meier survival analysis. In PH it is used for disease outbreak investigations, surveillance and to capture, manage and analyze health related data both statistically and geographically.

The basic operating system requirements are the common: Windows 98, NT, 2000, Me and XP. Apart from it being free with the manual, it is available online at http://www.cdc.gov/epiinfo, and it can also be downloaded from WHO website (www.who.int). Nevertheless, limitations are; It is also a stand-alone software running on desktop alone, It has limited GIS capacities because it can only capture and analyse health data, and it does not have the capacity for query.

SaTScan^{TM} was developed by Martin Kulldorf as free software, but with Information management services Incorporated. It was achieved with the financial support of organizations in the United States such as the National Cancer Institute (NCI), the National Institute of Child Health and Development (NICHD). Other supportive agencies were the Alfred P. Sloan Foundation (through the New York Academy of Medicine) and the Centres for Disease Control and Prevention (through the Association of American Medical Colleges). It was developed for epidemiological surveillance of diseases by detecting clusters of health and analysis of health events space, and space-time using scan statistics. As shown in figure 4 below, it has three main components which are used for all intended analysis.

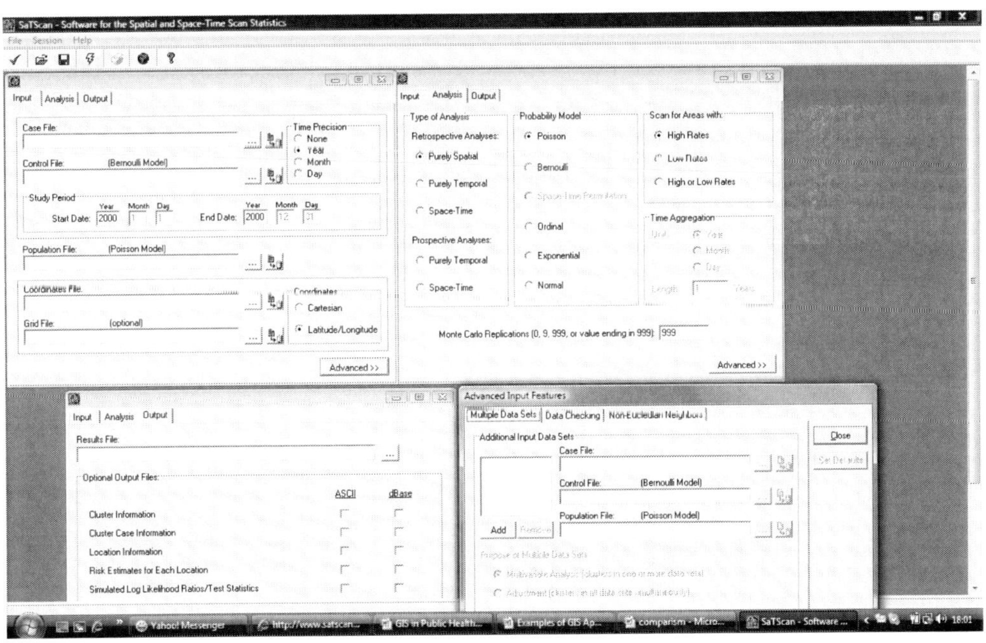

Source:www.satscan.org

Figure 4. Showing the SaTScanTM components.

The SaTScan^{TM} has some characteristics, among which is, its usefulness for geographical disease surveillance, the detection of spatial or space-time disease clusters, the testing of the statistical significance of diseases' cluster alarms, and also the performance of time-periodic diseases' surveillance (repeatedly), so as to detect disease outbreak. In PH, it has been effectively used to detect if a disease is distributed randomly in space and time. It has also been used to evaluate the statistical significance of clusters of high risk and low risk diseases, as well as perform repeated time-periodic disease surveillance for the detection of outbreak of diseases.

Its operating system requirement is any of the variants of the windows operating system such as: The Windows 98, NT, 2000, Me, and windows XP. Its recent test on window's Vista, was successful. It is often available for free from http://www.satscan.org with license agreement, and it is a very powerful software tool for space-time analyses. However, its limitations are like that of others; that is, it is a stand-alone software running on desktop alone, as well as have little or no GIS capacities. A review of other open source GIS applications, which is summarised in table 1shows that none of the application is web based and all runs on desktop. Apart from HealthMapper, others have little or no GIS capacity.

3. Current Research Trends in Public Health GIS

As at now, there are quite a few ongoing research projects in the field of GIS and Epidemiology. In Arkansas and North America, for instance there is research on the use of GIS to identify populations at risk for cancer. Also, finding the relationship between environmental factors and cancer is part of the research effort. The effort is aimed at monitoring the prevalence rate of cancer incidence and mortality in order to find more appropriate and timely interventions (Arkansas Central Cancer Registry, 2007;North American Association of Central Cancer Registries, 2007). Moreover, it has been reported that there is ongoing research on web based GIS, which will facilitate the monitoring and space-time clustering of Dengue hemorrhagic fever (DHF) in Indonesia and Southeast Asia (IDRC/CRDI, 2007).

In the United Kingdom, there are ongoing researches in the field of GIS and Epidemiology. The research focuses on development of a GIS to monitor air pollution at the Worcester. This uses GIS regression to generate predictive models of pollution concentrations as a function of population density, distance to roads, and land use data. Also, there is an ongoing research on how to use GIS to investigate the impact of air pollution on asthma development among children born in Boston area and investigate the spatial distribution of myocardial infection incidence rates in Worcester.

3.1. Benefits of GIS in Public Health

There are some contributions GIS has made to the field of PH which are discussed below. First, GIS has been useful in balancing patient privacy with data accessibility for health officers. Some of the epidemic disease data such as HIV/AIDS needs confidentiality because patients living with such diseases do not want people to identify them as carrying such a disease. This however, will be useful in a multi-ethnic setting like Nigeria, where there a multiple beliefs. Worst still, civilization as well as formal education is still far from most citizens, unlike in well advanced countries where their citizens are well informed. Thus they are able to cope with the stigma and trauma which goes with some diseases like HIV/AIDS mentioned earlier.

Secondly, GIS has reduced health data redundancy, as well as increase the integrity and accuracy of spatial health data. It has also improved health data efficiency by processing and analysing them within a short period of time. As a tool which finds relationship between people, their health and their environment; in PH officers using it are able to monitor and map areas at risk with the simple identification of risk factors. This is often realized by determining the geographical distribution and variation of disease and their associated factors. Also, with GIS spatial health data could be collected from different sources, such as maps, field work, and secondary data. These are integrated together using the same GIS application, and as a result better understandings of factors that contribute to the spread of diseases are established.

Thirdly, GIS could also help health officers to know when and where to intervene in specific locations, which will eventually improve the health care system and increase health facility accessibility. Health care providers often rely on it to manage health personnel and resources. In the developed nations, where it is being used, there are evidences of how It has been employed in such a way that the cost of health care delivery system has been well minimised and at the same time provide quality health care. Finally, even health planners could depend on it to know how patients are served by health personnel in order to determine the distance between patients, doctors and health facilities.

In Nigeria presently, there is this attempt to give quality health care services to the citizens, even at affordable costs. To this end the government has set up an agency, known as the National health insurance scheme (NHIS). So far, the scheme has been cumbered with various challenges, ranging from poor monitoring of health management officers (HMO) to proper management of HMO and beneficiaries of the scheme. Evidently, with the benefit of GIS discussed previously, GIS if embraced and deployed will do a lot in ensuring a hitch free and successful PH in Nigeria.

3.2. GIS in Public Health

a. GIS Web Services. Geo Web services, also popularly known as GIS web services is the distribution of spatial data to the user through a web browser and is one of the current researches in PH which need expansion. However, the use of web based GIS is still common among both public and private organisations, thus the need to share health related data online. The importance of web based systems, which are now being integrated with interoperability capacity, is an advantage in this regard. This as expected will give opportunity for cross platform, multi-architecture information system and thus allow open standard for computing platforms such as SQL, XML and its variants. Besides, Interoperability is a unique feature of geo web services, which refers to the ability of a system or part of a system to work with other system with little or no effort from the user (Sriphaisal & Pujari, 2006). Presently, few researchers are researching into Geo web service in PH. Lu(2004) proposed a system with interoperability capacity which will be used to prevent SARS virus and report the location of SARS to the health workers through the Internet. With this system the health worker can share SARS data over the Internet with stakeholders.

Another possible area of research in Geo web services is the integration of Artificial Neural Network, fuzzy logic and time series into Geo web services. If the integration of Artificial Intelligent and time series forecasting is possible, geo web service system will be able to support interoperability and at the same time predict accurate future trend or prevalence rate of diseases and environmental problem. The result of this will be a unique contribution to the field of health informatics and PH as a whole. The system is expected to assist stakeholders to be able to share health related data over the Internet as well as be able to predict the trend of diseases. A major challenge with this type of research, is how to bring together as well as harmonise the knowledge of statisticians or mathematician with that of GIS expert, which is required in order to come up with the geo web services that has inbuilt forecasting features.

b. Distributed Public Health GIS. There is a new generation of GIS known as the Distributed GIS (DGIS). It is a means of moving from the traditional two-tier client/server model to the three or n-tier client/server computing architecture. The DGIS is a system tool, which uses Internet and wireless networks for data and processing communication. In a DGIS, users do not need to bother to have a GIS software on their system, since it can be accessed from anywhere through the Internet or wireless connection. Also, in the DGIS, the client might be a laptop, a mobile phone, or a Personal Digital Assistant (PDA). An interesting side of the DGIS is that even if it is a mobile GIS, the one on a desktop or a wired GIS, so long as it is Internet based, which works on a wired or wireless Internet, it will still be compatible with an open architecture distributed computing.

The Internet GIS will often have a client and four types of servers, namely: The web server, the application server, the map and the data servers. Thus, with these components, the client/server will allow the user to interact with spatial health data. In the case of a mobile GIS, it has three components, which are client, servers (map, web, and data server) and network provider (Peng & Tsou, 2003). Apart from the DGIS being a cross platform, it is dynamic as well as a heterogeneous system, which function with Internet or wireless communication network connection. According to Sriphaisal et al., in DGIS client and server are the same, with the GIS nodes embedding GIS programs and geodata (Sriphaisal & Pujari, 2006).

The realization that in a DGIS, all the system that store data are linked together, and request for data can come from any of the systems located in different places (Bandopadhyay et al., 2003), underscores its relevance to PH. This couple with all the already discussed features of the DGIS confirms that the system will be useful for PH. This is in the sense that the health providers will (can) have all the required software on their server, while the health officers at different locations can access and run the GIS software any time as if is on their system.

c. Mobile Agent Based Public Health GIS. The mobile agent based in PH GIS, is an agent which is also called Geo-Agent in GIS. It is a system that takes autonomous action in certain environment so as to meet design objectives (Jenning, & Wooldrige, 2001). Mobile agent which is a special class of agent has ability to move from one point to another in a network. It has been used to monitor a lot of things on a network. It can be referred to as network mobile server (NMS). It is a recent development in computing used to manage network efficient applications so as to access information anywhere anytime so far there is wired or wireless connection. In a network, it is used to locate a particular resource and decide on where to send it to and with the aim of traffic reduction on the network. They, also move from one host to another on a network during their execution period to serve their creator or user. There are few works on GIS using mobile agent (Guan et al., 2002; Kalantari et al., 2003). Also, despite the fact that mobile agent is an aspect of information retrieval, reports on their use in spatial data analysis, is still very few. On the other hand, Mobile Agent will be a useful tool in PH GIS especially in a distributed GIS and GI-Service environment. With it, health related data can be searched for by mobile agent on the network and send it to where there is a need for it. Thus, the PH officer will have access to any data, whenever they need it and when there is a need to compare the trend of a particular disease in different locations.

4. Application of GIS as Solution to Public Health in Nigeria

4.1. Public Health in Nigeria

Nigeria had her independence in 1960, at which time the health care system was largely engaged in curative care and health care approach to providing health services to her citizens. The 1970's and 80's brought about large changes for health care in Nigeria with a dramatic expansion of the public health care system. At this same time, there was the third National Development Plan, which introduced a Health Sector Strategy that focused on Primary health Care (PHC) delivery. Along with this strategy, came the introduction of schools of health technology (SHT), and what is currently on ground came as a result of the National Health Policy (NHP) of 1988, which set up the health system in Nigeria. Also, in 1990, part of the goal of the policy became the establishment of a decentralized system, and a community-level based component with the action plan of training the PHC workers (Gustafsson-Wright& Van-der-Gaag, 2008).

There is also the National Health Council (NHC) that is chaired by a Minister in the Ministry of Health. Under the NHC, there are Commissioners of Health from all the states, who have the overall responsibility of health policy in the country. The responsibilities for policy guidance and technical support, national health management information systems, government service provision by tertiary and teaching hospitals and national laboratories and international health relations lies on them (Ademola et al., 2008). In addition, several health initiatives have been made since the late 1980's, with a view to monitor as well as handle different programs. Some of the programs includes: Hospital Management Boards (HMBs), National Agency for Food and Drug Administration and Control (NAFDAC), National Primary Health Care Development Agency (NPHCDA), National Programme for Immunization (NPI), Population Activities Fund Agency (PAFA), National Action Committee on AIDS (NACA) and National Health Insurance Scheme (NHIS). One of the challenges still encountered till date with the establishment of these programs is the coordination between parastatal agencies and programs and the federal and state ministries of health, which is responsible for carrying out effective health service provision (Gustafsson-Wright& Van-der-Gaag, 2008).

A supposed success story of the Nigeria's Health Sector strategy is the National Health Insurance Scheme (NHIS), which started in 1999. The scheme is designed to facilitate fair financing of health care costs through financial risk protection and cost-burden sharing for individuals. Another supposed success is the Health Insurance Fund/PharmAccess Programs (HIFPA). The HIFPA started in Nigeria in 2007 under the name Hygeia Community Health Plan (HCHP). Among its objectives is to provide coverage for the most common medical problems found among the target groups, which includes primary care, limited secondary care and medication, including HIV/AIDS voluntary counselling and treatment (HVCT). The local executing partner of the program is Hygeia. Hygeia is the largest Health Maintenance Organization (HMO) in Nigeria, with a local network of over 200 clinics and hospitals throughout Nigeria and around 200,000 paying members. Having had 20 years of experience in health care in Nigeria and as one of the HMOs executing Nigeria's new National Health Insurance Scheme (NHIS); it has contracted 19 clinics and hospitals for the Health Insurance Fund program where the scheme beneficiaries can obtain their medical services. However, the major problem with both NHIS and the HMOs is that of data capturing, organization, management, analysis despite the fact that data supposedly to exist (Gustafsson-Wright& Van-der-Gaag, 2008).

4.2. Public Health in Nigeria: Its Challenges

The successful implementation of the goals of the Public health sector in Nigeria is deviled by a number of challenges. Nigeria has so many programs, which could better lives, but there is still dearth of data. Where it exists, the efficient capture, storage, retrieval and analysis of it is not present. Another challenge is poor disease reporting and surveillance. In the advent of disease outbreak both the scope and type of the disease will remain a mystery since there is no proper approach in handling it. There is also the dearth of a reliable method of giving the public a blow-by-blow account of all for of contaminations that could endanger human health. Apart from the ones already mentioned, there are poor communication/links among stakeholders. In the case of diseases, which are contagious like the ones often spread by animals, monitoring them is not feasible. This is because, seasonal grazing (or communal grazing) often associated with the husbandry system practiced in Nigeria makes it impossible for effective monitoring (Ademola et al., 2008; Clarke et al., 1996), without the use of technology.

One of the basic objectives of healthcare Planning in any part of the world, according to (Murad, 2005), is to have an equivalent access to health care for all, regardless of peoples' ability to pay. This is means adequate Health care facilities' planning is needed. Other issues already surmounted using GIS include: (i) the assessment of spatial changes in health status, thus ensuring that health needs are satisfied (Land, 2004); (ii) in spatial epidemiology, using GIS to answer questions such as: Where are the incidences located?, what are the environmental characteristics of these areas?, what are the relations between health incidences and the environment at other locations?, and what patterns are evolving?(Worboys & Duckham, 2004); (iii) assessing health care facilities accessibility and utilization, in order to optimize resources, which has always been the worry of health authorities. This is often with a view to finding the best location for a health care facility. Also, results from this assessment allows three important factors that affect the level of accessibility in any facility location, which are; the capacity of the facility, the amount of demand for such facility, and the transportation network that communicate such demand to the relevant capacity, to be ascertained; (iv) evaluating the accessibility of existing health facilities. This is often with the purpose of determining the areas, which have poor accessibility for certain health facility and then proposals for improving such low level of health care accessibility are prepared; and (v) health care planning data, which is needed to evaluate existing location of a health service or prepare a new site location for a health care system. However, the huge impact of these PH care best practices using GIS still eludes Nigeria's PH care system, since it is still a burden. This is because Nigeria's PH sector need to realize the immense benefit GIS can be to it.

4.3. GIS: a solution to the Challenges in Nigeria's Public Health

Existing characterization of GIS, such as it being an "automated systems for the capture, storage, retrieval, analysis, and display of spatial data" (Clarke, 1995), and a useful technique for capturing, maintaining and analyzing the spatial data, considers what GIS can do in terms of tasks, rather than what it is. As a result GIS is considered as an important and useful tool in planning and evaluating any health care system (Clarke et al., 1996; Murad, 2005; Clarke, 1995). The aspect of capture, storage, and display capability of the GIS works exactly the same way with a database. GIS can accomplish everything that a regular database system can, such as enter and edit data and update information in the existing database. Also, Clarke et al. (1996) reported that data records in GIS can be retrieved in more than one ways, especially with the presence of the relational database manager, which allows easy searching, reordering, and selecting of data on the basis of its attributes and values. Obviously with these functional capabilities GIS can also be used for managerial purposes and well suited even for monitoring functions.

Also, Gesler reported how epidemiologists have traditionally used maps when analyzing associations between location, environment, and diseases (Gesler, 1986). They as well gave details of how GIS has been used as follows: (i) in the surveillance and monitoring of vector borne and water borne diseases in environmental health, (ii) in the modeling of exposures to electromagnetic fields, (iii) in the quantifying of lead hazards in a neighbourhoods (a challenge the PH in Nigeria struggled with recently in one of her northern states, where so many lives were lost), (iv) in the predicting of child pedestrian injuries, and (v) in the analysis of disease policy and planning. In the work of (Adebayo et al., 2008), several challenges were chronicled about PH in Nigeria. More specifically, mention was made of the fact that there are so many breeding grounds for insects and rodents resulting from the poor local waste management in public health. The lack of officially designated location for dumping of refuse was also bemoaned.

Nevertheless, Adebayo et al. recommended that appropriate and effective environmental health system, if it exists must address physical, chemical, and biological factors that is external to people, and all the related factors that can potentially affect health. Accordingly, it is expected to target preventing disease and creating health-supportive environments (Adebayo et al., 2008). This claimed will contribute to the improvement in quality of life and longevity, since improved health quality of life is important for productivity and the promotion of economic growth. Should this not be realized, according to the millennium development goal (MDG) will not be achieved. So, health is very strategic to achieving MDG thus the need for the use and deployment of GIS cannot be looked down, as it is a tool that could yield useful result (Adebayo et al., 2008).

Furthermore, In the work of Adekunleet al., (2007) the aim was to assess the levels of some physical, chemical, biochemical and microbial water quality parameters in twelve hand – dug wells in a typical rural area (Igbora) of southwest region of Nigeria. They suggest the regular monitoring of groundwater quality, abolishment of unhealthy waste disposal practices and the introduction of modern techniques was recommended for better analysis. Waste disposal practices cannot just be abolished, without convincing evidences, especially in a large scale of the PH consequences. Hence the need for modern techniques as suggested by (Adekunleet al., 2007), which can give faster and more accurate results, even on a large scale bases.

The work of Facchinelli (2001), showed the possibility of using GIS to successfully identify heavy metal sources on a regional scale. That the issue under consideration hinges on the health of humans make the need and urgent one and thus requires techniques or methods provided by GIS. According to Scholton, et al., (1990), health and ill-health always have and always will have a spatial dimension, hence epidemiologist and other medical sciences have explored the power of maps in helping human mind assimilate and understand the spatial dynamics of disease. It is thus pertinent to suggest the use of GIS in Nigeria's PH sector, as its application has been in implicated also in Public and environmental health (Scholton, et al., 1990)].

Finally, the human resources crisis in Africa including Nigeria, which is especially acute in the public health field, according to Ahearn & De Rooy, (1996), could be solved through the use of GIS. What needed are just a few well trained hands, and with the deployment of relevant GIS and Information and communication technology (ICT) facilities a lot would be achieved more than what an uncountable trained PH workers can achieve.

CONCLUSION

In conclusion, GIS is an important tool in epidemiology and is being used for disease visualization, exploration, interpretation, monitoring, surveillance, modeling and spatial relationship.

There is a need for developing country like Nigeria which is characterized with various diseases such as malaria, cholera, tuberculosis, fever and AIDS to adopt and use GIS in tackling her PH related problems. The system will not only be useful as a decision support system, but (with the inclusion of geo web services) to minimise, prevent, control and manage the epidemics that are troubling the citizenry. The argument that no country can attain a high level of economic development with a population crippled by high infant and maternal mortality, pervasive illness of its workforce, and low life expectancy; and that in essence, good health and physical well being are essential to the formation and maintenance of human capital and are key components for economic growth and sustained poverty reduction, is a food for thought.

Thus, effective use of GIS may lead to reduction of poverty in any region. Thus, for a developing nation like Nigeria, GIS is strongly recommended as a solution to the many challenges being faced by the PH sector in Nigeria.

ACKNOWLEDGMENTS

I hereby acknowledge the referees. I also acknowledge the effort of Titilope, Iyinoluwa and Iyanuoluwa during the period of developing this chapter.

REFERENCES

Adebayo, A., Ogunfowokan, A. A., & Olaogun, A., 2008. Challenges to better health in local areas in Nigeria: Environmental health officers experience in Ondo State. *Sudanese Journal of Public Health*: July 3 (3).

Ademola, A. I., McCrindle C. M, E, Fasina, F. O., & Godfroid, J., 2008. Evaluation of Problems and possible solutions linked to the surveillance and control of bovine brucellosis in sub-Saharan Africa, with special emphasis on Nigeria. *Journal of veterinaria Italiana*, 44 (3), 549-556.

Adekunle, I. M., Adetunji, M. T., Gbadebo, A. M.,& Banjoko, O. B., 2007. Assessment of Groundwater Quality in a Typical Rural Settlement in Southwest Nigeria. International *Journal of Environmental Research and Public Health*, 4(4), 307-318. ISSN 1661-7827.

Ahearn SC, & De Rooy C., 1996. Monitoring the effects of Dracunculiasis Remediation of Agricultural Productivity using satellite data. International. *Journal of Remote Sensing*. 3(2).

Arkansas Central Cancer Registry2007.*Arkansas Central Cancer Registry* [online] Available fromhttp://www.healthyarkansas.com/arkcancer/arkcancer.html[Accessed 30 Oct 2007].

Bandopadhyay, S. , Ghosh, A. & Sarkar R., 2003. Design of an efficient Distributed GIS Application. *TENCON 2003: Conference on Technologies for Asia-Pacific Region* 15-17 Oct 2003.p.1162-1166.

Boulos K.N., 2003. Web GIS In Practice: An Interactive Geographical Interface to English Primary Care Trust Performance Ratings for 2003 And 2004 *International Journal of Health Geographic*, 3(16) [online]. Available from at http://www.ij-healthgeographics.com/content/3/1/16 [Accessed 07/July 2007].

Boulos M. K., .2005. Web GIS in Practice III: Creating a Simple Interactive Map of England's Health Authorities using Google Maps API, Google Health KML, and MSN Virtual Earth Map Control. *International Journal of Health Geographic* 4(22) [online]. Available from http://www.ij-healthgeographics.com/content/4/1/22 [Accessed 07/July 2007].

Clarke K. C. 1995. Analytical and computer cartography. 2nd ed. Englewood Cliffs, NJ:Prentice-Hall.

Clarke, K. C., McLafferty, S. L., & Tempalski, B.J., 1996. Perspectives On Epidemiology and Geographic Information Systems: A Review and Discussion of Future Directions. *Journal of Emerging Infectious Diseases*. 2(2)— April-June 1996.

Colak E. & Yomralioglu T., 2005. Using GIS to produce Cancer Incidence Maps: A Case Study of Trabzon Turkey, GIS Development, Weekly Publication.

Cromely E.K. & Mclafferty, S. L., 2002. *GIS and PH*. New York: The Guilford Publication, Inc, ISBN 1-57230-707-2.

ESRI, 1999.*GIS for Health Care Today and Tomorrow* [online]. Available from http://www.esri.com/news/arcuser/0499/umberlla.html [Accessed 24/October 2007.

Facchinelli, A., Sacchi, E., &Mallen, L. 2001. Multivariate Statistical and GIS-based approach to identify heavy metal sources in soils. Elsevier *Journal of Environmental Pollution,* 114, 313 – 324.

Garb J. Ganai. S., Boyd, C. & Wait R., 2007. Using GIS for spatial analysis lesions in the human body, *International Journal of Health Geographic* 2007, 6(11).

Gesler W., 1986. The uses of spatial analysis in medical geography: a review. *Soc. Sci. Med.* 23:963-73.

Glass G., Schwartz B., Morgan J., Johnson D., Noy P., & Isreal E. , 1995. Environmental risk factors for Lyme disease identified with geographic information systems. *American Journal of PH* 85(7) p 146-156.

Guan J., Zhou S. & Bian F., 2002.A Mobile Agent and GML Based Framework for Integrating Distributed GIS; Integrated System for Spatial Data production, Custodian and Decision Support, ISPRS Commission II, Symposium 2002, Xi'an P.R. China August 20-23.

Gupta R & Shriram R. 2004. Disease Surveillance and Monitoring using GIS: Proceedings of Map India 2004 [online] Available from www.gisdevelopment. net/application/health/planning/pdf/min04054.pdf[Accessed 23 Nov 2007].

Gustafsson-Wright, E., &Van-der-Gaag, J., 2008. An Analysis of Nigeria's Health Sector by State: Recommendations for the Expansion of the Hygeia Community Health Plan. Report produced by the Amsterdam Institute for International Development (AIID). August, 2008. [40] World Bank. 2005. Nigeria Health, Nutrition and Population Country Status Report. Volume II. Main Report.

Hakre S., Masuoka P., Vanzie E., Roberrts DR., 2004. Spatial correlations of mapped malaria rates with environmental factors in Belize, Central America, International Journal of Health Geographic 3(6) [online] Available from http://www.ij-healthgeographics.com/content/3/1/6 [Accessed 23 Nov 2007].

Harris D., 2003. System Analysis and Design for the Small Enterprises, 3rd edition Thomson Course Technology.

Hirschheim R., Klein H., & Lyytinen K., 1995. Information System development and Data Modelling: Conceptual and Philosophical Foundations, Cambridge University Press.

IDRC/CRDI., 2007. Web Based Integrated DHF Surveillance System in Sleman District, Yogyakarta [online] Available from http://www.idrc.ca/en/ev-68229-201-1-DO_TOPIC.html [Accessed 6 Dec, 2007].

Jenning, N.R. & Wooldrige M., 2001. Applications of Intelligent Agent, Queen Mary and Westfield College, University of London.

Kalantari S. M., Alesheikh A.A., & Talebzadeh A., 2003.Promoting Distributed GIServices Using Mobile Agent Technology [online]. Available from http://www.gisdevelopment.net/technology/gis/ma03199.htm [Accessed 29/Oct 2007].

Kitron U. & Kazmierczak J.,1997. Spatial analysis of the distribution of Lyme disease in Wisconsin.*American Journal of Epidemiology.*145(6) p.5558-566.

Land F., 2004. The Darker Site of Knowledge Management.*The Software Practitioner,*14(5).

Laymon P., 1999. Spatially Enabling Vital Health Data, ESRI: GIS and Mapping Software, [online] Available from http://www.esri.com/news/arcuser/0499/vital.html [Accessed on 29/ Oct. 2007].

Lightsone A., Dhillon P., Peek-Asa C. & Kraus F., 2001. A Geographic Analysis of motor vehicle collisions with Child pedestrians in Long Beach; California: Comparing intersection and midblock incident. Locations.*Injury Prevention.*7(2). p. 155-160. [online] Available from http://injuryprevention.bmj.com/cgi/reprint/7/2/155.pdf [Accessed 24/October 2007].

Lu, x., 2004.Infrastructure for web GIS based interoperable SARS information System; Computer Supported Cooperative Work in design, 2004. Conference proceedings; Vol 1:26-28 May 2004.

Murad, A. A., 2005. Using GIS for Planning Public General Hospitals at Jeddah City.JKAU: *Environnemental Design Science,* Vol. 3, pp: 3 – 22, 2005.

Mutitanon W, Kongthong P., Kongkanon, C., Yoksa S. , Gonzalez J., & Babazan, P., 2007. Spatial and Temporal dynamic of Dengue Hemorrhagic Fever Epidemics (Nakhon Pathom Province, Thailand, 1997-2001), Map India 2007 held 22-25 January 2007 at *Hyderabad International Convention centre Hyderabad*, India.

North American Association of Central Cancer Registries, 2007. North American Association of Central Cancer Registries. [online] Available from http://www.naaccr.org/GIS [Accessed 30 Oct, 2007].

Omumbo J., Ouma J.., Rapuoda B., Craig M., LesSueur D. & Snow R., 1998. Mapping malaria transmission intensity using geographical information systems: an example from Kenya. *Annals Tropical Medicine and Parasitology* 92(1). p. 7-21.

Peng T-R & Tsou M-H., 2003. Internet GIS: Distributed Geographic Information Services for the Internet and Wireless Networks, New Jersey: Hoboken- Wiley & Sons.

Public Health Agency of Canada, 2005.Disease Surveillance [online].Available from www.phac-aspc.gc.ca.dsol-smed [Access on 22 Oct 2007].

Public Health Agency of Canada, 2013.Notifiable Disease online. Available from http://dsol-smed.phac-aspc.gc.ca/dsol-smed/ndis/ [Access on 3rd June, 2013].

Pillay R., 2007. Using GIS to spatially portray the prevalence of HIV/AIDS and it demographic Consequences in selected countries in Sub –Sahara Africa, Map India 2007 held 22-25 January 2007 at Hyderabad International Convention centre Hyderabad, India.

Ramirez A., Olugasa B. & Bickett-Weddle D., 2004. Geographic Information System and its Role in Biological Risk Management. [online] Available from http://www.cfsph.iastate.edu/BRM. [Accessed 22/Oct 2007].

Reinhardt M., Elias J., Albert J., Frosch M., Vogel U., & Harmsen D., 2007. EpiScanGIS: A Geographical Information System for Laboratory Surveillance of Meningococcal Disease in Germany. *European Congress of Clinical Microbiology and Infectious Disease*, 17th . Germany, 31 March-04 April 2007.

Scholten H. & Lepper M. ,1991. The benefits of the application of geographical information systems in public and environmental health. *WHO Statistical Quarterly*, 44(3).

Scholton, H. J., & De Lepper, M. J. C., 1990. The Benefit of the Application of Geographic Information Systems in Public and Environmental Health. Consultation onEpidemiological and Statistical Methods of Rapid Health Assessment/WHO, ESM/CONS.RA/90.13. Geneva, 26-27 Nov., 1990.

Shuai J., Buck P., Sockett P., Aramini J., & Pollari F., 2006.A GIS-driven integrated real time surveillance pilot system for national West Nile dead bird Surveillance in Canada. *International Journal of Health Geographic* 2006, 5:17.

Shukla S. & Goel R., 2007. A GIS based strategic disease prediction model to support Rural Health service system, Map India 2007 held 22-25 January 2007 at Hyderabad *International Convention centre Hyderabad*, India.

Sriphaisal W. & Pujari A. K., 2006. A Comparative Assessment of GIServices Architecture, [online]; Available from http://www.gisdevelopment.net/technology/gis/index.htm [Accessed 17 Aug 2007].

Thomson M., Connor S., D'Alessandro U., Rowlingson B., Diggle P., Cresswell M., & Greenwood B., 1999.Predicting Malaria infection in Gambian children from satellite data and bed net use surveys: the important of spatial correlation in the interpretation of results. *American Journal of Tropical Medicine and Hygiene*, 61(1) p. 2-8.

Vyas A. & Kalsaria S., 2007. Evaluating the Immunization Reach and Coverage: Use of GIS in the context of Rural Households and PH System, Map India 2007 held 22-25 January 2007 at Hyderabad International Convention centre Hyderabad, India.

Worboys M. & Duckham M., 2004. *GIS A Computing Perspective.* 2nd ed., CRC Press.

World Health Organisation 2005. PH mapping and GIS, [Online] Available from http://www.who.int/health_mapping/en [Accessed 22/Oct 2007].

In: Health, Violence, Environment and Human Development … ISBN: 978-1-62948-038-1
Editors: A. Cotte Poveda and C. I. Pardo Martínez

Chapter 4

HEALTH-POVERTY TRAP IN NIGERIA: IMPLICATIONS FOR ECONOMIC DEVELOPMENT

Kanayo Ogujiuba ***and Oluwasola Omoju***
Research Division,
National Institute for Legislative Studies, National Assembly,
Abuja, Nigeria

ABSTRACT

The relationship between poverty and health has long been recognised in development economics. It is widely believed that reduction in poverty can lead to improvement in health status, and improved health on the other hand can enhance productivity, income and facilitate poverty reduction and vice-versa. However, while most studies indicate a relationship between these two phenomena, very few have examined the link from a causality point of view.

This is the main aim of this chapter. This chapter examines the causal relationship between health and poverty in Nigeria and the implication of such relationship for economic development in Nigeria. Using the trend analysis and granger causality test, we find that there is a health-poverty trap in Nigeria, signifying a vicious circle between health status and poverty. It was also found that the relationship between health and poverty in Nigeria originates from the latter. The chapter further explains that the health-poverty trap could have negative effect on productivity, human and physical capital, savings and investment, trade, etc. Thus, the Nigerian government needs to make deliberate and conscious effort to break the vicious circle of poverty and health in order to achieve its development goals.

JEL: I15, I32, O20, C32

Keywords: Health, Poverty; MDGs; Poverty-Trap; Granger-Causality; Nigeria

---

*Corresponding Author Email: kannyog@gmail.com; who also, is a Research Associate at the Statistics and Population Studies Department; University of Western Cape, South Africa.

1. INTRODUCTION

The high level of poverty and other ills associated with it has attracted the attention of world leaders and the need to address the needs of the world's poor population necessitated the launch of the Millennium Development Goals. The Millennium Development Goals (MDGs) were initiated in 2000 to address the multi-faceted nature of poverty in developing countries. Apart from hunger and poverty, high infant and maternal mortality, environmental hazards, high malaria and HIV/AIDS prevalence, low literacy levels and gender inequality are some of the development challenges that the MDGs aim to address. Among other things, the MDGs targets to halve the number of people living below the poverty line by 2015; reduce by two-third and three-quarter respectively the rate of maternal and child mortality; and reduce the number of deaths resulting from preventable diseases such as malaria, tuberculosis, measles, HIV/AIDS, etc. Though the nexus between the MDGs is clear, the role of health in attaining the other MDGs has been acknowledged (Khanum and Singh, 2007). Moreover, the relationship between health and poverty has received substantial attention in development literature. Thus, there is a consensus that poverty reduction can lead to improvement in health status through increased access to better nutrition and health services. On the other hand, improved health enhances the productivity and income earning potentials of individuals and consequently facilitates poverty reduction. Furthermore, improvement in health status could also increase the ability to obtain education which has the capacity to improve lifetime earnings and reduce poverty.

Studies on the relationship between health and poverty are in abundance[1]. However, very few studies have focused on the causality between health and poverty. In other words, researches are limited on whether it is the level of poverty that influences health status or otherwise or both influences each other simultaneously. Majority of the researches conducted on this subject were done in other countries (Deaton, 2008; Hassan et al., 2011; Jackman et al., 2012; Parikh and Sharma, 2005; Starfield, 1992). Similar studies that were conducted in Nigeria, Babatunde (2011) and Riman and Akpan (2010) had some shortcomings. Riman and Akpan (2010) uses only life expectancy as the measure of health and the data used covers only from 1980 to 2004. This might be inappropriate since life expectancy does not adequately depict health status. On the other hand, Babatunde (2011) examines the relationship between health and economic growth; and since there are strong evidences of non-inclusive growth in Nigeria, the causal relationship between health and growth may not reflect health-poverty nexus. Therefore, the null hypothesis that is tested in this chapter is - there is no significant causal relationship between health and poverty in Nigeria. The alternative hypothesis is - there is significant causal relationship between health and poverty in Nigeria.

The contributions of this chapter to the health-development debate in Nigeria are that it examines the relationship between health and poverty from a causality angle; uses different proxies to measure health status; covers longer time-period and uses current data; and provide the implications for economic development. The main objective of the chapter is to examine the dynamic causality between poverty and health status using different proxies for health status and macro-level data from 1980 to 2010. The specific objectives are: i. To briefly

[1] These studies and several others have established that there is a significant long-run relationship between health and poverty.

review Nigeria's progress towards the Millennium Development Goals' poverty and health targets using available statistics; and ii. To empirically investigate the causality between poverty and health indicators in Nigeria.

The methodological approaches employed entail both analytical and econometrics techniques. The analytical technique involves trend analysis of time-series data. This is used to examine the first objective of this chapter – review the extent of achievement of MDGs health and poverty targets. Examining the level of achievement of MDG goals at the micro level requires a baseline study which involves substantial time and financial commitment. However, due to time and financial constraints, this chapter uses macro-level data. Thus, trend analysis is an appropriate technique to analyse the extent of progress made. This technique is unique and suitable because it provides a clear picture of the trend of the variable/phenomenon under investigation over a period of time (i.e. what it was, what it is now, and the possibility/likelihood of achieving what is desired).With respect to examining the causal relationship between health and poverty, we employ the granger causality test. This is because it is the most common way to test for causal relationships between variables. Using the granger causality to test for the existence of causal relationship between variables for an individual economy avoids the problem associated with the assumption of homogenous economic structure. This technique gives a clear insight about the variable(s) which significant efforts should be concentrated to break the health-poverty trap in Nigeria.

1.1. Brief Overview of Health and Poverty Situation in Nigeria

As at 2000, the Nigerian health system was ranked 187th among 191 countries according to the World Health Organisation. Communicable and non-communicable diseases account for 72% and 21% of deaths in Nigeria. By 2003, only 13% of Nigerian children aged 12-23 months were fully vaccinated (FMH, 2005). In 2007, Nigeria has one of the largest stocks of human resources in the health sector in Africa (USAID, 2007). As at the period, the country has 27 doctors and 170 nurses per 100,000 population compared to sub-Saharan average of 15 doctors and 72 nurses. Despite this, health care indicators have not met up with country targets and international benchmark. There are also significant differences in the health outcomes in rural and urban areas, among northern and southern states and across income groups. For example, under-five mortality in rural areas at 243 per 1000 live births is considerably higher than the level in urban areas which stands at 153 per 1000 live births. The number of women having access to birth assistance in urban area is 59% while those in rural area is 26%. The Nigerian health system is presently performing poorly. Over the years, various administrations – military and civilian – have made significant effort to promote the health of Nigerians through health reforms, policies and strategies. Particularly, President Obasanjo Administration (1999–2007) embarked on a fundamental reform of the health sector with a view to attaining the Millennium Development Goals and other national health policy targets. However, these reforms and polices have failed to yield result.

Despite the vision of the Nigerian Ministry of Health to reduce mortality and morbidity due to communicable diseases, reverse the prevalence of non-communicable diseases, meets global targets on the elimination and eradication of diseases and improve the quality of life of Nigerians, the Nigerian health situation is still in a despicable condition. Today, Nigeria still has one of the highest rates of infant and maternal mortality in the world[2]. Immunization coverage, especially in the northern part of the country, is one of the lowest in the world. Health care facilities and infrastructure such as clinics, beds, drugs, equipment, etc. are grossly inadequate to serve the teeming population. Health care personnel are also in short supply, particularly in rural areas. The number of death caused by preventable diseases such as malaria, measles, poliomyelitis, tuberculosis, etc., is still considerably high. The cost of health care, especially in private hospitals, where a higher standard of medical care is offered, is extremely high. The level of funding of the health sector has not kept up with the requirements of international organizations (WHO) and has contributed to worsening the health outcome of the populace.

The present state of health outcome in Nigeria has been aggravated by the high level of poverty persisting in the country as well as the poor state of the health sector, particularly at the primary health care level. High poverty level has retained a growing number of the population in a situation of ill health. On the other hand, sustained ill health has limited their opportunities to improve their income and pull out of poverty. Over the years, poverty level in Nigeria has oscillated. In 1980, poverty level stood at 28.1%. It increased to 46.3% in 1985, before falling to 42.7% in 1992. By 1996, poverty incidence had increased drastically to 66.9%. However, due to the various poverty-alleviating measures initiated by the government at the beginning of the new democratic dispensation, the national poverty rate decreased to 54.4% in 2004 (see Table 1). Nevertheless, poverty rose again between 2004 and 2010, from 54.4% to 69.0%, and further to 71.1% in 2011 (NBS, 2010).

Table 1. Trend, structure, dimension of poverty in Nigeria

Criteria/Year	1980	1985	1992	1996	2004	2010
NATIONAL POVERTY RATE	27.2	46.3	42.7	66.9	54.4	69.0
URBAN POVERTY RATE	17.2	37.8	37.5	59.3	43.2	61.8
RURAL POVERTY RATE	28.3	51.4	46.0	71.7	63.3	73.2
ZONES						
South-South	13.2	45.7	40.8	58.2	35.1	63.8
South East	12.9	30.4	41.0	53.5	26.7	67.0
South West	13.4	38.6	43.1	60.9	43.0	59.1
North Central	32.2	50.8	46.0	64.7	67.0	67.5
North East	35.6	54.9	54.0	70.1	72.2	76.3
North West	37.7	52.1	36.5	77.2	71.2	77.7
EDUCATIONAL LEVEL OF HOUSEHOLD HEADS						
No Education	30.2	51.3	46.4	72.6	68.7	n.a
Primary	21.3	40.6	43.3	54.4	48.7	n.a
Secondary	7.6	27.2	30.3	52.0	44.3	n.a
Higher than Secondary	24.3	24.2	25.8	49.2	26.3	n.a

Source: Nigeria Bureau of Statistics.

Examining the rural-urban dimension of poverty in Nigeria, statistics shows that rural areas have consistently had higher poverty level. In 1980, rural poverty level stood at 28.3%, compared to 17.2% in urban areas. The gap between rural and urban poverty widened in

[2] The number of child birth attended to by skilled personnel is still comparably low.

1985, as rural and urban poverty increased to 51.4% and 37.8% respectively. Between 1985 and 1992, there was reduction in the level of rural poverty, partly because of the rural-focus of the various poverty alleviation programmes initiated by the government during this period. The success of these programmes were, however, beset by poor targeting mechanism, programme inconsistency, poor implementation, corruption, and other institutional impediments (Adogamhe, 2010; Ogwumike, 2002; Ugoh and Ukpere, 2009). The poverty rates in both rural and urban areas have increased significantly thereafter. In terms of the regional distribution of poverty in Nigeria, evidence shows that the northern part of the country has the highest share of poverty. In 1980, the South-Eastern part of Nigeria had the lowest poverty rate, 12.9% while the North Western part had the highest, 37.7%[3]. The tide, however, changed in 1992, when the South, except the South-South region, experienced increase in poverty rates and the North the reverse. By 1996, all the regions witnessed ample increase in poverty level, but with the North West having the largest change. As at 2004, poverty level has drastically reduced in the South, while it still remain relatively high in the North, almost doubling the rates in the South.

Data from the National Bureau of Statistics provide evidence for clear relationship between poverty and education. Poverty is high among households whose head has no formal education. While the general level of poverty has increased over the years, the increase is skewed towards less educated households. In 1980, the poverty rate was within the same range (21-30%) for all households irrespective of the educational status of the head, except households headed by graduates of secondary school, who had a poverty rate of 7.6%. By 1992, poverty rate had become inversely related with the educational status of the household head. Households whose head's educational status is higher than secondary had a poverty rate of 25.8%. This is relatively low compared with 30.3%, 43.3% and 46.4% respectively for households headed by graduates with secondary, primary and no formal education. The trend still persists as at 2004, with poverty rate in households with heads having no, primary, secondary and above secondary education standing at 68.7%, 48.7%, 44.3% and 26.3% respectively.

2. Literature Review

2.1. Millennium Development Goals

One of the objectives of this chapter is to examine Nigeria's progress towards meeting the Millennium Development Goals (MDGs). The United Nations Millennium Development Goals (MDGs) was launched in 2000 to address the development needs of the world's poor population. The MDGs are eight international development goals that recognised the complexity as well as the multi-faceted nature and dimension of the challenges facing the poor, moving away from the conventional measure of income to concepts and indicators that capture overall human welfare. The MDGs are goals that were set by the international community with the aim of improving socio-economic conditions and quality of life of the world's poor. These goals were agreed by all member states of the United Nations and international organisations to be achieved by 2015.

[3] All the regions experienced large increases in poverty rates between 1980 and 1985.

Specifically, the MDGs has eight (8) goals, eighteen (18) targets and forty-eight (48) indicators to assess and monitor progress towards their achievement. However, the MDGs acknowledged the important role of health in poverty reduction and attainment of the other goals, as three out of the eight goals are health-related. The Millennium Development Goals are outlined as follow:

- Eradicate extreme poverty and hunger
- Achieve universal primary education
- Promote gender equality and women empowerment
- Reduce child mortality
- Improve maternal health
- Combat HIV/AIDS, malaria and other diseases
- Ensure environmental sustainability
- Develop a global partnership for development

The specific targets for each of the MDGs that are related to health and poverty include:

- Halve between 1990 and 2015, the proportion of people whose income is less than one dollar a day
- Achieve decent employment for women, men, and young people
- Halve between 1990 and 2015, the proportion of people who suffer from hunger
- Reduce by two-thirds, between 1990 and 2015, the under-five mortality rate
- Reduce by three quarters, between 1990 and 2015, the maternal mortality ratio
- Achieve, by 2015, universal access to reproductive health
- Halve halted by 2015 and begun to reverse the spread of HIV/AIDS
- Achieve, by 2010, universal access to treatment for HIV/AIDS for all those who need it
- Have halted by 2015 and begun to reverse the incidence of malaria and other major diseases

2.2. Health – Poverty Relationship: Empirical Literature

The relationship between health and poverty has long been discussed in the literature, particularly after the pioneering work of Schultz (1961), who argues that health is an important driver of quantity and quality of life. Poor health shortens the working life of an individual and reduces productivity and lifetime income of such individuals. Good health enhances prosperity by enhancing the educational outcomes and human capital capacity of individuals and the effect of education on socio-economic development (Barro, 1996; Schultz, 1999). An improvement in health status will result in an improvement in national income and reduction in the poverty level (Barro and Sala-i-Martin, 2004). Bloom and Canning (2003) argued that health affect poverty by enhancing productivity and income, spend longer time in the labour force and earn more income, invest more in training and education that would enhance their productivity and income, and save more in expectation of longer life. On the other hand, one of the main effects of poverty is poor health; and this has been reflected in the high level of infant and maternal mortality and low life expectancy (Ucha, 2010).

According to the World Health Organisation estimates, those living in poverty are more likely to die early than those with higher income (Government of Sindh Health Department, 2005). However, the World Bank and WHO (2005) posit that while the relationship between poverty and health is indisputable, the health of poor people can be improved without a significant increase in their income. This requires improved access to basic public services, such as clean water, sufficient and safe food, decent housing, adequate sanitation and improved education. The relationship between inequality and health has also attracted the attention of researchers. There seems to be a general consensus on the impact of inequality on the health status of the population (Fotso, 2006; Hong et al., 2006; Houweling et al., 2003; Rimanand Akpan (2010)[4].

Strauss and Thomas (1998) investigated the link between health, nutrition and development. They found that increase in the level of income will enhance access to better nutrition, healthcare and ultimately lead to better health. In another study on the relationship between poverty, health and economic growth in fifteen India states, Gupta and Mitra (2003) found that per capita income has a positive impact on health, and the relationship between health and poverty in India is bi-directional. This finding is however contrary to Anand and Ravallion (1993) who had concluded from a study of human development in poor countries that income level does not influence life expectancy as much as health expenditure does. Jackman et al. (2012) examine whether poverty have any influence on the health status and patterns of communities in the eastern region of Trinidad and Tobago using both qualitative and quantitative approaches. The findings pointed to a considerable negative association between poverty and improved health status of the populace. In the course of examining the poverty-health nexus in Pakistan, Hassan et al. (2011) expressed poverty as a function of health. Applying the ordinary least square method, the paper finds that health has a strong negative relationship with poverty in Pakistan. It concluded that policies directed towards improving the health status of the populace have a strong impact on poverty reduction. The Commission on Macroeconomics and Health examine the causal relationship between health and poverty and found a bi-directional relationship (WHO, 2001).

Some studies have investigated the link between poverty and disability. Filmer (2008) examined the relationship between health and disability in fourteen low and medium income countries[5]using household survey data. He found that being disabled is associated to being in the poorest two quintiles of the population in eight countries. Hoogeven (2005) investigated the link between households headed by disabled persons and the incidence and severity of poverty using cross-sectional survey data for Uganda. He found that the incidence of poverty is worse in households headed by disabled persons. In contrast to these studies, Gureje et al. (2006) examine the relationship between disability and poverty among the Yoruba-speaking areas of Nigeria using cross-sectional survey. They found no relationship between poverty and the likelihood of disability. In fact, in a study of the relationship between disability and poverty in South Africa using a case-control analysis, Loeb et al. (2008) found that the relationship between disability and poverty is inverse.

---

[4] These studies find that increasing level of inequality has an adverse effect on the health status of the population.

[5] (Bolivia, Cambodia, Chad, Colombia, India, Jamaica, Romania, Burundi, Mongolia, Indonesia, Mozambique, South Africa and Zambia)

Some studies have also gone further to examine the link between poverty and different types of health issues and diseases. Lanre-Abass (2008) examines the link between poverty, medical practise and maternal mortality in Nigeria. The paper concludes that poverty limits the ability of women to get proper and adequate antenatal care. In the same vein, Family Health Care (2005) argued that reproductive ill health is both a cause and effect of poverty. Yusuf et al. (2010) investigated the relationship between poverty and prevalence of childhood fever in Nigeria using a multi-level analysis. The determinants of fever among under-five children were analysed using data obtained from the 2008 DHS data sets. They found a distinct positive relationship between poverty and vulnerability to fever. According to their results, the prevalence of fever was highest among children from the poorest households and those without bed nets. WHO (2006) established a causal link between malaria and poverty[6]. Poor housing and sanitation, lack of basic education, inability to afford simple preventive measures and lack of resources to seek timely health care are some of the transmission mechanisms through which poverty causes malaria. Furthermore, Starfield (1992) associates low socio-economic status with the high mortality and morbidity rates as well as low birth weight among children. According to Bhutta (2004), child mortality is common in poor countries. This was buttressed by Aber et al. (2007), Fotso (2006), Hong et al. (2006) and Wood (2003) who claimed that within each country, children from poor households are most likely to be malnourished, disabled, sick or die. In Bangladesh, Begum (1997) found that access to quality healthcare among poor and non-poor households/category stands at around 25% and 40% respectively. Obi et al. (2010) examine the relationship between poverty and HIV/AIDS in Abia State of Nigeria. They found that poverty has no significant effect on the incidence of HIV/AIDS. Research on poverty and new born survival conducted by the FMH, Save the Child and ACCESS (2009) confirms that health and poverty in Nigeria are interlinked. According to the studies, poor families have poorer nutrition, have limited access to safe drinking water, better sanitation, health care and are vulnerable to illness.

At the home front, Riman and Akpan (2010) in a study of the relationship between poverty, health expenditure and health status in Nigeria using granger causality and the vector error correction model found that causality runs from life expectancy, which is an indicator of health status, to poverty. In examining the relationship between economic growth and health in Nigeria using the three-stage least square method, Babatunde (2011) found that there is a reverse causality between health and economic growth; and growth-oriented and poverty reduction policies would lead to improvement in the health status of Nigerians. The Nigerian DHS for 2003 found that over 30% of Nigerian women do not have access to maternal care primarily because of financial constraints (National Population Commission and ORC Macro, 2004). Ajakaiye and Nwabu (2007) developed a framework for the link between reproductive health, economic growth and poverty reduction in sub-Saharan Africa. They found that the significance of the link between reproductive health, growth and poverty is dependent on the availability of employment opportunities, markets for labour intensive products, favourable macroeconomic environment and pro-poor institutions.

From the brief overview of the literature on the subject matter, it is obvious that there is a significant relationship between poverty and health in Nigeria, but there is no consensus on the direction of causation between the variables. While some studies found that there is uni-directional causality, others showed a bi—direction relationship. Some other studies also

[6] According to the report, poor households are prone to malaria which in turns keeps them in a state of poverty.

argue that the relationship between the variables is dependent on a number of factors. It is also evident from the review that poverty shows different degrees of relationship with different types of health issues. While poverty exerts a significant relationship with health issues such as malaria, infant mortality and maternal mortality, it has no significant relationship with health problem like HIV/AIDS. The current literature is lacking on the implication of the link between the two variables on economic development in Nigeria. Thus, this chapter examines these missing links. That is, it investigates the causal relationship between health variables and poverty in Nigeria and the implications of such relationships for economic development in Nigeria.

2.3. Theoretical Framework

The theoretical framework for this chapter is situated in the Lucas model of the Endogenous Growth Theory (Lucas 1988). The endogenous growth theory explains long-run economic growth of an economy on the basis of endogenous factors as against exogenous factors of the neo-classical growth model. The theory emphasizes technical progress resulting from the rate of investment, the size of the capital stock, and the stock of human capital. The Lucas Endogenous Growth Model is based on investment in human capital. The model assumes that investment in education leads to the production of human capital which is a vital determinant of long-run economic growth. It distinguished between the internal and external effect of human capital. The internal effect is the increase in the productivity of the worker while the external effect is the spillover effect on the productivity of capital and other workers in the economy. The functional form of the Lucas model in which output is generated via a production function is as follows:

$$Y = A(K^{\alpha})(uhL)^{1-\alpha};\ 0 < \alpha < 1, \tag{1}$$

where A is the technical coefficient, K and L are the inputs of physical and human capital used to produce the output Y. The variable u is defined as the proportion of total labour time spent working, and h is the stock of human capital. The Lucas model posits that it is the average level of skills and knowledge in the economy that are crucial for long-run economic growth (Jhighan, 2008). This implies that poor countries require significant investment in human capital to break free from the poverty trap.

In traditional development economics literature, poor countries are caught in a poverty trap and they need a "big push" in terms of foreign aid and investment that will lead to their takeoff into growth. A 2005 United Nations Millennium Project Report[7] argued that poor countries are caught in a poverty trap and requires a "big push" in terms of basic investment in public administration, human capital, and infrastructure to escape the trap. Similarly, Sachs (2005) argued that a combination of customized investment is required for African countries to break out of the poverty trap. Empirical researches have however failed to produce convincing evidences that aid spur growth. In fact, Easterly (2005) and Rajan and Subramanian (2005) posit that growth is lower in aid-intensive countries; and despite increase in aid-GDP ratio in Africa, the continent's growth rate has fallen over time.

[7] United Nations Millennium Project, Overview Report, 2005, p. 19.

There are various models of the poverty trap. Easterly (2005) posits that countries could be caught in poverty traps in a number of ways as shown by various poverty trap models. Lucas (1988) model depicts poverty trap through a situation where low average skills in the labour market could discourage new workers from acquiring higher and better skills, thereby perpetuating a state of low skill trap. The skill trap could also perpetuate a productivity and income trap. Workers that have maintained a low skill level will also have their productivity level stagnated and hence their income. In other words, lack of improvement in workers' skills level will result in stagnation in productivity level and income. The stagnation in income levels will discourage existing and new entrant workers from acquiring skills, thereby perpetuating the poverty—trap. Kundu et al., (2007) also developed an overlapping generation poverty-trap model where illness is linked to household income, child education and future family income. The model links health, education and poverty and how this phenomenon interacts to create a poverty trap. According to this model, a prolonged period of illness or premature death of an earning member reduces family income, ability to invest in child education, the future income-earning potential of the child, and future household income. Fall in family income as a result of poor health or death of an income earner will adversely affect the household's expenditure including child education. The possible fall in investment in child education may likely affect the child's performance and academic attainment, which will in turn adversely affect the ability of the child to earn adequate income to meet the household's needs in the future. In turn, the low future household income will limit the next generation's access to education and further lower their income. This cycle continues thereby creating a health-education-poverty link induced poverty trap. The Kundu-Reitschuler-Emanuel model was adjusted to develop a framework for health-poverty trap for this chapter.

Health-Poverty trap is a situation where poverty results in poor health outcomes and poor health outcome in turn leads to more poverty. Poverty has been identified as a major barrier to human development. It is also seen as one of the major causes of high infant and maternal mortality in developing countries, as it deprives women and children of adequate health care due to their inability to afford ante- and post-natal care (Lanre-Abass, 2008). Since, high level of poverty impacts negatively on health, poor health outcomes would also undermine economic growth and development prospects, thereby creating a heath-poverty trap[8]. Poor health imposes a direct burden on the society and creates a vicious circle of poverty-deprivation-ill health-poverty in a mutually reinforcing manner (Begum, 1997).

Poverty perpetuates a state of poor health and poor health in turn impedes efforts to reduce poverty. With this cause-and-effect relationship between poverty and ill health, a health-poverty cycle is established (Teklehaimanot and Mejia, 2008). Healthy individuals are likely to be more productive, work longer, earn higher, afford the basic necessities of life such as food, clothing, shelter, healthcare, etc. and be healthier and prosperous. On the other hand, disease-ridden individuals have the possibility of having low productivity due to absenteeism, work lesser hours, earn lower income, have lower savings, may not be able to afford necessities of life including health care, and remain in poverty. In another dimension, health enhances education outcomes, which in turn enhance human capital, productivity, income and living condition.

---

[8] Improvement in development is unattainable without ensuring better health outcomes.

In summary, the link between poverty and health is explained through various channels (Aghion et al., 2010; Babatunde, 2011) and is illustrated in Figure 1 below. Firstly, it is believed that better health will lead to higher life expectancy; improved life expectancy will result in higher lifetime savings; high savings will results in economic growth, which is expected to translate to reduction in poverty level. Secondly, better health outcomes will reflect in human capital formation with expected effect on economic growth and poverty. From the diagram below, good health will lead to better learning ability and educational outcomes. Improvement in learning abilities and educational outcomes will result in human capital and technological development and consequently economic growth and poverty reduction. Good health will also enhance productivity or work duration directly or through its effects on educational outcome and learning ability. Improved productivity levels and ability to work longer hours will result in increased earnings which will boost household income and government tax revenue.

A good fiscal outlook for the government will potentially enhance economic growth and ultimately help to reduce poverty. Going backward, increased earning, improved economic growth and considerable reduction in poverty levels will further enhance good health. On the contrary, this also applies to a situation of poor health. Poor health will lead to poor learning ability and educational outcome, with adverse effects on human capital development, average working hour and productivity.

Lower level of productivity and human capital development will result in lower earning, income and economic growth. This situation will perpetuate a state of poverty which will also have a negative effect on health outcome. Thus, the theoretical relationship between health and poverty is bi-directional.

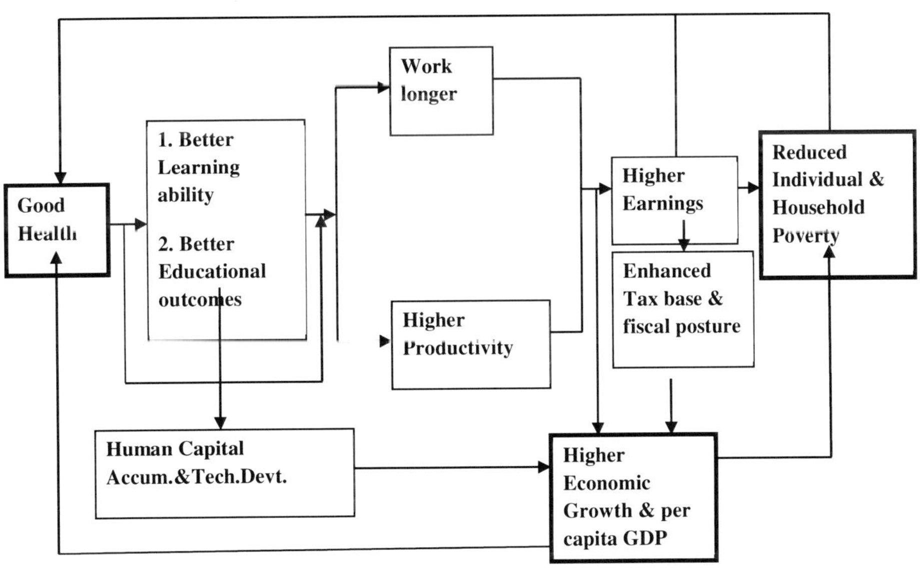

Figure 1. Health-Poverty Link -Source: Extracted from Babatunde (2011)[9].

[9] The figure was extracted with the consent and permission of the author

3. METHODS

The chapter uses secondary data to achieve the objectives of this research. The data are obtained from various sources such as the World Bank Development Indicator Database, World Health Organisations, UNICEF, National Action Committee on Aids, National Bureau of Statistics, Central Bank of Nigeria, website of international NGOs, the literature and other sources. The data sets include life expectancy, poverty rates, per capita health expenditure, doctor-population ratio, and infant mortality. Others are under-five mortality rates, maternal mortality rates, malnutrition prevalence rates, TB prevalence rates, proportion of stunted and under-weight children, neonatal mortality rate, and female literacy. The former variables were used for the granger causality test while the latter were used for trend analysis. Life expectancy (LEXP) is the number of years an individual is expected to live at birth. Poverty rate (POV) is the level of poverty that is prevalent in the society. Per capita health expenditure (PCHEXP) is the ratio of health expenditure to the population. That is, the average amount spent on the health on an individual. Doctor per capita (DOC) is the number of doctors divided by the population. In other word, the number of patients/population that a doctor is expected to attend to in a particular time period. Infant mortality (INF) is the number of children that die per 1000 live births. The time period of the data sets ranges from 1980 to 2010.

The empirical methodology adopted encompasses both theoretical and econometric analysis. The theoretical analysis is used to assess Nigeria's progress towards the Millennium Development Goals, which is the first objective of the chapter. Here, the trend of health- and poverty-related MDGs are assessed between 2000, when the MDGs were initiated and now, and at the same time ascertain the possibility of meeting the 2015 deadline of the MDGs. In other words, we examined the MDGs health and poverty-related targets to see where Nigeria was in 2000, where she is now and the likelihood of meeting the 2015 target. The second objective is examined using econometrics methods[10]. Understanding the health-poverty linkage from a policy viewpoint is done using the granger causality technique. Applying the ordinary least square or correlation coefficient would only give information about the measure of fit as well as the degree of the relationship between the two variables; but will be silent on the direction of causality, which is crucial in terms of appropriate policy interventions. In order to address this shortcoming, the granger causality test was employed to investigate the causality between health and poverty in Nigeria.

The granger causality is the most common way to test for causal relationships between variables. It has gained acceptance due to its simplicity, robustness and extendability (Hiemstra and Jones, 1994; Liu and Bahadori, 2012). It is used to determine whether one time series is useful in forecasting another. In order word, the test will provide information on which of the variables causes each other. Causal relations are required by policy makers to know the consequences of the various actions they take. The idea behind granger causality is that variable X granger-causes variable Y if variable Y can be forecasted using the past values of both X and Y than it can be predicted by using past values of Y alone. Specifically, a time series X is said to granger-cause Y if it can be shown through a series of t-and F-test on lagged values of X (and with lagged values of Y also), that those X values provide

[10] The econometrics methods used in this chapter is granger causality test.

statistically significant information about future values of Y (Granger, 1969). The granger-causality is mathematically expressed as thus:

$$y_t = \alpha_1 + \sum_{i=1}^{n} \beta_i x_{t-i} + \sum_{j=1}^{m} \gamma_j y_{t-j} + e_{1t} \ldots \quad (1)$$

$$x_t = \alpha_2 + \sum_{i=1}^{n} \theta_i x_{t-i} + \sum_{j=1}^{m} \delta_j y_{t-j} + e_{2t} \quad (2)$$

Based on the stated equations above, the null and alternative hypothesis are:

$$H_O: \sum_{i=1}^{n} \beta_i = 0 \text{ or } x_t \text{ does not cause } y_t$$

$$H_1: \sum_{i=1}^{n} \beta_i \neq 0 \text{ or } x_t \text{ does cause } y_t$$

Situating our variables in the model assuming that y = POV and x = HEALTH gives equ. 3 and 4

$$POV_t = \alpha_1 + \sum_{i=1}^{n} \beta_i HEALTH_{t-i} + \sum_{j=1}^{m} \gamma_j POV_{t-j} + e_{1t} \ldots \quad (3)$$

$$HEALTH_t = \alpha_1 + \sum_{i=1}^{n} \beta_i HEALTH_{t-i} + \sum_{j=1}^{m} \gamma_j POV_{t-j} + e_{1t} \quad (4)$$

The granger causality tests examine two time-series to identify whether a variable (series X) comes before the other variable (series Y), Y comes before X, or if the movements are simultaneous. Thus, according to Sims (1972), granger causality does not necessarily depict causality but instead identifies which variable precedes the other. This chapter makes use of the bivariate granger causality test. The probable outcomes of the granger causality test are that health granger cause poverty, poverty granger cause health, or both granger-cause each other. The model adopted follows that of Hassan et al. (2011) with minor adjustments.

4. RESULTS

4.1. Review of MDG Health and Poverty Progress

The level of poverty in Nigeria over the years has shown no remarkable reduction despite efforts and measures aimed at poverty alleviation (see Table 2). The first of the MDGs is to halve by 2015 the number of people living in extreme poverty. The poverty level in Nigeria has witnessed substantial swings over time. As at 1980, poverty level in Nigeria was 28.1%. The poverty level increased to 46.3% in 1985, before plunging to 42.7% in 1992. The poverty rate skyrocketed to 66.9% in 1996. The high poverty rate in the mid-1990s propelled the government to initiate poverty alleviation programmes such as the National Poverty Eradication Programme (NAPEP), etc., in the early 2000s. These programmes were partly successful as the national poverty rate fell to 54.4%. They were encompassing, focusing on education, health, rural development, women empowerment, employment generation, etc.

Table 2. Trend of Poverty, 1980-2011

Criteria/Year	1980	1985	1992	1996	2004	2010	2011
NATIONAL POVERTY RATE	27.2	46.3	42.7	66.9	54.4	69.0	71.1
URBAN POVERTY RATE	17.2	37.8	37.5	59.3	43.2	61.8	n/a
RURAL POVERTY RATE	28.3	51.4	46.0	71.7	63.3	73.2	n/a

Source: NBS.

As a result of the encircling nature of these programmes, rural and urban poverty rates also declined from 71.1% and 59.3% in 1996 to 63.3% and 43.2% in 2004 respectively. However, due to the inconsistency of these programmes, poor implementation, corruption and other institutional challenges, the level of national, rural and urban poverty increased to 69%, 73.2% and 61.8% respectively in 2010. Infact, based on a recent report by the National Bureau of Statistics, poverty level in Nigeria stands at 71.1%, with the northern part of the country sharing the largest burden. Going by this trend, it is obvious that poverty rate in Nigeria has grown worse than when the MDGs were initiated and the country seems not to be in line to meet the MDG goal of halving the proportion of people living in abject poverty by 2015. In terms of halving the proportion of people that suffer from hunger, Nigeria has also not done considerably well.

Recent improvements in agriculture and health services have helped to reduce the proportion of underweight children from 35% in 1990 to 23.1% in 2008. Despite the considerable reduction in the proportion of children suffering from malnutrition in Nigeria, the regional differences is not encouraging; with the supposedly poor regions – North West, North East and North Central – still having a high level of child malnutrition. From the table below, there is still high level of underweight and stunted children in the Northern part of Nigeria compared to the South, which is a vivid illustration of the strong link between poverty, hunger and malnutrition (see Table 3).

Moreover, considering the high level of poverty, the continued dependence on food importation and limited access to health services, the goal of halving the number of people that suffer from hunger by 2015 may not be realistic in Nigeria.

Table 3. Regional distribution of some health and literacy indicator, 2009

Zone	NW	NE	NC	SW	SS	SE
Proportion of stunted children %	53	49	44	31	31	22
Proportion of underweight children %	20	22	9	9	7.5	8.6
Neonatal mortality rate	55	61	55	39	53	34
Female Literacy among 15-24 years old	21	39	55	85	85	88

Source: FMH, Save the Child and ACCESS, 2009.

NW: North West NE: North East NC: North Central SW: South West SS: South South SE: South East.

Nonetheless, Nigeria has made consistent progress in reducing child mortality. Under-five mortality rate has plunged from 214 deaths/1000 live births in 1990 to 157 deaths/live births in 2008.

Available statistics shows that there have a been a gradual and consistent decline in the incidence of under-five mortality over the years, even though some parts of the country – northern Nigerian – still have high incidences. The regional disparity in the incidence of infant mortality could be attributed to differences in incomes level, education status, access to medicare, cultural cum religious practices.

The overall improvements made in under-five mortality reduction were due primarily to interventions by the government, NGOs and international organisations. Even at that, Nigeria may not fully meet the target of reducing the under-five mortality rate by two-third in 2015 except substantial efforts are geared towards promoting more investments in health infrastructure and human resources as well as enhancing access to health facilities, especially in rural areas and northern part of the country (see Table 4).

Commendable progress has also been made in the area of maternal mortality. Maternal mortality fell from 1100 deaths/100000 live births in 1990 to 630 deaths per 100000 live births in 2010. Similar to under-five mortality, the progress made in maternal mortality varies from states to states and between rural and urban areas. However, the overall improvement at the national level has been encouraging.

This development has been achievable through increased maternal education and enlightenment and government policies towards enhancing maternal health in the country. Looking at the state of maternal health in 2010, the prospect of meeting the 2015 MDG maternal health target is not bright[11]. Government needs to initiate measures to extend access to health care and maternal health programs to rural areas, especially in the northern part of the country.

Also efforts to reduce HIV/AIDS prevalence rate in Nigeria has not very been successful. HIV prevalence rates increased consistently from 1.8% in 1991 to 5.8% in 2001. Thereafter, the prevalence rate reduced to 4.6% in 2008 and 3.7% in 2011, primary due to government intervention mechanisms such as increased enlightenment, prevention of mother to child infection as well as assistance from international organisations and NGOs. According to statistics for 2012, HIV prevalence rate in Nigeria had increased to 4.1%. Furthermore, the prevalence rates differ from state to state, with Benue, Akwa-Ibom, Bayelsa, FCT, and Anambra States topping the chart.

According to UNDP MDG Report, there has been a sharp fall in malaria prevalence rates in Nigeria. This is basically due to the widespread development in the distribution and use of insecticide-treated nets. On the contrary, significant progress has not been made in the fight against tuberculosis.

As at 1991, TB prevalence rates in Nigeria stands at 129. However, this figure skyrocketed to 182 in 2003 before it began to show gradual reduction to 158 in 2007, 145 in 2008 and 133 in 2010. Going by this trend, the goal of reversing the incidence and prevalence of the disease is still far from being achieved, as the prevalence rate today is higher than what it was in 1991.

[11] The situation may be aggravated by the fact that the proportion of birth attended by skilled personnel is still low.

Table 4. Trend of Health Indicators in Nigeria, 1990-2011

Years	1990	1992	1994	1996	1998	2000	2002	2004	2006	2008	2010	2015 (Pro-jected)
Under-5 mortality rate/1000	214	214	213	207	200	188	175	162	150	139	129	72
Years	1990	1993	1995	1999	2000	2003	2005	2007	2008	2010	2012	2015
Maternal mortality rate/100000	1100	n/a	1000	n/a	970	800	820	n/a	n/a	630	n/a	275
Malnutrition prevalence (wasting)	35.1	35.1	n/a	27.3	n/a	27.2	n/a	25.7	26.7	23.1		
Years	1991	1993	1996	1999	2001	2003	2005	2007	2008	2010	2011	2012
HIV Prevalence rates	1.8	3.8	4.5	5.4	5.8	5.0	4.4	n/a	4.6		3.7	4.1
TB Prevalence Rates	129	132	143	165	178	182	175	158	145	133		

Source: Under-5 mortality – World Bank Database; Maternal mortality – WHO/UNICEF/UNFPA and World Bank, 2010; Malnutrition Prevalence – UNICEF/WHO Joint Global Malnutrition Analysis, 2011; HIV/AIDS Prevalence Rates – National Action Committee on Aids, 2012; Tuberculosis Prevalence Rates – US Embassy in Nigeria, Nigeria TB Factsheet, January 2012.

4.2. Analysis and Discussion of Granger-Causality Results

The result of the granger causality test is shown in the table below

Table 5. Summary of Pair wise Granger Causality Test Results

Null Hypothesis	Obs	F-Statistic	Probability
POV does not Granger Cause DOC	29	1.50523	0.24219
DOC does not Granger Cause POV	29	0.19420	0.82478
PCHEXP does not Granger Cause INFM	29	14.2680	8.3E-05
INFM does not Granger Cause PCHEXP	29	0.23914	0.78916
POV does not Granger Cause INFM	29	3.50706	0.04611
INFM does not Granger Cause POV	29	2.34170	0.11775
PCHEXP does not Granger Cause LEXP	29	23.0926	2.6E-06
LEXP does not Granger Cause PCHEXP	29	0.93307	0.40715
POV does not Granger Cause LEXP	29	5.55559	0.01040
LEXP does not Granger Cause POV	29	0.93679	0.40575
POV does not Granger Cause PCHEXP	29	1.24122	0.30693
PCHEXP does not Granger Cause POV	29	0.58446	0.56515

- Empirical findings from our analysis show that there is no direct causal link between doctor-population ratio and poverty in Nigeria. This shows that the number of doctors available to take care of the population does not have a direct effect on the poverty level. Similarly, poverty levels do not have direct effect on the availability of doctors. This could be as a result of the inelastic nature of the supply of doctors. Moreover, the availability of doctors does not mean people will have access to healthcare facilities. Access to healthcare is also determined by availability of medical facilities and ability to afford payment for medical services. Statistics shows that Nigeria has one of the highest ratios of doctor per capita in the world but as the result of the granger causality shows, it does not have effect on the poverty situation. This clearly shows that other more important and significant factors influences poverty in Nigeria.
- Per capital health expenditure granger causes infant mortality and life expectancy in Nigeria. This implies that changes in per capita health expenditure have significant causal effect on child health and overall quality of life. Health spending in terms of provision of health facilities and infrastructure improves child health. Provision of free medical treatment and drugs for children, regular immunization, expansion of health facilities to rural areas, distribution of free mosquito nets, and general measures towards eradicating diseases that affect children's health are part of measures and initiatives to enhance child health. This could be the reason why in recent times some state governments initiate free healthcare for children within certain age. Emphasis has also been placed on regulation immunization against killer diseases such as polio, measles, meningitis, etc. Similarly, increase in per capita health expenditure is likely to enhance an individual's access to medicare and thus its health status. Improvement in health status will increase productivity, income and ability to afford basic necessities of life which will in turn determine life expectancy.

- Poverty granger causes infant mortality and overall life expectancy. Though there is a two-way bi-directional relationship between health and poverty in theory, empirical evidence from these analyses shows that it is poverty that firstly causes poor health before poor health may further lead to sustained poverty situation. Similarly, the level of poverty to an extent determines the likely number of years an individual will spend. Lack of adequate income cripples an individual's ability to afford good nutrition and medicare, and therefore results in poor health. This is because it is the availability of income that guarantees access to the basic necessities of life including food and medicare. Children whose parents are poor are prone to health problems due to lack of adequate nutrition and healthcare. This result is also buttressed by the fact that the Northern regions of Nigeria which have the highest poverty rates also have high level of disease burden and infant mortality than other regions. Poverty could also be accountable for low level of educational achievements in developing countries including Nigeria, which may have indirect effect on health outcome. Moderate level of education may make an individual to be conscious of good hygiene and health practises, which may influence their health status and outcomes.

4.3. Health-Poverty Trap: Implications for Economic Development in Nigeria

One of the major implications of the health-poverty trap for economic development is its negative impact on total factor productivity[1]. The combination of poor health and poverty presents a great productivity loss for individuals and the aggregate economy. People who have diseases and are poor may not have the opportunity to work, study, or may have their productivity adversely affected. This will consequently have a negative on aggregate productivity, economic growth and development.

Health-poverty trap impacts economic development through demographic changes. There is thus, an apparent relationship between reproductive health and poverty. Even in Nigeria, statistics from the National Bureau of Statistics shows that large families tend to be poorer. Poor people usually tend to have more children and fewer resources to invest in the health and education of each child. Such children are more likely to experience both physical disability and cognitive deficiencies. The implication of this circle is a continuous trend of intergenerational poverty. Moreover, the demographic changes associated with poor reproductive health and poverty, could lead to high level of dependency and economic stagnation.

Poor health and poverty individually and collectively have substantial adverse effect on human capital accumulation. Individuals that are poor and unhealthy would have low capacity to acquire education, with a negative impact on human capital. A country with low human capital will have low capacity for innovation, research and development and consequently economic development. This implies that given good macroeconomic policies, good health will promote human capital in the form of education, on-the-job training, technological development, etc.

Similarly, the health-poverty trap will also have a negative impact of physical capital accumulation. The role of physical capital, in the form of infrastructure, in economic

[1] This refers to the productivity of capital, labour and technological advancement.

development is clearly recognised in the development literature. A fall in the level of productivity as a result of consistent poverty and health problems would lead to decline in income, economic growth, private sector investment and government fiscal posture. Reduction in government tax revenue will also affect government's ability to invest in physical infrastructure and capital. This will in turn lead to decline in economic activities and growth, promote poverty and poor health and sustain the vicious cycle. Fall inpersonal and corporate tax revenue will limit government ability to spend on pro-poor sectors such as housing, education, social security, etc. Poor health and poverty constitute economic burden to individuals and governments.

There is substantial evidence that poverty and health status have a strong impact on businesses' decisions to invest. Businesses want to invest in places with healthier population because their costs of production are lower and productivity is higher. Domestic and foreign investments are determined by a number of factors of which health and income are key[2]. Low labour productivity serves as a disincentive for investment. Furthermore, increasing level of epidemic and diseases is likely to discourage foreign investment, as it dampens their growth prospects and increase the health risks for their personnel. Howbeit, the preponderance of poor health and poverty will have adverse effect on savings and investment. Poor households consume a higher proportion of their income and devote little to savings and investment. The incidence of poor health will further increase the proportion of household income that is consumed, leaving very little for saving and investment. Low savings and investment level will retard economic growth and development.

Sustained poverty and poor health over a long period of time could also have political implications. Countries that are simultaneously caught up in the web of poverty and poor health may be prone to epidemic, violence and terrorism. As noted by Alesina et al. (1996) and Collier and Hoeffer (2004) poor economic conditions could increase the possibility of political instability and civil wars. The present case of Nigeria shows that violence, kidnapping and other social vices are common in poverty-stricken regions. The prevalence of poverty and poor health situations also reveals the ineffectiveness of government's policies.

CONCLUSION

This chapter examines the health-poverty trap in Nigeria and its implication for economic development. Development economists have long recognised the strong link between the two economic phenomena. It is believed that poverty results in poor health and poor health also lead to perpetuation of poverty. The chapter also presents an overview of the Millennium Development Goals, particularly with respect to health and poverty related goals. It examines the various transmission mechanisms through which poverty and health affect each other and the implication of such interactions for economic development.

The conceptual and theoretical frameworks adopted are the Millennium Development Goals and the Health-Poverty Trap. The analytical approach entails theoretical, descriptive and econometric methods. From the analysis, it was found that empirically, and in the case of Nigeria, it is poverty that granger cause health status. In other words, the initial level of poverty determines the health status/situation of the population. Other findings from the data

[2] Investors will invest in a region or country where there is prospect of a large market.

analysis include: there is a causal relationship from per capita health expenditure to infant mortality and life expectancy; there is a causal relationship from poverty to infant mortality and life expectancy; and there is no causal link between poverty and per capita health expenditure. The implication of these findings is that between poverty and health, the prime issue that needs to be addressed for the overall human development is poverty. If the problem of poverty is appropriately addressed in Nigeria, it will have a far-reaching effect on other development indicators and outcomes include health status. The health-poverty trap affects economic development in a number of ways. It could lead to fall in productivity, high dependency ratio, low human capital accumulation, declining physical capital accumulation, low savings and investment, decline in trade and investment flows, fall in tax revenue, and political instability, with subsequent effect on economic development. Thus, the Nigerian government needs to initiate a multi-pronged approach to combat poverty. Deliberate and conscious efforts also need to be taken to break the vicious circle of poverty and health and achieve development goals.

This chapter has made an attempt at explaining the causal relationship between poverty and health in Nigeria using the traditional granger causality test. Among other things, it found that poverty causes poor health, and poor health may latter perpetuate the state of poverty, thereby creating a health-poverty trap with serious socio-economic implications for development. However, it did not examine which health situations are caused by poverty and which are not. For example, while some studies found that poverty is a major cause of malaria and infant mortality, others found that it is not a major cause of HIV/AIDS. Thus, future studies should critically and comprehensively examine the relationship between poverty and different health issues. This will provide policy makers with the necessary insights and approaches to addressing poverty and the various health challenges in the country. Also, the two-variable granger causality test used in this chapter does not consider the effects of other variables that affect health and poverty and also ignores the non-stationary nature of the time-series. Therefore, future studies on health-poverty relationship in Nigeria should note these shortcomings as a basis for improvement.

REFERENCES

Aber, J.L., Bennett, N.G., Conley, D.C., Jiali, L., 1997. The effects of poverty on child health and development. *Annual Review of Public Health*, 18, 463-483.

Adogamhe, P.G., 2010. Economic policy reform & poverty alleviation: A critique of Nigeria's strategic plan for poverty reduction, Poverty & Public Policy, 2(4), 49-80.

Aghion, P., Howitt, P., Murtin, F., 2010. The relationship between health and growth: When Lucas meets Nelson-Phelps. *Bruegel Working Paper*, 2010/04, 1-24.

Ajakaiye, O., Nwabu, G., 2007. Reproductive health, economic growth and poverty reduction: A framework. Research report presented on9th December, in Arusha, Tanzania.

Alesina, A., Ozler, S., Roubini, N., Swagel, P., 1996. Political instability and economic growth. *Journal of Economic Growth*, 1, 189-211.

Barro, R., 1996. Health, human capital and economic growth. Paper prepared for the Program on Public Policy and Health, organised by the Pan African Health Organisation and World Health Organisation, Washington.

Barro, R., Sala-i-Martin, X., 2004. Economic Growth, second ed. Prentice Hall, New Delhi.

Begum, S., 1997. Health dimension of poverty in rural Bangladesh: Some evidence, in: Rahman, H.Z., Hossain, M., Sen, B. (Eds.), Dynamics of Rural Poverty in Bangladesh. Bangladesh Institute of Development Studies, *Dhaka*, pp. 1987-1994.

Bhutta, Z.A., 2004. Beyond Bellagio: Addressing the challenge of sustainable child health in developing countries. *Archive of Diseases in Childhood*, 89, 483-487.

Bloom, D., Canning, D., 2003. The health and poverty of nations: From theory to practice. *Journal of Human Development*, 4(1), 47-71.

Collier, P., Hoeffer, A., 2004. Greed and grievances in civil war, *Oxford Economic Papers*, 56, 563-595.

Deaton, A., 2008. Policy implications of the gradient of health and wealth. *Health Affairs*, 1-5.

Easterly, W., 2005. Reliving the 50s: The big push, poverty traps, and take-offs in economic development, *Center for Global Development Working Paper* No. 65, August.

Family Care International, 2005. Millennium Development Goals and sexual and reproductive health. Briefing Cards, *Family Care International*, New York.

Federal Ministry of Health, 2005. Draft health promotion policy for Nigeria, Federal Ministry of Health, Abuja.

Federal Ministry of Health, Save the Children and ACCESS, 2009. Saving newborn lives in Nigeria: Situation analysis and action plan for newborn health in the context of the integrated maternal, *Newborn and Child Health Strategy,* Abuja.

Filmer, D., 2008.Disability, poverty and schooling in developing countries: Results from 14 household surveys. *World Bank Economic Review*, 22(1), 141-163.

Fotso, J.C., 2006. Child health inequities in developing countries: Differences across urban and rural areas. *International Journal of Equity in Health*, 5(9).

Government of Sindh Health Department, 2005. Health policy for the Province of Sindh: Paving the way for health sector reforms. Karachi, India, March.

Granger, C.W.J., 1969. Investigating causal relations by econometric models and cross-spectral methods, *Econometrica, 37*(3), 424-438.

Gupta, I., Mitra, A., 2003. Economic growth, health, and poverty: An explanatory study on India, in: Misra, R., Chatterjee, R., Roa, S. (Eds.), Indian Health Report, Oxford University Press, New Delhi.

Gureje, O., Ogunniyi, A., Kola, L., Afolabi, E., 2006. Functional disability in elderly Nigerian: Results from the Ibadan study of aging. *Journal of the American Geriatrics Society,* 54(11), 1784-1789.

Hassan, A., Malik, S., Chaudhry, I.S., Khalil, S., 2011. Poverty-health nexus: The case of Pakistan. *Middle Eastern Finance and Economics*, 11, 142-149.

Hiemstra, C., Jones, J.D., 1994. Testing for linear and non-linear granger causality in the stock price-volume relation. *The Journal of Finance*, 49(5), 1639-1664.

Hong, R., Banta, J.E., Betancourt, J.A., 2006. Relationship between household wealth inequality and chronic childhood malnutrition in Bangladesh. *International Journal of Equity in Health*, 5(15).

Hoogeven, J., 2005. Measuring welfare for small but vulnerable groups: Poverty and disability in Uganda, *Journal of African Economies*, 14(4), 603-631.

Houweling, T.A., Kunst, A.E., Mackenbech, J.P. 2003. Measuring health inequality among children in developing countries: Does the choice of the indicator of economic status matter? *International Journal of Equity in Health*, 2(8).

Jackman, C., Bolastig, E.V.C., Pierre, K., 2012. Defying the tyranny of averages: Unshackling the health-poverty nexus towards equitable health policy development in Eastern Trinidad. Paper Presented at the 2nd UNESCO MOST Forum of Ministers of Social and Sustainable Development of the Caribbean, held between 21-23 May, 2012 in Port-of-Spain, Trinidad and Tobago.

Jhighan, M.L., 2008. The Economics of Development and Planning, thirty-ninth ed. Vrinda Publications, New Delhi.

Khanum, S., Singh, A., 2007. Health, poverty and human security: Illustrations from malaria in the SEA region. *Regional Health Forum*, 11(1), 33-44.

Kundu, T., Reitschuler, E., Emanuel, L., 2007. Alleviation poverty: A proposal to mitigate the economic cost of disease. University of Oslo Working Paper, Retrieved from http://www.sv.uio.no/esop/english/research/publications/working-papers/alleviating poverty.pdf.

Lanre-Abass, B., 2008. Poverty and maternal mortality in Nigeria: Towards a more viable ethics of modern medical practice. *International Journal of Equity in Health*, 7(11).

Liu, Y., Bahadori, M.T., 2012. A survey on granger causality: A computational view. Retrieved online from http://www-bcf.usc.edu/¬liu32/granger.pdf.

Loeb, M., Eide, A.H., Jelsma, J., Ka Toni, M., Maart, S., 2008. Poverty and disability in Eastern and Western Cape Provinces, South Africa, *Disability and Society*, 23(4), 311-321.

Lucas, R.E., 1988. On the mechanics of economics development. *Journal of Monetary Economics*, 22, 3-42.

NBS, 2006.Core Welfare Indicators Questionnaire Survey. *National Bureau of Statistics*, Abuja.

NBS, 2012. Nigeria poverty profile 2010. National Bureau of Statistics, Abuja. Retrieved from http://www.tucrivers.org/tucpublications/Nigeria%20Poverty%20Profile%202010.pdf

National Population Commission, ORC Macro, 2004. 2003 Nigeria demographic and health survey. National Population Commission and ORC Macro, Calverton, Maryland.

Obi, R.K., Okangba, C.C., Nwanebu, F.C., Ndubuisi, U.U., Mgbemene, I.C., Braide, W., 2010. Relationship between HIV/AIDS and poverty: A case study of two cities in Abia State, Nigeria. *Current Research Journal of Biological Sciences*, 2(6), 356-360.

Ogwumike, F.O., 2002. An appraisal of poverty reduction strategies in Nigeria. CBN *Economic & Financial Review*, 39(4).

Parikh, J., Sharma, S., 2005. The energy, poverty, health and gender nexus – A case study from India. ENERGIA News, 8(2).

Rajan, R.G., Subrmanian, A., 2005. Aid and growth: What does the cross-country evidence really show? NBER Working Paper No. 11513, April.

Riman, H.B., Akpan, E. S., 2010. Causality between poverty, health expenditure and health status: Evidence from Nigeria using VECM, *European Journal of Economics, Finance and Administrative Sciences*, 27, 120-129.

Sachs, J.D., 2005. The End of Poverty: Economic Possibilities for Our Time. The Penguin Press, New York.

Schultz, T.W., 1961. Investment in human capital. *The American Economic Review*, 51(1), 1-17.

Schultz, T.P., 1999. Health and schooling investment in Africa. *Journal of Economic Perspectives*, 13, 67-88.

Sims, C.A., 1972. Money, income and causality. *The American Economic Review*, 62(4), 540-552.

Starfield, B., 1992. Effects of poverty on health status. *Bulletin New York Academy of Medicine*, 68(1), 17-24.

Strauss, J., Thomas, D., 1998. Health, nutrition and economic development. *Journal of Economic Literature*, 36, 766-817.

Teklehaimanot, A., Mejia, P., 2008. Malaria and poverty. *Annals of the New York Academy of Sciences,* 1136, June, 32-37.

Ucha, C., 2010. Poverty in Nigeria: Some dimensions and contributing factors. *Global Majority E-Journal*, 1(1), 46-56.

Ugoh, S.C., Ukpere, W.I., 2009. Appraising the trend of policy on poverty alleviation programmes in Nigeria with emphasis on National Poverty Eradication Programme (NAPEP).*African Journal of Business Management*, 3(12), 847-854.

UN Millennium Project Report, 2005. Investing in development: A practical plan to achieve the Millennium Development Goals - Overview report, United Nations, New York.

USAID, 2007. Confronting HIV/AIDS, TB, and malaria: A situation analysis of human resources health in Nigeria – Emerging challenges and opportunities. *Health System* 20/20 Brief, June.

WHO, 2001. The report of the Commission on Macroeconomics and Health. *World Health Organisation*, Geneva.

WHO, 2006.The African Malaria Report. *World Health Organisation*, Geneva.

Wood, D., 2003. Effect of child and family poverty on child health in the United States. Paediatrics, 112, 707-711.

World Bank, WHO, 2005. Dying for change – Poor people's experience of health and ill-health, July.

Yusuf, B.O., Adeoye, B.W., Oladepo, O.O., Peters, D.H. and Bishai, D., 2010. Poverty and fever vulnerability in Nigeria: A multilevel analysis. *Malaria Journal*, 9(235).

In: Health, Violence, Environment and Human Development ... ISBN: 978-1-62948-038-1
Editors: A. Cotte Poveda and C. I. Pardo Martínez

Chapter 5

EXPLAINING THE VIOLENCE AND CRIME IN COLOMBIA: A CRIMINOMETRIC APPROACH

Alexander Cotte Poveda*
Department of Economics,
University of Göttingen, Göttingen, Germany
Faculty of Accounting and Administration, University of La Salle,
Bogotá, Colombia

ABSTRACT

Violence is a significant development constraint that generates economic problems, limits public and private investments, and damages the country's infrastructure. This paper offers an explanation of violence through an empirical analysis of Colombian departments that takes into account categories of violence and variables of economic development and deterrence of violence. We use different data sets to measure violence and economic development, and we employ a dynamic panel model for a sample of 32 Colombian departments over the period 1993-2007. We find that the aggregate-level production per capita, education, deterrence variables and employment rate show a negative effect on violence, whereas GINI, unemployment rate, hectares under drug cultivation and lagged rate show a positive effect on violence. Moreover, the objective conditions and their interrelationships have been important in the trends of violence in Colombian departments. The findings demonstrate the importance of generating social policies and strategies against violence to increase economic growth and development, productivity, and security for the population across Colombian departments.

JEL: O1, 040, I30, C33

Keywords: Economic development, categories of violence, deterrence variables, Dynamic Panel Data, Colombia

---

* The author is grateful for the support provided by Deutscher Akademischer Austausch Dients (DAAD), the University of Göttingen and the University of La Salle. Any remaining errors are the responsibility of the author.

1. INTRODUCTION

Decreasing violence and increasing economic growth and social development are the main challenges facing several developing countries like Colombia, which has been affected by violence in the last decades. Several studies show that high levels of violence in a country indicate significant institutional failures (Koonings and Kruijt, 2004, WB, 2003, Broekman, 2000). Violence can have different sources (Soriano, 2000): (I) economic causes associated with societal pressure to seek a larger share of real income and the stock of national wealth; (II) interest of illegal groups in the appropriation of income derived from national resources or illegal activities such as drug trafficking; and (III) differences in ideas or opinions about how society should be organised or in political ideologies.

Violence has been studied in terms of different categories such as political violence and economic violence. Several studies have indicated that the category of political violence has increased in recent decades and that the main root causes include poverty, inequality and decreases in economic growth and state capacity (Nafziger and Auvinen, 2002, Sambanis, 2004, Besley and Persson, 2009). Various studies have demonstrated that economic violence is more severe in poorer countries; this type of violence has negative effects on investment and economic growth, and there is a strong relationship among the factors of economic violence and economic insecurity as well as a general lack of opportunities (Benson and Fox, 2002, WHO, 2004, Moser and Mcilwaine, 2005, Fisman and Miguel, 2008).

However, there are many gaps in the literature with respect to violence and its inter-relationships with economic development as well as to the main causes that generate different categories of violence. Therefore, the purpose of this paper is to contribute to a better explanation of violence through an empirical analysis that takes into account categories of violence, variables of economic development and deterrence of violence using a case study of Colombian departments.

In recent decades, Colombia has shown an increase in violence across departments that has been explained by various phenomena such as drug trafficking, conflicts between guerrilla and paramilitary groups over economic resources such as oil and metals, and disputes over territorial limits. Gaviria and Velez, (2001) Holmes et al., (2002), Sánchez et al., (2003) and Cotte, (2007) have illustrated the dynamics and trends of Colombian violence and have concluded that there are significant connections between coca production, illegal groups and violence.

Other studies have explained Colombian violence as the result of so-called “objective conditions,” which are understood as a series of political, social and economic realities that have created significant decay in the conditions of existence for wide sectors of society. For example, Sánchez and Nuñez (2001) show that the difference between the most violent and least violent Colombian counties is explained by socioeconomic variables such as poverty and inequality and by objective conditions such as political exclusion and lack opportunities; Echandia (2003) argues that Colombian violence has traditionally been explained through the existence of “objective conditions” present in remote regions where the insurgency appropriates peasant demands to engage in violence related to land tenancy or state violence; Palalu and Sánchez (2006) analyse the determinants of violence between 1974 and 1982 and demonstrate that the increase in violence during this period coincides with objective conditions such as poverty and inequality. Nevertheless, these studies have not analysed the relationship between objective conditions and categories of violence. In contrast, this study seeks to analyse the different categories of violence and their relationships with objective conditions using data panel analysis that includes different statistic tests to determine the robustness of the estimations and the use of dynamic panel data models from the Colombian departments between 1993 and 2007.

The chapter is organised as follows: Section 2 discusses the relevant literature, Section 3 presents the methodology and a description of the data available for analysis, Section 4 describes the results and Section 5 concludes the paper and presents recommendations for further research.

2. Literature Review

The definitions of violence are diverse. For example, violence can be understood as the existence of economic, cultural, social, judicial, and political structures that cause the oppression of human beings and impede their liberation and total human realisation. This is termed the "violence of the structures" (Wood, 2004, Scheper-Hughes and Bourgois, 2004). Alternatively, violence can be understood as the use of weapons to impose force on others to compel their submission, which is commonly known as "armed violence" (Geneva Declaration, 2008, OECD, 2009). Criminology approaches violence as social or individual conduct that involves destructive aggression, which causes the illicit use of force to achieve a purpose. Buvinic et al. (1999) define violence as "the use or threat of use, of physical or psychological force, with the intention of doing harm". Through its various manifestations, including homicide, theft, kidnapping and domestic violence, violence is one of the largest obstacles to the development and welfare of the population of developing countries.

Violence has been analysed through different approaches that have generated widely accepted theories such as economic theories, theories of rational choice, sociological or structural theories and descriptive approximations. These various approaches are explained as follows:

a. Economic theory assumes that there is an implicit relationship among rationality, strategy, violence, conflict and the economy (Schelling, 1960). In Colombia, this theory has been studied by Gorbaneff and Jacome (2000) and Castillo and Salazar (2001) using game theory. They found that violence is the result of the rational action of armed agents who have learned to survive in extreme conditions of uncertainty, scarce solidarity and lack of transparent rules with respect to relationships among individuals and different social groups. Violence and armed conflict are expected to be the result of the learning and adaptation process of armed organisations and the civil population in a context of increasing anarchy and the loss of a state monopoly over weapons and violence (Giugale et al., 2003).
b. Theories of rational choice are based on an individual's choice to conform to or to break the law. Such a theory was developed by Rubio (2001)[1], where the rational actor evaluates the possible risks and benefits associated with illegal conduct.

[1] Rubio (2001) developed this theory based onclassical 19th century criminological thinkers such as Bentham (1789) and Beccaria (1764) and the recent studies of Fielding et al. (2000).

Empirical studies that have analysed these theories show evidence in favour of the economic determinants of violence and conflict, suggesting that the level of economic development of countries is negatively related to the levels of conflict or violence (Rubio, 2001). Likewise, the causes and the time span of violence and conflicts are affected by various processes, including economic and social factors, the system of causalities and geographic features (Camatari, 2006).

c. Sociological or structural theories suggest that violence and conflict are a framework in which contradictions between material forces of production and the relationships of production historically manifest themselves. According to these theories, though their roots are in economic domination, violence and conflict always present themselves as related to some form of political domination (Tejerina, 1991). These theories are based on the social, political and economic conditions that determine individual behaviour where political conditions (e.g., the type of regime or the opportunities for participation) or economic conditions can determine situations of conflict or violence and where the probability of an internal war depends directly on the relative situation of the masses and the elites (Durkheim, 1982, Marx, 1853).
d. Descriptive approximations emphasise the detailed analysis of societies involved in conflicts to highlight peculiarities that are susceptible to generalisation. In this context, the need to move from a classical model of war to an analysis of civil conflicts is highlighted. The gradual transformation of a war subjected to rules into confrontations in which virtually "anything goes" makes an analysis of civil conflicts difficult to perform. As such, increasing importance is given to war as a phenomenon with its own internal dynamics (Rubio, 2001).

Table 1. Categories of Colombian violence

Categories	Definition	Manifestation
Political	Commission of violent acts, motivated by the desire, either conscious or unconscious, to obtain or maintain political power.	Guerrilla conflict, paramilitary conflict, political assassinations, armed conflict between political parties.
Economic	Commission of violent acts motivated by the desire, either conscious or unconscious, for economic gain or to obtain or maintain economic power.	Street crime, carjacking, robbery or theft, drug trafficking, kidnapping, assaults during economic crimes.
Social	Commission of violent acts motivated by the desire, either conscious or unconscious, for social gain or to obtain or maintain social power.	Interpersonal violence such as spousal and child abuse, sexual assault of women and children, arguments that get out of control.

Source: Moser (2000).

Taking into account these theories, Moser (2000) proposes three categories for the study of Colombian violence: political, economic and social violence, specified in terms of the primary motivating factor, either conscious or unconscious, for gaining or maintaining political, economic, or social power through force or violence (Table 1). These categories allow the analysis of the dynamics of different types of violence using an approach that is both conceptually and operationally integrated. The categories also allow the determination of adequate strategies to decrease violence according to its category; e.g., political violence requires peace negotiations, whereas economic violence requires that design of social policies that address topics such as the labour market, social opportunities and inclusion.

This study analyses general violence and two categories of violence, political and economic, for the Colombian while taking into account different variables that could cause violence and their interrelationships with economic growth and development.

3. Data and Methodology

3.1. Data

This chapter uses Colombia as a case study. We have used data published by the National Police of Colombia, the Colombian defence ministry, the DNP (National Planning Department), the Colombian treasury ministry, and the DANE (Colombian Department of Statistics). We build a data panel at the level of Colombian departments to analysis different categories of violence and determinate factors. The analysis is performed for the time period 1993-2007.

3.2. Methodology

The different categories of violence and their relationships with objective conditions can be modelled by the following function:

$$V = F\begin{pmatrix} LV & P & GDP & LM & DV & ID & EDU & GINI \\ + & + & - & \pm & - & \pm & - & + \end{pmatrix}$$

where V represents violence and its categories; LV is lagged violence; P is the population of a department, GDP is the aggregate-level production per capita by department; LM represents the relevant characteristics of the labour market such as the employment rate, employment per industry and unemployment; DV is composed of deterrence variables such as the number of police officers and the number of captures or apprehensions by department; ID represents variables pertaining to illegal drugs, such as hectares under drug cultivation and hectares of drugs eradicated by the department; EDU represents education variables such as education coverage by department; and GINI is a measure of income inequality by department. The sign below a variable signals its expected effect on violence and its categories. Such a formulation is in line with the general economic literature on violence (e.g., Becker, 1968, Durkheim 1982, Fajnzylber, 2002, OECD, 2009).

To examine the different categories of violence and their relationships with objective conditions, we employ the Generalised Method of Moment (GMM) for dynamic panel data models in this study to be a model consistent with and efficient enough to measure the trends of violence, economic development objective conditions over time. This model is dynamic because the explanatory variable set includes a lag of the dependent variable and some explanatory variables that are potentially jointly endogenous in the sense of being correlated with the error term. Taking endogeneity into account, it applies lagged explanatory variables as internal instruments, where it controls for endogeneity by using GMM. Arellano and Bover (1995), Blundell and Bond (1998) encompass a regression equation in differences and levels, each one with its specific set of instrumental variables[2]. The general regression model for the indicator of violence is as follows:

$$y_{i,t} = \beta_1 y_{i,t-1} + \beta_2 X_{i,t} + \eta_i + \varepsilon_{i,t} \quad (1)$$

Equation (1) and a GMM procedure are applied to obtain consistent estimates of the variables of interest and to correct for bias caused by endogenous explanatory variables. A Sargan test of over-identifying restrictions is also applied to assess the overall validity of the instruments. The models used in this study are as follows:

$$\widehat{\Psi}_{i,t} = \beta_1 \widehat{\Psi}_{i,t-1} + \beta_2 SI_{i,t} + \beta_3 X_{i,t} + \eta_i + \varepsilon_{i,t} \quad (2)$$

where $\widehat{\Psi}_{i,t}$ is the category of violence in the period *t* for the department *i*, $\widehat{\Psi}_{i,t-1}$ is the lagged category of violence, $SI_{i,t}$ represents the various social indicators (the GINI Index and the Unsatisfied Basic Needs measurement in the period *t* for the department *i*). $X_{i,t}$ is a vector that contains indicators related to the following measurements: the economic development (GDP per capita, budget execution, deterrence variables of department *i* in the period *t*; illegal drug trade (hectares of land under drug cultivation eradicated or cultivated) for the department *i* in the period *t*. Lastly, η_i and $\varepsilon_{i,t}$ are the fixed effects and the idiosyncratic error terms, respectively. Specification tests support the dynamic model. Similarly, the Sargan test is calculated to support the specific purpose of each Colombian department.

4. Results

This section provides estimates from the dynamic panel model. The results of the estimations show the same coefficients and trends in the study of violence and its categories as well as their relationships with objective conditions. The results suggest that violence depends on various factors. GDP-PC, education and deterrence variables show a negative effect on violence, whereas GINI and the lagged dependent variable show a positive effect on violence. Labour market and illegal drugs can show either a positive or negative effect depending on the analytical approach. Moreover, the objective conditions and their

[2] The instrumental variables allow driving two issues. First, it can resolve the problem of simultaneity and reverse causation caused by the likely endogeneity of the regressors used in this type of equation. Second, it reduces the estimation bias caused by the underreporting of corruption and homicide rates.

interrelationships have been important in the trends of violence in Colombian departments (Tables 2and 3).

In the majority of models, the results of the lagged dependent variables show a positive and significant impact on violence and its categories, which should demonstrate the existence of violence inertia over time, indicating that violence is persistent over time. Therefore, changes in crime rates tend to persist over time, even after the original causes of the change have disappeared (Fajnzylber et al., 2000, Levinson, 2002).

a. Violence. Table 2 shows the results of violence measured as the rate of homicides, the rate of political homicides and the number of cases of collective homicides, which show that the number of police officers has a negative influence on violence, whereas illegal drugs, measured as hectares under drug cultivation, have a positive and significant influence on violence. The former results concur with those of Soares and Naritomi (2007) and Mousumi and Zakir (2009), who demonstrate that the number of police officers is associated with a reduction of the incidence of violence.

In the latter result, violence arises through increased cultivation of coca or other illegal drugs (Angrist and Kugler, 2007 and Hofmann, 2009). Moreover, in the Colombian case, narcotics traffickers have generated a new set of values for Colombian society. This process is evidenced by the consumerism and the loss of institutional legitimacy that are reflected in the generalized crisis of state authority suffered by this country in the mid-1980s and late 1990s. This crisis progressively destroyed all chances of institutional intervention because the drug traffickers are opposed to institutional loyalties of any kind and demonstrate that anyone can reach power through the use of violence (Camacho and Lopez, 2000).

Analysing violence as the homicide rate, the results show that the deterrence variables, education, budget execution, GDP-PC and market labour variables all have negative effects on violence, whereas the lagged rate of homicides, population, GINI and illegal drug cultivation have positive effects on violence.

The lagged rate of homicides, population, GDP-PC, employment per industry and budget execution are the variables with more significant effects on violence in Colombian departments (see Table 2). In the analysis of the number of cases of collective homicides, the results indicate that the lagged rate of collective homicides, population GINI and illegal drug cultivation all have positive effects on violence; whereas deterrence variables have negative effects on violence (see Table 2).

In the majority of models, the results of the lagged dependent variables show a positive and significant impact on violence and its categories, which should demonstrate the existence of violence inertia over time, indicating that violence is persistent over time. Therefore, changes in crime rates tend to persist over time, even after the original causes of the change have disappeared (Fajnzylber et al., 2000, Levinson, 2002).

These results demonstrate that violence is closely related to deterrence variables and to economic growth. Deterrence variables are determined by the state presence, where violence tends to correlate with critical variables such as a weak state presence and a lack of effective justice, which concurs with the Colombian case (Chernick and Bailey, 2005). According to World Bank (2007), in the context of Latin America, economic growth is impeded by the high levels of violence and insufficient opportunity. Therefore, violence increases when the application of justice is a weak, economic opportunity is scarce, and education is deficient.

b. Political violence. Economists working in this category of violence highlight the state monopoly on coercion and force and see political violence as related to the state's failure to maintain that monopoly (Solimano, 2004). The results show that deterrence variables, education, GDP-PC and labour market variables have negative effects on political violence, whereas the lagged rate of political homicide, population, GINI, and illegal drug cultivation have positive effects on this category of violence (see Table 2).

Table 2. Dynamic panel data estimation for violence and political violence

Parameter	The rate of homicides	The rate of political homicides	The number of cases of collective homicides
Constant	1.109 (1.967)	-0.283 (7.069)	1.076 (1.004)
Lagged variable	0.533*** (0.082)	-0.372*** (0.058)	0.214*** (0.067)
Population	0.295** (0.154)	1.211*** (0.338)	0.394*** (0.154)
GDP per capita	-0.073** (0.036)	-0.410 (0.292)	
Education	-0.118 (0.117)	-0.384** (0.219)	
Captures	-0.054 (0.072)	-0.449** (0.243)	-0.147 (0.171)
Number of police officers	-0.054 (0.072)	-0.654** (0.343)	-0.008 (0.132)
Hectares under drug cultivation	0.038** (0.022)	0.189*** (0.080)	0.00003 (0.00002)
Budget execution	-0.211*** (0.058)	-0.085 (0.154)	
Employment rate	-0.331 (0.324)	-0.906 (1.388)	
Hectares under opium cultivation	0.014 (0.020)		
Employments per industry	-0.137* (0.077)		
GINI		16.85 (27.76)	15.73*** (6.530)
Observations	96	209	243
Specification test (p-values)			
Sargan test	0.081	0.061	0.083
Serial correlation			
Second - order	0.139	0.340	0.942

Notes: All models are estimated using the Arellano-Bover/Blundell-Bond linear dynamic panel-data system GMM estimations. Figures in the parentheses are standard errors. *** Significant at the 1% level, ** Significant at the 5% level, * Significant at the 10% level. Sargan and Serial correlation tests are *P* values.

The variables of economic growth, such as GDP-PC and budget execution, show negative effects on political violence, whereas the GINI index shows a positive. This implies that increases in economic growth are linked with decreases in political homicide rates but that departments with high levels of income inequality exhibit comparatively high political homicide rates (Messner et al., 2002). In previous studies, high levels of political violence have been shown to cause an economic recession, impose financial constraints on the government, and damage the country's infrastructure (Li, 2006). Such findings are in line with our results in the Colombian case.

Table 3. Dynamic panel data estimation for economic violence

Parameter	Cases of robberies	The number of kidnappings	Displaced population
Constant	8.085*** (1.855)	0.902 (1.119)	5.531** (2.699)
Lagged variable	0.603*** (0.092)	0.528*** (0.088)	0.145 (0.105)
Hectares under drug cultivation	0.027 (0.062)	0.138*** (0.049)	0.033 (0.064)
Population	13.70 (10.37)	2.178*** (0.594)	
Education	-0.219 (0.203)	-0.258*** (0.104)	
Number of police officers	-0.742*** (0.213)	-1.106** (0.494)	
GINI	2.486*** (1.009)		1.837*** (0.728)
NBI	5.102 (12.52)		0.612 (0.631)
Captures		-0.206* (0.125)	-0.248*** (0.080)
Unemployment rate		0.755*** (0.199)	
Political Violence			0.156*** (0.070)
Hectares eradicated of drugs			-0.0007 (0.049)
Observations	93	98	121
Specification test (p-values)			
Sargan test	0.741	0.637	0.287
Serial correlation			
Second - order	0.900	0.051	0.217

Notes: All models are estimated using the Arellano-Bover/Blundell-Bond linear dynamic panel-data system GMM estimations. Figures in the parentheses are standard errors. *** Significant at the 1% level, ** Significant at the 5% level, * Significant at the 10% level. Sargan and Serial correlation tests are P values.

c. Economic violence. This category of violence is analysed through three approaches: the number of kidnappings, cases of robbery and displaced population (see Table 3). The results show that the lagged rate of the dependent variable, population, GINI and unemployment all have positive effects on economic violence, whereas deterrence variables and education have a positive effect on this category of violence. The lagged rate of dependent variables, population and deterrence variables are the most significant variables for economic violence.

The results of the size of the population show a positive correlation with economic violence. This may be because departments with population heterogeneity have weak social ties, poverty and high population turnover, making them more conducive to economic violence. This explanation is applied by Schichor (1979) in the context of U.S. and McCall and Nieuwbeerta (2007) in the context of European countries.

Kidnapping. Table 3 shows the results of the estimations for economic violence measured as the number of kidnappings. In Colombia, the trends in kidnapping rates show that the rates increased during the second half of the 1980s, that they peaked during the 1990s, and that they have recently fallen. However, the current rates are still significantly high (Montenegro and Pedraza, 2009). Kidnapping in this country is linked to politically motivated (guerrilla) groups, and this phenomenon has generally been a rural activity with urban victims, which means that hostages are usually non-residents of the place where the incident occurs (Rubio, 2004).

The results of the analysis of the kidnapping variable indicate that deterrence variables and education have an inverse relationship with the number of kidnappings, whereas the lagged rate of kidnappings, population and hectares under drug cultivation and unemployment rate have a direct relationship with kidnapping events. Variables such as the lagged rate of kidnappings, population, number of police officers, and market labour show significant effects on kidnapping.

Market labour, measured as unemployment rates, indicates that higher unemployment rates increase the number of kidnappings. In previous literature, an increase in kidnappings is seen when unemployment and economic recession affect the population at large (Rettberg et al., 2010, Raphael and Winter, 1998), and these results show that such a finding is supported in the Colombian case.

Robbery. Economic violence, measured as the number of robberies, shows that the lagged rates of robbery and GINI have positive effects on robbery, whereas education, the number of police officers and education have negative effects on robbery (see Table 3). These results indicate that an increase in education significantly reduces subsequent violence and robbery, yielding sizeable social benefits because education should have a significant and large influence on individual propensities to commit violent acts (Machin and Vujic, 2006). According to Lochner (2007), there are four primary reasons that education might affect violence: (I) education increases wage rates, which increase the opportunity costs of violence; (II) education may directly affect the financial rewards of crime; (III) education may alter preferences for risk-taking or patience; and (IV) education may affect the social networks or peers of individuals.

Displaced population. Colombia has experienced more than four decades of internal violence resulting in the displacement of millions of people; estimates range between 1.8 million and 3.7 million internally displaced individuals over the past 20 years (WFP, 2008). The results show that the lagged rate of the displaced population, and GINI have positive effects on the displaced population, whereas deterrence variables have a negative effect on the displaced population (see Table 3). The results of deterrence variables, measured as the number of captures and hectares of drugs eradicated, should indicate the importance of the presence of the state to decrease economic violence measured as the displaced population. Moreover, violence reduces social investments that alter the development and economic growth of departments, decreasing the quality and conditions of life and generating more displacement and violence, which concurs with Nafziger et al., 2000.

All findings reported in this paper are of particular interest in the formulation and development of social policies and strategies against violence to increase economic growth and development, productivity, and security for the population across all Colombian departments. These policies and strategies ought to include investments in education, increasing opportunities in the labour market, strengthening the justice system, and generating an effective state presence in all Colombian regions.

CONCLUSION

In this chapter, we attempted to explain and analyse the different categories of violence and their relationships with objective conditions using a dynamic data panel model in the Colombian departments between 1993 and 2007. This study analyses general violence and two categories of violence, political and economic, in the Colombian case, taking into account different variables that could cause violence along various categories and examines their interrelationships with economic growth and development.

To examine the different categories of violence and their relationships with objective conditions, we employ a dynamic panel data model. We find that the aggregate-level production per capita, education, deterrence variables and employment rate show a negative effect on violence, whereas GINI, the unemployment rate and that lagged rate show a positive effect on violence. Moreover, the objective conditions and their interrelationships are important factors influencing the trends of violence in the Colombian departments.

The results demonstrate that violence is closely related with deterrence variables and economic growth. Deterrence variables are determined by state presence, and violence tends to correlate with critical variables such as a weak state presence and a lack of effective justice. Economic growth is impeded by high levels of violence and insufficient opportunities. Therefore, violence increases when the application of justice is a weak, economic opportunity is scarce, and education is deficient.

In the case of political violence, the results show that deterrence variables, education, budget execution, GDP-PC and labour market variables have negative effects on political violence, whereas population, GINI, and illegal drug cultivation have positive effects on this category of violence. These results indicate that increases in economic growth are linked with decreases in political homicide rates and that departments with high levels of income inequality exhibit comparatively high political homicide rates.

The results of economic violence show that the lagged rate of the dependent variable, population, GINI and unemployment have positive effects on economic violence, whereas deterrence variables and education have a negative effect on this category of violence. The lagged rate of the dependent variables, population, the numbers of police officers and education have the most significant effects on economic violence.

The findings demonstrate the importance of generating social policies and strategies to decrease violence and to increase economic growth and development, productivity, and security for the population across Colombian departments. These policies and strategies ought to include investments in education, increasing opportunities in the labour market, strengthening the justice system, and generating an effective state presence in all Colombian regions.

REFERENCES

Angrist J., Kugler A., (2007). Rural Windfall or a New Resource Curse? Coca, Income, and Civil Conflict in Colombia. http://econ-www.mit.edu/files/35.

Arellano M., Bover O., 1995. Another look at the instrumental variable estimation of error-components models. *Journal of Econometrics* 68, 29–51.

Beccaria C., 1764. On crimes and punishments. HPC Classics Series. Hackett Publishing, 1986.

Baum C., (2001). Residual diagnostics for cross-section time series regression models. The Stata Journal 1, 101–104.

Becker, G., (1968). Crime and punishment: an economic approach. *Journal of Political Economy* 76, 169– 217.

Benson M., Fox G., (2002). Economic Distress, Community Context and Intimate Violence: An Application and Extension of Social Disorganization Theory. *Final Report* 193434. the National Institute of Justice, Office of Justice Programs, U. S. Department of Justice.

Besley T., Persson T., (2009). The Logic of Political Violence. Paper 091222. http://people.su.se/~tpers/PoliticalVilolence_paper091222.pdf.

Bentham, J., (1789). An Introduction to the Principles of Morals and Legislation. Latest edition: *Adamant Media Corporation*, 2005.

Blundell R., Bond S., 1998. Initial conditions and moment restrictions in dynamic panel data models. *Journal of Econometrics* 87, 115–143.

Broekman D., (2000). A state failure-violence-resource capture triangle: Comparing the Angolan and Colombian experiences. The UNISA centre for Latin American studies 16, 4-34.

Buvinić, M., Morrison A., Shifter M., (1999). Violence in Latin America and the Caribbean: A Framework for Action", Technical Study, Inter-American Development Bank, Washington DC.

Camacho A., Lopez A., (2000). Perspectives on Narcotics Trafficking in Colombia. III. The Political Economy of the Drug Trade. *International Journal of Politics, Culture and Society*, 14, 151-182.

Camatari, D., (2006). The new wars in Africa: armed conflicts and natural resources *Documents and academic researches* 22.

Castillo M., Salazar B., (2003). Rationality, preferences and irregular war. *Colombian Economic Journal* 1, 16/33.

Chernick M., Bailey J., (2005). Democracy and violence, early warning and conflict prevention. Implications for international assistance. *Georgetown University and United Nations Development Programme.*

Cotte, A., (2007). Growth, Inequality and Poverty: An Analysis of the Violence in Colombia, Bogotá, Universidad de La Salle (Available at SSRN: http://ssrn.com/abstract=1012487)

Driscoll J., Kraay A., (1998). Consistent covariance matrix estimation with spatially dependent panel data. *Review of Economics and Statistics* 80, 549-560.

Drukker D., (2003). Testing for serial correlation in linear panel-data models. *The Stata Journal* 3, 168–177.

Durkheim, E., (1982). The rules of sociological method. New York: Free Press. (Original work published 1895).

Echandía, C., (2003). The Colombian intern conflict: last changes and implications in the process of violence. http://www.santafe.edu/files/gems/obstaclestopeace/echandia. pdf (In Spanish).

Fajnzylber P., Lederman D., Loayza N., (2000). Crime and Victimization: An economic perspective. Economia, Fall 2000. *Journal of the Latin American and Caribbean Economic Association* 1, 219-248.

Fajnzylber P., Lederman D., Loayza N., (2002). What causes violent crime?. *European Economic Review* 46, 1323-1357.

Fielding N., Clarke A., Witt R., (2000). The economic dimensions of crime. *Palgrave Macmillan.*

Fisman R., Miguel E., (2008). Economic Gangsters: Corruption, Violence, and the Poverty of Nations. Princeton University Press.

Gaviria A., Vélez C., (2001). Who bears the burden of crime and violence in Colombia?. FEDESARROLLO and World Bank.

Geneva Declaration, (2008). The Global Burden of Armed Violence report. Geneva Declaration Secretariat. http://www.genevadeclaration.org/fileadmin/docs/Global-Burden-of-Armed-Violence-full-report.pdf.

Giugale, M., Lafourcade, O., Luff, C., (2003). Colombia: The Economic Foundation of Peace. World Bank, Washington DC.

Gorbaneff Y., Jacome F., (2000). The Armed Conflict in Colombia: An Application of The Game Theory. Working Paper SSRN: http://ssrn.com/ abstract= 240742ordoi:10.2139/ ssrn. 240742.

Greene, W. (2000). Econometric Analysis. Upper Saddle River, NJ: Prentice–Hall.

Hausman, J., (1978). Specification tests in econometrics. *Econometrica* 46, 1251–1271.

Hoechle D., (2007). Robust standard errors for panel regressions with cross–sectional dependence. The Stata Journal 7, 281-312.

Hofmann K., (2009). The Impact of Organized Crime on Democratic Governance – Focus on Latin America and the Caribbean. Friedrich-Ebert-Stiftung. Department for Development Policy. Dialogue on Globalization. *FES Briefing Paper* 13, 2-9.

Holmes J., Gutiérrez S., Curtin K., (2002). Drugs, Violence and Development in Colombia: A Department Level Analysis. University of Texas at Dallas. *Latin American Politics and Society.*

Koonings K., Kruijt D., (2004). Armed actors, organized violence and state failure in Latin America: a survey of issues and arguments. Armed actors, organised violence and state failure in Latin America. Zed Books.

Levinson D., (2002). Encyclopedia of crime and punishment. Vol. 3 Crime and Violence in Latin America. Sage Publications.

Li Q., (2006). Chapter 11 Political Violence and Foreign Direct Investment. Book series: *Research in Global Strategy Management* 12, 225-249.

Lochner L., (2007). Education and Crime. Department of Economics, University of Western Ontario. *The International Encyclopedia of Education*, 3rd Edition.

Machin S., Vujic S., (2006). Crime and Education: New evidence from Britain. http://www.iza.org/conference_files/SUMS2007/vujic_s3348.pdf.

Marx, K., (1853). New York Daily Tribune article on the death penalty. www.marxists.org/archive/marx/works/1853/02/18.htm

McCall P., Nieuwbeerta P., (2007). Structural Covariates of Homicide Rates. A European City Cross-National Comparative Analysis. *Homicide Studies* 11, 167-188.

Messner S., Raffalovich L., Shrock P., (2002). Reassessing the Cross-National Relationship between Income Inequality and Homicide Rates: Implications of Data Quality Control in the Measurement of Income Distribution. *Journal of Quantitative Criminology* 18, 377-395.

Montenegro S., Pedraza A., (2009). Falling Kidnapping Rates and the Expansion of Mobile Phones in Colombia. CEDE documents 32. http://ssrn.com/abstract=1544475.

Moser, C., (2000). Violence in Colombia: Building sustainable peace and social capital. Colombia. *Essays on Conflict, Peace, and Development*. The World Bank.

Mousumi D., Zakir H., (2009). Determinants of crime rates: Crime Deterrence and Growth in post-liberalized India. MPRA Paper No. 14478. http://mpra.ub.uni-muenchen.de/14478/

Nafziger, E., Stewart, F., Väyrynen, R., (2000). War, Hunger, and Displacement: The Origins of Humanitarian Emergencies; Vol. 1 & 2. Queen Elizabeth House Series in Development Economics and UNU/WIDER Studies in Development Economics. Oxford: Oxford University Press.

Nafziger E., Auvinen J., (2002). Economic Development, Inequality, War, and State Violence. World Development 30, 153–163.

Organisation for Economic Co-operation and Development (OECD), (2009). Conflict and Fragility Armed Violence Reduction: Enabling Development. www.oecd.org.

Palau, M., Sánchez F., (2006). Conflict, decentralisation and local governance in Colombia, 1974-2004. Document Cede-University of Los Andes. Mayo.

Raphael S., Winter R., (1998). Identifying the effect of unemployment on crime. Discussion Paper 98-19. University of California, San Diego.

Rettberg A., Leiteritz R., Nasi C., (2010). Entrepreneurial Activity and Civil War in Colombia. Exploring the Mutual Determinants between Armed Conflict and the Private Sector. Working Paper No. 2010/06. UNU-WIDER project on Entrepreneurship and Development.

Rubio, M., (2001). Violence and conflict in the nineties. *Coyuntura Social*, 22, May. (In Spanish).

Rubio M., (2004). Kidnapping and Armed Conflict in Colombia. Paper presented at the PRIO Workshop on "techniques of violence in civil war". http://uniset.ca/terr/art/colombiakidnapping.pdf

Sambanis N., (2004). Poverty and the Organization of Political Violence: A Review and Some Conjectures. Yale University. Political Science.

Sánchez, F., Díaz A., Formisano M., (2003). Conflict, violence and criminal activity in Colombia: a spatial analysis. *Economies Files* No. 219.

Sánchez, F., Nuñez J., (2001). Determinants of violent crime in a highly violent country: The Colombian Case. Cede - University of los Andes (In Spanish).

Shichor D., Decker D., O'Brien R., (1979). Population density and criminal victimization. Some Unexpected Findings in Central Cities. Criminology 17, 184-193.

Solimano A., (2004). Political violence and economic development in Latin America: issues and evidence. Economic Commission for Latin America and the Caribbean Economic Development Division.

Schelling T., (1960). The Strategy of Conflict, Harvard U Press.

Scheper-Hughes N., Bourgois P., (2004). *Violence in war and peace.* Volume 5 of Blackwell readers in anthropology.

Soares R., Naritomi J., (2007). Understanding High Crime Rates in Latin America: The Role of Social and Policy Factors. The conference: Confronting Crime and Violence in Latin America: Crafting a Public Policy Agenda, organized by the Instituto Fernando Henrique Cardoso (iFHC) at the John F. Kennedy School of Government, Harvard University.

Soriano, A., (2000). Colombia Essays on Conflict, Peace, and Development. The World Bank Washington, D.C.

Tejerina B., (1991). Sociology theories of conflict. *Spain Journal of Sociology Researches*, 55, 47-63.

Wood J., (2004). Violence and crime in nineteenth-century England: the shadow of our refinement. Volume 1 of Routledge studies in modern British history.

Wooldridge J., (2002). *Econometric Analysis of Cross Section and Panel Data*. Cambridge, MA: MIT Press.

World Bank (WB), (2003). Breaking the Conflict Trap Civil War and Development Policy. A World Bank and Oxford University Press Policy Research Report.

World Bank (WB), (2007). Crime, Violence, and Development: Trends, Costs, and Policy Options in the Caribbean. A Joint Report by the United Nations Office on Drugs and Crime and the Latin America and the Caribbean Region of the World Bank. Report No. 37820.

World Food Bank (WFB), (2008). Food Assistance to Internally Displaced Persons and Other Highly Food-Insecure Groups Affected by Violence. *Executive Board.* http://www.wfp.org/eb.

World Health Organization (WHO), (2004). The Economic Dimensions of Interpersonal Violence. *Department of Injuries and Violence Prevention.*

In: Health, Violence, Environment and Human Development ... ISBN: 978-1-62948-038-1
Editors: A. Cotte Poveda and C. I. Pardo Martínez

Chapter 6

WATER AND POVERTY: A STUDY OF THE COLOMBIAN ORINOQUÍA REGION

Gustavo Correa Assmus*

Faculty of Agricultural Sciences, University of La Salle,
Bogota, Colombia

ABSTRACT

Economic progress is not comprehensible when its variables are dissociated. In contrast, a maximum balance must be pursued in the articulation of these variables when the conservation of a strategic resource, such as water, which is unquestionably necessary for the sustenance of life on earth and is a key factor in overcoming poverty, is at stake. The present manuscript explored the relationship between water and poverty and interpreted the expansion of hydraulic welfare to be the result of the interaction between access to water and the public investment that facilitates water access.

The present study also examined the Colombian Orinoquía region and its variables, such as population, land ownership, and hydraulic supply and demand, as a case study for determining the necessary conditions for secure access to water.

Keywords: Water, poverty, resource allocation, access to water, Orinoquía

1. INTRODUCTION

The present manuscript is aimed to examine the relationships between water, poverty, and development. The theme is relevant not only due to the current combination of variables but also from the perspective of the people living behind the figures, bio-economic models,

* Reflections on the doctoral thesis: Water, Poverty, and Development in Colombia: an Analysis of the Last Few Decades.

and theories, whose day-to-day existence is deprived of the opportunity to enjoy a greater quality of life[1].

The present study first presented an initial overview of the investigations and rationales that contribute to the interpretation of the sophisticated relationships between water and poverty as a situation to be resolved by both socio-economic and environmental development. Then, the present study addressed the construction and behaviour of the expansion curve for hydraulic welfare in Colombia, primarily based on the investment in water coverage infrastructure. Next, the case of the Colombian Orinoquía region, comprising the Departments of Arauca, Casanare, Meta, and Vichada, was examined from the perspective of the socio-environmental status quo of the regional water supply and demand. In the third section, the present study found that an abundant natural water resource supply does not necessarily imply an improved quality of life.

Finally, the conclusions of the present study suggested that certain environmental conditions and the construction of favourable socio-economic circumstances can lead to regional opportunities of varying magnitudes and characteristics, which may promote environmentally friendly social and economic development.

2. Conceptual Theoretical Framework

The relationship between water and poverty has been studied by the science of economics using various approaches. There are those who have viewed the topic as a problem related to equality, to be addressed through state interventions. Others have considered the relationship to be an issue within the area of agrarian production and food security that is subject to the framework of rural policies. And then there are those who have approached the subject from the perspective of health. More recently, the relationship between water and poverty has been addressed as a matter of socio-environmental responsibility. In the face of climate change, this approach has tied the issue to middle- and long-term implications for welfare, wealth, and development. These perspectives, which each contain analytical biases, are discussed below.

Some authors, such as Boch, Hommann, Sadoff, and Travers (2000), have suggested the importance of governance through state interventions to guarantee the rational use of water for public health. Similarly, Sánchez-Triana, Ahmed, and Awe (2007) made a brief examination of Colombia, in which they identified the social costs of inadequate water, not only from the loss of heath due to the use of grey water (contaminated) but also from the inadequate management of water. The Asian Development Bank (ADB) (2004) has also considered the strengthening of state governance to be important for water-related matters to guarantee the enforcement of policies, norms, and laws that regulate social order in the use and conservation of water.

After studying samples in the communities of Amran and Zabid in Yemen to explore aspects of water supply, sanitation, water quality, and public health, Klasen, Lechtenfeld, Meier, and Rieckmann (2011) stressed the importance of integrating cooperative work with investment in hydraulic sanitation infrastructure to improve the quality of local life. An

[1] Bio-economy is defined in the present manuscript as a pluri-dimensional situation in which the development of the economic system is based on service to mankind, assuring the dynamic reproduction of natural conditions to guarantee that the biosphere functions optimally with the economy and nature (Passet, 1996).

efficient water supply for urban and rural homes has been considered to be of great importance by Kulindwa and Lein (2008). Just as poverty can be defined in absolute and relative terms, human relationships with water can be composed of complex absolute and relative interactions, as is evident when comparing those who live in urban centres to those who live in rural communities. Aderinwale and Ajayi (2008) explored this theoretical explanation in Nigeria and concluded that poverty impacts the water quality, just as supplying grey water to people has effects on poverty. Similarly, Kulindwa (2008), in a study of Tanzania, suggested that water supply infrastructure projects at the rural level are a good economic mechanism for eliminating the gap between the urban poor and the rural poor, as well as the gap between urban and rural communities.

In the case of Colombia, Pérez, Smits, Benavidez, and Vargas (2004), presented a case study of the town of Dagua in the Department of Cauca concerning the multiple uses of water. These authors warned that the inadequate management of water eventually increases the inherent risks to the water supply, which can significantly and simultaneously affect the qualities of both peasant life and the natural environment.

From the perspective of equality and gender, it is a global premise that the responsibility for water-gathering in communities with a lack of urban-level water service and in rural areas falls to women and very young boys and girls. In this respect, Bhat, Pomane, and Kulkarni (2012), stressed that there is a structural inequality that is linked to the presence of social conflict arising due to water scarcity in some regions of the world. However, Hemson (2008) analysed South Africa and noted that water security in rural homes tends to be managed by women rather than men. Nonetheless, Hemson suggested that this situation increases poverty because the women must devote much time to procuring water, whereas if access to water were adequate and in quality conditions, women could dedicate that time to other skills, such as procuring more economic resources for their families and providing better care and education to their children.

The issue of growing desertification was studied by Morales and Parada (2005), with Brazil, Chile, and Argentina as references. They constructed a set of indicators that established the interdependence between poverty, increased land desertification, and subsequent environmental degradation. Using an econometric model, they found that the desertification of productive soils in Latin America produced environmental migrants, a negative socio-economic impact on the region.

It is clear that, for all societies, water is indispensable for production, particularly in agriculture. The Inter-American Development Bank (IDB) (2003) proposed that the social dialogue on water and poverty be simultaneously focused on two issues: first, the need to satisfy the basic needs of the population because secure access to water improves worker productivity due to improved health; and second, the investment in water as a production factor to promote growth and generate jobs. According to the United Nations Development Program (UNDP) (2006), there are 2 cornerstones for human development: first, water for life in the home, and second, water as a means of food production. These two foundations have yet to be achieved for a large part of humanity.

Based on their experience in Zimbabwe, Robinson, Mathew, and Proudfoot (2004) suggested that the task of approaching peasant communities to rationalise the multiple uses of water and promote productivity in each locality should be the responsibility of governments. Similarly, Barker, Van Koppen, and Shah (2000) evaluated the scarcity of water in southern Asia and Sub-Saharan Africa and emphasised the importance of irrigation systems and technological progress as a means of alleviating rural poverty based on agrarian production. Lein (2008) observed that decreased poverty in Bangladesh could be explained by agricultural changes and, more precisely, by achievements in water management. Rawnborg, Hanjra, Smith, and Hussein (2007) identified a common denominator in the sustainability of rural homes, which allowed residents to improve productivity, food safety, and individual and collective health, while mitigating financial needs and the multiple dimensions of poverty. That common denominator was access to secure water.

At present, considerations regarding access to water and violence are of great concern. Moriarti, Butterworth, Van Koppen, and Soussan (2004), observed that mobility in poor communities results in settlements on the outskirts of cities. There, procuring water for homes presents difficulties that create an informal context of economic survival marked by violent episodes. That the lack of water or its scarcity is one of the causes of violence cannot be ignored[2]. This analysis was discussed by Welzer (2010) when he made the Malthusian prediction that, increasingly, "more people will have a smaller resource base to survive, which can unleash violent conflicts between those who aspire to get food from the same piece of land or drink water from the same source that is running out."

These sources of water originate in the hydro-climate context that has historically modelled life on Earth. In recent decades, climate change has clearly tended toward global warming and extreme seasonal summer and winter cycles. These tendencies primarily affect the poorest communities because the poor depend, to a large extent, on a hospitable and stable climate (UNEP, United Nations Environmental Programme, 2007)[3].

According to the UNEP (2010), the vulnerable situation in Latin America is due not only to an obvious increase in the various climate events but also to the increased exposure of people, eco-systems, and productivity systems to climate risks[4]. Although Latin America's responsibility for climate change is only 12%, the future outlook for the region is somewhat alarming[5].

In Colombia, evidence of climate change is characterised by temperature increases of approximately 3.2ºC by the end of the millennium. Precipitation is expected to decrease by up to 4.0 mm/yr in 20% of the national territory, and deficits for crop production and human quality of life are predicted. The other 80% of the territory can expect average precipitation increases of approximately 10% in the first half of the century (Institute of Hydrology, Meteorology and Environment, IDEAM, in Spanish) (2010b).

Two of the Millennium Development Goals (MDGs), which were adopted at the Millennium Summit held in the year 2000, were to eradicate extreme poverty and hunger and to ensure environmental sustainability. The first goal focused on people as holders of rights to be met through integral human development. Moreover, the document declared that poverty is, to a large extent, a problem of social inefficiency that is detrimental not only to those directly affected by needs and "anti-freedoms" but to all of society (ECLAC Economic Commission for Latin America and the Caribbean, 2003). The second millennium goal was

[2] One example is the social uprising that occurred in the city of Yopal, the capital of the Department of Casanare (Colombia), in March, 2013 as a result of the destruction of a treatment plant due to a severe winter.

[3] A hospitable climate is directly related to the comfort indicator and its impact on human productivity.

[4] The impact of climate change is manifested in changes in variables, such as the distribution and intensity of precipitation, temperature levels, the melting of glaciers, and a higher sea level.

[5] Today, it is assumed that climate change is fundamentally anthropogenic. Therefore, responsibilities are measured according to greenhouse gas production.

oriented toward the concept of the sustainable development of total natural resources. In the particular case of water, the lack of access to secure water is considered to significantly diminish the useful human potential for the progress of a nation, to infringe on human rights, to restrict opportunities to achieve a better quality of life, and, therefore, to exacerbate poverty.

In accordance with previous studies, the present study analysed the relationships between water and the state, health, supply, gender, desertification, production, climate change, violence, quality of life, and poverty. However, the development factor has been defined in previous studies to be a random element that is negatively affected by the effects of the described relationships. Some studies have examined sustainability in depth, while others have focused more on the perspective of economic growth.

3. Methodological Approach

Based on the qualitative analyses from various studies and rationales that have clearly established socio-environmental relationships between water and poverty, the relationship between investment (C) in access to secure water and demand for water (D) was graphically established. This relationship led to an expansion path relating the points of union (C, D) by means of a curve (DHW, similar to an isocline) that indicated the development in terms of hydraulic welfare obtained by the population, which was defined by the possibility of access to drinkable or secure water.

Then, the Colombian Orinoquía region was taken as a case study. Using the given base variables, relationships were determined that allowed us to address the following: whether coverage indices were a reflection of better quality of life due to water supply; whether a low scarcity index resulted in better conditions of access to secure water; and whether hydro-climate impacts equally affected producers according to their land-ownership categories.

Returning to economic theory and the perception of the Colombian reality led to a descriptive rationale that articulated the water and poverty variables from individual or regional configurations. At this point, another set of elements intervened to restrict essential freedoms in the quest for socio-economic development. The information and data employed were retrieved from international or national public or private entities, according to the criterion of institutional reliability.

4. Discussion of Results

According to Pearse and Turner (1995), environmental strains and tensions, including the degradation of water, are currently present in all economic systems, regardless of wealth or political ideology. Moreover, it would appear that contemporary society is not interested in water itself but rather in the services that water provides. Perhaps for this reason, the conservation/degradation issues have been studied in terms of immediate needs, while the complex and reciprocal causality relationships that exist between poverty and the degradation of water, i.e., that poverty is a causal agent of water degradation and water degradation is a causal agent of poverty (Morales and Parada 2005), have been ignored.

From this perspective, the degradation of water quality and quantity affects productivity regarding quality of life and future opportunities for a significant part of the population, thus marking poverty as a restrictor of socio-economic development[6]. In turn, poverty, which is characterised by economic, cultural, educational, social, and sanitary restrictions, similarly hinders access to water in terms of quality and quantity, thus impacting water use and management, while also affecting development[7].

For this reason, examining the behaviour of hydraulic welfare as a function of investments in access to secure water in Colombia (Figure 1) generates points of intersection between the curves for secure water demand (D) and investment (C). An expansion path can be constructed from the intersection point that reflects the progressive behaviour of hydraulic welfare (DHW). According to data from the office of the Colombian ombudsman (2009), from 1997 to 2005, investment and demand increased over time[8]. Although the DHW curve clearly indicates the existence of periods in which investment resulted in significant increases in access to secure water (see Q2, Q3), responding to the economic rationale of maximising efficiency, in the following periods, significant investments did not result in significant increases in demand (access) for water (see Q4, Q5). This situation may be explained by the renovation of infrastructure, in some cases, but in others, it is not explainable. Therefore, technological and social interventions in hydraulic welfare should act innovatively on the investment variable (C) because that is where the development process (DHW) can be maximised to generate significant increments in meeting the demand for water (Q).

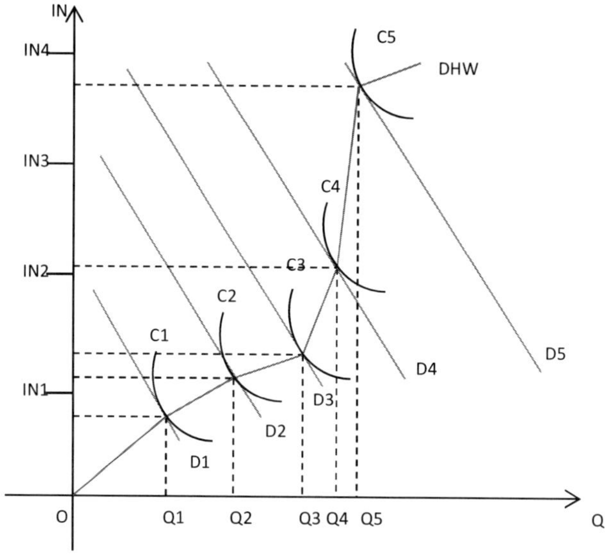

Source: Based on data from the Office of the Ombudsman, 2009.

Figure 1. Development curve for water welfare.

[6] Sánchez-Triana, Ahmed, and Awe (2007) estimated that, in Colombia, the cost of degradation of natural resources, including water, was approximately 3.7% of the Gross Domestic Product (GDP).

[7] Sánchez-Triana, Ahmed, and Awe (2007) estimated that 9% of the population in Colombia lacks access to a secure source of water.

[8] Investment for the period of 1997-2005 increased from 7 billion to 37 billion annually, while access to secure water grew from a rate of 59% to 65% of the population.

The Orinoquía region is a natural area of Colombia that is part of the third most abundant watershed for surface waters on the planet (Lasso, Usma, Trujillo, and Rial, 2010). The region consists of 254,335 km2 distributed between savannah and piedmont regions[9]. The Orinoquía region extends to the east, between the Arauca River in the north and the Guaviare River in the south, and from the eastern slopes of the Oriental Range in the west to the Orinoco River in the east. As a result of successive geological upheavals that occurred 2 million years ago, 4 types of terraces or sedimentary deposits (ecological sub-regions) were formed, structuring a plains landscape: the piedmont, the high plains or altillanuras, the flood plains or llanurasaluviales, and the sandy wind-swept relief areas[10].

The inhabitants of this area represent 3.17% of the national population, (see Table 1); 51% of the inhabitants are men, and 49% are women. Seventy-one per cent of the regional population reside in regional capitals, and the other 29% reside in rural areas, except in the Department of Vichada, where the rural population constitutes approximately 62%. The populations have index of unsatisfied basic needs (UBN) values of 35.6% in the Department of Arauca, 35.5% in Casanare, 25% in Meta, and 66.8% in Vichada. Most of these UBN figures are above the national average of 27.7%, signifying substantial regional poverty.

Table 1. Population in the Orinoquía Region

DEPARTMENTS	URBAN POPULATION	% TOTAL	RURAL POPULATION	% TOTAL	TOTAL	% NATIONAL POPULATION
ARAUCA	140,445	61	91,673	39	232,118	0.54
CASANARE	200,952	68	94,401	32	295,353	0.68
META	571,055	73	212,113	27	783,168	1.82
VICHADA	21,035	38	34,873	62	55,872	0.13

Source: National Administrative Department of Statistics, hereafter referred to as DANE (DANE: Departamento Administrativo Nacional de Estadísticas) 2008.

The region's aggregate production represents 7% of national GDP, 59% of which consists of proceeds from the production of oil. The remaining 41% is distributed, from highest to lowest, among agricultural products, livestock, commerce, and construction (DANE, 2008). Land ownership is concentrated in small and micro farms (see Table 2).

The hydro-climate of Colombia's Orinoquía Region (IDEAM, 2005a) is characterised by a monomodal precipitation pattern of 2,000 to 3,000 mm/yr. The winter season takes place from April to November and is succeeded by a dry period from December to March. There are, on average, 150 to 200 days of rain per year. Wind speeds range from 2 to 3 m/s, which equals between 40 to 60 km/h (IDEAM, 2006). There is no significant elevation in the region. Most of the land lies below 500 MASL, with temperatures between 24 and 28°C and a hot climate comfort level, due to the hot thermal floor; it receives sunshine for between 1,600 and

[9] The piedmont is a fertile strip of 36,023 km^2, including the 3,600 km^2 of the Macarena mountain range, between the mountain and savannah ecosystems that border on the occidental part of the region. The piedmont is currently undergoing a process of climate transition involving a greater intensity of rainfall.

[10] Also called the "arenales" or sandy areas, these are desert savannahs of low productivity but of great scenic value. The management of these lands is complex due to the low fertility of their soils. They form part of the high plains and savannah marshlands.

2,300 hours per year (IDEAM, 2005b)[11,12,13]. Temperatures gradually decrease from Puerto Carreño to the piedmont.

Surface run-off in the Orinoquía region amounts to 21,399 m^3/s, with an output of 55 $l/s/km^2$ and an average run-off sheet of 1,928 mm. Underground aquifers produce between 20 and 60 l/s. The region also has a surface of 97,870 ha that is covered by permanent marshland and 16,600 ha that is covered with swamps, for a total annual hydrological volume of 674,839 Mm3 that sustains vegetal, animal, human, and economic life in the region.

Evaporation presents 3 well-differentiated regions: the piedmont and its area of influence, with evaporation from 1,100 to 1,300 mm/yr; the plains in the Departments of Vichada, southern Casanare, and western Meta, with evaporation from 1,500 to 1,700 mm/yr; and the remaining region, with evaporation from 1,300 to 1,500 mm/yr. These factors ensure relative humidity values of 77% in the summer and 85% in the winter. The ozone column in the Orinoquía varies from 240 to 280 Dobson Units (DU).

Table 2. Land ownership

DEPART-MENTS	AREA (Km^2)	MUNICIPA-LITIES	MICRO-FARMS (%)	SMALL FARMS (%)	MEDIUM-SIZED PROPERTY (%)	LARGE PROPERTY (%)
ARAUCA	23,818	7	43	43	12	2
CASANARE	44,640	19	71	21	6	2
META	85,635	29	75	19	5	1
VICHADA	100,242	4	63	28	8	1

Sources: Social Action 2010; Agustín Codazzi Geography Institute (IGAC, in Spanish) 2008.

Additionally, the rivers crossing the Colombian Orinoquía region from west to east have high stream flows.[14] These rivers are as follows: the Casanare, at 1,199 m3/s; the Meta, at 4,700 m3/s; the Vichada, at 1,290 m3/s; and the Guaviare, at 5,031 m3/s. Other important but lesser rivers include the Arauca, at 740 m3/s, and the Tomo, at 991 m3/s. Stream flows are fed by rainfall, which makes the rivers navigable, particularly from April to November, along approximately 2,559 km.

This navigable river period coincides with production and commerce cycles such that the rivers can alleviate the economic conditions of the population by compensating for deficient road infrastructure to some extent.

Although the hydraulic system corresponds to an accentuated monomodal precipitation model that requires rational resource use, the data define a system of water supply and demand that is characterised by considerable abundance to meet demand, along with a low-risk scarcity index (see Table 3).

[11] Except for the piedmont, where altitudes of up to 1,100 metres above sea level can be found. Higher altitudes belong to the Andina Region, according to Romero, Cabrera, and Ortiz, (2008).

[12] In the presence of "El Niño", temperatures may increase from 0.21 to 0.50°C, while under the influence of "La Niña", temperatures may fluctuate between a decrease of 0.20 and an increase of 0.20°C over the normal temperature.

[13] Sunshine is determined according to the Hill and Morikofer-Davos method

[14] Rivers with speeds of more than 1,000 m^3/s are considered to have high flows, while those with lower speeds have low flows.

Table 3. Water supply and demand

DEPART-MENT	SUPPLY (Mm^3/yr)	DEMAND (Mm^3/yr)	SCARCITY INDEX	PER CAPITA SUPPLY (m^3/yr)	PER CAPITA DEMAND (m^3/yr)
ARAUCA	55,587	29	0.10	707,995	68
CASANARE	59,254	52	0.10	287,931	64
META	171,268	91	0.20	400,053	65
VICHADA	305,722	5	0.00	10,588,951	64

Sources: IDEAM 2005a; IDEAM 2010a; Office of the Ombudsman, 2009.

Thus, the water supply, whether measured in Mm3 per Department or in m3 per capita, is abundant enough for both agricultural use (60%) and domestic use (28%), which together account for 88% of the regional water demand. However, conditions of equality and secure access create a contradictory situation, particularly for a region that benefits from the proceeds of oil royalties. This situation is compatible with previous empirical findings on the inverse relationship between natural wealth and economic development (the Colombian paradox)[15]. Economic and political structures, keen to obtain income from the limited endowment of natural resources instead of reorienting rational expectations toward the creation of new wealth, contribute to a breach of productivity which may sustain poverty in the long-term (see Table 4)[16].

Table 4. Secure access to water

DEPARTMENT	URBAN COVERAGE AQUEDUCT (%)	URBAN COVERAGE SEWAGE SYSTEM (%)	QUALITY RISK (%)	HYDROLOGICAL MORBIDITY (%)	SERVICE HOURS (%P/H)
ARAUCA	83	69	21	7	71/12H
CASANARE	55	45	35	9	94/20H
META	64	55	55	7	83/17H
VICHADA	49	4	42	19	75/6H

Sources: Office of the Ombudsman, 2009; IDEAM 2001; IDEAM 2010a.

The first aspect that deserves attention is that both aqueduct and sewer system coverage are generally inadequate and hardly reach rural zones; the proportions that do are insufficient for the analysis[17]. The second item of interest involves the weak indicators for the aqueduct and sewage systems for the Department of Vichada, which conspire to sustain risk and

[15] Among the 17 mega-diverse countries in the world identified by the UNEP, Colombia is in 2nd place. However, according to the ETHOS Index (2011), Colombia is in 78th place among the 187 poorest countries in the world.

[16] Sánchez-Triana, Ahmed, and Awe (2007) have determined that, due to hydraulic impacts and incidences, the average social cost of lack of access to secure water and hydraulic sanitation is approximately 1.9 billion pesos per year, of which 70% is absorbed by health impacts and 30% is absorbed by other effects.

[17] It has been argued that low population densities and the great distances involved in offering hydraulic services would result in excessively high costs.

morbidity indices[18]. The third item of interest is that a high percentage of the regional populations (between 70% and 90%) have aqueduct service, but the service does not run regularly or continuously. Services are operative from between 6 hours per day to a maximum of 20 hours per day. These circumstances assume a greater significance when it is observed that 63% to 88% of the regional population is poor and must seek hydraulic survival in natural sources with insecure waters that are, in many cases, far from their homes.

However, the indices of usage for average and dry years indicate vulnerability and a low hydraulic potential due to a scarce population residing in the large territory (population/territory)[19]. Moreover, the comfort index (hot-humid) and west-east wind velocity create an unfavourable environment for human productivity. However, the per capita water consumption levels do not vary significantly from those of other regions in the country (270 l/hab/day/urban and 140 l/hab/day/rural).

Weather series and models indicate a moderate situation with respect to the effects of climate change and the erratic phenomena of "El Niño" and "La Niña". The perspective of a gradual increase in temperature of up to 3°C by the end of the millennium (IDEAM, 2010b), along with a radicalisation of climate behaviour, suggest the need to take precautionary measures against the potential risks of climate change for the regional economy. Appropriate technology for the hydraulic management of surface and underground waters should be implemented for development.

Conclusion

The Colombian Orinoquía region is an extensive savannah containing reserves of significant renewable and non-renewable natural resources. This fact is promising for the creation of urban, agricultural, agro-industrial, and eco-touristic centres that put man in touch with natural spaces while complying with fair and intergenerational socio-economic bio-development, based on regional ecological potential and sensitivity.

In hydro-climatic terms, the region presents a clear monomodal pattern requiring optimal management to protect the many diverse adaptations that the flora and fauna in the area have undergone over hundreds of years to survive long winters, flooding, and periods of harsh drought.

Additionally, the thin ozone column implies that, in the not so distant future, the region will need to take measures to prevent the generation of greenhouse gases, to protect against ultraviolet rays, and to confront erratic climate phenomena and their accentuated impact on the winter-summer periods.

In favour of the balance between water, poverty, and development, there is an abundant hydraulic supply of both surface and underground water available to satisfy demand. Nevertheless, the management and conservation of this resource require that traditional canons regarding how water is used be modified to overcome regional poverty as a form of "anti-freedom" that restricts human and bio-economic progress in the Orinoquía region.

[18] In recent studies on the quality of water from the aqueducts, health risks, including cloudy water, residual chlorine, total coliforms, and Escherichia coli, have been detected in Vichada, as well as in the other departments in the region.

[19] It has been estimated that surface run-off decreases by approximately 37 to 48% in summer.

From a socio-environmental perspective, political access to water needs to be differentiated from real access. Political access considers coverage to be an access indicator that is based only on the quantity of infrastructure that reaches a given number of homes containing an average number of members. In contrast, real access takes into account the quantity and quality of water. Therefore, real access not only considers investment in infrastructure (C) but also the security of receiving water in the optimal hygienic and sanitary conditions (D) that are necessary to avoid morbidity and eventual mortality, factors that ultimately subtract from the condition of coverage. Thus, in the present study, the coverage indicator was considered to be inappropriate for establishing the regional and national progress in areas of water service. Firstly, the political indicator includes the autonomous efforts of the population to supply themselves with the water they need from natural sources, without processing, by means of hoses (gravity permitting) or by hauling on the heads of women and children as though these families were receiving public water service. Secondly, this indicator does not represent the true daily experience of the population in supplying itself with water (see Figure 2).

Thus, there exists an integral water coverage, in which the conditions of service are optimal in quality and quantity, including regularity, continuity, and duration of the service. However, there is also deficient coverage, which restricts access to water. The objective of secure access is not only to obtain access to water but also to obtain access to clean, fresh, uncontaminated, drinkable water whenever it is needed.

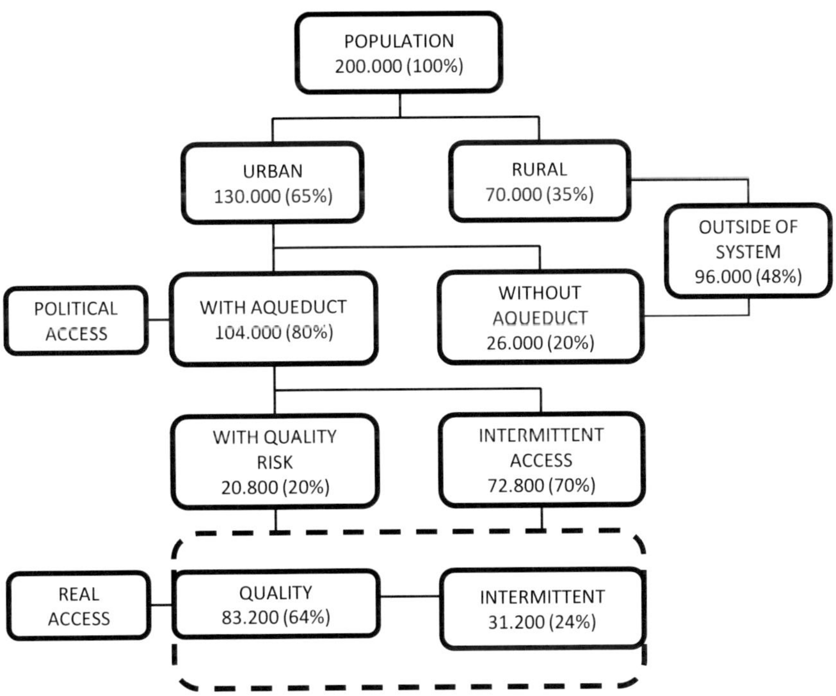

Source: Based on observations of the Colombian Orinoquía region.

Figure 2. Political and real access to water.

References

Acción Social. 2010. [Social Action] Unidades Agrícolas Familiares, Tenencia y Abandono Forzado de Tierras en Colombia. [Family Agricultural Units, Land Ownership and Forced Abandonment of Lands in Colombia.] Bogotá: Espacio Creativo Impresores. Pp. 384.

Banco Interamericano De Desarrollo Bid. [Interamerican Development Bank Idb] 2003. Agua y pobreza. [Water and Poverty] Kyoto, Tercer Foro Mundial del Agua. GIRH, GWP y CARE. Pp. 67.

CEPAL. 2003. Hacia el objetivo del milenio de reducir la pobreza en América latina y el Caribe. [Toward the millennium goal of reducing poverty in Latin America and the Caribbean] Santiago de Chile. CEPAL. Pp. 78.

DANE. 2008. Censo general 2005. [General Census] Bogotá. Dane. Pp. 498

Defensoría Del Pueblo. 2009. [Office of the Ombudsman] Diagnóstico del cumplimiento del derecho humano al agua en Colombia. [Diagnosos of the Fulfilment of the human right to water in Colombia] DESC.Pp. 456.

Ethos Fundación. 2011. Índice Ethos de pobreza. [EthosPovertyIndex] México. Ethos Fundación. Pp. 71.

Hemson, David. 2008. Easing the burden on women? Water, cholera and poverty in South Africa.New York. CROP. Pp. 144 – 167.

IDEAM. 2001. El medio ambiente en Colombia. [Environment in Colombia] Bogotá. IDEAM. Pp. 543.

IDEAM. 2005a. Atlas climatológico de Colombia. [Climate Atlas of Colombia] Bogotá. IDEAM. Pp. 219.

IDEAM.2005b. Atlas de radiación solar de Colombia. [Solar radiation atlas of Colombia] Bogotá. IDEAM. Pp. 175.

IDEAM. 2006. Atlas de vientos y energía eólica de Colombia. [Wind and wind energy atlas of Colombia] Bogotá.IDEAM.Pp. 168.

IDEAM. 2010a. Estudio nacional del agua ENA 2010. [National water study ENA 2010] Bogotá.IDEAM. Pp. 420.

IDEAM. 2010b. Segunda comunicación nacional ante la convención marco de las naciones unidas sobre cambio climático. [Second national communication at the United Nations Framework Convention on Climate Change] Bogotá. IDEAM. Pp. 447

IGAC. 2008. Atlas básico de Colombia. [Basic atlas of Colombia] Bogotá. IGAC. Tomo 2. Pp. 704.

Lasso, Carlos; Usma, José; Trujillo, Fernando y RIAL, Anabel. 2010. Biodiversidad de la cuenca del Orinoco. [Biodiversity in the Orinoco Basin Bogotá]. Instituto de Investigación de Recursos Biológicos Alexander von Humboldt. Pp. 609.

Lein, Haakon. 2008. Water, agricultural development and rural poverty in Bangladesh. New York. CROP. Pp. 87 – 102.

Morales, Cesar y PARADA, Soledad.2005. Pobreza, desertificación y degradación de los recursos naturales. [Poverty, desertification and degradation of natural resources] Santiago. CEPAL.Pp. 267.

Passet, René. 1996. Principios de Bioeconomía. [Principles of Bioeconomy] Madrid. Ed. Argentaria. Pp. 163.

Pearse, David y Turner, Kerry.1995.Economía de los recursos naturales y del medio ambiente. [Economics of natural resources and the environment] Madrid. Ed. Celeste. Pp. 448.

Pérez, Mario; SMITS, Stef; Benavidez, Alberto and VARGAS, Silena. 2004. Multiple use of water, livelihoods and poverty in Colombia: a case study from the ambichinte micro catchment. Holland. IRC. Pp. 75 – 93.

Perz, Stephen; Aramburú, Carlos y Bremner, Jasón.2003. Cambios poblacionales y uso del suelo en la cuenca amazónica. [Population change and land use in the Amazon Basin] Lima. Consorcio de Investigación Económica y Social. Pp. 11 – 52.

PNUD. 2006. Más allá de la escasez: poder, pobreza y la crisis mundial del agua. [Beyond scarcity: power, poverty and the global water crisis] New York. PNUD. Pp. 422.

PNUMA. 2007. Geo 4, Medio ambiente para el desarrollo. [Environment for development] Dinamarca. Phoenix Desing. Pp. 540.

PNUMA. 2010. Geo ALC 3, Perspectivas del medio ambiente: América Latina y el Caribe. [Perspectives on environment: Latin America and the Caribbean] Panamá. PNUMA. Pp. 375.

Romero, M.; Cabrera, E Y Ortiz, N. 2008. Informe sobre el estado de la biodiversidad en Colombia 2006-2007. [Report on the state of biodiversity in Colombia 2006-2007] Bogotá. Instituto de Investigación de Recursos Biológicos Alexander von Humboldt. Pp. 181.

Welzer, Harald. 2010. Guerras climáticas. [Climate Wars] Buenos Aires. Katz Editores. Pp. 342.

In: Health, Violence, Environment and Human Development ... ISBN: 978-1-62948-038-1
Editors: A. Cotte Poveda and C. I. Pardo Martínez

Chapter 7

AN EVALUATION OF THE ENVIRONMENTAL PERFORMANCE OF BUS RAPID TRANSIT AND THE CONTRIBUTION TO PUBLIC POLICY IN EMERGING CITIES USING BOGOTA AS A CASE STUDY

***Luis Gabriel Carmona Aparicio*[1] *and Adriana Ocampo Garcia*[2]**

[1]Master in Energy Efficiency and Industrial Ecology Program, CIRCE – Centre of Research for Energy Resources and Consumption, University of Zaragoza, Zaragoza, Spain

[2]Environmental Engineering Specialization, Faculty of Chemical Engineering, University of Santander (UIS), Bogota, Colombia

ABSTRACT

This chapter examines the relationship that exists between public transport policies and the environment in an urban setting. The case study used is that of the *TransMilenio* Bus Rapid Transit (BRT) network of Colombia's capital city, Bogota. In order to comprehensively evaluate the impact of the city's public transport project, the authors identify key indicators relating to environmental performance along with best practices and the lessons learned since the conception of the project back in 1998. The quantitative methodologies, to give weight to the qualitative analysis, include that of the Life Cycle Analysis and Landscape Assessment. The results presented indicate that whilst a BRT network provides a more sustainable option than conventional bus systems, challenges remain. In the case of Bogota these include the development of policies and practices which serve to improve urban spaces and energy efficiency whilst leading to a reduction in atmospheric contamination.

Keywords: Sustainable Transport, Bus Rapid Transit, TransMilenio, Public Policy, Environmental performance

[1] Email: lugacapa@gmail.com.
[2] Email: adrianaocampo@gmail.com.

1. Introduction

A great proportion of the global population is concentrated in cities. Indeed, since 2008 half of the people on Earth were registered as living in an urban setting, a figure which is expected to rise to 60% by 2030 (WHO, 2012). Modern society is thus increasingly characterized by urban growth where a transport service is an essential component of development. This is because regardless of a city's exact configuration, its citizens and visitors require modes of transport and services, motorized or otherwise, for a variety of reasons: be it education, work or leisure. Arguably:

> "An advanced city is not one where the poor can drive around in car but one where the rich use public transport" - Enrique Peñalosa, ex-mayor of Bogota (2011).

One way in which to achieve this is to build or retrofit an integrated city with a sustainable transport network vision, given that it is the transport sector that contributes to the productivity and quality of life of the average citizen, particularly where development in the past has been characterized by socio-economic imbalance and poor organization.

Bogota, Colombia's capital city provides perhaps one of the greatest examples of where the transformation of the transport system, revolutionized not only the transport sector but also the social-economic and political structure as a whole (Pardo, 2009; Rodríguez, 2009; Estupiñan, 2007). It is thus perhaps not surprising that the city has become the reference point for emerging and developing nations. This chapter, using the *TransMilenio* program as the case study, provides an overview of transversal motifs associated with *Bus Rapid Transport* (BRT) and the potential implementation of an *Integrated Public Transport System* (IPTS).

With this in mind, the authors compiled the necessary information by reviewing existing literature and complementing it with by field work and direct observation[3]. The work presented here is not however an exhaustive account of the planning, operations and maintenance of a BRT system's effect on the environment. It contains many factors peculiar to Bogota. As such application of any results presented here will be subject to each given city's or urban area's cultural, socio-economic and environmental aspects.

That said, the results of this undertaking illustrate, in a didactic way, the multiple relationships that exist between a transport project and the environmental aspects that need to be examined under a given territory's policies. The authors thus provide the following: i. A brief description of the public environmental policies that should be taken into account for the successful deployment of a BRT or IPTS; ii. A general vision of the different project stages of a transport system from an environmental perspective; iii. A summary of innovations and lessons learned throughout the project life cycle; iv. Conclusions and recommendations which serve to support the orientation of those taking decisions within the realm of sustainability.

At this stage, it is important to clarify that although this chapter is written predominately from an environmental perspective, the socio-economic dimensions are by no means less important given that the definition of sustainability is a balance of all three pillars fundamental to modern society. Certainly transport projects require a financial structure to guarantee the stability and function of the project throughout its life, just as much as they need to facilitate social inclusion.

---

[3] The authors have worked for 7 years on the TransMilenio project in a position of employment.

2. Literature Review

The literature review, using the *TransMilenio* project as the basis, focuses on those features relevant to public transport policy, specifically mobility and environmental impacts which are this chapter's two central themes. Mobility in cities is heavily associated with the consumption of resources (time, energy, space, materials and monetary) and the generation of negative consequences, often referred to as "externalities." These externalities consist of those effects generated by society without the provision of any type of compensation to Nature or ecosystem users. In the case of the transport sector, they typically include atmospheric and noise pollution (Vasconcellos, 2010).

Currently two simplified definitions exist that have found acceptance internationally. These are those circulated by the EMBARQ Centre for Sustainable Transport of the *World Resources Institute* (WRI) (Gutiérrez, 2012):

Bus Rapid Transit (BRT)

High demand routes which run metro type services but with buses instead of trains. In many cases they complement other feeder services and tend to co-exist with conventional forms.

Integrated Public Transport System (IPTS)

Public transport systems with an integrated tariff, in the sense that a unified system of fare collection and ticketing exists within a designated urban nucleus. Integrated operation and management permits door to door trips. Some may also have BRT routes, metros and other types of subsystems.

Specifically, the BRT *TransMilenio* system located in Bogota, Colombia, has been recognized at the global level as a leader of mobility within what is now termed the megacity. It is structured as a network of trunk lines for the mass transport of passengers in articulated buses. Such buses typically have 160 seated/standing capacity[4]. The system control is centralized and there are exclusive high speed lines constructed for the sole use of the bus network. Feeder services, which cover circular routes of around 4 km (Chaparro, 2002) compose 50% of all passengers that use the BRT service (see Table 1). In terms of the totality, users come from 318 neighborhoods. The *TransMilenio project* was constructed in phases, beginning in 2000 with Phase I, followed by Phase II, five years later. In total seven lines were operational in the first two phases. These spanned some 84 km, covering some 512 km if feeder zones are also considered. At the time of publication, Phase III is operational although incomplete. Some feeder zones, fare tariff and collections have however been integrated since 2012. Three more phases with five trunk lines is scheduled some time into the future.

[4] Something which would require between 40 to 100 private vehicles or three normal buses.

Table 1. Main characteristic of the *TransMilenio* BRT Project

Operating bus Terminals	7
Intermediate stations in operation	6
Single stations in operation	108
Scrapped vehicles until 2010	7.104
Trunk buses Euro II, III y IV until 2010	1.256
Feeder Buses until 2010	517
Bus Depots	7

Source: www.transmilenio.gov.co

All the fleet, including that of the feeder service, operate with one the following technological innovations bought in by the *EURO II, EURO III, EURO IV* or *EURO V*, which are standards of the acceptable limits for exhaust emissions in new vehicles sold in the member states of the European Union (the exact technology is dependent on the phase in which they were introduced). The contracts between the District and the operators companies set the type of vehicle to be linked to the BRT project. All vehicles have a catalyst converter installed and all consume low sulfur diesel (<50 ppm), which since 2009 had to legally include a proportion of biodiesel which stood at 7% as of 2011.

Additional key facts include:

- Together with Curitiba, Brazil, Bogota is home to one the first complete BRT systems found in Latin America.
- It has high average transit speed (from approximately 15 kph to 26.7 kph) (Cain *et al.*, 2006).
- Its load capacity in peak times can be as high as 40,000 passengers/per direction/per hour, which is almost equal to that and in some cases greater than that of rail systems across the globe (Hook, 2008).
- It integrates the majority of aspects that characterize a BRT: line and station exclusivity (no other vehicles are allowed to use the designated areas), intelligent transport systems, electronic and automatic fares, clean bus technologies, etc.
- Up and until the first day of operation the project was self-financed in that it didn't receive any subsidies with which to guarantee the continuation of the service, even though the price per passenger was extremely competitive (0.79 USD/trip with respect to a range of 0.11 to 1.33 USD/trip in those cities that do receive governmental subsidies) (Hidalgo and Carrigan, 2010).
- It was the first large-scale transport system registered under the *United Nations Framework Convention on Climate Change* Clean Development Mechanism (CDM) in 2006, after developing approved methodology (AM0031 for BRT systems) (Rosenthal, 2009).

Ever since the first "BRT" system, in Curitiba, Brazil, sowed the seeds in 1970s (Lindau, 2012) there has been a strong interest in BRT application. As it stands (of 2013) there are currently 143 such projects operating across the globe, on every inhabited continent. Yet it was arguably Bogota's *TransMilenio Project*, conceived in 1998 and operational in 2000, that turned this interest into exponential construction as can be seen by Figure 1. It has since served as a motor for development in emerging nations (Deng & Nelson, 2013; Hidalgo & Gutiérrez, 2013; Mejía-Dugand et al., 2012; Schalekamp & Behrens, 2010; Venter, 2013; Goldman & Gorham, 2006). Furthermore, although one cannot say that they are fully established, the transport concepts related to BRT and IPTS have evolved steadily since the launch of the *TransMilenio Project* (Wright & Hook, 2007).

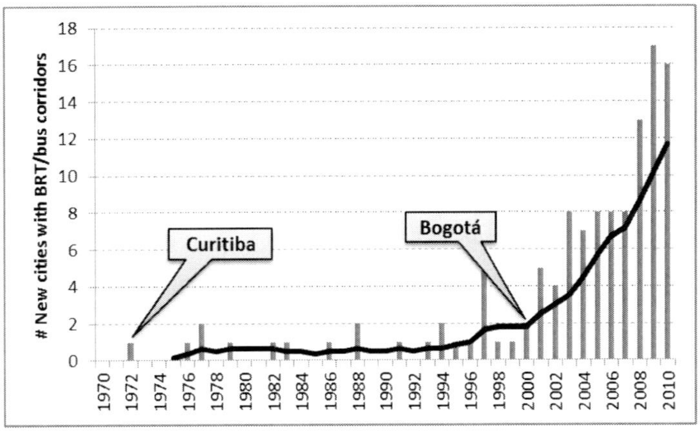

Source: brtdata.org, 2012

Figure 1. BRT implementation around the world.

2.1. BRT Serving as a Catalyst for Sustainable Transport Policies

Public policies are understood to be a collective of instruments which can include objectives, directives, strategies, targets, programs, actions and norms through which a State can identify and focus on a real or perceived need whether it economic, environmental, social or cultural in nature. Policies also support the planning and implementation of programs or mediatory actions in that they facilitate group participation of (Arroyave, 2011).

To facilitate the abatement of the externalities derived from transport and in doing so improve the quality of life in cities it is first necessary to identify the general principles that need to be applied. Such principles, in terms of sustainable transport, were established by Withelegg (1986):

- Transport must reduce its environmental impacts to within the Earth's carrying capacity.
- Any calculation of transport's contribution must include the whole productive cycle (the abstraction of raw materials including fuel, vehicle, production and maintenance, infrastructure construction and maintenance, and the disposal of wastes).
- The necessary changes to mobility patterns must be equitably distributed, among societies and between those individuals constituting those societies.
- Decisions on how changes are to occur must be taken at the most appropriate level.

The *International Environmental Agency* (IEA) (2010) were among the first to give priority to the following policies in the transport sector, with the aim of reducing the consumption of materials and atmospheric emissions. Specifically they looked into:

- Fuel economy of heavy-duty vehicles
- Fuel-efficient tires
- Eco-driving

The agency also set sectorial challenges to be solved in the short term. These include: better information through vehicle labeling, fiscal incentives and modal shift. In order to promote the implantation of these policies the IEA along with many other institutions published various White Books, to debate the future of transport in cities. In all cases, without exception, the IEA encouraged the adoption of integrated and intelligent transport systems and strategies which look to curve the number of conventional fuel vehicles in operation or at least reduce the frequency of their use. Such advice correlates strongly to the need of BRT.

The BRT ALC center, sponsored by the Volvo Research and Education Foundation (VREF), study the complexity of policy design in urban mobility systems, which has the purpose of enhancing the adoption and implementation of BRT systems. They have defined a group of policies and measures called "Energy and Environment", which deals with energy, environmental and sustainability issues. It includes measures relating to environmental and energy certification, alternative fuels and IPTS technologies (Filipe, 2013).

As in Bogota, whereby the district government also promotes the following complementary programs and practices as part of the sustainable transport model:

- Circular bicycle lines and routes[5]. On Sundays and Bank Holidays, motorized traffic is suspended in certain areas, in order to promote cycling as a leisure activity (Prada, 2011).
- Opening of pedestrian zones and walkways at the expense of motorized vehicles.
- Car free day: A day where no private car is allowed access to roads. This is done in order to evaluate the effect cars have on city congestion levels and to promote other transport modes.

Other BRT systems have served as the backbone of new policies include the following:

- Modal integration with bicycles and other forms of non-motorized vehicles (Shafiq-Ur Rahmana, et al., 2012).
- Development of planning policies to facilitate urban concentration and the protection of green belts around the city, as achieved in Seoul, Korea (Jun, 2012).

[5] Circular bicycle lines are a road corridor built exclusively for transit riders and tricycles. Their function is to provide an alternative mode of transportation. Circular bicycle routes are road segments serving the community for the practice of recreational activities with specific operating hours.

2.2. Specific Externalities BRT

Literature available on the subject of the environmental aspects BRT focuses predominately on either atmospheric contamination or fuel consumption which comes as no surprise as they are the two most significant impacts. In the authors' opinion the scope should be amplified and more holistic in nature to avoid only a surface exploration of the planning and design aspects. Weak overviews should be thus developed into management strategies which consider the accumulative and synergetic effects, seeing that the total impact is often larger than the sum of all the individual impacts (CTS Mexico, 2011). This section now describes each of the major externalities which are to be subjected to a holistic analysis in the result section.

Atmospheric Emissions

A vehicle requires a given quantity of space which it occupies whilst producing a great number of contaminants. Diesel represents 74% of the energy units employed in the mobilization of passengers travelling on Latin American public transport. The rates of morbidity and mortality in the largest Latin American cities, including Bogota, have been shown to correlate to the degree of air contamination, something which translates into elevated costs for health treatment (between 4 and 20 USD/per person/pa for public transport) (CAF, 2010; WHO, 2006).

The principal atmospheric contamination in Bogota is connected to particular matter originating from industry and the use of heavy duty vehicles. One strategy which the authors believe can be used to mitigate this problem is a systematic organization of the city's public transport network. It is expected that this could generate various benefits through the:

- Reduction of emission levels. The particulate matter from the PM 2.5 group could be reduced from 1.2 0.9 g/km to only 0.3 g/km with the purchase of new fleets for the *TransMilenio* system. Should this occur, the quality of combustion coupled with the installation of particulate control systems could generate reductions of up to 60% annually (Beherentz, 2009). Experiences in others cities operating a BRT, likewise, have shown that similar actions can significantly influence the concentration of PM10 (Nugroho et al., 2010).
- Contaminant reduction in the areas close to bus routes.
- Contaminant reduction in the bus' interior which brings obvious benefits both to the driver and passengers.

Energy Consumption

The energy used by each person in a transport network is dependent on the exact mode of transport utilized. Specifically it relates to the number of passengers a given vehicle can carry at any one time or the number of kilometers covered per passenger. To compare, Latin American BRT systems can transmit anywhere between 5.3- 10 people per kilometer whilst traditional public transportation can only manage 0.6-3.2 passengers (CAF, 2010). Therefore the evaluation of energy consumption is an important component in the creation of appropriate public transport policies, planning and practices, especially as in the case of fuel it is both a costly and scarce resource.

Landscape

There are various components that should be considered including vegetation cover and silviculture generally. Landscape aesthetics is a key factor which constitutes a great percentage of the assessment. According to the German geographer Carl Troll (2010) the landscape must be seen as a holistic entity where a synergy is created. Any assessment must therefore ensure all elements (physic-biological, natural or atrophic) are integrated. It must be without limits, configured by the observer as a scene which carries meaning, an order and a message. This message is being lost in Bogota, where the international standard of one tree per three inhabitants (there are currently only 0.16 trees/per inhabitant, SDA, 2010) is far from being met – currently there exists a deficit of 1,400,000 trees. This fact indicates structural weakness in municipal policy, particularly in the planning and follow-up processes which should ensure correct procedure has been followed. It is an issue that could be avoided or at least lessened if one is prepared, in the planning stage, to search for and take the necessary remedial actions to protect key aspects. Such an undertaking may also serve to encourage urban re-design and improvements. In this way pollution, caused by the transport sector, can also be minimized and the quality of life of citizens heightened.

Materials

Other externalities that need to be considered in terms of energy consumption and emissions are the manufacture of materials such as glass, metal, rubber or plastic, required for a vehicle fleet or the minerals, rocks and asphalt used in the construction of roads. For example, an articulated bus consumes 3,2-4,5 ton/bus of steel, around 1,5 ton/bus of iron, between 0,2-1,6 ton/bus of aluminium, 400 kg/bus of rubber, and around 100 to 530 kg/bus of plastics and other metals such as copper and lead (Simonsen, 2010, Danielsson, 2001).

Waste

The operation of a transportation system implies the generation of hazardous and conventional waste in back-office processes such as vehicle maintenance. Waste typically includes oil (215 - 915 kg/bus/pa), batteries (0,72 – 1,75 unit/bus/pa), tires (0,207 unit/bus/pa), electronic components, carton, etc. All are generated in the *TransMilenio project* (Romero, 2011). The vehicle itself also becomes a complex waste requiring some form of disposal or recycling at the end of its useful life, which is normally once it has completed over 1,000,000 km.

Water

BRT standards demand a clean fleet, which mean that all operating vehicles require daily wash cycles. In the Brazilian city Sao Paulo, for example, there are 15,064 buses circulating which are washed at the end of each service day. Indeed the transport companies involved in providing the fleet consume approximately 2,200,000 m3 of water per year in this activity alone, with cycles of between 300 to 500 L/bus-day (Almeida, 2010). Water use in bus manufacturing at 69 m3 per bus, is also an important point for consideration (Volvo, 2001).

2.3. Tools to Measure Externalities: The LCA and Landscape Assessment

A project's LCA is a process which evaluates, during the entirety of a production process or service, its resource consumption and flows which have a potential impact on the environment and/or human society. Its ultimate aim is to facilitate decision making and the establishment of objectives and programs that will reduce or at least control the aspects highlighted (ISO, 2006). Such a process would be helpful in the design of an IPTS and/or BRT, as it helps define environmental scoping and encourage integrated policies which also serve to reduce the possibility of conflict of interests between the various parties involved.

The environmental impact of public transport systems has been extensively studied using the LCA method, but have been up until now conducted with fuel and emissions in mind. For example, McKenzie et al., (2012) indicate that the CNG and Hybrid buses have lower lifecycle GHG emissions than diesel ones, but that any emissions savings come at an increase in cost, especially capital costs. Kliucininkas et al., (2012) meanwhile, in explaining the comparative life cycle assessment of fuel chains suggested that biogas-powered buses and electric trolleybuses be considered as the best alternatives for the modernizing of the public transport fleet in Kaunas, Lithuania. Aranda et al., (2010) compared several means of transport concluding that buses are one of the most energy efficient forms. In all cases, the respective authors promote the development of sustainable transport policies based on measurable results.

The UK Transport Carbon Model (UKTCM), which also is based on a LCA, is particularly relevant to this chapter given its attempt to integrate transport, energy, environmental impacts and emissions. It provides annual projections of demand for different transport modes up to 2050 and supports the prioritizing of policy interventions into the short, medium and long term (Brand, 2012).

Whilst there are other LCA methodologies such as TREMOVE, TRENDS, ASTRA, GEM-E3 and POLES, which can be applied to transport policies and practices, the authors rejected their inclusion in this chapter because of their focus on areas, not relevant to the material presented here. Readers particularly interested in such themes are asked to consult Burgess et al., (2005).

Finally, in relation to the landscape, it is recognized by the *European Landscape Convention* (Council of Europe, 2000) as a significant element adding to the quality of life: whether it urban or rural. There are numerous ways in which to evaluate the environmental quality landscape. Martí Vargas and Pérez González (2002) indicate that in general, almost all the models agree in three points: visibility, landscape fragility and landscape quality. The authors would also like to state that landscape can be analyzed and classified using qualitative terms based on subjective observations which may also involve a quantified study, through the systematization of information in a way that allows for weighting. This can be done via one of two methods (Aguió et al., 1995):

- Assessment is carried out by experts, whether direct (through contemplation of landscape) or indirect (analysis and description of landscape components or through aesthetic categories). It is independent of landscape users.
- Assessment relies strongly on landscape users or evaluations concerning the observer. In this case, it is easier to obtain a more "democratic" review of an area, *i.e,*

a representative opinion, where there are three lines of inquiry: psychophysical, psychological and phenomenological.

Both can be used for landscape assessment of a transportation project with the exact characteristics relating to the purpose of the study.

3. METHODS

The authors applied the following methodology:

1) Compilation of secondary information including academic papers, books and reports. The criteria applied in the selection of such sources relates closely to the themes mentioned in the introduction.
2) Systematic analysis of content and the identification of key words and phrases with the aim of obtaining a wider understanding and enrichment of existing knowledge. An inductive reasoning was applied to produce the conceptual framework.
3) The primary data obtained came from public institutions and other actors, using tools such as databases, software analysis, field work and direct observation.
4) A comparison of the practices used in the case study in respect to a reference point (a conventional transport scheme) was undertaken to identify factors of success, examples of innovation, relevant cases, lessons learned and barriers to implementation. The figures and percentages presented in the text correspond to those obtained empirically by the authors during their time employed as members working on the *TransMilenio project*. Any figure that does not come from the authors is properly cited in the text and later in the bibliography located at the end of the chapter.
5) Finally the authors provide an estimation of the environmental contributions using informatic tools for the modeling of a service or a product from a LCA perspective and Landscape assessment. All indicators were selected on a qualitative basis.

All of the above were done in such a way to facilitate the adoption of new transport policies relating to the environment.

The methodology used for the evaluation of the environmental impact of the project from a lifecycle viewpoint is the ReCiPe 2008 with a Hieratical perspective (Spielmann et al., 2007). The database and structure was taken by the one provided by *Ecoinvent* for the transport sector. The calculating tool is the LCA software *Simapro 7.3*[6]. The analysis was done in stages: manufacturing, operation, maintenance and disposal of the bus and construction, operation/maintenance and deconstruction of the road. The Ecoinvent methodology (Spielmann et al., 2005) establishes that in order to link various transport components to the reference flow of one passenger-kilometre (pkm), so-called demand factors

[6] The LCA evaluation was completed by the authors under the academic license granted as part of the Research Centre for Energy Resources and Consumption- CIRCE, University of Zaragoza, Zaragoza-Spain

d_j are determined. Cumulative Life Cycle Inventory - LCI results for a transport service, per pkm are calculated as follows:

$$x_i^T = \sum_{j=1}^{n} \frac{x_i^j}{r(p_j)} \cdot d_j$$

where n denotes the number of transport components and $x_i^j / r(p_j)$ indicate the cumulative interventions of a certain component related to its reference flow. The project is analyzed using a black box calculation of energy and matter.

In total there are 35 indicators considered in the methodology, 18 are mid-point and 17 are end-point. The mid-point indicators include: *Climate change* (kg CO2 eq), *Ozone depletion* (kg CFC-11 eq), *Human toxicity* (kg 1,4-DB eq), *Photochemical oxidant formation* (kg NMVOC), *Particulate matter formation* (kg PM10 eq), *Ionising radiation* (kg U235 eq), *Terrestrial acidification* (kg SO2 eq), *Freshwater eutrophication* (kg P eq), *Marine eutrophication* (kg N eq), *Terrestrial ecotoxicity* (kg 1,4-DB eq), *Freshwater ecotoxicity* (kg 1,4-DB eq), *Marine ecotoxicity* (kg 1,4-DB eq), *Agricultural land occupation* (m2a), *Urban land occupation* (m2a), *Natural land transformation* (m2), *Water depletion* (m3), *Metal depletion* (kg Fe eq) and *Fossil fuel depletion* (kg oil eq).

The end-point indicators used are: *Climate change - Human Health* (DALY), *Ozone depletion* (DALY), *Human toxicity* (DALY), *Photochemical oxidant formation* (DALY), *Particulate matter formation* (DALY), *Ionising radiation* (DALY), *Climate change Ecosystems* (species/yr), *Terrestrial acidification* (species/yr), *Freshwater eutrophication* (species/yr), *Terrestrial ecotoxicity* (species/yr), *Freshwater ecotoxicity* (species/yr), *Marine ecotoxicity* (species/yr), *Agricultural land occupation* (species/yr), *Urban land occupation* (species/yr), *Natural land transformation* (species/yr), *Metal depletion* ($ surplus), *Fossil fuel depletion* ($ surplus)[7].

For the landscape assessment, using the *Methodological Guide for the Evaluation of Environmental Impacts (Conesa, 2005)*, through direct observation of trunks lines, a Relative Value (RV) was obtained, derived from two parameters: "Current state of the visible section or area" and the "Level of vegetation development". The value perpendicular to the RV then permits a landscape quality calculation, which are graded from 0.00 to 0.33 Low; 0.34 to 0.66 medium; 0.67 to 1.00 high. These values are also expressed as a percentage.

The second landscape assessment, using the methodology stated in the *Matrix of the Functions of Urban Vegetation in Infrastructural Projects and Urban Public Space* (IDU *et al.*, 2003), has the ultimate aim of selecting the most appropriate tree species to complete the following functions. Six out of a possible ten functions were selected for the assessment based on their relevance to the transport sector:

- Main functions:
  - F1 Aesthetic, cultural and symbolic provision

[7] Indicators such as water depletion, occupied area and transformed area, are only evaluated as mid-point factors due to the fact that they are still not accounted for in a quantitative way, which is something which would permit their use as an end-point indicator.

   - F3 Attenuation or minimization of particulate matter, winds, bad odors and disease-carrying pests.
- Complementary functions:
   - F2 Physical and psychological wellbeing, through the possibility of recreation, education and rest
   - F4 Space and sub-space configuration.
   - F5 Valorization of private property and public space.
   - F9 Carbon Dioxide Capture

To obtain a score (1-10) for each trunk line, one gives weighting to the results of each function for each separate tree species. It shouldn't be less than 8 for the principle functions and no less than 6 for complementary ones. The minimal total sum should be at least 40, meaning that all functions are provided. In the ideal case, the total is 60.

Finally, the qualitative environmental analysis was based on an adapted ABC methodology from the *Guide for Environmental Aspect Analysis* in an Organization by *Centro Nacional de Producción Más Limpia* (León, 2001) ABC qualitative rating for the letter A corresponds to a high impact, B a medium impact and C to a low impact. An index per stage and per impact is also included. The environmental index per process is calculated by weighting the qualitative grade given to each impact by an index: 1 (A), 0.5 (B) and 0.1 (C) and then divided by the total number of stages. The environmental impact index per impact is calculated by weighting each qualitative grade given to each stage by an index 1 (A), 0.5 (B) and 0.1 (C) and dividing by the total number of impacts.

4. RESULTS

For the development of this section an overall explanation is provided. A general description of the specific case study investigated is given as are the actions implemented and the lesson(s) learned. The section ends by measuring the BRT contribution to sustainable transport policy through an evaluation of environmental impacts and landscape alterations.

4.1. Public Transport Policy

Colombia has two means in which it can pass public policy, either through *the National Council of Economic and Social Policy –CONPES-* or the *Ministry of the Corresponding Administrative Sector* (Article 58 of the Colombian Law 489 of 1998).

The authors will now go on to analyze the transversal public policies of the transport sector which coincide with the environment. Firstly the authors undertake an environmental component classification, using examples harmoniously employed for the development of the BRT in Bogota. In addition, a summary of other policies linked to the development of the BRT e.g., the integration of the modes of transport, is provided.

Table 2. Thematic Classification of those policies related to public transport

Classification	Subcategory	Objective
Urban Planning, Public Space and Landscaping,	National regulations	To orientate and administrate the physical development of the territory and land use. To consolidate cities into more compact spaces which are more sustainable, more equitable and more able to manage and finance their development.
	Organization of the Public Transport System	To promote the implementation of integrated public and / or mass transport – such as IPTS/BRT-. Increase the quality of life and productivity of cities and to integrate further urban development processes.
	Modal integration and non-motorized mechanisms	To encourage the reduction of private transport, whilst at the same time ensuring inclusivity and quality in the provision of public transportation. To incentivize the use of other mechanisms of motorized or non-motorized vehicles.
	Landscaping	Promote the recognition, valorization, management and planning of sustainable landscapes to ensure their protection
Energy, Air Quality and Climate Change	Energy Efficiency	Incentivize the rational and efficient use of energy, during all stages from its production to consumption.
	Renewable Energy	Advocacy of renewable and non-conventional energy sources such as solar, geothermal, small hydropower and energy derived from biomass and that coming from the oceans.
	Fuel quality	To incentivize the use of clean fuels based on their components, such as, hydrogen, CNG, Liquefied Petroleum Gas (LPG), Diesel up to 50 ppm sulfur and/or with biodiesel blends, gasoline mixtures with alcohol or denatured anhydrous ethanol fuel..
	Gas emissions and atmospheric pollution levels	Achieve adequate air quality levels for the protection of human health and wellbeing.
	Climate Change	Mitigation of climate change, with the sale of the verified reduction of GHG emissions. Adaptation and resilient practices.
	Noise pollution	Maintain a permissible decibel level according to those conditions and characteristics subscribed to the sector, in a way in which protects, within a margin of safety, the health and welfare of the exposed population.

Table 2. (Continued)

Classification	Subcategory	Objective
Efficient Use of Materials and others resources	Materials and supplies	Changing societal production and consumption patterns and moving them towards a greater level of environmental sustainability. Generate a critical mass of companies that employ good sound practice and supply or produce sustainable goods and services. Regular use and restriction of materials and products. Develop legislation that permits the closure of material cycles.
	Water	Guarantee the sustainability of water resources through efficient use and management.
	Dangerous Wastes	Ensure the prevention, reduction and source separation, collection, storage, transportation, use and /or recovery, treatment and / or disposal, import and export of general or hazardous waste
	Special Waste	Guarantee selective collection and environmental management of special waste such as tires, e-waste, debris, etc.
Public Health	Transport safety	Increase levels of safety through the intervention of driver behavior, vehicles, infrastructure, traffic rules, etc.
	Environmental Health	Contribute to the generation of environmental and social conditions that improve the quality of life and health.

Of all the previous policies Bogota's transport sector has placed a higher priority on those issues relating to air quality, fuel quality and dangerous wastes. Figure 2 shows a timeline of all policies and their derivations that have been applied.

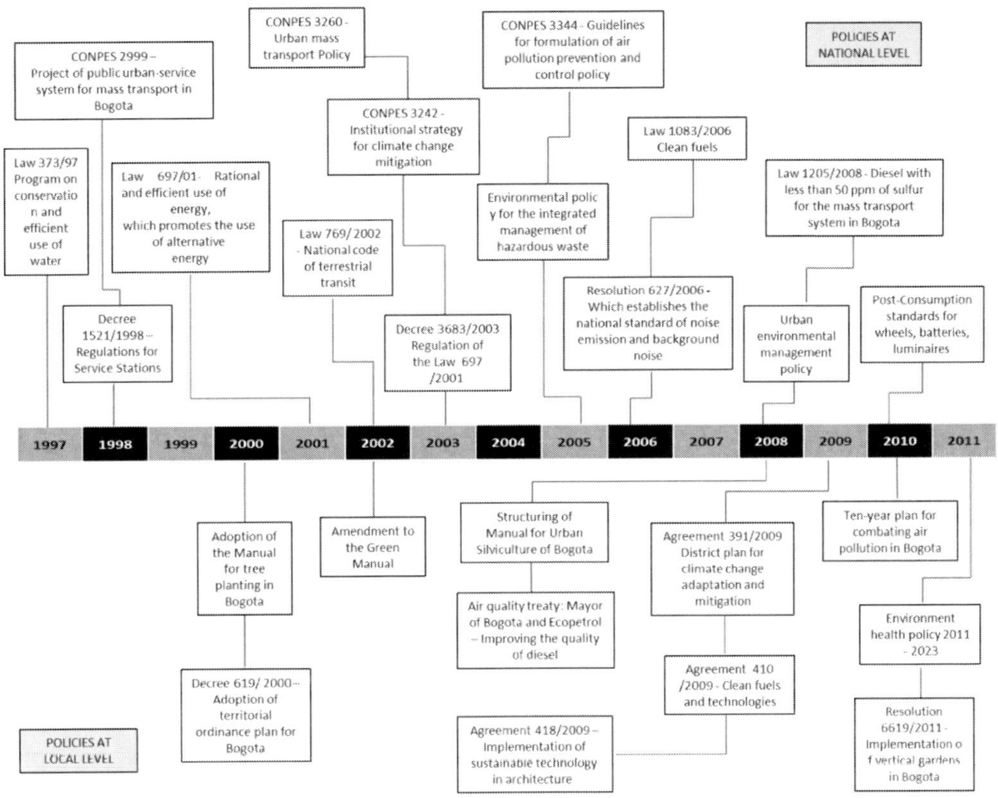

Figure 2. Timeline of relevant policies for Bogota BRT project.

4.2. The Life of a Public Transport Project

Public policies and planning schemes relating to mobility should identify all LCA stages of a public transport project. Figure 3, based on the authors observations within the BRT *TransMilenio*, shows the various stages that constitute a transport project. It also shows the system boundaries as well as identifying the interaction that can exist between the environmental indicators and the policies necessary for each mode of transportation. Among the inputs considered are materials, energy and the human and spatial resources needed to ensure the successful operation of a public transport service. The outputs meanwhile, are both the mid-point and end-point products whose units are typically given as an equivalent contamination (e.g., kg CO2 eq, kg Oil eq, m2*yr, etc.), or as a measure of the damage caused to a receptor. They can also be used to define protection zones (e.g., Disability-adjusted life year - DALY, Loss of species during a year - species*yr, increased cost - $).

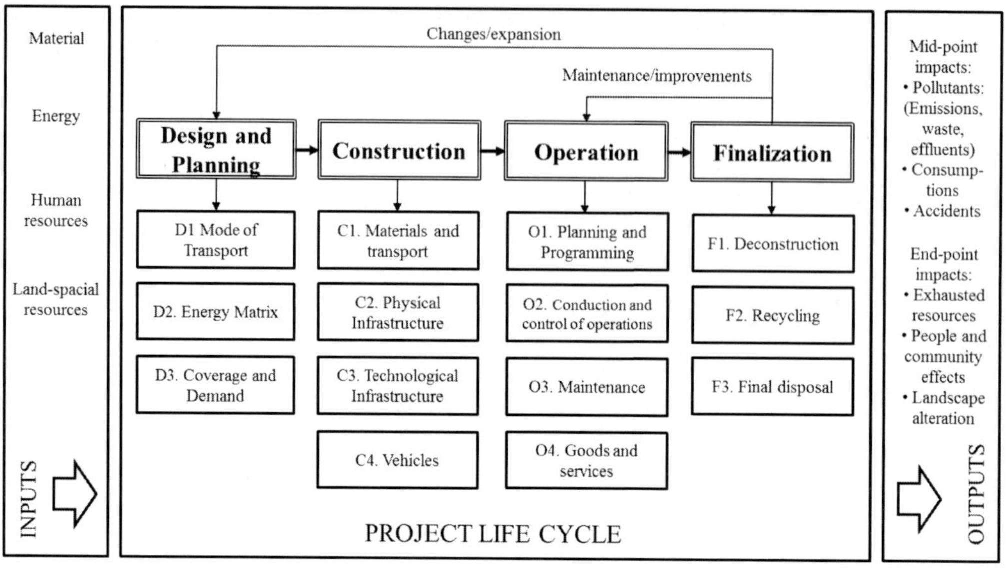

Figure 3. Life cycle of a transportation project.

The model is composed of the following phases as shown in Table 3.

Now the authors go on to analyze the aforementioned additional externalities which serve to make a model of transport more sustainable throughout the entire life cycle of a given service. In undertaking such a task one can avoid transferring contaminant elements from one process to another, as might occur in the scrapping of vehicles. In this case, while such an action might reduce atmospheric emissions it might also create a new problem such as additional volumes of dangerous waste.

Table 4 highlights the qualitative relevance of each environmental impact is shown. Albeit that the design phase (D1-D3), does not directly generate an environmental impact it remains an underlying factor in the management of resources, contamination and health effects and the avoidance of latent failures. The decisions taken at this stage are also highly significant because of the difficulty in modifying them later on. One must also recognize that planning and policy is restricted and influenced by economics, politics and technological development.

In relation to the stage results, the design of the routes considered in the coverage and demand evaluation, the selection of the mode of transport and the maintenance and operation of the buses, presents the biggest impact, not only from an environmental perspective but also in socio-economic terms.

In relation to the environmental impact index and according to the literature review, the majority of the significant impacts are located in the design and operation phases (the latter invokes the driving of the bus and vehicle maintenance), which are atmospheric contamination, climate change, combustion of fossil fuels, electricity, dangerous wastes, the consumption and pollution of water resources, accidents, public health and key changes to mobility.

Table 3. Description of phases and stages of a transport life cycle project

Phase	Stage	Convention	Scope
Design and Planning	Mode of Transport	D1	Definition of the mode of motorized transport (e.g., bus, train, tram, etc.) and modal integration.
	Energy Matrix	D2	Selection of the energy source, fuel and technology used for the vehicle fleet.
	Coverage and Demand	D3	Determination of the population and the geographical area attended based on the planning routes.
Construction	Materials and Transport	C1	Determination of the origin of the prime materials utilized in construction, in function of the chosen suppliers and the distances that need to be covered in order to move them from their location until that of the project.
	Physical Infrastructure	C2	Includes the construction of lines, stations, terminals and other auxiliary buildings that help maintain proper and normal operations.
	Technological Infrastructure	C3	Considers the manufacture and acquisition of the equipment and elements needed in the collection of fares, fleet control and the provision of internal and client information.
	Vehicles	C4	Conformity of fleet manufacture, technical, safety and environmental specifications. For example in the case of buses, are they to be bi-articulate or micro etc.
Operation	Planning and Programming	O1	Consists of the design of routes, their characterization and distribution and the assignation of vehicles and personnel in a way that meets customer expectations and ensures that the service runs in a secure and timely manner – guaranteeing the wellbeing of employees and users, in addition to resource optimization.
	Conduction and control of operations	O2	Whether the part of the service with direct contact with users occurs under controlled and safe conditions. It involves the gauging of line operation to ensure a level of punctuality and continuality in either normal or contingency plan operating conditions. There is a provision of feedback for those interested in maintenance and service improvements.

Table 3. (Continued)

Phase	Stage	Convention	Scope
	Maintenance	O3	Covers the activities of preventative, predictive and corrective maintenance in a way in which guarantees fleet availability and its adequate use, according to service standards and the optimization of resources.
	Goods and Services	O4	Includes those goods and services which are requisites to a reliable service. Includes physical infrastructure, general services and installation security and proper administration of technology.
	Deconstruction	F1	Activities relating to the demolition of physical infrastructure and the disassembly of vehicles and other equipment.
Finalization[1]	Recycling	F2	Activities relating to the valorization of all those elements in the previous stages.
	Final disposal	F3	Diversion of waste to landfill or incineration

[1] In the final stage of these types of projects there is generally a testing of the possibility of new transport models or improvements to the service under the current working parameters.

This is in short why an LCA is integral to the environmental and sustainable practices of projects as through it one can validate the results and justify the weightings ascribed, as quantitative values are assigned to qualitative aspects and subsequently problems and their remedial actions are prioritized.

Table 4. Qualitative environmental relevance of impacts per stages and per components using ABC methodology

COMPONENT		PROJECT STAGES	D1	D2	D3	C1	C2	C3	C4	O1	O2	O3	O4	F1	F2	F3	Impact index
ABIOTIC COMPONENT	Material and energy	Hazardous substances				A	B	B	B			A	M				0,20
		Hazardous waste				M	A	B	A			A	M	A	A	A	0,51
		Minerals		A	B	A	B	B	B								0,17
		Electric power		A		M	M	M			A	A	M				0,36
		Fossil Fuels	A	A	A	M	B	B	B	A	A	A					0,49
	Soil	Soil loss			A		A										0,14
		Soil pollution				M	M		M			A	B	M		A	0,29
		Use alteration	A		A		A					M		A			0,32
	Water	Water consumption	M			M	M		M			A	M	B	M	B	0,30
		Water pollution				M	M		M			A	M		M	A	0,32
	Air	Air pollution (greenhouse and MP)		A		A			A		A	A					0,36
		Climate change	A	A	M				A	A	A	A					0,46
		Increased noise		M	M		M		M		A	M					0,25
	Landscape	Impaired visual quality	A		A		A							A		M	0,32
BIOTIC COMPONENT	Flora	Impact of vegetation	M		A		M										0,14
		Involvement of endemic	B		B		B										0,02
	Fauna	Alteration of terrestrial and aquatic fauna	B		B		B										0,02
SOCIOECONOMICAL AND CULTURAL COMPONENT	Social Dimension	Accident	A						M	A	A	A					0,32
		Public health	A	A		B	M		B		A	A					0,34
		Conflict with communities	M				M				B	B					0,09
	Economic Dimension	Alteration of the demand for goods and services	M		A		M			A	M						0,25
		Alteration to the local economy	M		A		M			A	M						0,25
		Alteration to employment conditions	M		A		M			M	M						0,21
	Spacial Dimension	Social infrastructure impact	A		A		A										0,21
		Utility infrastructure impact	A		A												0,14
		Access impact	A		A		B										0,15
		Impaired mobility	A	A	A					A	A						0,36
	Cultural Dimension	Disturbance to cultural heritage	B								B						0,01
		Psychosocial effects	A								A						0,14
Environmental relevance index per project stages			0,38	0,24	0,41	0,10	0,17	0,00	0,10	0,21	0,31	0,38	0,00	0,10	0,03	0,10	

4.3. Contributions of TransMilenio System

From this point on the authors will describe those factors with the greatest relevance to the environment in relation to the *TransMilenio* project.

4.3.1. Planification and Design

4.3.1.1. Selection of Vehicle Typology

A determinant factor during the planning process is the choosing of the fleet that is to be utilized. This is usually within a given range of options such as fuel type technology which includes engines designed to an agreed standard. For the vehicles of the *Transmilenio* system, selection was done according to a set of sustainable criteria which led to the use of engines meeting the regulatory standards *EURO* or even Compressed Natural Gas (CNG). The standard incorporated has changed over time as environmental regulations have become more stringent and attitudes have greened.

The first ever bus fleet met the *Euro II* design (300 HP/10 liters). Engines operating to this standard produce a higher torque (1100 and 1400 r.p.m), which permits a reduction of the maximum r.p.m from the typical 2100 to the much lower value of 1700. This contributes to an important fuel saving compared to traditional bus fleets. For those vehicles in operation since 2006, engines meeting the *Euro III* standard were installed. In these newer buses, the quantity of fuel supplied is computer controlled which guarantees a more complete combustion, maximum power and a reduction in the quantity of emissions. The decision to meet the *EURO* standard, although successful, was more of a market based decision relating to technology availability, with only limited quantitative data and analysis.

As such, the authors propose that any further acquisition of fleets is subject to a comprehensive LCA which evaluates all the environmental implications of vehicle inputs and outputs. The case of the former particularly, is often one which is overlooked. An example of this is the loss of engine efficiency which accompanied the decision in 2009 to add a low quality biofuel to the conventional fuel and in a separate issue, the reduced performance of those engines which meet the *Euro III* standards, due to the sacrifice of efficiency (in the order of approximately 112 MJ/bus/year) derived from a lowering of emissions. At the time, decision makers could have considered alternatives such as an *Euro IV* fleet, which were already available on the market as of 2007 and were shown not to have this drop in efficiency. This problem was eventually solved in 2010 when the leadership opted for all new buses to be fitted with the *Euro IV* standard. One of its main innovations is the SCR (Selective Catalytic Reduction), in which a mixture of urea and water known as AdBlue ® is injected into the exhaust gases. AdBlue and the exhaust gases pass through a catalytic converter in which nitrogen oxides are converted to harmless nitrogen gas and water vapor, thereby reducing emissions. *Euro V* buses will run once the ITPS begins its operations.

Apart from these diesel based fleets, bus operators had in 2003-2006 investigated the possible use of CNG under the prototype IKARUS. Although promising in terms of cleaner emissions its overall performance was far from convincing and prevented any further development.

4.3.2. Construction

4.3.2.1. Landscape Management

The implementation of transport projects often changes the surrounding landscape and therefore it clearly adds an important dimension that needs to be considered right from design and planning. This is because it takes into account various elements including the objective of the urban services, the identification of potentially affected areas, and the spatial, natural and physical infrastructures of a given project.

For *TransMilenio* there exist three constructions: bus depot, terminal stations and trunk lines that typically alter the landscape, through a reduction in soil quality and an increase in grey urban areas at the expense of natural greenery. To avoid excessive alternation to the landscape, a series of criteria and methodologies were developed which serve to maximize spaces available for tree planting, support tree health and promote green zones in the urban environment. Given that in such projects "landscape" only tends to focus on silviculture the authors propose that in the future a holistic urban environmental management scheme is undertaken to harmonize all elements of urban space, both natural and artificial.

4.3.2.2. Design of System Infrastructure

The *TransMilenio* project, apart from the buses and their routes, requires supporting structures to ensure the proper and efficient working of the network. Such structures are identified in Table 1. In this section the authors would like to highlight one of the many lessons learned: the design of the bus depots.

Unfortunately during construction of the bus depots the following issues were not taken into consideration leading to various environmental problems including noise pollution and the accidental mixing of grey and black water:

- Soundproofing of engine compressors
- Internal management of wastes, such as recollection routes, the transportation of bulky objects and storage areas for conventional or dangerous wastes
- Provision of natural light
- Pneumatic and mechanical systems for the driving and drainage (via pumps) of new and used oil. Also the installation of dykes capable of holding 110% of the tank volume
- Perimeter grates to contain and conduct waste water from maintenance and wash zones to the waste water treatment system
- Implementation of a hanger cabin for the control of volatile organic compounds (VOCs).

To solve the above problems the authors ask that the design of new bus depots be revised, taking into account the distribution of parking spaces, maintenance areas and the location of fuel tanks and cleaning areas.

4.3.3. Operation

4.3.3.1. Efficient Fuel and Emission Factors

Apart from the identification and the evaluation of environmental aspects and impacts, legal requisites and material and energy balances, the management of the *TransMilenio* project established a further five factors (see Figure 4) that must be managed and controlled to reach the proposed objectives of improved fuel efficiency and emission control:

1) Bus fleet typology and maintenance plans: bus operators implemented maintenance plans to optimize the performance of those components, such as the fuel, injection and exhaust systems that influence combustion and consequently the generation of atmospheric emissions. They contemplated the efficiency of combustion, the longevity of lubricants and the opacity of each individual bus. In all maintenance plans, with support from vehicle manufactures, it was necessary to develop a fleet acclimatization plan in order to improve performance via engineering changes to certain systems. These plans apart from helping to reduce emissions have helped identify and address premature failures and poor bus reliability.

2) Operation management: the operators highlighted innovations in the planning process such as automatic measures using genetic and heuristic algorithms that optimized different routes.
3) Fuel station control: In order to fulfill the legal requisites and the accreditation of the *Ministry of Mines and Energy* (Ministerio de Minas y Energía) the service stations must operate according to maintenance and metrological assurance plans, daily tracking and inventory control. With respect to energy efficiency the fuel must be filtered to avoid the possibility of solids diminishing the effectiveness of fleet injection systems.
4) Human talent: Each operator managed human resources and built competence into the team, for amongst other things driving in a pro-environmental way, through proper selection processes, training, performance, development, recognition and reward. The training program imparts theory and practice in economic driving techniques and skills. There is a certification of competence authorized by professional institutions which provides an employee with the possibility of obtaining proper training and work-related qualifications.
5) Information Systems: All data collected by the monitoring system, their analysis and validation must be administrated through software that leads to the intelligent fleets. Other support applications such as inventory control and performance based measurements must also involve information technology.

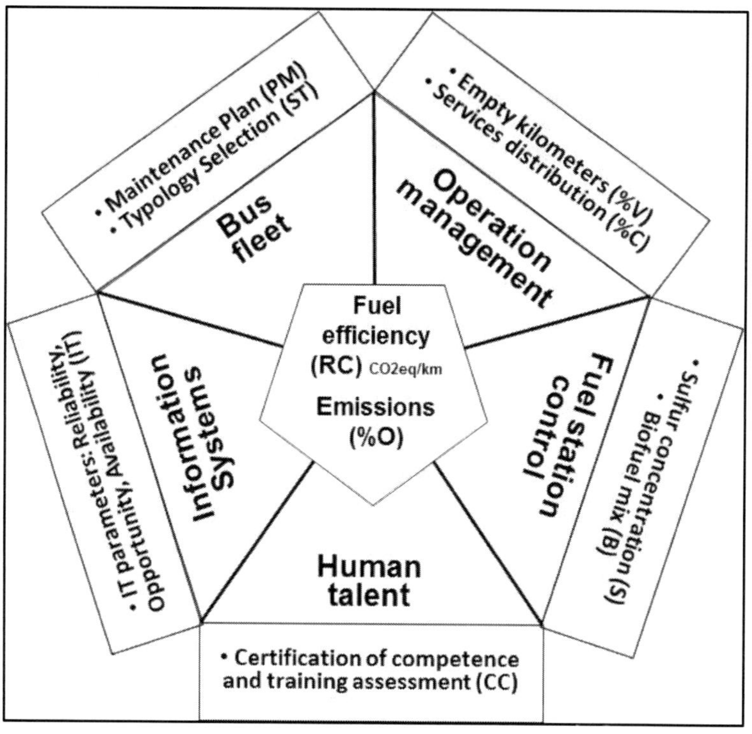

Figure 4. Management model for the efficient use of fuel and the control of atmospheric emissions.

In an analysis of the correlation between the measured variables of each of the five factors and the fuel efficiency and emission reductions, the authors determined the cause-effect relationship using the following hierarchy of importance, ranked from high to low impact: *For fuel efficiency:* 1. Biofuel mix, 2. Empty kilometers by percentage, 3. Typology fleet selection, 4. Maintenance plan, 5. Certification of competence, 6. Information Systems and 7. Sulfur concentration in fuel. *For Opacity*: 1. Maintenance Plan, 2. Information systems 3. Sulfur concentration in fuel, 4. Typology fleet selection, 5. Certification of competence, 6. Biofuel mix and 7. Empty kilometers by percentage.

The permanent monitoring of these variables has shown there to be a strong correlation between the attainment of a lower degree of emissions and higher fuel efficiencies with the successful application of the five aforementioned factors. Recent alterations to the BRT service which have helped (or in some cases hindered) the delivery of the two main objectives (Figure 4). These include the modification of maintenance routines and practices, fleet typology modifications (via the use of engines designed to the varying standards: *Euro II* through to *Euro III* and *IV*), a mixing of biofuels *B5* and *B7* with conventional fuel, sulfur content reductions, technological renovations in software relating to opacity and fleet control systems, and the restructuring of training content and methodology. As most contributed positively to the emission control, despite the aging of the fleet, the program successfully led an emission level well below that stipulated by law. Fuel combustion efficiency was also maintained. The adoption in 2004 of a significantly modified preventative maintenance practice led to a financial saving of some USD 1 million which also translated to the prevention of approximately 65 Ton CO2eq per bus from entering the atmosphere between 2005 and 2007.

4.3.3.2. Clean Development Mechanism

Together with Corporación Andina de Fomento, Grütter Jürg, Beratung/Consulting, the *Transmilenio Project* developed the "Baseline Methodology for Bus Rapid Transit Projects" which was approved by the UN in 2006. The UN also sanctioned the Project Design Development "Bus Rapid Transit System for Bogotá, Colombia: TransMilenio Phase II to IV" in the same year as a large scale urban transport with the aim to reduce the greenhouse effect.

The *TransMilenio* project was also the first of its kind registered under the United Nation's (UN) Clean Development Mechanism (CDM) having obtained the verification and certification of emission reductions from the period 2006-2011, corresponding to Phase II and beyond. Emissions released under Phase I (2001-2006) were registered in an international voluntary emission market. As of 2011, 2.134.079 tons of CO2eq, have been prevented from entering the atmosphere. This figure can be broken down into 431,300 tons CO2eq for Phase II and 1,702,779 tons of CO2eq in Phase I.

4.3.3.3. Management of Waste Resources

The current waste classification permits the separation of 36 different waste streams which include conventional and hazardous, either recyclable (56%) and non-recyclable. Figure 5 shows the distributional proportion of wastes generated by the operations of companies providing transport services. The largest volume of waste is from used oils and muds stemming from vehicle wash downs. Next are the tires and metal scrap followed by "others"[1].

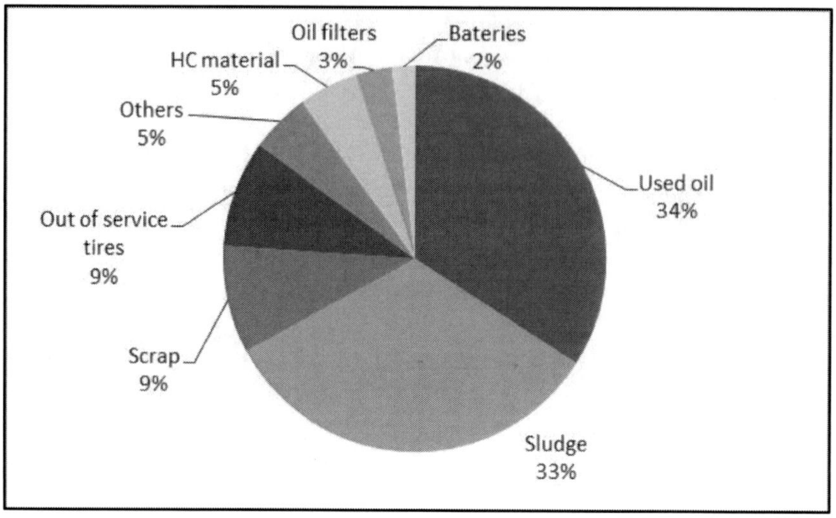

Figure 5. Distribution of waste streams in the project.

For used oils, the best way in which to manage them is, as with all forms of waste, is through the prevention and optimization of their life cycle and useful life. To do this three actions can be undertaken, firstly prescribed preventative maintenance intervals must be respected with a maximum flexibility of ±500 km, secondly the substitution of one oil type with another and thirdly the replacement of oil-based lubricant with one of the same type, all of which serve to prolong scheduled maintenance, from every to 7,500 km to every 10,000 km. The actions also result in a reduction of 3.5 tons of used oil per bus over its lifetime (assuming that a useful life equates to 1,000,000 km).

Oil filters are a key lesson learned in the program. The Puradyn filter (the bypass technology of this filter is <8 μm) was introduced to the fleet in an effort to extend the useful life of engine lubricants. Unfortunately laboratory tests showed that the new filter contributed to a higher quantity of dissolved metals in the lubricant than would have otherwise been found, should the original filter have been used. Another important finding was greater part fatigue upon using the new filter which led to a higher likelihood of environmental problems: excessive generation of emissions and residues and subsequently more frequent corrective maintenance procedures.

After the oils, mud represents the largest waste residual. In the maintenance procedures it is broken down into inert coarse sands (13%), fine sands mixed with preliminary treatments (24%), mud with high hydrocarbon content, originating from chassis maintenance and cleaning (27%) and flocculant sediment, coming from other physico-chemical treatments (36%). The amount of mud produced is directly proportional to the quantity of wastewater treated. Dehydration offers the greatest benefits in environmental, operative and financial terms due to the:

[1] e-wastes, rubber, plastics, fluorescents, liquid refrigerant and typical household recyclable materials i.e. paper, cardboard, cans etc.

- A minimal 50% reduction of the mud generated (reduced from 574 to 260 kg/bus/yr)
- Reduction in drying times by 97% (reduced from15-20 days upon a dry bed located in a zone with a temperate climate to just four hours)
- Improved quality of re-used water. Also an increased useful life – from the original 45 days to 60 days
- Improved process effectiveness via the reduction of preliminary steps needed in the water treatment process
- The avoidance of waste streams mixtures *i.e.* hazardous with conventional

4.3.3.4. Efficient Use of Water

Within a program of efficient water use there have been important goals reached in relation to the reduction of consumption, changes in culture and process optimization. The most common practices adopted in the improved water efficiency program of the *Transmilenio project* was the substitution of equipment such as traditional taps for ones with sensors or reduced flow, the use of high pressure, low flow hoses, the collection and use of rainwater for the washing of buses, the use of trickle irrigation technology for the watering of green zones, promotion of dry cleaning practices, where possible and the monitoring and control of leaks. In total all such activities lead to an annual reduction of potable water by 10% and permitted the re-use of 70% of the water used in cleaning activities. On average, this represented a saving of 28 m^3/bus/pa, which is by no means negligible when one considers that the current use of potable water per bus has been reduced to 34 m^3/pa.

4.3.3.5. Management of Chemical Risk

The transport sector has the potential to benefit from many vehicle advances in environmental innovation. An example of this is the implementation of prime material and supply control systems or *Painting Preparation System* (PPS). These systems involve the fragmentation of each section of a bus which requires painting and the exact calculation of the necessary quantities needed. This has led to a 26% reduction in the amount of chemical used in the bodywork maintenance process. It has also subsequently meant that there has been a 40-60% reduction in the generation of both conventional and dangerous wastes.

Another key point is the use, where possible, of biodegradable certified products.

4.3.3.6. Efficient Use of Electricity

The bus operators in 2009-2010 undertook performance field tests and provided recommendations for the development and implementation of LED technology which was to be used for the internal illumination of buses. It was hoped that through the introduction of such technology, the use of fluorescent tubes would be avoided (they contribute to a large proportion of dangerous wastes). Another important factor in their introduction was the possibility of increasing the longevity of the useful life of both electric and electronic components. Less material used is then spent on spare parts (e.g., alternators, batteries and starter motors), waste collection and disposal.

Further savings occurred in the bus depots with the following factors contributing to a 650kWh/bus/yr cutback:

- Energy inventory undertaken with the aim to establish an energy balance of the different processes and baseline reduction
- Operation and monitoring of capacitor banks in order to reduce reactive energy
- Reduced number of lighting hours through the application of light sensors which switch off internal lights when sufficient luxes (natural light) are detected
- Installation of transparent ceilings, in hangers for example to lower artificial light consumption on sunnier days
- Use of motion sensors in moderately used zones such as bathrooms and basements
- Use of twin florescent tubes with mirror reflectors
- Breaking up of areas requiring lighting with the installation of additional circuit breakers and switches
- Improved control of pneumatic line leakage through inspection and maintenance
- Correct circuit layout, voltage lines and electric systems generally, were guaranteed through the inspection by qualified personnel in accordance with the *Technical Regulation of Electric Installations* (Reglamento Técnico de Instalaciones eléctricas, RETIE)

4.3.4. Finalization

Taking into account that is only stage yet to be experienced by Bogota's BRT project, the finalization activities the following are still at the planning stage:

- **Vehicle scrapping:** Although Colombia nationally has performed scrapping activities for many years and taken advantage of scrap metal, there remains the challenge of developing recycling and evolving it further from an ecological and efficiency perspective.
- **Deconstruction:** On a global scale an extremely limited quantity of construction debris is recycled. The majority of it still finds its way to landfill or is used as filler without really considering the impact of such actions (Banias et al., 2011). The authors recommend that the procedure of separating the recyclable concrete from the rest of the waste stream (wood, paper, cardboard and metals) is carried out through sifting and trituration processes, in order to obtain a commercial product of value.

It is noteworthy that to date, the *TransMilenio* system has no defined roadmap with which to support the successful completion of Phase I, especially if one considers that many of its buses are close to completing, at one million service miles, their useful life. This fact is indicative of one of the existing weakness in district planning. It also serves as an opportunity to assess the environmental impact of the *TransMilenio* project's first phase. Such an undertaking should generate empirical knowledge and help guarantee environmental standard compliance throughout its entire lifecycle.

The authors now proceed, with all of the previous information in mind, to the landscape assessment and LCA, in order that they may effectively evaluate the contributions of various transport policies and practices.

4.4. Landscape Evaluation

Further to the discussion presented in 4.3.2.1, it is clear that any transport project will by its very nature alter the quality of the surrounding landscape. The evaluation of BRT *TransMilenio* project Phase I and Phase II presented here takes a detailed look at how silviculture and greening of spaces contributes to those urban areas of Bogota affected by the bus network. In order to do this the authors undertook a quantitative observation, assigning two matrices scores representative of landscape quality and the function of urban vegetation.

For the landscape assessment, using the *Methodological Guide for the Evaluation of Environmental Impacts (Conesa, 2005),* a landscape quality calculation was obtained based on the relative value through the field observation, as shown in Figure 6.

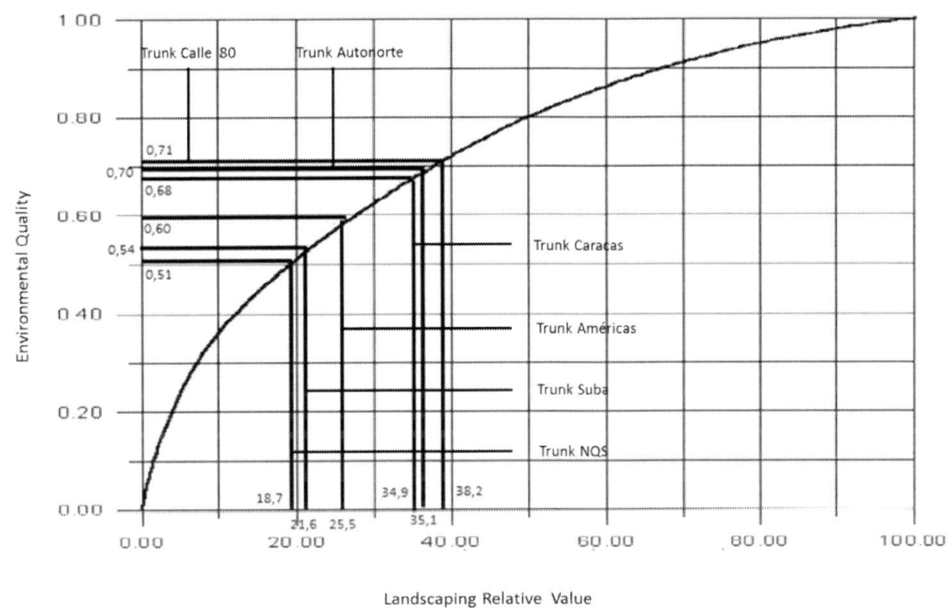

Figure 6. A modified matrix of the transformation of environmental quality showing the authors' results.

Figure 6 indicates that Bogota's urban landscape affected by Phase I and Phase II has a quality valued at between 51-71%. Four trunk lines are situated in the "medium" quality range leaving only two occupying the high quality range. The average value is 63% but those landscapes which relate to Phase II are in better condition than those of the first phase, an observation which indicates changes to project policy and practices. The most significant conclusions of the landscape assessment are:

Positive aspects:

- Healthy tree groups with a good age structure and a variety of tree species that have reached > 10-15 m, something which serves to support dust and odor control whilst offering pleasant aesthetics.
- Conservation areas where vegetation cover provides a feeling of wellbeing.

Negative aspects:

- Excessively concreted areas where tree planting is scarce.
- Some areas lack biodiversity and are monotonous.
- Some green urban spaces are not used to their full capacity *i.e.* weak biodiversity or a lack of managed vegetation.
- Areas where small bushes dominate instead of trees which prevent optimal land use function.

These results show that whilst the published technical guides and manuals have successfully navigated certain landscape aspects, there remains significant enhancement potential via improved planning and better maintenance processes and interventions.

Following on from the second landscape methodology evaluation, the *Matrix of the Functions of Urban Vegetation in Infrastructural Projects and Urban Public Space was used.* As Table 5 shows, the values for F1 are for the most part higher than those recommended in the *Matrix* whilst for F3, given that the value is lower than 8, most areas fail to achieve their principal function. With the exception of F2, all other values were lower than the recommended minimum. In the authors' opinion *Bogota District Council* needs to develop a public policy which serves to address this failing and commit to a re-naturalization program which would enhance the city's green spaces of and the wellbeing of its citizens.

4.5. Evaluation of an Environmental Impact in Agreement with a Project LCA

With the mainly information obtained from the previous sections, regarding consumption and emissions taken from the innovations and lessons learned in the BRT *TransMilenio* project, one is able to calculate which introductions have provided the best net contribution, with respect to the baseline (traditional public transport in the absence of the environmental improvements). Through which one can establish a correlation between the public policy categories as shown in Table 6.

An evaluation undertaken using the LCA ReCiPe methodology was completed for the characteristics of the current project. The results (Figure 7) indicate that it is the operation phase, especially the driving of the buses in normal service (*O2*) that heralds the biggest impact. Indeed *O2* contributes almost to 90% of the total impact in 9 of the 18 mid-point indicators and 33.3 % of the impact in a further six indicators. It is therefore an essential policy point, given that all of the variables associated are designated as high or medium concerns. The maintenance of the vehicle fleet, that of the electrics and the bodywork in particular, the cleaning and the generation of dangerous wastes, meanwhile has a large impact especially for those activities linked to "Ionising radiation", "Water depletion", "Freshwater eutrophication" and "Agricultural land occupation". For its part, road use impact is strongly associated with "Urban land occupation" and is a critical factor in the design of the service to ensure that the greatest number of potential clients is served by the BRT system.

Table 5. Functional Rating for Bogota's urban silviculture associated with the BRT Network

Trunk line name	F1 Aesthetic, cultural and symbolic provision	F2 Physical and psycholo-gical wellbeing	F3 Attenuation or minimization of particulates, winds, odors and disease-carrying pests	F4 Space and sub-space configurati on	F5 Valorization of private property and public space	F9 Carbon Dioxide Capture	Total
Calle 80	8,1	8,0	6,5	6,1	6,1	5,2	39,9
Autopista Norte	8,2	7,6	5,7	7,0	6,1	5,7	40,2
Caracas	7,9	6,7	5,8	4,2	3,8	7,0	35,4
NQS	8,6	8,0	6,3	7,3	7,1	6,0	43,2
Américas-Calle 13	6,8	6,6	4,5	5,0	5,3	4,9	33,0
Suba	9,1	8,3	7,0	6,8	7,8	6,4	45,4

Table 6. Relationship between policy categories and impact indicators

Classification	Mid-point Indicators	End -point Indicators
Urban planning, public spaces and landscaping	Natural land transformation Landscaping quality	Ecosystems Species/yr
Energy, Air quality and climate change	Climate change Ozone depletion Particulate matter formation Photochemical oxidant formation Ionizing radiation Fossil fuel depletion Noise	Human Health DALY Ecosystems Species/yr Resources Surplus cost
Efficient use of resources and generation of wastes	Water depletion Metal depletion Marine eutrophication Terrestrial ecotoxicity Freshwater ecotoxicity Marine ecotoxicity Terrestrial acidification Freshwater eutrophication	Human Health DALY Ecosystems Species/yr
Public Health	Human toxicity Vehicle Accidents	Human Health DALY

In the construction phase the principal impacts are those originating in vehicle manufacture. Of particular note is the "Metal depletion" that occurs during the production of the chassis and bodywork, albeit that this depends on the exact technology one is employing: bi-articulate, articulate or conventional. Another key issue associated with this activity is the hazardous nature (including bioaccumulation, toxicity) of the chemical substances employed.

In terms of the end-term indicators the detrimental impacts, the order of magnitude is greatest for the following indicators: "Fossil fuel depletion", "Climate change - human health", "Particulate matter formation", "Climate change-ecosystems" and "Human toxicity". Such results demonstrate the importance of technically evaluating decisions simultaneously with the writing of public transport policy.

A good example of this is whether the adoption of *Euro III* designed technology should be placed in buses, given that it must reduce energy efficiency by 8.5% in order to cut emissions. Likewise, the introduction of conventional/biofuel mixes of low quality, which although a green policy, results in a reduction of fleet efficiency by 1% for every additional 1% of biofuel added.

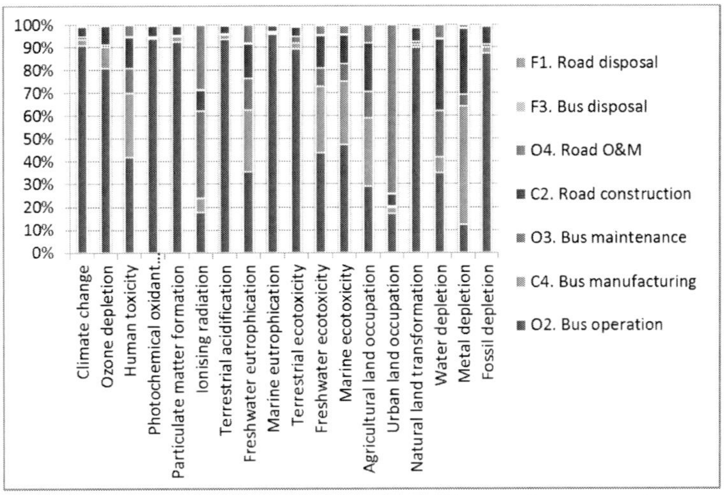

(a) Characterization of Mid-point indicators by categories

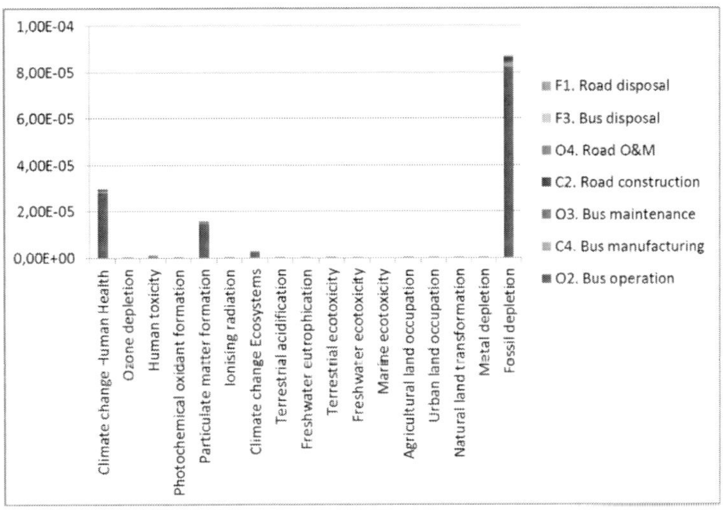

(b) Normalization of End-point indicators by categories

Figure 7. Impact evaluation by categories (a) Mid-point (b) End-point.

Table 7 presents the environmental contribution of TransMilenio through the mid and end-point indicators, comparing the current parameters of the BRT with that of the baseline. The unit measure is 1 passenger-kilometer (pkm). For example in the climate change mid-point indicator, while the baseline has a value of 1,39 kg CO_2 eq/pkm, BRT's is lower at 0,285 kg CO_2 eq/pkm.

Table 7. Comparing of the indicators between project and line base per unit measure is 1 pkm

Policies Classification	Indicator Class.	Indicator	Unit	Base Line	BRT	Impact Reduc-tion
Energy, air quality and climate change	Mid-point	Climate change	kg CO2 eq	1,39	2,85x10-01	80%
		Ozone depletion	kg CFC-11 eq	5,50x10-07	5,63x10-08	90%
		Photochemical oxidant formation	kg NMVOC	1,29x10-02	3,22x10-03	75%
		Particulate matter formation	kg PM10 eq	3,64x10-03	8,05x10-04	78%
		Ionising radiation	kg U235 eq	1,22x10-01	1,21x10-02	90%
	Endpoint	Terrestrial acidification	kg SO2 eq	8,65x10-03	1,86x10-03	78%
		Fossil depletion	kg oil eq	9,95x10-01	1,19x10-01	88%
		Climate change Human Health	DALY	1,95x10-06	3,99x10-07	80%
		Ozone depletion	DALY	1,34x10-09	1,45x10-10	89%
		Photochemical oxidant formation	DALY	5,02x10-10	1,26x10-10	75%
		Particulate matter formation	DALY	9,47x10-07	2,09x10-07	78%
		Ionising radiation	DALY	1,99x10-09	1,99x10-10	90%
		Climate change Ecosystems	Species/yr	1,11x10-08	2,26x10-09	80%
		Terrestrial acidification	Species/yr	5,02x10-11	1,08x10-11	78%
		Fossil depletion	$	1,60x10+01	1,92x10+00	88%
Urban planning, public spaces and landscaping	Mid-point	Natural land transformation	m2	1,01x10-03	1,23x10-04	88%
	End point	Natural land transformation	Species/yr	1,48x10-09	1,81x10-10	88%
Efficient use of resources and generation of wastes	Mid point	Freshwater eutrophication	kg P eq	2,16x10-04	1,38x10-05	94%
		Marine eutrophication	kg N eq	5,07x10-04	1,14x10-04	78%
		Terrestrial ecotoxicity	kg 1,4-DB eq	2,34x10-04	3,43x10-05	85%
		Freshwater ecotoxicity	kg 1,4-DB eq	6,76x10-03	4,50x10-04	93%
		Marine ecotoxicity	kg 1,4-DB eq	7,18x10-03	5,03x10-04	93%

Policies Classification	Indicator Class.	Indicator	Unit	Base Line	BRT	Im-pact Redu-ction
		Agricultural land occupation	m2a	6,73x10-03	4,05x10-04	94%
		Urban land occupation	m2a	6,76x10-03	1,27x10-03	81%
		Water depletion	m3	5,67x10-03	5,91x10-04	90%
		Metal depletion	kg Fe eq	1,38x10-01	6,08x10-03	96%
		Freshwater eutrophication	Species/yr	9,48x10-12	6,09x10-13	94%
		Terrestrial ecotoxicity	Species/yr	2,98x10-11	4,36x10-12	85%
		Freshwater ecotoxicity	Species/yr	1,76x10-12	1,17x10-13	93%
	Endpoint	Marine ecotoxicity	Species/yr	5,75x10-15	4,03x10-16	93%
		Agricultural land occupation	Species/yr	7,67x10-11	4,62x10-12	94%
		Urban land occupation	Species/yr	1,31x10-10	2,44x10-11	81%
		Metal depletion	$	9,87x10-03	4,35x10-04	96%
Public Health	Mid point	Human toxicity	kg 1,4-DB eq	2,89x10-01	1,95x10-02	93%
	Endpoint	Human toxicity	DALY	2,02x10-07	1,36x10-08	93%

The reductions in environmental burdens relate mainly to the greater capacity of the system vs. Traditional transport (5.1 vs. 1.6 passenger/km; SDM, 2011), evolution of vehicle technology and the incorporation of best practices collected in this chapter.

Comparing the two columns of Table 7 and taking into account the number of passengers transported from 2000-2012, it becomes clear that the main fuel, emission and resources use reductions are as follows: 4.4 Mton of CO2-eq (6299 DALY), 3.5 Mton of oil-eq (*i.e.* \$56 billion (USD) are required, using current technology, to extract and replace the fuel used); 1,1 MTon 1,4-DB eq, 20 MTon *Fe* eq, 11 Ton PM-eq and 0,2 MTon m^3 H_2O. These data demonstrate once again that the contribution of BRT systems in large cities such as Bogota, support, if not enhance environmental performance and policies for sustainable mobility.

4.6. Challenges Ahead of the New BRT Phases and IPTS

Bogota's BRT system has led to the improved environmental development of the city, despite the fact that it has moved beyond its load capacity. The implementation of an IPTS and future phases of the BRT, is now urgently required. This involves, amongst other things, an evaluation of transport alternatives such as rail (Acevedo et al., 2008).

Moreover, a strengthening of the planning of the system's environmental aspects needs to occur. For example, as Phase 1 and 2 contracts did not stipulate the need for any formal certifications such as *ISO 14001* or *OHSAS 18001* international standards, there was a severe lack of homogeneity across the *TransMilenio* system and its standards of operation. This is however perhaps not surprising, given its pioneering nature (first transport based CDM registered and the world's first fully operational BRT project). Over the last 12 years there have been series of complex challenges requiring ingenious innovations. With the further development of the network into a fully functioning IPTS many more are envisioned, these include:

- Eventual replacement of 10,500 of the existing 18,000 strong fleet within the next decade with greener buses, either because they have a higher carrying capacity or the fuel used results in lower emissions.
- The scrapping of an additional 7830 buses either because they are part of an aging fleet or because they were made obsolete by improved planning and integration of the transport system generally.
- Promote the strengthening of institutional and technical support to ensure public relevance and the continuity of strategic plans and practices.
- Tweaking of the current network for improved environmental performance: installation of particulate filters in those buses that are to form part of the IPTS; Measurement of contaminant parameters to include factors apart from opacity; Promotion of dry washing and the increasing of wash cycles; Substitution of solvent based paints with those of a water base.
- The continuation of consolidated waste management with plans regarding end life (tires, batteries and other forms of e-waste) and the initialization of arrangements with manufactures and suppliers to ensure that wastes are properly dealt with from the beginning of the cradle to the grave.

- The introduction and integration of complementary modes of green transport. Any transport solution should not be worked into isolated activities, but rather serve as a component within a fully integrated system.
- The use of alternative technologies such as hybrid and fully electric buses.
- The need for new city planning and designs to increase and promote sustainable urban infrastructure (green roofs and vertical gardens).
- Intervention to recuperate and improve lost or poorly managed urban spaces.
- Sustainable architecture education and training
- Introduction of renewable energy in urban spaces.

With the inclusion of the authors' suggestions, Bogota will once more be the vanguard of sustainable mobility in emerging countries, for the benefit of all global citizens, now and into the future.

CONCLUSION

The *TransMilenio* system as a pioneer in the field of transport has revolutionized national public policies relating to the quality of fuel, the mitigation of climate change and the control and management of atmospheric emissions. In addition, through various investigations and field testing Bogota's BRT Network has contributed to the development of not only local and national policy but innovations in transport networks and technologies across the globe (including in processes and vehicle technologies, CDM methodology, transport integration, planning guide).

Many challenges do remain however, despite the greener promise of BRT and IPTS compared to traditional forms of mass transport. For one thing, authorities need to strengthen norms and regulations with the aim of reducing the energy intensity of the transport sector. They should also be increasingly involved in the promotion of more efficient technologies given that fuel combustion contributes to 90% of the adverse impacts. This could be achieved, for example, in the development of collaborative projects between government and industry.

The LCA presents another way of addressing environmental aspects in its provision of indicators which support the development of public policy. Its results show that the BRT reduces environmental impacts by up to 75% (depending on the exact aspect considered). At the same time the values obtained strongly reflect the necessity to prioritize policies and practices, which in the case of the *TransMilenio project* are energy efficiency, climate change mitigation, emissions and landscape aesthetics, taking into consideration the end-point indicators and the landscape quality evaluation. For the latter to be fully successful there needs to be inter-institutional leadership and coordination for the improvement of those indices involved. Landscape also need to be moved to the forefront of transport-related decisions and should not always be regulated to an issue of secondary importance.

The good practices and lessons learned presented in this chapter serve as a reference point for the adoption of policy better adjusted to the recent advances in the transport sectors across the globe but especially in rapidly developing cities. This chapter is also indicative of the benefits that modern quantitative analysis can bring to the sustainable transport debate and the development of adequate policies with which to make the objectives of such debates a reality.

ACKNOWLEDGMENT

The authors would like to thank Kai Whiting for his translation of the original text and the provision of helpful advice and editing, without which this chapter would not have been possible. Also special thanks to the maintenance team of the bus operating company in Bogota, Colombia.

REFERENCES

Acevedo, J., Bocarejo, J.P., Lleras, G., Rodríguez, A., Echeverry, J.C., Ospina, G., 2008. El transporte como soporte al desarrollo de Colombia - Una Visión 2040. Universidad de los Andes. Versión Preliminar (*in Spanish*).

Aranda, A., Valero, A., Zabalza, I., Scarpellini, S., Llera, E., Energy efficiency in transport and mobility from an eco-efficiency viewpoint. Energy, 36, 1916-1923.

Arroyave, S., 2011. Las políticas públicas en Colombia. Insuficiencias y desafíos. Universidad Nacional, Sede Medellín. Revista del Departamento de Ciencia Política, Forum Nro. 1 enero – julio de 2011. (*in Spanish*).

Behrentz, E. 2009. Relevancia Ambiental del Sistema de Transporte Público: Bogotá como Caso de Estudio – Memoria Foro de Movilidad Sostenible: Una Construcción Multidisciplinaria. Bogota. (*in Spanish*).

Brand, C., Tran, M., Anable, J., 2012. The UK transport carbon model: An integrated life cycle approach to explore low carbon futures. Energy Policy, 41, 107–124.

Burgess, A., Becker, J.F.F., Snelder, M., Bröcker, J., Schneekloth, N., Szimba, E., Kraft, M., Krail, M., Nielsen, O., Hansen, C., Martino, A., Fiorello, D., Christidis, P., Chen, M., Vilcan, A., Tardieu, P., 2005. Report on Policy Requirements and Selected Relevant Models/Methods, TRANS-TOOLS Deliverable1, Funded by 6th Framework RTD Programme. TNOInro, Delft, TheNetherlands.

Cain, A., Darido, G., Baltes, M.R., Rodriguez, P., Barrios, J.C., 2006. Applicability of Bogotá's TransMilenio BRT System to the United States. Federal Transit Administration, Washington.

Centro de Transporte Sustentable de México (CTS México). 2011. Informe Institucional, 2009-2011. EMBARQ. México D.F. (*in Spanish*).

Chaparro, I., 2002. Evaluación del impacto socio económico del transporte urbano en la ciudad de Bogotá. El caso del sistema de transporte masivo, Transmilenio. Comisión Económica para América Latina y el Caribe - CEPAL. Santiago de Chile. (*in Spanish*)

Conesa, V., 2005. Guía Metodológica para la Evaluación del Impacto Ambiental. Madrid. (*in Spanish*).

Corporación Andina de Fomento. 2010. Observatorio de Movilidad Urbana para América Latina. Bogotá.

Council of Europe, 2000. The European Landscape Convention. Florence.

Danielsson, P., Gunnarsson, C., 2001. Desing for the environment – What, why and how at volvo? Event Memory. Ravel Conference, Stockholm.

Deng, T., Nelson J.D., 2013. Bus Rapid Transit implementation in Beijing: An evaluation of performance and impacts. *Journal of Transportation Economics*, 39, 108-113.

Duarte, E., 2004. Una visión de transporte urbano sostenible en Colombia. Universidad Nacional de Colombia. Bogotá (*in Spanish*).

Estupiñan, N., Rodriguez, D.A., 2008. The relationship between urban form and station boardings for Bogota's BRT. *Transportation Research*, Part A, 42, 296–306.

Filipe, L.N., Macário, R., 2013. A first glimpse on policy packaging for implementation of BRT projects. *Transportation Economics*, 39, 150-157.

Goldman, T., Gorham, R., 2006. Sustainable urban transport: Four innovative directions. *Technology in Society*, 28, 261–273.

Gutiérrez Aparicio, L. 2012. Una mirada a la modernización del transporte público urbano en América Latina – Memoria de evento. 2012. Madrid. (*in Spanish*).

Hidaldo, D., Carrigan, A., 2010. Modernizing Public Transportation, Lessons Learned from Major Bus Improvements in Latin America and Asia. world Resources Institute. Washington.

Hidalgo, D., Gutiérrez, L., 2013. BRT and BHLS around the world: Explosive growth, large positive impacts and many issues outstanding. Transportation Economics, 39, 8-13.

Hook, W., 2008. Bus Rapid Transit: An International View.Institute for Transportation and Development Policy. New York.

Instituto de Desarrollo Urbano (IDU), Jardín Botánico de Bogota José Celistino Mutis (JBB), Departamento Técnico Administrativo del Medio Ambiente (DAMA). 2003. Guías de procedimiento y lineamientos ambientales de diseño para obras de infraestructura en Bogotá. Alcaldía Mayor de Bogota. Bogota. (*in Spanish*).

International Energy Agency. 2009. Transport, energy and CO2. Francia.

International Standards Organization - ISO, 2006. ISO 14040: environmental management–life cycle assessment–principles and framework.

Jardín Botánico de Bogotá José Celestíno Mutis, 2002. Complemento al Manual Verde. 2002. Alcaldía Mayor de Bogota. Bogota. (*in Spanish*).

Jun, M.J., 2012. Redistributive effects of bus rapid transit (BRT) on development patterns and property values in Seoul, Korea. *Transport Policy*, 19, 85–92.

Kliucininkas, L., Matulevicius, J., Martuzevicius, D., 2012. The life cycle assessment of alternative fuel chains for urban buses and trolleybuses. *Journal of Environmental Management*, 99, 98-103.

Kojima, K., Ryan L., 2010. Energy efficiency policy recommendations. International Energy Agency. Paris.

León, R., 2001. Análisis de los aspectos ambientales de una organización. Centro Nacional de Producción Más Limpia. Medellín. (*in Spanish*).

Lindau, L.A., Hidalgo, D., Facchini, D., 2012. Curitiba, the cradle of Bus Rapid Transit. Integrated Transport Systems and BRT systems alliance (available in http://www.sibrtonline.org/downloads/built-environment-curitiba-oct19-4db0b5ac230da.pdf).

McKenzie, E.C., Durango-Cohen, P., 2012. Environmental life-cycle assessment of transit buses with alternative fuel technology. Transportation Research, Part D, 17, 39–47.

Mejía-Dugand S., Hjelm, O., Baas, L., Ríos R.A., 2012, Lessons from the spread of Bus Rapid Transit in Latin America, *Journal of Cleaner Production*, in press, 1-9.

Ministerio de Ambiente, Vivienda y Desarrollo Territorial 2008. Política de Gestión ambiental Urbana. Bogotá. (available in http://www.minambiente.gov.co/documentos/politica_de_gestion_ambiental_urbana.pdf) (*in Spanish*).

Nugroho, S.B., Fujiwara, A., Zhang, J., 2010. The influence of BRT on the ambient PM10 concentration at roadside sites of Trans Jakarta Corridors. *Procedia Environmental Sciences*, 2, 914–924.

Pardo, C., 2009. Los cambios en los sistemas integrados de transporte masivo en las principals ciudades de América Latina. División de Recursos Naturales e Infraestructura, Comisión conómica para América Latina y el Caribe (CEPAL), de la Organización de las Naciones Unidas. (*in Spanish*).

Prada, A., 2011. El futuro de la movilidad en Bogotá. Event Memory. (available in http://www.celat.org/eventos/2011/movilidad/presentaciones/presentacion_alfonso_prada.pdf).

Perez, L., Martí, J.R., 2002. La valoración de la fragilidad visual del paisaje en la planificación territorial. I Congreso de Ingeniería Civil, Territorio y Medio Ambiente. Agapea. Madrid. (available in http://www.ciccp.es/webantigua/Icitema/ Comunicaciones/Tomo_ll/T2p1441.pdf) (*in Spanish*).

Rodriguez, D.A., Brisson, E.M., Estupiñan, N., 2009. The relationship between segment-level built environment attributes and pedestrian activity around Bogota's BRT stations. *Transportation Research*, Part D, 14, 470–478.

Romero, E., 2011. Diseño de un modelo de control y manejo ambiental apropiado de los residuos generados por las operaciones de mantenimiento en las empresas de buses del Sistema TransMilenio. Escuela Colombiana de Carreras Industriales. Facultad de Postgrados. Bogota (*in Spanish*).

Rosenthal, E., 2009. Buses May Aid Climate Battle in Poor Cities. New York Times (available in http://www.nytimes.com/2009/07/10/world/americas/10degrees.html?_r=0)

Schalekamp, H., Behrens, R., 2010. Engaging paratransit on public transport reform initiatives in South Africa: A critique of policy and an investigation of appropriate engagement approaches. *Transportation Economics*, 29, 371-378.

Secretaría Distrital de Movilidad – SDM, 2011. Movilidad en cifras 2010. Press Release. Bogota.

Shafiq-Ur Rahmana, M., Timms, P., Montgomery, F., 2012. Integrating BRT Systems with Rickshaws in Developing Cities to Promote Energy Efficient Travel. Procedia - *Social and Behavioral Sciences*, 54, 261–274.

Simonen, M., 2010. Energi- og utslippsvirkninger av produksjon av Volvo 8500 busser. Unpublished paper. (Available in http://transportDokumentasjon/pdf/Buss/Volvo8500.pdf) (*in Norwegian*).

Solari, F.A., Cazorla, L., 2009. El paisaje como referente de diseño. Universidad de Palermo. Buenos Aires. (*in Spanish*).

Spielmann, M., Bauer, C., Dones, R., Tuchschmid, M., 2007.Ecoinvent Report 14: Transport Services. Swiss Centre for Life Cycle Inventories. Villigen and Uster.

Spielmann, M., Scholz, R.W., 2005. Life Cycle Inventories for Transport Services - Background Data for Freight Transport. *International Journal for Life Cycle Analysis*, 10, 1.

Troll, C., 2010. Ecología del Paisaje. Journal of environmental research. Sermanat. 2010-2(1):94-105, México D.F. (*in Spanish*).

United Nations Department of Economic and Social Affairs/Population Division. 2012. World Urbanization Prospects: The 2011 Revision. New York. (available in http://esa.un.org/unup/pdf/WUP2011_Highlights.pdf).

Vasconcellos, E.A. 2010. Análisis de la Movilidad Urbana, Espacio, Medio Ambiente y Equidad. Corporación Andina de Fomento. Bogotá. (*in Spanish*).

Venter, C., 2013. The lurch towards formalisation: Lessons from the implementation of BRT in Johannesburg, South Africa. *Transportation Economics*, 39, 114-120.

Volvo, 2001. Environmental product declaration. Volvo FH12 and Volvo FM12, Euro 3. Volvo. Göteborg.

Walters, J., Overview of public transport policy developments in South Africa. Transportation Economics, 39, 34-45.

Whitelegg, J., 1986. Critical Mass: Transport, Environment and Society in the Twenty-First Century. Pluto press.

World Health Organization. 2006. Health risks of particulate matter from long-range transboundary air pollution. Copenhagen.

Wright, L., Hook, W., 2007. Bus Rapid Transit Planning Guide. Institute for Transportation & Development Policy. 3rd edition.

In: Health, Violence, Environment and Human Development ... ISBN: 978-1-62948-038-1
Editors: A. Cotte Poveda and C. I. Pardo Martínez

Chapter 8

EFFECTS OF URBANISATION AND SUBURBANISATION ON HEALTH IN THE BOGOTÁ REGION

***Clara Inés Pardo Martinez*[1] *and William H. Alfonso Piña*[2]**
Faculty of Administration, Universidad del Rosario, Bogotá, Colombia
Faculty of Science Policy and Government, Urban Development and Management – Ekística, Universidad del Rosario, Bogotá, Colombia

ABSTRACT

This chapter seeks to analyse and determine how urbanisation and suburbanisation affect health, taking as a case study the urban agglomeration of Bogotá and neighbouring municipalities for the study period of 1998-2012. This analysis is conducted using several indicators to characterise trends in population, urbanisation and suburbanisation and their effects on health, which is assessed as total deaths in Bogotá and Savanna. The indicators used for this study include the population, urban density, number of deaths and main causes of death, which are calculated for Bogotá and every neighbouring municipality selected. Some municipalities (Chia, Cajica and Cota) demonstrate how, in the process of suburbanisation and urbanisation, consolidation with different conditions and levels of development affect the health of the population, with increases in deaths by disease and cancer. This study's findings are important in that the evidentiary aspects of urbanisation and new populations on the neighbouring municipalities of Bogotá can be considered for formulating comprehensive regional developmental policies to improve welfare and habitability, particularly for vulnerable populations.

Keywords: Urbanisation, Suburbanisation, Health, Bogotá Region

[1] Email: cipmusa@yahoo.com, clara.pardo@urosario.edu.co.
[2] Email: william.alfonso@urosario.edu.co.

1. INTRODUCTION

Cities throughout the world are highly diverse with differing amounts of concentrated national economic and political power and scientific, political and media attention. Analysing the effects of urbanisation and suburbanisation on health is complex due to difficulties in separating the impact of these processes from other variables, such as population, geographical extension, social inequalities and multiple and fragmented land occupation (WHO, 2009). Moreover, today's sustained growth of cities and the surrounding municipalities, where close to 50% of the world's population resides compared to only 15% in 1900, is partly a consequence of rural-urban migration to seek better opportunities and to reduce vulnerabilities. Lower rates of diseases, higher individual incomes, greater job opportunities and better access to health care, social services, and cultural activities are often found in urban regions; however, access may not be evenly distributed among the population, generating large social gaps and tensions (Tellnes, 2005, McGranahan et al., 2005, UN, 2006).

Patz et al. (2005) show that urban populations with lower incomes or in poverty are exposed to important vulnerabilities. It is estimated that over 900 million people, one-third of the global urban population and more than 70% of the urban population of developing countries, live in slum-like conditions, with an estimated increase to approximately 2 billion by 2020. This situation is characterised by low incomes, poor housing and basic services, no effective control of pollution and ecosystem degradation. The main health problems for this group have increased and include air pollution, water-borne and vector-borne infectious diseases, floods, storms and landslides.

Urbanisation and suburbanisation generate a profound effect on people's living conditions and health status, with the main feature being differences in lifestyle. Not only changes in food habits, physical activities and work patterns but also changes in leisure-time activities and travelling patterns cause changes in morbidity and mortality patterns. The majority of these factors are related to a rise in the risk of chronic diseases and infectious diseases. Moreover, urban environments impact almost every aspect of human health and welfare, whereas cities are associated with both positive and negative effects on public health (McMichael, 2000, Tellnes, 2005).

Increases in urbanisation and suburbanisation in the cities of developing countries have generated increases in the number of people living in slums and unhealthy environments, which has become a rising concern. High levels of environmental pollution, high construction densities and loss of social connections often have negative effects on the health of urban populations (Harpham, 2009, Stephens et al., 2008).

The relationship between urbanisation and health has been analysed from different perspectives. For example, Moore et al. (2003) indicated an association between urban health hazards and the health risks characterised by substandard housing, crowding, air pollution, insufficient or contaminated drinking water, inadequate sanitation and solid waste, disposal services, vector-borne diseases, industrial waste, increased motor vehicle traffic and stress associated with poverty and unemployment, among other conditions. They proposed the need for available, accessible, relevant health data and the use of such data to inform policy, to target and evaluate interventions, and to include the health sector in urban planning and decision-making with environmental regulators, urban zoning authorities, energy and transportation planners, housing authorities, and municipal service providers. Graham et al. (2004) investigated environmental health risks associated with planned and unplanned growth in peri-urban communities in Northern México. They found that households in both planned and unplanned areas were vulnerable to poor environmental health conditions, but more risk factors and negative health outcomes were associated with unplanned communities. Wells and Donofrio (2011) described the relationship between urban planning and human health, demonstrating that effective city planning influences improvements in public health and the welfare of the population. Smit et al. (2011) studied the relationship between urban planning/design and health equity, particularly in cities in low- and middle-income countries, suggesting that the appropriate planning/design and/or retrofitting of built environments can facilitate and promote safe outdoor physical activity and can, thus, contribute to better health outcomes. These studies show the importance of identifying urban factors that may affect health outcomes and improve the welfare of the population.

In the case of Bogotá, studies of urbanisation and suburbanisation have focused on historical aspects, showing the transformation process from Spanish colonisation and modernisation over the last few decades to suburbanisation and metropolisation (Mertins, 2004). Changes in mobility between Bogotá and the neighbouring municipalities showed a relative homogeneity in the social composition of the municipalities analysed, which contrasts with a widening of the inequalities of daily mobility (Dureau and Gouëset, 2011), causing the peripheral expansion of Bogotá due to the flexible systems of popular housing production and public transportation availability (Montezuma, 1997).

Several studies have focused on urbanisation and suburbanisation and their effects on health. However, studies on cities in developing countries are limited. This chapter's objective is to explore the effects of urbanisation and suburbanisation on health by studying Bogotá and its neighbouring municipalities using different approaches.

The remainder of this chapter is organised as follows. In the next section, we present a literature review. The third section introduces the data and methods used in this study. In the fourth section, a description of the Bogotá Region is presented. The fifth section illustrates the main results of this analysis. Finally, the last section concludes the paper.

2. Literature Review

This section provides a description of urban health that is based on the framework proposed by Galea et al. (2005) in which multiple levels of influence shape population health. Hence, social and physical environments that explain an urban context are formed by municipal factors, such as government and civil society, and national and global trends set the context in which local factors operate.

The framework also assumes that urban environment (physical, social, economic, and political) directly or indirectly affects all strata of residents. With the aim of considering these factors and how they affect the health of urban populations, this framework suggests mechanisms through which these variables may influence the conditions that are the primary social and economic determinants of the health of urban populations (see Figure 1).

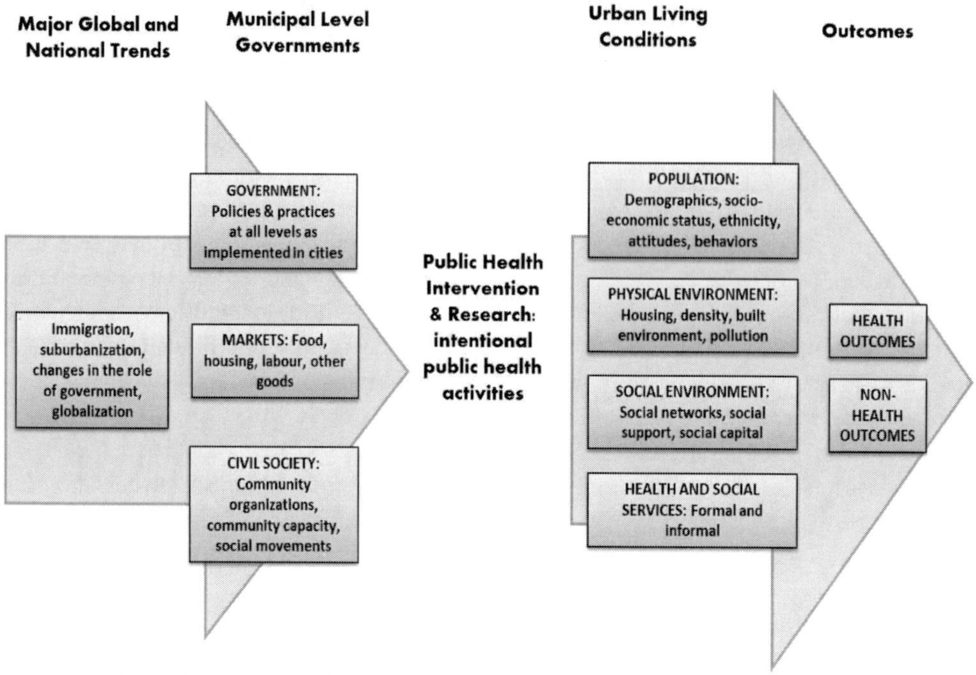

Source: Based on Galea et al. (2005).

Figure 1. Framework for urban health.

To understand urban health, it is key to shift the focus of inquiry away from disease outcomes towards urban exposures, namely, the characteristics of an urban context that influence health and welfare in cities. Moreover, the urban context is complex and requires studying interactions at multiple levels as well as cause-and-effect relationships (Perrow, 1999, Vlahov and Galea, 2003).

Urbanisation and suburbanisation should generate the following emerging health problems according to Ritter (2007): environmental, housing, social and lifestyle (see Table 1). These problems are integrated in urban areas, and one problem can cause another.

3. Data and Methods

3.1. Data

This study is applied to Bogotá and its neighbouring municipalities from 1998 to 2012. The data necessary to conduct this analysis include population, increase of urban areas, urban developed area, mortality rates, main causes of mortality, health-care coverage, unsatisfied basic needs and built area. These data are provided by the Departamento Nacional de Estadística (Colombian Department of Statistics, or DANE) and the Departamento Nacional de Planeación (National Department of Planning DNP), Instituto Geografico Agustin Codazzi (Geographic Institute Agustin Codazzi) and the Governor of Cundinamarca.

Table 1. Emerging health problems due to urbanisation and suburbanization

Emerging Health problem	Description	Consequences
Environmental	Problems related to Global change and overpopulation that include air, water, and noise pollution, ozone depletion, food safety, natural resource depletion, and climate changes.	•Poor air quality can trigger asthma and allergies or contribute to physical inactivity •An unclean water supply can cause the transmission of infectious diseases though the water supply or through food (waterborne and foodborne diseases) •Climate changes can cause deaths from extreme heat or cold •Noise can cause sleep disturbances, and hence poor performance at work and in school •Second-hand smoke and exposure to carcinogens can cause cancer •Overall, poor environmental quality contributes to 25–33% of global ill health.
Housing	Living conditions affects Physical, mental and social health include lead exposure, noise, asbestos, mould growth, crowding, respiratory disease, spread of infectious diseases, accidents and mental illness.	Health impacts of inadequate housing conditions are a complex issue involving a variety of exposures (physical, chemical, biological, building, and social factors) and diverse health outcomes (asthma and allergies, respiratory diseases, cardiovascular effects, injuries, poisoning, mental illnesses, etc.).
Social	Social component includes overcrowding, lack of resources, poverty, unemployment, and lack of education and social services (e.g., crime, violence, drug use, high school drop-out rates and mental health problems).	Social problems can lead to health problems such as: - Accidents and cirrhosis of the liver caused by alcohol - Malnutrition caused by poverty - Suicide lack of mental-health services - Injury caused by drugs or stress

Table 1. (Continued)

Emerging Health problem	Description	Consequences
Lifestyle	These problems are causes by several factors such as lack of education, access to health care, or access to social services; poverty; stress and overcrowding (e.g., noncommunicable diseases such as heart disease, cancer, stroke, obesity and diabetes).	Many of the health problems are largely preventable i.e, diabetes, lung cancer, and hypertension. Education, social services programs, changes in systems (i.e., making low-fat foods available in school cafeterias and creating walking paths) are a few examples of how to combat these major contributing factors to disease.

Source: Based on Ritter (2007).

3.2. Methods

To evaluate the effects of suburbanisation and urbanisation phenomena on health in Bogotá and its neighbouring municipalities, it is necessary to calculate several indicators to determine population dynamics, urban growth trends, mortality rate and main causes of mortality during the period 1998-2012. The dynamic of urban development should reveal suburbanisation as a continual and complex change process and the associated environmental and social impacts (Whitehand and Larkham, 1992). The indicators used in this study are as follows:

- Population is measured as the number of inhabitants during the period of study to determine its trends in Bogotá and its neighbouring municipalities, with the aim of identifying areas with higher occupancy and growth related to Bogotá.
- Population density is an indicator for analysing how population trends may determine suburbanisation. This indicator was measured as the population per hectare over the sample period.
- Urban density allows for the identification of the types of processes that are shared between suburbanisation and urbanisation. This indicator was calculated as the number of properties per hectare for the period of study.
- Health is measured as the total deaths and main causes of mortality (recurrent diseases or homicides) as an indicator for analysing the relationship between mortality and changes in urbanisation and suburbanisation.

In order to understand the relationship between population, urbanisation and suburbanisation and health as explained by mortality, a correlation analysis is applied where the estimate of the product-moment correlation coefficient, ρ, is

$$\hat{\rho} = \frac{\sum_{i=1}^{n} w_i(x_i-\bar{x})(y_i-\bar{y})}{\sqrt[2]{\sum_{i=1}^{n} w_i(x_i-\bar{x})^2}\sqrt[2]{\sum_{i=1}^{n} w_i(y_i-\bar{y})^2}} \qquad (1)$$

where w_i are the weights, if specified, or $w_i = 1$ if weights are not specified. $\bar{x} = (\sum w_i x_i)/(\sum w_i)$ is the mean of x, and $\bar{y}$ is similarly defined (Snedecor and Cochran, 1989, Pearson, 1896). The unadjusted significance level is calculated as (Wolfe, 1997):

$$p = 2 * \left(n-2, |\hat{\rho}|\sqrt{n-2}/1-\hat{\rho}^2\right) \qquad (2)$$

Let v be the number of variables specified so that $k = v(v-1)/2$ correlation coefficients are to be estimated.

4. BOGOTÁ REGION AS CASE STUDY

The Bogotá region's Altiplano geology is characterised by a terrace of lacustrine origin with fluvio-lacustrine deposits that began in the tertiary and finished in the recent quaternary. The ground formation has volcanic ash influences that come from the volcanoes of the central cordillera. Ecological structures related to the areas of environmental importance and services for the territory of Bogotá with ecosystems, such as moorland, woodland ecosystems, wetlands and some arid and semi-arid zones, generate a great potential for eco-tourism due to their diversity. The groundwater availability from the localisation of aquifer sequences, which are geological structures that are capable of storing and providing water, generate a region with a wealth of groundwater that is localised in the hills adjoining the savannah, which is characterised by sandstone, with a secondary porosity of high to middle productivity.

This region uses diverse material and energy flows, including fuels (65,000 gallons / day, and electricity: 10,236 GW) water (300,000 m3 / day), food consumption (7,907 tons / day) and solid waste generation (4,276 tons / day). Mining for wall-building materials leads to exploitation in the nearby hills. This large internal market has generated an increase in the occupation of fertile soil, moving agricultural activities to low-quality soils. Moreover, a higher population concentration implies a new infrastructure, causing greater environmental impacts.

In the Bogotá region, foreign investments increased by 164% from 2002 to 2009, particularly in the mining and petroleum industries. In contrast, manufacturing and commerce decreased by 6.3% and 2.9%, respectively, which affected employment: 26% of the employed population works in the service and commerce sectors. Mining increased by 11.3% and employed 1% of the population.

This region has also increased its socio-spatial segregation (e.g., the residential segregation index increased from 13.1 in 2007 to 17.6 in 2011), generating a higher gap between localities and population growth and leading to problems in the quality of urbanisation, irrational land use, unequal access to infrastructure and services, increased pollution and environmental problems and inefficient traffic management.

Over the last few decades, the evolution of the Bogotá region has been characterised by the addition of several municipalities without a concept of region, which follows the open model of a metropolitan area regarding the region concept as a regional urban network. Suburbanisation in the Bogotá region has been characterised by an increase in the occupation and construction of isolated buildings as a result of an accelerated subdivision process of rural properties and by changes in formal urbanisation by using condominiums as primary residences. This process has influenced the phenomena of urban expansion, loss of the historical boundaries of nearby settlements, and conurbation with new occupation in the forest reserve, mountain areas and ecosystems of primary ecological structures. Likewise, in this region, industrial corridors have begun to appear that have been consolidated by construction in industrial areas and bodegas as well as floriculture construction (sheds and greenhouses) and agro-industrial sector construction along the main regional and national highways. As a result of these processes, the Bogotá region has occupied disperse forms, generating new neighbourhoods, isolated properties, and ways and roads among rural properties without clear rules or regulations, which have fragmented different ecosystems in terms of the soil loss, alteration of areas of environmental interest and affectations of landscape.

5. RESULTS

This section describes the main results of the relationship between urbanisation and suburbanisation and health in the Bogotá region, taking into account the indicators proposed in Section Three that were explained according to effects in this region and population.

A. Population

The population of the Bogotá region has increased by 8.5-fold in the last 60 years (from 883,412 habitants in 1952 to 7,571,345 habitants in 2012), and the population who previously lived on large rural properties in the municipalities around Bogotá now lives in urban zones. Initially, the population of Bogotá grew by 6%, whereas the municipalities of the Savanna of Bogotá grew by 2.7%. This growth changed progressively between 1993 and 2005. The population of Bogotá grew by 1.9% on average, whereas that of the other municipalities grew by 3.6% on average (Lizarazo, 2011). The increases in population have generated pressure on land use, affecting rural properties with accelerated subdivisions to localise condominiums and plan for the construction of industrial zones and informal housing areas.

Figure 2 shows an increasing trend in the population of the neighbouring municipalities, from 2003 (taking 1998 as the base year). Bogotá and La Calera show smaller increases, whereas Mosquera (from 26,538 habitants in 1998 to 78,658 habitants in 2012) and Chia (from 58,616 habitants in 1998 to 120,719 habitants in 2012) show larger increases. In 2012, Bogotá had a population of 7,571,345, whereas the neighbouring municipalities had a population of 1,137,299, with the most populated being Soacha (43%), Facatativa (11.2%), Chia (10.6%), Zipaquira (10.4%) and Mosquera (6.9%). These results concur with Mertins (2004), who studied suburbanisation phenomena in the Bogotá savannah.

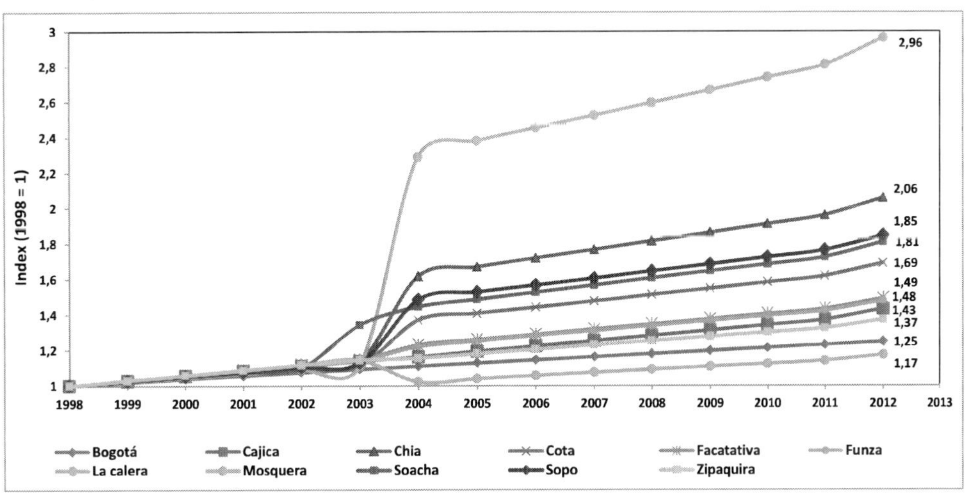

Figure 2. Population trends in Bogotá and neighbouring municipalities (1998-2012).

These trends show that due to urban land scarcity, the urban expansion of Bogotá is performed on fertile savannah, affecting soil and water resources with high environmental quality in several neighbouring municipalities. Hence, the result is a patchwork of developments or individual disperses occupations localised in zones without public services and facilities, with limited connectivity and transport, and with greater natural hazard risks (floods and landslides). Therefore, this population is more vulnerable and has fewer opportunities, which affects welfare, quality of life and habitability.

B. Population Density

The population density of Bogotá and its neighbouring municipalities measured as the population per urban hectare shows that Soacha is the municipality with the highest population density (194.96), followed by Bogotá (188.89) and Facatativa (188.57), whereas Funza (83.3), Mosquera (83.3) and Cota (96.4) have the lowest population densities, with almost 100 inhabitants per hectare (see Figure 3). Sopo, Soacha and Mosquera have larger increases in population density, whereas Bogotá showed smaller increases. This trend also confirms the suburbanisation and urbanisation process in the Bogotá savannah where Bogotá maintains these trends, while the other municipalities demonstrate greater changes in this indicator due to the migration from rural zones to urban zones as the population seeks new opportunities and increased welfare. However, this population tends to be localised in marginal zones with higher risks and lower sanitary conditions, generating higher poverty and inequality.

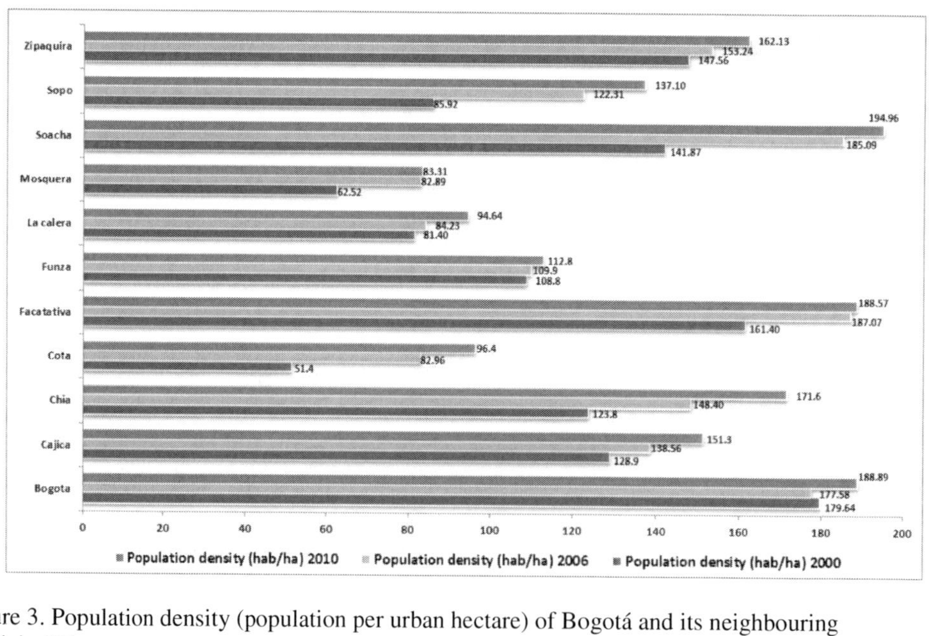

Figure 3. Population density (population per urban hectare) of Bogotá and its neighbouring municipalities.

C. Urban Density

This indicator measured the process of suburbanisation, which is determined when suburban areas are not greater than five properties per hectare (in contrast to urbanisation, which is greater than twenty-five properties per hectare). Chia, Cajicá and Cota demonstrate a suburbanisation process, whereas other neighbouring municipalities demonstrate an urbanisation process, with Bogotá, Soacha and Facatativa having the highest number of properties per hectare (see Figure 4). These results demonstrate that informal occupation has generated an increase in property subdivisions and a dense urbanisation process in the western corridor.

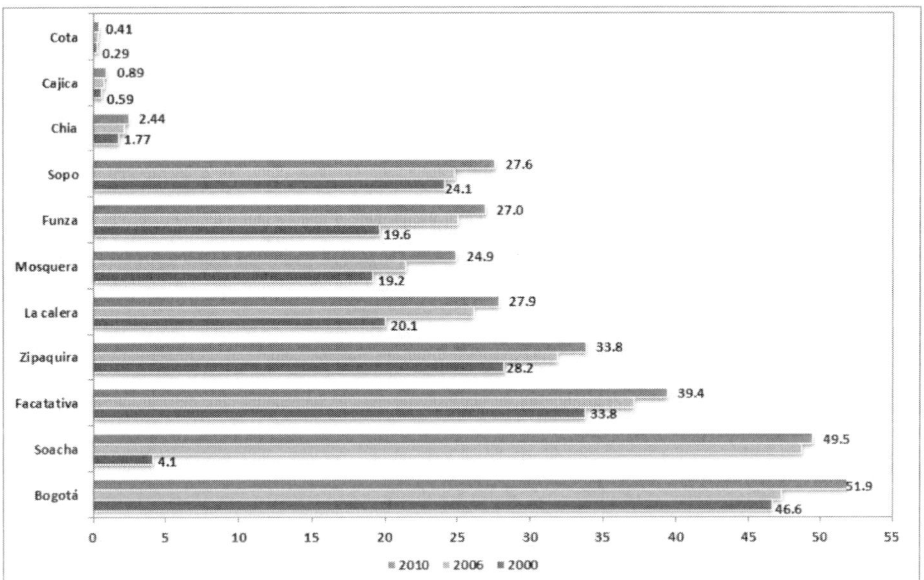

Figure 4. Urban density (properties per hectare) in Bogotá and its neighbouring municipalities.

D. Health

Health in Bogotá and its neighbouring municipalities is analysed by taking into account the number and causes of deaths in the region. Bogotá and Soacha have the higher number of deaths, whereas Cota and Sopo have the lowest number of deaths. Figure 5 shows a trend in the number of deaths, taking 1998 as the base year. Mosquera (from 25 deaths in 1998 to 195 deaths in 2012) and Funza (from 119 deaths in 1998 to 225 deaths in 2012) show smaller increases, whereas Bogotá (from 26,579 deaths in 1998 to 28,016 deaths in 2012) and Facatativa (from 399 deaths in 1998 to 416 deaths in 2012) show smaller increases.

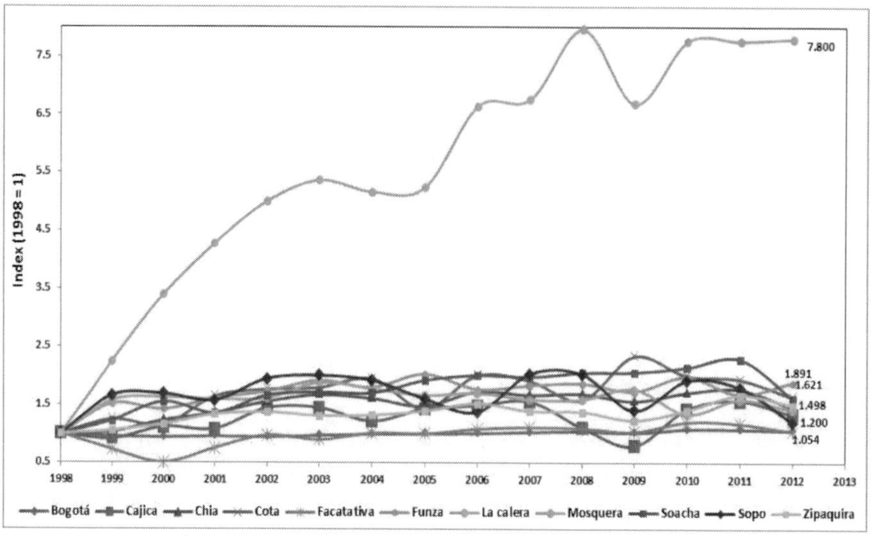

Figure 5. Trends in the number of deaths in Bogotá and its neighbouring municipalities (1998-2012).

Over the last decade, the number of deaths in Bogotá has remained relatively constant, with an average annual growth of 0.41%, whereas neighbouring municipalities have increased their average annual growth between 2-6%, except for Mosquera, which increased by 19%.

In Bogotá and its neighbouring municipalities, the main causes of mortality are cancer and heart disease. In the majority of municipalities, cancer has been the disease with the highest increase, and the trends in all of the municipalities are similar (see Figure 6). The relationship between the causes of mortality by disease and homicide indicate that in Bogotá and its neighbouring municipalities, diseases dominate compared to homicides. Bogotá and Soacha have the highest percentage of homicides. However, over the last few years, homicides have decreased in all of the municipalities have decreased homicides (see Figure 7).

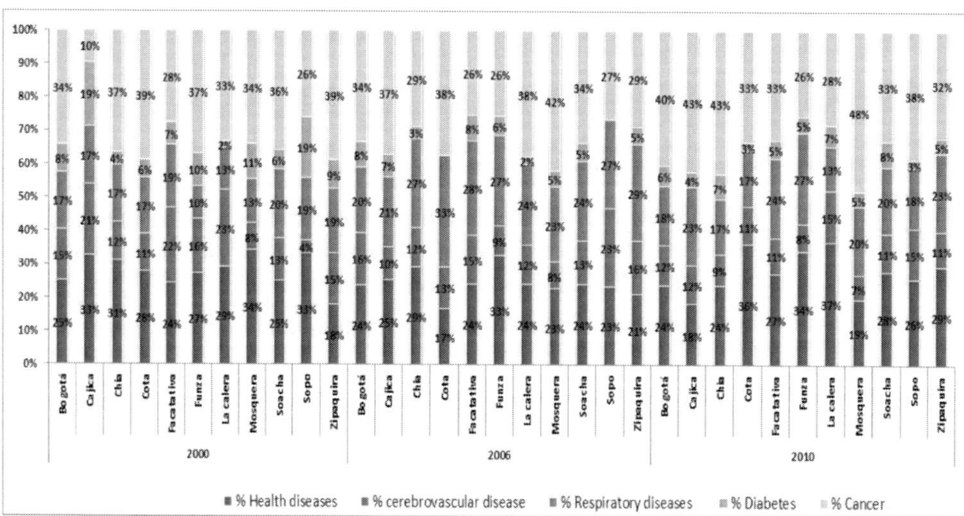

Figure 6. The main causes of deaths in Bogotá and its neighbouring municipalities.

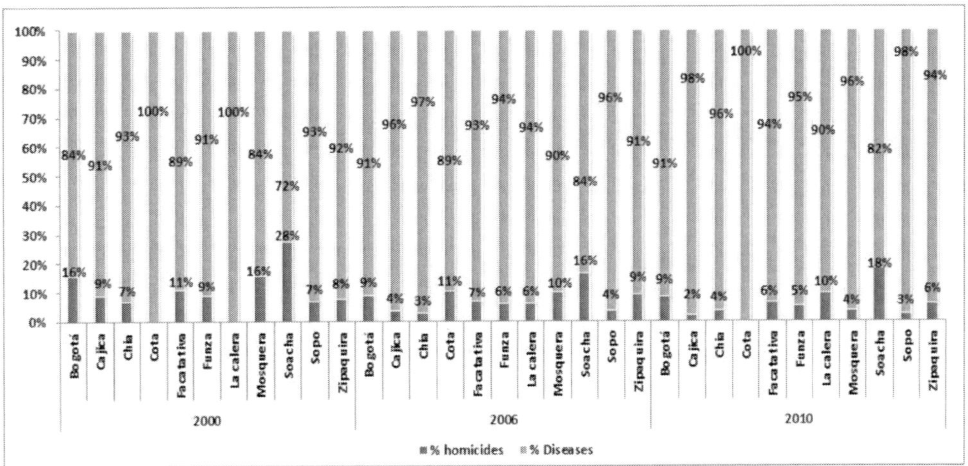

Figure 7. The relationship between diseases and homicides in Bogotá and its neighbouring municipalities.

E. The Relationship between Population, Urbanisation and Suburbanisation Processes and Health

To understand the relationship between population, urbanisation and suburbanisation and health in Bogotá and its neighbouring municipalities, a correlation analysis is applied with the main indicators as explained above.

The results of the indicators show that as the population grows, the process of urbanisation and suburbanisation affects the neighbouring municipalities of Bogotá and leads to an increased urban population, suburbanisation and mortality by causes that predominate in cities, such as cancer and health diseases, which agrees with the WHO (2002). Diseases such as cardiovascular diseases and cancer are rapidly increasing problems of urbanisation and suburbanisation for the socially disadvantaged. Perez (2003) indicated that the determining factors of a low quality of life, health conditions and promotion of diseases for new urban families are the following: *a*. the nutritional deterioration of the childhood population due to easy access to media and an the acquisition of food that is more expensive and of lower nutritional value; *b*. the deterioration of the urban environment, which generates health problems due to the lack of suitable urban infrastructure, increasing the effects of pollution; *c*. the overcrowding of small spaces with deplorable sanitary conditions; *d*. low educational levels replicating poverty conditions; *e*. the increase of infectious diseases, particularly respiratory and gastrointestinal diseases that are generated by the contamination of water, poor sanitation and hygiene practises; and *f*. sedentary behaviours and nutritional transitions that cause an increase in obesity as a risk factor related to heart and cardiovascular diseases.

Table 2 shows the correlation analysis for the Bogotá region using the indicators of population, urban density and health for the period of study. The results indicate a direct relationship between the analysed indicators, confirming that urbanisation and suburbanisation without adequate planning affects the health and welfare of the population, mainly by health inequalities in urban areas caused by slums and informal settlements where people live in deplorable conditions, which is characteristic of several neighbouring municipalities, including Soacha, Mosquera and Facatativa. Poverty and health inequalities within and between countries contribute greatly to national and global disease burdens (WHO, 2008).

Table 2. Correlations of population, population density, urban density and the number of deaths (1998-2012)

	Population	Population density	Urban density	Number of deaths
Population	1			
Population density	0.985*	1		
Urban density	0.881*	0.840*	1	
Number of deaths	0.999*	0.985*	0.882*	1

* Significant at 0.05 level.

Table 3 shows the correlation analysis taking into account the main causes of mortality (homicides, health diseases, cerebrovascular disease, respiratory diseases, diabetes and cancer) and the indicators of population density and urban density. The table demonstrates the direct relationship between the features of urbanism and suburbanism and the health of the population in Bogotá and its neighbouring municipalities. Here, urban development and town-planning are important for creating supportive social and physical environments for the welfare of health and health equity (WHO, 2008), primarily through migration from rural and urban areas in search of new opportunities. Moreover, urbanisation and suburbanisation also have a direct relationship on violence; therefore, it is important to decrease poverty and inequality to better guarantee safe conditions, particularly for populations that live in slums and informal settlements.

The correlation values in both correlation analyses for the selected indicators are all greater than 0.8 (or in statistical terms $R > 0.8$). The closer an R value is to 1.0, the stronger the relationship between the two variables analysed, confirming that health, population and urbanism are fundamental to developing adequate regional policies that decrease health inequalities and increase welfare and development. Hence, inequalities in health in urban settings reflect, to a great extent, inequities in economic, social and living conditions that have been a hallmark of most societies since urbanisation began (Marmot, 2006).

This study's findings are important for the formulation of regional policies, particularly for the Bogotá region, which, due to the availability of environmental resources and urban services, has resulted in higher urbanisation that is characterised by housing developments and limited production chains as well as expansion to nearby municipalities without adequate economic structures. Therefore, it is essential to improve the quality of life of those who live in slums and informal settlements, generating adequate infrastructure and facilities contributing to urban governance in ways that achieve better housing, water and sanitation, transportation, education, employment, healthier working conditions and access to health-promoting interventions and health services.

Table 3. Correlations of population density, urban density, and the number and causes of deaths (1998-2012)

	Population density	Urban density	Number of deaths
Population density	1		
Urban density	0.840*	1	
Number of deaths	0.985*	0.882	1
Homicides	0.941*	0.857*	0.958
Health diseases	0.981*	0.879*	0.995
Cerebrovascular disease	0.984*	0.880*	0.998
Respiratory diseases	0.980*	0.876*	0.993*
Diabetes	0.978*	0.879*	0.993*
Cancer	0.976*	0.871*	0.990*

* Significant at 0.05 level

CONCLUSION

This study describes the effects of urbanisation and suburbanisation on health in Bogotá and its neighbouring municipalities using a set of indicators and a correlation analysis. This study demonstrates that urbanisation and suburbanisation have increased the number of deaths per year, particularly in neighbouring municipalities, which confirms that incomplete urban processes increase the vulnerabilities of poor populations due to their predisposition to localise in zones that are not adequate for urban development.

Results show that Bogotá maintains similar trends for its indicators during the sample period, whereas the neighbouring municipalities have increased their urban areas and populations without adequate planning, which has generated higher poverty, inequality and vulnerability in immigrant populations from rural areas that live in slums and informal settlements. Moreover, Chia, Cajicá and Cota show a suburbanisation process that is characterised by a rapid process of urban occupation, whereas other neighbouring municipalities show more consolidated urbanisation. In Bogotá and its neighbouring municipalities, the main causes of mortality are cancer and heart disease, which are features of urban areas. Over the last decade, Bogotá has grown more slowly (1.9% on average), whereas neighbouring municipalities have grown more rapidly (3.6% on average), particularly Soacha, Facatativa and Mosquera. Hence, the city grows on its periphery, consolidating new clusters or urban agglomerations with poor health and habitat.

These results are important for the formulation of adequate regional policies to improve sustainability in urban areas with the aim of decreasing vulnerability in these zones and increasing health equality, which is fundamental for maintaining development and the welfare of populations, formulating urban policies that achieve better housing, water and sanitation, transportation, education, employment, healthier working conditions and access to health-promoting interventions and health services.

The relationship between urbanisation and suburbanisation and health has multiple determinants and interacting factors that operate at different scale levels and require further research, particularly for developing countries where cities grow without planning and increased slums and illegal settlements deteriorate the welfare and health of the population.

References

Dureau F., Gouëset V., 2011. Patterns of Urban Settlement and Inequalities of Mobility. The Evolution of Daily Mobilities Within Two Working Class Suburbs of Bogota: Soacha and Madrid (1993-2009). *Territorios* 25, 65-93.

Graham J., Gurian P., Corella-Barud V., Avitia-Diaz R., 2004. Peri-urbanization and in-home environmental health risks: the side effects of planned and unplanned growth. *International Journal of Hygiene and Environmental Health* 207, 447-454.

Galea S., Freudenberg N., Vlahov D., 2005. Cities and population health. *Social Science & Medicine* 60, 1017-1033.

Harpham T., 2009. Urban health in developing countries: what do we know and where do we go? *Health & Place*, 15: 107-116.

Lizarazo P., 2011. Cuadernos de desarrollo Económico. CUADERNO No. 7. La Integración de la Región Capital, hacia 2038. http://www.desarrolloeconomico.gov.co/index.php /cuadernos-de-desarrollo-economico/.

Marmot M., 2006. Harveian oration. Health in an unequal world. Lancet, 368:2081–2094.

McGranahan G., Marcotullio P., Balk D., 2005. Urban Systems. Ecosystems and Human Well-Being: Current State and Trends: Findings of the Condition and Trends Working Group. Washington: Island Press; 795–825.

McMichael A., 2000. The urban environment and health in a world of increasing globalisation: issues for developing countries. *Bull World Health Organ* 78, 17–26.

Mertins, G., 2004. The population suburbanization of Santafé de Bogotá: to savanna of Bogotá. Virtual library of Republic Bank. http://www.banrepcultural.org/blaavirtual/ geografia/geografia/a.htm.

Montezuma, R., 1997. Les transports urbains: l'organisation, la gestion et le processus d'urbanisation à Bogotá [tesis doctoral], París, École nationale des ponts et chaussées, Doctorado en Urbanismo y Ordenamiento Territorial.

Moore M., Gouldb P., Keary B., 2003. Global urbanization and impact on health. *International Journal of Hygiene and Environmental Health* 206, 269-278.

Patz J., Campbell-Lendrum D., Holloway T., Foley J., 2005. Impact of regional climate change on human health. *Nature* 438, 310–317.

Pearson K., 1896. Mathematical contributions to the theory of evolution—III. Regression, heredity, and panmixia. *Philosophical Transactions of the Royal Society of London, Series A* 187: 253–318.

Perez B., 2003. Effects of Urbanization on health of population. www.onu.org/NU/ informes/fnuap.htm.

Perrow C., 1999. Normal Accidents: Living with High Risk Technologies. Princeton: Princeton University Press.

Ritter L., 2007. Urbanization and Health in the Developing World. Education project of the Global Health Education Consortium.

Snedecor W., Cochran G., 1989. Statistical Methods. 8th ed. Ames, IA: Iowa State University Press.

Stephens C., Satterthwaite D., Kris H., 2008. Urban Health in Developing Countries, International Encyclopedia of Public Health. Oxford: Academic Press, 452-463.

Tellnes G., 2005. Positive and negative public health effects of urbanisation. *European Journal of Public Health* 15, 552–553.

United Nations, 2006. World Urbanization Prospects: The 2005 Revision. New York: Population Division, Department of Economic and Social Affairs, United Nations.

Vlahov D., Galea S., 2003. Urban health: a new discipline. *Lancet* 362, 1091-1092.

Wells N., Danofrio G., 2011. Urban Planning, the Natural Environment, and Public Health. Encyclopedia of Environmental Health Elsevier, Burlington, 2011, Pages 565-575.

Whitehand J., Larkham, P., 1992. Urban Landscapes: International Perspectives. *Routledge Geography and Environment Series* 333 p.

Wolfe F., 1997. sg64: pwcorrs: Enhanced correlation display. Stata Technical Bulletin 35: 22–25. Reprinted in Stata. Technical Bulletin Reprints, vol. 6, pp. 163–167. College Station, TX: Stata Press.

World Health Organizatio (WHO), 2002. *The World Health Report* 2002. Geneva.

World Health Organization (WHO), 2008. Our cities, our health, our future. Report to the WHO Commission on Social Determinants of Health from the Knowledge Network on Urban Settings Acting on social determinants for health equity in urban settings.

World Health Organziation (WHO), 2009. Megacities and urban health. Centre for health Development (WHO Kobe Centre – WKC). www.who.or.jp.

In: Health, Violence, Environment and Human Development ... ISBN: 978-1-62948-038-1
Editors: A. Cotte Poveda and C. I. Pardo Martínez

Chapter 9

VIOLENCE AND SOCIAL ASPECTS IN THE SEVEN MOST IMPORTANT CITIES IN COLOMBIA: EVIDENCE FROM A PANEL DATA MODEL

Alexander Cotte Poveda[1]*

Department of Economics, University of Göttingen, Göttingen, Germany
Faculty of Accounting and Administration, University of La Salle, Bogotá, Colombia

ABSTRACT

This work examines existing evidence in the Colombian case regarding the effects of poverty and inequality dynamics on violence in the seven most important cities in Colombia. The long-term and short-term implications of successive increments of poverty and inequality on violence are discussed. To this end, this manuscript offers a description of the main determinants of violence in these cities because they are considered important factors of social instability. To perform this analysis, approximations using Poisson panel data analysis were generated. Evidence supporting the hypothesis under study was found, namely, that factors related to inequality, poverty and human capital directly influence violence in the cities under study and have negative effects on the economic and social development of the country because of their dynamic effects over time and their incidence rates across society.

JEL: I30, O1, O40, C33

Keywords: Poverty, Inequality, Economic development, Growth, Socio-political instability, Violence, Panel Data

---

[1] Email: alexcotte@yahoo.com.

* The author is grateful for the support provided by Deutscher Akademischer Austausch Dients (DAAD), the University of Göttingen and the University of La Salle. Any remaining errors are the responsibility of the author.

1. Introduction

Recent literature on socio-economic violence has shown that the effects of violence and instability may influence economic activity and development. Moreover, the factors leading to violence have been discussed in several studies, demonstrating that these factors may be directly related to increases in poverty, income inequality and social development (Brush 2007). In this respect, recent evidence has demonstrated that the deficiencies observed in the social equipment, infrastructure and the environmental conditions of society, as well as its social, economic, cultural and political structural characteristics, are factors that increase or decrease crime and criminality in cities (Ergun et al., 2003). Therefore, the primary aim of this chapter is to analyse the varying effects of inequality, poverty and human capital on violence in the most important cities of Colombia from 1985 to 2006, where studies (particularly at the city level) are limited in the Colombian context.

Several cross-sectional studies have found a positive association between inequality and crime; urban violence may be the result of development dynamics that differ by country (Parsley, 2001). However, violence is generated by a variety of causes. Evidence has confirmed that economic, social and political conditions are determining factors of violence. Hence, whenever a country is prone to urban violence, it is possible that this society suffers from inequality, poverty and low human capital. In specific terms, the institutional structure of a society determines the incentives of its agents with respect to economic decisions, including the features and elements that may generate urban violence.

The motivation to study this topic is the sharp increase in the average rate and numbers of homicides and the differences in this rate across the seven most important cities in Colombia. Preliminary analysis of the data suggests stability in homicide rates across several cities, despite the variability of the associated national indicator. Regardless of whether the geographic distribution of homicide rates has undergone significant change, the sharp increase in the average rate of homicides in the cities included in this study may be explained through cyclical and dynamic factors that generally affect economic factors such as unemployment, economic growth, inflation, inequality and poverty.

This study seeks to use empirical analysis to determine the dynamic changes in poverty, inequality, and economic development in the Colombian cities and to study how these changes have influenced violence in the Colombian cities that are analysed. With this in mind, quarterly data on the main cities in Colombia are analysed using an econometric Poisson panel data model with balanced data for the period 1985-2006. In this study, different estimate types are applied to control heterogeneity that emerges across the cities and to address endogeneity problems involving the explanatory variables. Empirical research has analysed aspects associated with violence and instability in comparisons across countries and over time. However, few empirical studies have investigated the dynamic of violent behaviour and instability in urban areas, which is a particular feature of this analysis. This research contributes to the existing literature by analysing the particular case of Colombian cities and by using an econometric model that is key to determining evidence for trends of urban violence and socio-economic determinants from quantitative variables.

In this context, to understand the effects that phenomena such as poverty, inequality and human capital have on violence, as well as the impacts of different socio-economic factors on the relationship between criteria that characterise the development of a country such as

Colombia. This chapter provides an analysis that differs from other conventional approaches that have been used to analyse this topic because it uses cities as the unit of analysis. The rest of the chapter is organised as follows. Section 2 reviews the literature. Section 3 describes the data and methods used based on the studies of Winkelmann (2010), Cameron and Trivedi (2010; 1998), Allison (2009), Baltagi (2008), Greene (2007), Arellano (2003), Hsiao (2003) and Wooldridge (2002). Section 4 discusses the main findings and analyses the results. Section 5 concludes the chapter.

2. Literature Review

It is widely believed that factors such as inequality, poverty and human capital directly influence urban violence, generating negative effects on the overall economic and social development of the country. Indeed, various studies report these effects using different approaches. Jong (2007) found that political instability has four dimensions: politically motivated violence, mass civil protest, instability within the political regime, and instability of the political regime. Other authors have studied the empirical correlations and theoretical linkages between political instability and economic growth, demonstrating the negative and significant relationship between these variables (Cotte, 2007; Darby et al., 2004; Ghate et al., 2003; Ades et al., 1997). Grogger (1990) studies and describes the short-term deterring effect of capital punishment. Poisson and compound-Poisson regression models are estimated to control for seasonal fluctuations and to measure the effect of executions on daily homicide count. In particular, he investigates whether the daily number of homicides in California in the early 1960s was lower on days that followed an execution (or on days leading up to one, as they were usually reported in the newspapers with a lead) than on other days. Using Poisson and negative binomial regression models, the null-hypothesis of no effect cannot be rejected.

Kelly (2000) examines the impact of inequality and crime using data from urban counties. Data are extracted from the 1991 FBI Uniform Crime Reports, which include violent crimes and property crimes. Kelly developed a Poisson quasi-likelihood estimation and found that for violent crime, the impact of inequality is large, but that it was not possible to reject the hypothesis that inequality causes violent crime for one data set. As the empirical analysis shows for counties with large populations, high-income households are less likely to live near low income ones, but inequality still induces violent crime.

The research of Plassmann and Tideman (2001) used a generalised Poisson process to examine the dynamic effects of right to carry laws on the number of various crimes: reported homicides, rapes, and robberies, using data for the U.S. states. They conclude that such laws appear to have statistically significant deterrent effects on the numbers of reported murders, rapes, and robberies.

Soares (2004) analysed the determinants of heterogeneity in crime rates across countries, finding that reductions in inequality and increases in growth and education are associated with reductions in crime rates. Moreover, in the context of violence in Indonesia, Zulfan et al. (2007) found that an emphasis on human development in the early phase of development has a strong violence-reducing impact.

In several developing countries, the extreme deprivation and oppression, high levels of inequality and poor social conditions and development are triggered by irregular armed groups that have sought to achieve political power through violence (Bodea and Elbadawi (2008), Moser and Clark (2001)). Violence in cities has been investigated using different approaches. For example, Bailey (1984) evaluated the relationship among poverty, inequality and homicide rates in the context of the USA through regression analysis, finding that these factors are determinants of homicides in cities. Loftin and Nash (1985) also studied the effects of poverty on homicide rates in the largest cities in the USA with instrumental variables and OLS estimates, demonstrating that poverty increases the homicide rate. McCall and Nieuwbeerta (2007) made a comparative analysis of homicide rates for European cities using OLS regression techniques, showing that cities' deprivation and population structure indexes are strong predictors of homicide rates. These studies have demonstrated through different approaches that homicide rates are related to differences in the social and economic factors characterising those cities. However, these researchers did not analyse the effects of human capital, development, inequality and growth in violence across specific cities in a developing country such as Colombia.

In the context of Colombia, studies have focused specifically on the analysis of inequality and quality of life index measures, in part concluding that inequality and poverty may partially explain the increase of violence in the last decade in the country (Gutierrez et al., 2002; Valenzuela, 2002; Rubio, 2000; Sarmiento, 1999). Furthermore, other studies show that the effect of volatility on economic growth in the last decade negatively affected the most vulnerable population, which led to a deterioration of many major social indicators such as poverty and social welfare and resulted in a low rate of economic growth (CGR et al., 2004, Garay, 2002).

Research on urban violence in Colombia has investigated the relationship among violence, socio-economic variables, drug trafficking, armed actors and the efficiency of justice using different econometric techniques (Sanchez and Nuñez, 2001). For example, Gaviria and Velez (2001) evaluated the distribution of crime and violence across victims using probit models; Bourguignon et al. (2002) analysed the effects of income distribution on crime with a panel of data of fixed effects; and Cotte Poveda (2011a, 2011b) studied the effects of economic development, inequality and poverty on urban violence using several panel data models. These studies have demonstrated that several socio-economic factors have effects on crime and violence in Colombian cities. However, despite the valuable contributions of previous studies, the effects of inequality, poverty and human capital on Colombian cities have not been analysed from an empirical approach.

The relevance of the chapter is that it contributes to the literature by analysing violence and economic development using a sample from a developing country (Colombia), which is characterised by a stable democratic government and little racial or religious conflict. However, this country has experienced armed conflict for decades, which has generated high rates of violence. Violence in Colombia is committed by a variety of irregular armed actors, as a result of a dangerous combination of narcotrafficking, guerrillas and paramilitary forces that operate in the name of social justice and democracy but seek only economic power (Sweig (2002)). Moreover, unlike previous studies, the model applied in this study includes social conditions, arrests and drug trade variables to determine the relationship between violence and economic development using an empirical approach. Taking into account previous studies, our understanding of poverty, human capital and inequality with respect to urban violence is limited in the case of Colombia. This chapter seeks to analyse and describe the main determinants of violence in the seven most important cities in Colombia and their relationship with social instability using a fixed-effects Poisson model and Generalized Method of Moment (GMM) for dynamic panel data models.

3. Empirical Strategy and Model Specification

3.1. Data

Data are grouped quarterly for the period from 1985-2006 for the seven most important cities in Colombia, namely, Bogotá, Medellín, Cali, Pasto, Manizales, Barranquilla and Bucaramanga. A panel is constructed from 616 observations. The dependent variable is the number of murders per 100,000 inhabitants. The primary data source is the National Policy of Colombia Thought Centre of Criminalist Research (DIJIN) (Centro de Investigaciones Criminológicas, DIJIN) and the information systems SIEDCO and CERAC. Other data sources used in this study include the Colombian defence ministry, the DNP (National Planning Department), the Colombian treasury ministry, and the DANE (Colombian Department of Statistics).

Explanatory variables are calculated from the National Survey of Households as follows: GDP per capita – aggregate-level production per capita (GDPPC by city and year); Poverty – the percentage of the population living in poverty (POV by city and year); Indigence – percentage of population living as indigent (IND by city and year); GINI – coefficient of GINI or the GINI Index by city and year; GINI Property evaluation – measured as the GINI coefficient with respect to concentration of property (GINIPE by city and year); GINI surface – measured as the GINI coefficient with respect to the concentration of land (GINISF by city and year); Primary Education – measured as primary education coverage (PRIEDU by city and year); and Secondary Education – measured as secondary education coverage (SEEDU).

Following the recent literature on this topic, the model includes aggregate-level production by city with the aim of checking the development level of each city. When the development level is checked for every city, it is possible to see the dynamic effects of inequality, poverty, and human capital on violence. Because it is important that to show the trends in the distribution of income in Colombia, we use data from nationwide household surveys periodically undertaken by the DANE (Colombian Department of Statistics). Our period of study, which runs from 1985 to 2006, is characterised by the realisation of two different surveys: the ENH (National Household Survey) and the ECH (Continuous Household Survey).

3.2. Model Specification

The econometric model used in this chapter is a fixed-effects Poisson model and Generalized Method of Moment (GMM). In this analysis, a fixed-effects Poisson model is utilised because the dependent variable (the number of murders per 100,000 inhabitants) is a count. A fixed-effects model is particularly useful in situations with omitted variables, which can be captured within the fixed effects. We utilise a city-level fixed-effects Poisson model to test whether violent activity is motivated by poverty, human capital, inequality or socio-economic development or whether it is in response to other variables. Examples of panel data where the dependent variable is a count are varied. See Winkelmann (2010), Cameron and Trivedi (2010; 1998), Allison (2009), Baltagi (2008), and Greene (2007). The general Poisson panel regression is given by:

$$\Pr(Y_{it} = y_{it} / x_{it}) = \frac{e^{-\lambda_{it}}\lambda_{it}^{y_{it}}}{y_{it}}, \lambda_i = \exp\ (\alpha + x_{it}'\beta) \tag{1}$$

where

$$y_{i,t} = 0, 1, 2,... ; i = 1,..., N ; t = 1,...., T$$

with i denoting the cities and t denoting time. The most common specification is the log linear model is:

$$\ln \lambda_{it} = \mu_i + x_{it}' \beta \tag{2}$$

where μ_i denotes the unobservable individual specific effect. For the fixed effects specification,

$$E(y_{it} / x_{it}) = \mathrm{var}(y_{it} / x_{it}) = \lambda_{it} = e^{u_i + x_{it}'\beta} \tag{3}$$

The marginal effect of a continuous variable x_k is given by,

$$\frac{\partial E(y_{it}/x_{it})}{\partial x_k} = \lambda_{it}\beta_k \tag{4}$$

In this case, one can write the likelihood function as the product of the marginals,

$$L(\beta, \lambda_{it}) = \sum_{i=1}^{N}\sum_{t=1}^{T}[-\lambda_{it} + y_{it}(u_i + x_{it}'\beta) - lny_{it}!] \tag{5}$$

The first-order conditions of this loglikelihood are given by

$$\frac{\partial L(\beta/\lambda_{it})}{\partial \beta} = \sum_{i=1}^{N}\sum_{t=1}^{T}(y_{it} - \lambda_{it})\, x_{it} = 0 \tag{6}$$

and

$$\frac{\partial L(\beta/\lambda_{it})}{\partial u_i} = \sum_{t=1}^{T}(y_{it} - \lambda_{it}) = \sum_{t=1}^{T} y_{it} - e^{u_i} e^{x_{it}'\beta} = 0 \tag{7}$$

for i = 1,.....,N. Solving for u_i in terms of β in this model gives

$$\widehat{u_i} = \ln\left[\frac{\sum_{t=1}^{T} y_{it}}{\sum_{t=1}^{T} e^{x'_{it}\beta}}\right] \quad (8)$$

This equation shows a conditional Poisson likelihood, which maximises the joint probability of (y_{i1}, y_{i2},...., y_{iT}), and conditioning on their sum yields a likelihood that is free of ui. In fact, the sum of T independent Poisson distributions, each with parameter λ_{it}, is a Poisson with parameter $\sum_{t=1}^{T} \lambda_{it}$,

$$Pr[\sum_{t=1}^{T} y_{it}] = \frac{\exp(-\sum_{t=1}^{T} \lambda_{it})(\sum_{t=1}^{T} \lambda_{it})^{\sum_{t=1}^{T} y_{it}}}{(\sum_{t=1}^{T} y_{it})!} \quad (9)$$

Because u_i is a fixed parameter, the joint probability is the product of the marginal products, which is given by:

$$Pr[y_{i1}, y_{i2}, \ldots, y_{iT}] = \frac{\exp(-\sum_{t=1}^{T} \lambda_{it}) \prod_{t=1}^{T} \lambda_{it}^{y_{it}}}{\prod_{t=1}^{T} y_{it}!} \quad (10)$$

Hence, the conditional likelihood is,

$$Pr[y_{i1}, y_{i2}, \ldots, y_{iT} | \sum_{t=1}^{T} y_{it}] = \frac{\exp(-\sum_{t=1}^{T} \lambda_{it}) \prod_{t=1}^{T} \frac{\lambda_{it}^{y_{it}}}{\prod_{t=1}^{T} y_{it}!}}{\frac{\exp(-\sum_{t=1}^{T} \lambda_{it})(\sum_{t=1}^{T} \lambda_{it})^{\sum_{t=1}^{T} y_{it}}}{(\sum_{t=1}^{T} y_{it})!}} = \frac{(\sum_{t=1}^{T} y_{it})!}{\prod_{t=1}^{T} y_{it}!} \prod_{t=1}^{T} p_{it}^{y_{it}} \quad (11)$$

where

$$P_{it} = \frac{\lambda_{it}}{\sum_{t=1}^{T} y_{it}} = \frac{e^{u_i + x'_{it}\beta}}{\sum_{t=1}^{T}(e^{u_i + x'_{it}\beta})} = \frac{e^{x'_{it}\beta}}{\sum_{t=1}^{T} e^{x'_{it}\beta}} \quad (12)$$

As is clear from this conditional likelihood, the joint probability is free of ui. In addition, zero counts in every period do not contribute to this conditional log likelihood.

We employ the Generalized Method of Moment (GMM) for dynamic panel data models in this study to be a model consistent with and efficient enough to measure the trends of violence in the cities. A Sargan test of over-identifying restrictions is also applied to assess the overall validity of the instruments. In addition the second test examines the hypothesis that the error term is not serially correlated. Generalized Method of Moments Estimation (GMM) procedure are applied to obtain consistent estimates of the variables of interest and to correct for bias caused by endogenous explanatory variables.

Models for count data and Generalized Method of Moment (GMM) have been used in different areas of applied economics, for example, in social economics, economics of crime, health economics, management, and industrial organisation. The foundational building block in this model framework is the Poisson regression model (Greene, 2007). The Poission fixed-effects model and Generalized Method of Moment (GMM) is attractive because of the ease with which the normal mixture model can be extended and adapted to new models and formulations, in this case, to the analysis of violence and socio-economic indicators.

4. EMPIRICAL FINDINGS AND ECONOMETRIC RESULTS

4.1. Description of the Main Trends in Homicides and GINI Coefficient in Colombian Cities Selected

First, we describe the main trends in homicide and GINI coefficients in the Colombian cities selected. The sample mean of homicides is 276.6, and the sample variance is 298.92 = 89341. In the case of the GINI coefficient, the sample mean is 0.49, and the variance is 0.0412 = 0.001, so there is great overdispersion. However, the homicide rate in countries in Latin America and the Caribbean is high in 2008: the rate in Honduras was 60.9, the rate in Jamaica was 59.5, the rate in Venezuela was 52, the rate in El Salvador was 51.8, and the rate in Colombia was 38.8. The size of the total violence in Colombia is astonishing. The homicide rate in Colombia in 2008 is 7.4 times higher than those of other violent Latin American countries, such as Argentina and Uruguay, 23 times that of the Canada, and, on average, 48 times higher than the homicide rates of Germany, Switzerland, Spain, and Sweden (UNODC, 2010). In some cities, violence has spread at a high rate. Medellin, Colombia's second largest city, experienced over 500 murders per 100,000 inhabitants in the early 2000s.

The seven Colombian cities have an average annual rate between 15 and 16 homicides per 100,000 inhabitants. During the sample period, in all Colombian cities, the year with the highest homicide rate was 2001, which had rates between 36 and 42 homicides per 100,000 inhabitants, whereas 1992 and 1993 were the years with the lowest homicide rates, with average annual rates between 6 and 9 homicides per 100,000 inhabitants. The density estimate shows that in recent years have reduced homicides in the cities of Colombia (see Figure 1) and National Institute of Legal Medicine and Forensic Science (2012). The wide variation in homicide rates during the sample period raises the question of whether criminological theories and associated homicide relationships established in earlier homicide studies are supported when using data based on a sample of Colombian cities.

Figure 2 reports the trends and the density estimate of GINI coefficients for the main seven cities for the period of analysis. In 1985 and 1986, the cities exhibit a downward trend in their GINI coefficients during the 1980s and early 1990s, which is subsequently reversed starting in the mid-1990s. In the cases of Bogotá, Medellin, Cali and the general aggregate of the seven cities, the corresponding GINI coefficients appear to have moved upwards in 1990s and 2000s. For the period of the 1990s, that most of the GINI coefficients exhibit an increase, indicating that the economic and financial reforms implemented in the 1990s contributed to the deterioration in income distribution in the cities of Colombia.

In general terms, to analyse the changing trends of the GINI coefficient with respect to 1990 and 2006, variations observed cannot predict long-term optimistic trends in income distribution in cities; in this chapter's analysis, most of the variations in the GINI coefficients are in the positive direction, reflecting a deterioration in inequality, the density estimate shows the considerable inequality in income (see figure 2).

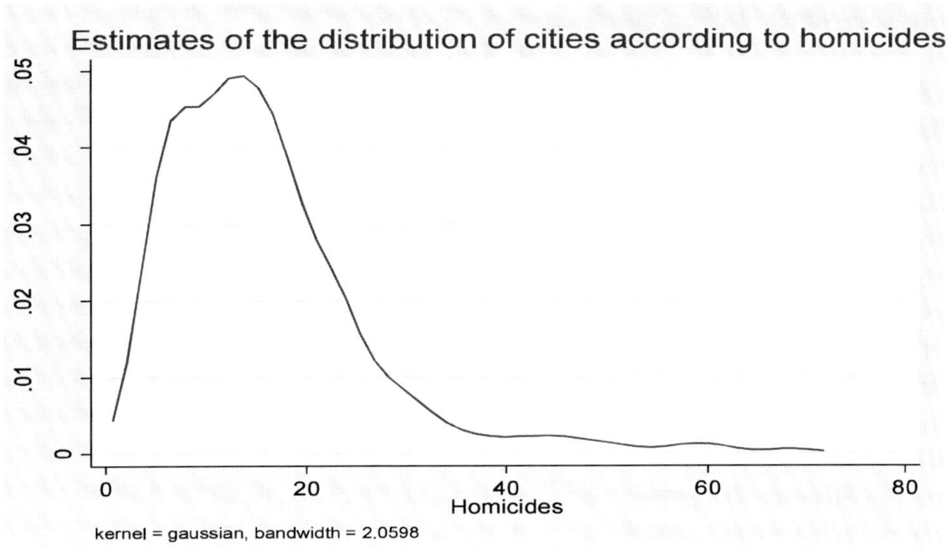

Figure 1: Homicides in cities in Colombia.

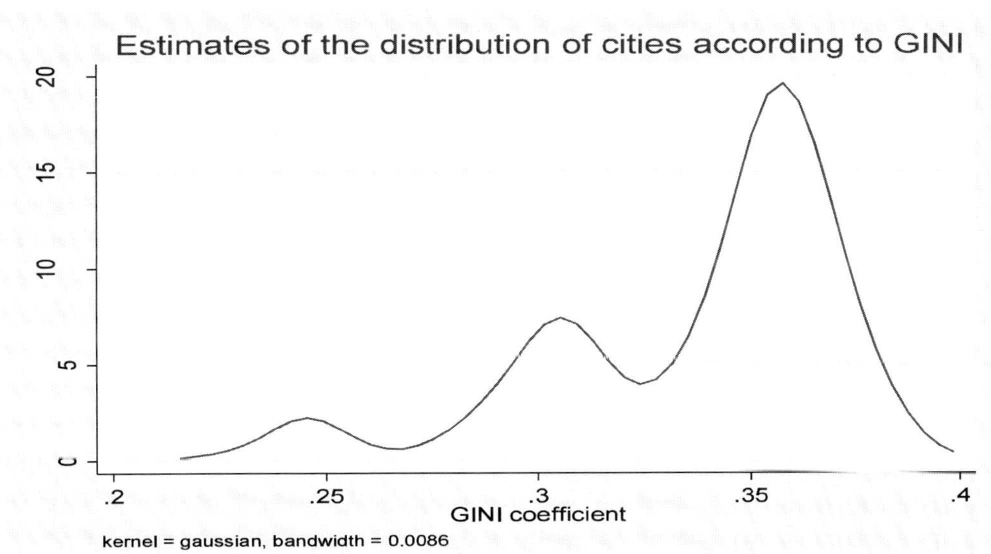

Figure 2. GINI coefficients in cities in Colombia.

4.2. Results of the Econometric Model

The following simple linear dynamic specification forms the basis for subsequent estimation:

$$V_{i,t} = \exp\,(\alpha + \beta\ V_{i,t-1} + \upsilon\ GDPPC_{i,t} + \gamma\ POV_{i,t} + \delta\ IND_{i,t} + \eta\ GINI_{i,t} + \psi\ GINIPE_{i,t} + \sigma\ GINISF_{i,t} + \phi\ PRIEDU_{i,t} + \lambda\ SEEDU_{i,t}) \quad (13)$$

Note that Vit is the number of homicides in the period t for the city i; Vit-1 is the lagged coefficient of the homicide numbers; GDPPCit is the aggregate-level production by city; POVit is the poverty level by city; INDit is the indigence level by city; GINIit is the coefficient of the Gini index in period t for city i; GINIPEit is the coefficient of the Gini index according to property evaluation in period t for city i; GINISFit is the coefficient of the Gini index according to surface in period t for city i; PRIEDUit is the average primary education level of the population by city; and SEEDUit is the average secondary education level of the population by city.

The specifications of equation (13) will be estimated in terms of level of violence. In Table 2, the different relationships between homicides, level of economic development of cities, poverty, income distribution, and human capital are shown. Table 2 reports the results of regression models using a dynamic panel for the homicide numbers by city. The results show several findings that confirm previous studies. The lagged homicide rate has a positive and significant impact on the current homicide numbers, which suggests evidence of criminal inertia over time. This fact coincides with the forecasts of the theoretical model of crime developed in recent years. Although the coefficient size of the lagged homicide rate decreases when it is controlled with specific effects, this factor continues to be significant, indicating that specific factors for each city explain only part of criminal inertia.

The GDP per capita has a negative and significant coefficient, meaning that cities with higher GDP per capita may experience higher effectiveness in the reduction of violence, which concurs with Cotte (2010) and Holmes and Gutierrez (2006). These results are important in the development of different macroeconomic policies that promote the increase of employment through directed investment and government programmes, with effects on economic growth and a decrease in violence, Carranza et al. (2010).

The coefficients of the estimations show that poverty and an unequal distribution of income have positive effects on the violence in Colombian. Recently, Holmes et al. (2010) argued that poverty, social inequality, socio-economic variables and narco-trafficking are causes of violence in Colombia. Economic inequality, as measured using the GINI index, suggests that higher inequality increases the incidence of homicide. These results remain valid when the lagged homicide rate is included and are strengthened when controlling for urban growth. Moreover, the combinations of significant effects due to the economic cycle, as well as the income distribution, indicate that the decrease in the poverty rate and the rate of indigence may be associated with large decreases in the homicide rate (Da Mata et al., 2007). Table 1 shows the principal results of the different estimations that were performed. The specifications show that in models 1, 2, and 3, the coefficients of all variables have the correct sign, with appropriate levels of significance.

Table 1. Dependent variable: Homicides

Parameter	[1]	[2]	[3]	[4]	[5]	GMM
	0.278***	0.276***	0.275***	0.283***	0.279***	
Homicides lagged one period	-0.013	-0.013	-0.013	-0.013	-0.013	0.719***
						-0.018
GDP per capita	-0.007***	-0.013***	-0.013***	-0.014***	-0.013***	-0.102*
	-0.002	-0.002	-0.002	-0.002	-0.002	-0.052
	0.064***	0.066***	0.069***		0.062***	
Poverty	-0.012	-0.012	-0.012		-0.012	0.032
						-0.022
	0.041***					
Indigence	-0.014	0.019	0.019		0.023*	0.124
		-0.014	-0.014		-0.014	-0.108
		0.989***	0.978***	1.000***	1.007***	
GINI		-0.081	-0.081	-0.08	-0.082	0.972***
						-0.122
				1.712***		
GINI Property evaluation			0.879	-0.576	0.713	2.975
			-0.579		-0.586	-3.413

Table 1. (Continued)

Parameter	[1]	[2]	[3]	[4]	[5]	GMM
				3.394***		
GINI surface				-0.104		
Primary Education					-0.348***	-0.473
					-0.109	-0.337
Secondary Education					-0.083**	-0.093**
					-0.039	-0.047
Constant						1.555***
						-0.118
Log likelihood	-14290.74	-14217.6	-14216.46	-13695.53	-14209.27	Sargan test: 0.4871
Wald chi(2)5	456.86	601.16	603.79	1635.12	618.01	Serial correlation
Prob >(chi2)	0	0	0	0	0	Firs – order: 0.008
No. Groups	7	7	7	7	7	Second – order: 0.253
No. Obs	616	616	616	616	616	616

Notes: Figures in the parentheses are standard errors.
* Significant at the 10 percent level.
** Significant at the 5 percent level.
*** Significant at the 1 percent level.

Finally, the results of estimates demonstrate the important effect of human capital on violence. First, note that the term "human capital" refers to the increases in productivity or efficiency that society acquires with improving levels of education or training that provide improved productivity. The benefits that are generated by increasing levels of education or technological innovations that are liberally diffused are thought of as a social effect. Human capital does not refer to changes in individuals. This finding indicates that those economies with higher levels, or higher averages, of human capital are more productive. In other words, human capital is also reflected in social productivity rates and economic and social stability.

The results for human capital are measured using education level, primary education coverage and enrolment in secondary education, all of which show a negative and significant impact on violence. Thus, the higher the level of human capital in a city, the lower the city's homicide rate will be, and the negative coefficient of education shows that the inverse of this relationship is also true, indicating that education plays an important role in the decrease and control of violence. In the Colombian case, the research of Vélez et al. (2002) has determined that another effect of violence is the reduction of the human capital stock by the decrease in investments in human capital.

CONCLUSION

This study analyses the effects of violence (measured as homicide numbers) on human capital and socio-economic variables in Colombian cities, taking into account different interrelationships of violence on socio-economic development, poverty and inequality. The main findings of this study indicate that there are direct effects of economic dynamics on urban homicides. Crisis periods of economic activity generate an escalation in the homicide numbers, whereas in growth periods, the homicide rate tends to decrease. Likewise, the results show that economic shocks, such as those occurring in several Colombian cities due to drug traffic, may help explain the increase in homicide numbers and the decrease in the homicide rate for the adoption measures.

To examine the different relationships between violence and its causes with objective conditions, we employ a city-specific, fixed-effect, panel Poisson regression with the aim of capturing all of the characteristics specific to each city (e.g., the degree or level of development, poverty or inequality). The results suggest that the increase in the homicide rate may occur over time after an initial event. Therefore, cities may suffer from a prolonged wave of violence. In addition, inequality, poverty and human capital are key variables that determine the level of urban violence. Policy makers should consider a combination of economic dynamics and redistributive politics focused on decreasing inequality and poverty and increasing human capital with the aim of decreasing violence. Finally, with respect to criminal inertia, the results indicate that the lagged homicide rate responds to explanatory variables. All of the findings of this study are important in the formulation of policies that increase human capital and decrease poverty and inequality, which is fundamental to incentivise economic growth and development.

References

Ades A., Chua H., 1997. Thy Neighbor's Curse: Regional Instability and Economic Growth. Journal of Economic *Growth* 2, 279–304.

Allison, P. D. 2009. Fixed Effects Regression Models. Quantitative Applications in the Social Sciences. Newbury Park, CA: Sage.

Alvarez, J., Arellano., M., 2003. The time series and cross-section asymptotics of dynamic panel data estimators. *Econometrica* 71, 1121-1159.

Arellano, M., 2003. Panel data, econometrics. Oxford, University Press.

Arellano, M., Bover, O., 1995. Another look at the instrumental-variable estimation of error-cpmponents models. *Journal of Econometrics* 68, 29-52.

Arellano, M., Bond., S., 1991. Estimation of dynamic models with error components. *Journal of the American Statistical Association* 76, 29-52.

Bailey W. 1984. Poverty, Inequality and Homicide rates. Criminology 22: 531–550.

Baltagi, B., 2008. Econometric Analysis of Panel Data, Fourth edition. Chichester: Wiley.

Blundell, R., Bond, S., 1998. Initial conditions and moment restrictions in dynamic panel data models. *Journal of Econometrics* 87, 115-143.

Bourguignon F, Nuñez J, Sanchez F. 2002. What part of the income distribution does matter for explaining crime? The case of Colombia. Working paper 2003–04. Delta and World Bank, Paris; CEDE, Universidad de los Andes, Bogota.

Brush, J., 2007. Does income inequality lead more crime? A comparison of cross-sectional and time-series analyses of United States counties. *Economics Letters* 96, 264-268.

Cameron, A. C., and Trivedi P. K. 2010. Microeconometrics using stata. Stata press.

Cameron, A. C., and Trivedi P. K.. 1998. Regression Analysis of Count Data. Cambridge: Cambridge University Press. C.

Carranza, J., Dueñas, X., Gónzalez, C., 2010. Lo dicen los datos: La violencia homicida en Colombia es un resultado del ciclo económico. Documento de Políticas Públicas, Policy Paper 2010-002. http://www.icesi.edu.co/polis/images/contenido/pdfs/dpp_2010-002.pdf.

Cotte Poveda A. 2011a. Economic Development, Inequality and Poverty: An Analysis of Urban Violence in Colombia. *Oxford Development Studies* 39: 453–468.

Cotte Poveda A. 2011b. Socio-Economic Development and Violence: An Empirical Application for Seven Metropolitan Areas in Colombia. *Peace Economics, Peace Science and Public* Policy 17, Article 7.

Cotte, A., 2010. Estimating effectiveness of the control of violence and socioeconomic development in Colombia: an application of dynamic data envelopment analysis and data panel approach. *Social Indicators Research.* DOI 10.1007/s11205-010-9772-7.

Cotte, A., 2007. Growth, Inequality and Poverty: An Analysis of the Violence in Colombia, Bogotá, Universidad de La Salle (Available at SSRN: http://ssrn.com/abstract=1012487).

Contraloría General de la República (CGR), Centro de Investigaciones para el desarrollo (CID), 2004. Welfare: Macroeconomics and Poverty. Universidad Nacional de Colombia. Facultad de Ciencias Económicas. (In Spanish).

Da Mata, D., Deichmann, U., Henderson, V., Lall, S., Wang, H., 2007. Determinants of city growth in Brazil. *Journal of urban economics.* 62, 252-272.

Darby J., Li C., Muscatelli V., 2004. Political uncertainty, public expenditure and growth. *European Journal of Political Economy* 20, 153–179.

Ergun N., Giritlioglu, C., Yirmbesoglu, F., 2003. Social change and criminality in Istanbul. Working Papers, ERSA Congress.

Frees, E., 2004. Longitudinal and panel data. Analysis and applications in the social sciences. Cambridge University Press.

Fuertes, A,. Smith, R., 2008. Panel time series. Mimeo, School of Economics Mathematics and Statistics Birkbeck University of London. http://www.ems.bbk.ac.uk/faculty/smith/PTS08.pdf.

Gamboa, L., García. A., Otero, J., 2009. Statistical inference for testing Gini coefficients: An application for Colombia. Working Papers No 65. http://www.urosario.edu.co/urosario_files/eb/ebcedbcf-1571-487e-8d27-dfcdcdcd7df0.pdf.

Garay J., 2002. Colombia between exclusion and development. Contraloria General de la Republica (In Spanish).

Gaviria A, Vélez C. 2001. Who bears the burden of crime and violence in Colombia? FEDESARROLLO and World Bank.

Gorgens, T., Skeels, C., Wourtz, A., 2008. Effcient estimation of non-linear dynamic panel data models with application to smooth transition models. Mimeo NZAE Annual Conference 2008. http://www.nzae.org.nz/conferences/2008/100708/nr1215381424.pdf

Greene, W., 2007. Functional Form and Heterogeneity in Models for Count Data. Now Publishers Inc.

Grogger, J.T. 1990. "The deterrent effect of capital punishment: an analysis of daily homicide counts," *Journal of the American Statistical Association* 85: 295-303.

Gutiérrez, J., Gallo, D., 2002. Violence and criminality in Sta Fe de Bogota: Possible determinant and relationship of double causality. *Journal Estudios de Economia y Ciudad* 10.

Hojman, D., 2004. Inequality, unemployment and crime in Latin American cities. Crime, Law & Social Change 41: 33–51.

Holmes, J., Gutierrez, S, Curtin, K., 2010. Guns, Drugs, and Development in Colombia. University of Texas Press.

Holmes, J., Gutierrez, S. 2006. The Illegal Drug Industry, Violence and the Colombian Economy: A department level analysis. *Bulletin of Latin American Research* 25, 104-118.

Hsiao, C., 2006. Panel data analysis – advantages and challenges. IEPR working paper 06.49. http://college.usc.edu/econ/IEPR/Working%20Papers/IEPR_06.49_%5bHsiao%5d.pdf

Jong-A-Pin, R., 2009. On the measurement of political instability and its impact on economic growth. *European Journal of Political Economy* 25, 15-29.

Kelly, M. 2000. "Inequality and crime," Review of Economics and Statistics 82: 530-539.

Loftin C, Nash R. 1985. An errors in variable model of the effect of poverty on urban homicide rates. *Criminology* 23: 269–287.

Mansoob, S., Zulfan, M., 2007. Socio-Economic Determinants of Everyday Violence in Indonesia: An Empirical Investigation of Javanese Districts, 1994–2003. *Journal of Peace Research*. 44, 6, 689-709.

McCall P, Nieuwbeerta P. 2007. Structural Covariates of Homicide Rates. A European City Cross-National Comparative Analysis. *Homicide Studies* 11: 167–188.

National Institute of Legal Medicine and Forensic Science (2012) Description of behaviour of Colombian homicides 2010, available at: www.medicinalegal.gov.co/images/stories/root/FORENSIS/2010/HOMICIDIO.pdf (accessed 3 Jan 2013).

Parsley, J. Travis, 2001. Basic Examination of the Correlation Between Crime Rates and Income Inequality. Regional Research Institute at West Virginia University Research Paper, vol. 19.

Plassmann, F. and Tideman T., 2001. "Does the right to carry concealed handguns deter countable crimes? only a count analysis can say," *Journal of Law and Economics* 44: 771-798.

Rubio M., 2000. Violence and Conflict in Colombia. Paz Publica, Universidad de los Andes, IUDEC, Universidad Carlos III de Madrid (In Spanish).

Sanchez F, Nuñez J. 2001. Determinants of violent crime in a highly violent country: Colombian case. Documento CEDE 2001–02 (In Spanish).

Sarmiento, A., 1999. Violence and Equity. Departamento Nacional de Planeacion. *Journal Planeacion y desarrollo* 3, 47-80 (In Spanish).

Soares R., 2004. Development, crime and punishment: accounting for the international differences in crime rates. Journal of Development Economics 73, 155– 184.

Sweig, J., (2002). What kind of war for Colombia? *Foreign Affairs* 81, 122-141

United Nations Office on Drugs and Crime (UNODC). 2007-2010 Annual Report.

Valenzuela P., 2002. Reflection about recently interpretations of Colombian violence. *Journal Reflexion Politica* 8, 125-146.

Vélez, C., Santa María, M., Millan, N., De la Briere, B., 2002. Two decades of economic and social development in urban Colombia: a mixed outcome. Archivos de Economía 192. http://www.dnp.gov.co/PortalWeb/Portals/0/archivos/documentos/DEE/Archivos_Economia/192.PDF.

Winkelmann, R., 2010. Econometric analysis of count data. Springer.

Wooldridge, J., 2002. Econometric analysis of cross section and panel data. The MIT Press.

Zulfan M., Mansoob S., 2007. Socio-Economic Determinants of Everyday Violence in Indonesia: An Empirical Investigation of Javanese Districts, 1994–2003. *Journal of Peace Research* 44, 689–709.

In: Health, Violence, Environment and Human Development ... ISBN: 978-1-62948-038-1
Editors: A. Cotte Poveda and C. I. Pardo Martínez

Chapter 10

IN SEARCH OF SUSTAINABLE DEVELOPMENT OF LA LIBERTAD REGION, PERU: A SYSTEM DYNAMICS INTEGRATION OF ECOLOGICAL, ECONOMIC AND SOCIAL ISSUES

Alfonso Martínez Valderrama[1], Silvio Martínez-Vicente[2] and Ricardo A. Rodríguez-Ulloa[3*]
[1]Simulacion Dinámica, S.L., Spain
[2]Consejo Superior de Investigaciones Científicas (CSIC), Instituto Andino de Sistemas – IAS, Perú
[3]CENTRUM Católica Business School, Pontificia Universidad Católica del Perú, Perú

ABSTRACT

The goal of this chapter is to build up a simulation model for the sustainable development of La Libertad Region in Peru, considering System Dynamics (SD) as a methodology of study. The model allows simulate diverse strategies to get economic, environmental and social results for this Peruvian region, expressing those results in a series of quantitative and qualitative indicators, looking for a sustainable development of it along to a medium / large time horizon, which can be directly controlled by the users of the model developed, through levers or management inputs, that can be specified in: 1) Public Investment; 2) Tax rates for families and businesses; 3) Transfers/ Subsidies to families; 4) Subsidies to enterprises by economic sectors; and 5) Land use policies; allowing to make strategic decisions within certain conditions, which are not controlled by the user but need to be considered in different simulated scenarios. Once the manageable levers and the external conditions have been fixed a particular scenario is arranged. In this chapter only the Base scenario and a HDI maximization scenario are compared.

The paper starts with an introduction where the stakeholders concerned with the sustainable of La Libertad region are introduced on and some qualitative and quantitative

* Email: rrodriguezu@pucp.pe.

information on La Libertad Region is shown. Afterwards the applied methodology, based on a system dynamics approach is presented, describing the model and sub-models built for the study. The model allows test diverse scenarios to support Peruvian Government investment policies for sustainable development of La Libertad Region.

Keywords: Simulation model, system dynamics, public policies, HDI, climate change

1. INTRODUCTION

While 21st century draw on becomes more evident that human institutions, both locally and globally are facing with growing economic, social and ecological challenges whose nature is progressively complex. Since the mid-1980s there is a growing increase in the interrelationships between these three factors, and on the inability of policies that do not recognize the interdependencies between the economy (including technology), social (including politics) and the environment.

The complexity of causal structures of these three supra-systems is characterized by: a). each effect has many causes, b). there exits causal feedback loops, c). time delays between actions and reactions and the acquisition of information by the actors involved, existing many non-linear relationships in between them.

On the other hand, the dynamic approach of the model introduces the temporary nature of the problems, emphasizing the importance of a long-term view, having into account the diverse worldviews of stakeholders affected by the transformation process to be implanted in the region. The stakeholders considered are (see Figure 1): 1) citizens, 2) the economic, social and environmental authorities, 3) State public institutions, 4) La Libertad's private institutions as the Chamber of Commerce, NGOs, INICAM - Research and Municipal training Institute, etc., and 5) International Agencies such as the IDB or United Nations.

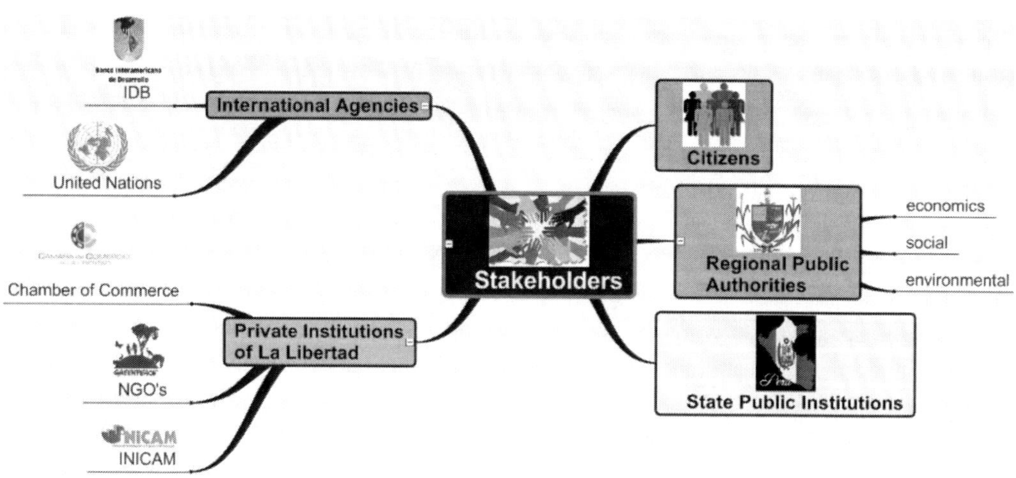

Figure 1. Mental map of stakeholders of La Libertad Region, Peru.

Preliminary Diagnosis of the Situation

The main problems faced by La Libertad region with regard to sustainable development in the middle and long term in the economic, social and environmental fields are listed below:

a) According with census data from 2005, La Libertad region is the 3rd region with more population in Peru with more than a million and a half inhabitants, representing more than 5% of Peru's population. In 2005 La Libertad had a Human Development Index (IDH) of 0.605 (8th region) while in 2002 it was of 0.585 (12th region). The most developed municipalities are primarily those of the coastal part, as shown in the following map (see Figure 2).
b) Between years 2001 and 2004 poverty indicators show a Total Poverty Index close to 50% of the population, and a slightly ascending Extreme Poverty Index over 20% of the population.
c) In 2005, the literacy rate was 91.2% (12th region). The schooling rate is 80.8% (19th region), and the index of educational achievement of 87.7% (13th region).
d) In 2005, the average life expectancy of La Libertad was 72.7 years (5th region), while Familiar Income per capita was $329.2 (8th region).
e) In 2005, the contribution of La Libertad to the Peruvian´s GDP does not exceed 10% in any of the sectors. The agricultural sector is the most important with a participation of 10% of the regional GDP.
f) In 2005 La Libertad was the 12th region in number of passengers with more than 120,000; in number of lodgings is the 5th region (more than 1000), and in number of rooms is the 4th (with more than 6500). For a region with a relatively high proportion of coastline these tourism indicators are not too high and could be improved.

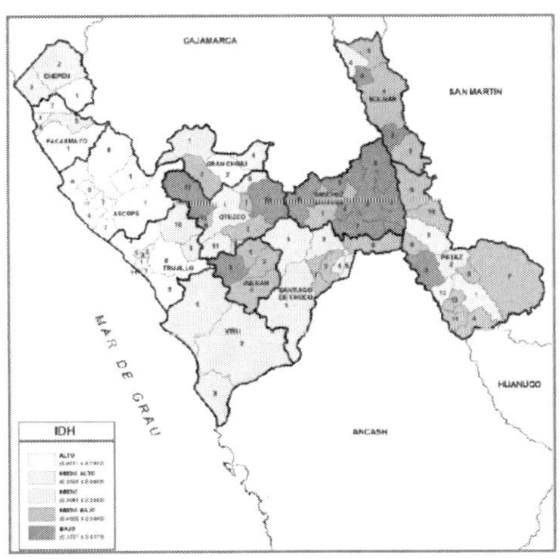

Figure 2. Map of La Libertad Region, Perú.

The main objective of the study is to help to plan strategies, policies, actions and projects that allow to fulfill the Millennium Development Goals by the 2015 and to achieve sustainable development in the region in the coming decades.

For accomplish this objective, a system dynamics simulation model is elaborated. The model allows simulate different strategies in order to improve the economic, environmental and social results of La Libertad region, showing those results in a series of qualitative and quantitative indicators.

The basic objectives of this type of models are two: first, to reproduce the overall behavior of the socio-economic system through the interconnected functioning of the multiplicity of partial mechanisms comprising it; secondly, to have a tool for territorial planning capable of simulating the impact on spatial areas previously delimited, of different strategies of economic policy. The impacts are measured on a number of variables of interest (economic, sectorial, labor market, demographic variables, land uses, infrastructure, development or environmental indicators).

2. Applied Methodology: Simulation Model with System Dynamics

Strategies are based on an optimal set of decisions with time horizon for medium and long term, which are directly controllable by user of the model to be developed, through levers or inputs, that materialize in: 1) public investment: origin of resources according to level (State or regional), by functional distribution and type of spending (infrastructure or complementary); 2) Tax rates for families and businesses; 3) Subsidies to families; 4) Subsidies to enterprises by economic sectors; and 5) land use policies.

Strategic decisions can be made within certain conditions, which are not controlled by the user but need to be considered in the different simulated scenarios, composed by a set of external factors that might occur in the uncertain future; these factors are: 1) Demographic factors (rates of birth, of potentially active population, immigration and emigration of reference, for an unemployment rate of equilibrium); 2) Characteristics of households (members per household, income recipients per household); 3) Labor & Productive characteristics (activity rates and employment distribution according to gender and educational level, sectorial productivity, wages by economic sector, other average income per capita according to household poverty status); 4) Macro-economic conditions (exchange rate, GDP deflator, interest rate, inflation, oil imports variation); 5) Trends in tourism; 6) Climate change (average precipitation, random effects of disasters resulting from El Niño like phenomenon).

Once the manageable levers and the external conditions have been fixed, a particular scenario is arranged. In this model some possible scenarios could be: 1) Base Scenario; 2) HDI maximization scenario; 3) Tourism dynamic scenario; 4) Accelerated climate change scenario; 5) Energy dependency reduction scenario; 6) Intensification of mining activity; 7) Any combination of those scenarios. For this chapter only the Base scenario and a HDI maximization scenario are compared.

Finally, quantitative and qualitative indicators and results are obtained: 1) regional GDP growth rate, 2) change rate of Population and Employment, 3) Unemployment and Employment rates, 4) GDP and Income per capita, 5) Households by poverty condition, 6) Structure of Gross Value Added (GVA) by branches of activity, 7) Occupied Population by economic sector or educational level, 8) Surfaces by type of land, and 9) Other indicators such as: HDI, Governance Index, Forest Cover Index or Water quality Index.

2.1. General Description of the System Dynamic Model

The following sub-models can be distinguished: 1) demographic; 2) labor market; 3 y 4) real and nominal economy; 5) public sector; 6) GVA sectorial distribution; 7) land uses; 8) environment, hydric resources and climate change; and 9) development indicators.

The model works with all sub-models or blocks interacting simultaneously, although for expository reasons, variables have been grouped into blocks with a certain degree of arbitrariness. The overall structure of the aggregated model may be seen in the following diagram (see Figure 3).

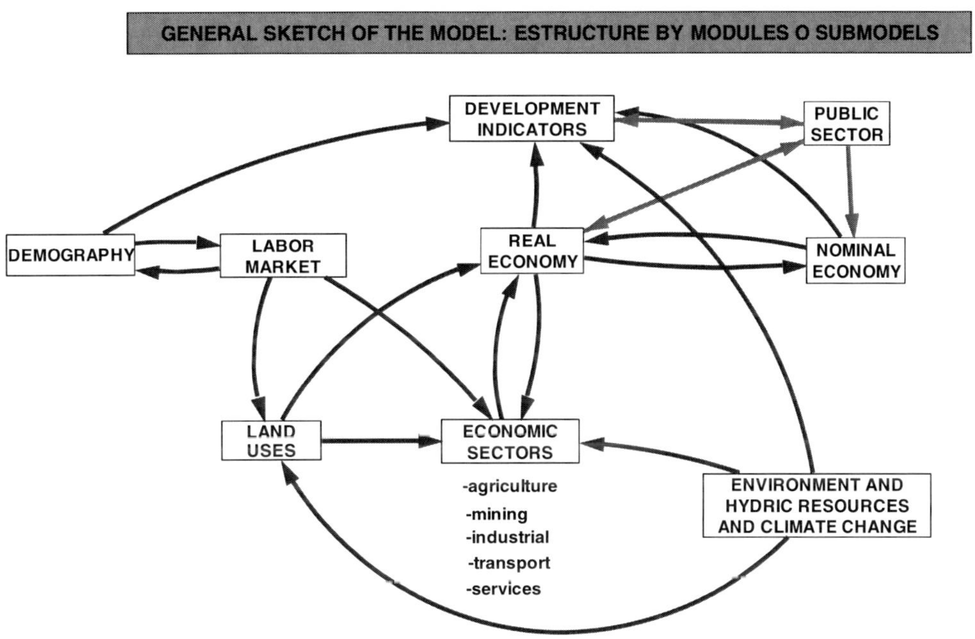

Figure 3. Overall view of the aggregated system dynamic model for studying the sustainable development of La Libertad Region, Peru.

Demographic Sub-model

The purpose of the demographic block is to calculate the evolution of the total population and its structure by age cohorts and gender. The level of total population is equal to births plus net migration less deaths. In turn, flows of births, deaths and migrations are calculated as the product of the level of population by the rates of birth, mortality and immigration / emigration respectively. In/emigration rate is a de/ increasing function of the unemployment rate, which is the ratio between the unemployed and the active population (see figure 4 stock and flow diagram).

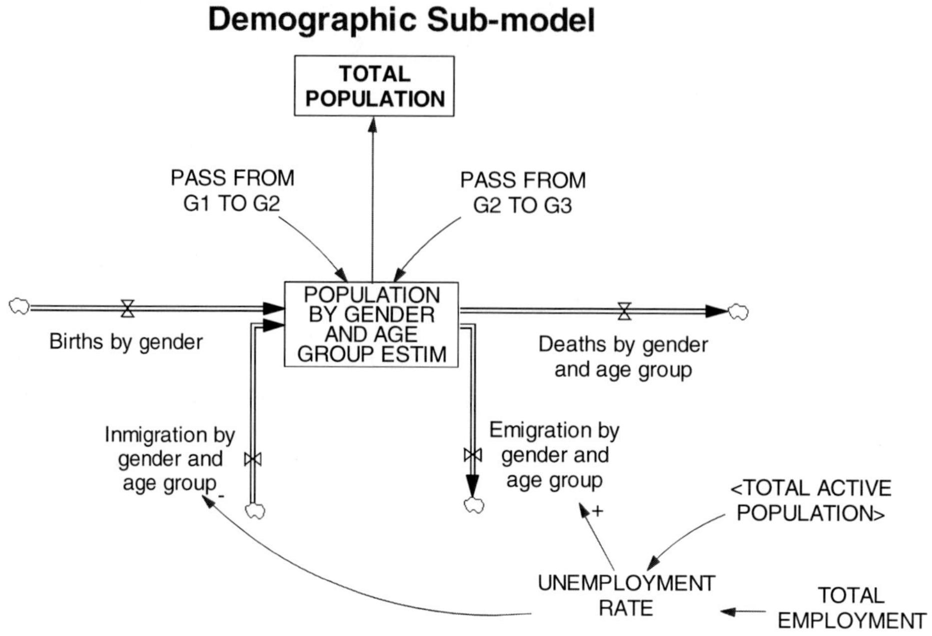

Figure 4. Demographic sub-model for the study of the sustainable development of La Libertad Region, Peru.

Labor Market Sub-model

The basic purpose of this block is to determine the Unemployment as the difference between Total Employment and the total Active Population. The most relevant equation determines the Active population, which is the product of the potentially active population by a rate of activity.

Total Employment and Sectorial Employment variables belong to the sub-model of the real economy, but in simple terms are calculated as the ratio of the gross value added by the productivity, plus the amount of employment induced by the implementation of projects in the mining or other similar activities.

Real Economy Sub-model

The fundamental objective of this block is to generate the evolution of GDP in real terms. Subsidiarily, the GVA in real terms and its distribution are calculated by sectors.

The value of real GDP is determined by a change rate estimated according to a modified version of the neoclassical model of economic growth with a Cobb-Douglas production function with diminishing returns. It is assumed the hypothesis of that the variations of the capital stock is similar to the net investment of each period. In addition, the Total Factor Productivity (TFP) is a function of the estimated value of reference and the effects of public investment in telecommunications and transport that generate induced effects common to all branches of activity. Also, the GVA in real terms is equal to GDP less taxes to companies plus subsidies to enterprises.

The total investment is made up of the total public investment and private investment. Private investment is a function of private savings (product of disposable income by the net savings propensity) plus an extra private investment (function of tourism and general GVA returns and of the Foreign Direct Investment –FDI-). The net savings propensity is a function of a time trend, of the variations in the interest rate and the exchange rate (much of the consumption goes to imported goods).

Total public investment is composed of the State investment and regional investment in the region. It should be noted that the model distinguishes between scheduled and executed public investment. The last is obtained as a product of the former by the Degree of realization of the investment, which, in turn, is a function of the proportion of investment in institutional management.

Economic Sector or Sectorial GVA Distribution Sub-model

In this block the distribution of the real GVA by sectors is carried out, multiplying the real total GVA by the fraction allocated to each sector. This fraction is variable over time, depending on the effects of subsidies and public investment in each branch of activity. The connection between the sub-models of the real economy and the nominal economy is via the deflator of GDP (with base year in 1994), which is considered an exogenous variable.

Nominal or Monetary Economy Sub-model

The fundamental objective of this sub-model is to determine the change in families income and their personal distribution. Calculations are performed in current money, since it is as well as taxes or subsidies are executed both to businesses and families.

Disposable income is equal to the salaries of employees plus the net operating profit plus net subsidies to families. In turn, the employee's remunerations are the product of sectorial employment by the average wage for each sector. The average wage is an exogenous variable which is part of the boundary conditions of each scenario. Both non-productive (families, self-employed) taxes and subsidies / transfers to families are determined as the product of the GVA by the average tax/ subsidies rate.

This sub model contains a part intended to calculate the family (and per capita) distribution of the income according to poverty condition: households in extreme poverty, households in relative poverty and non-poor households. The median household incomes are made up of the remuneration of labor and other average household incomes whose distribution is modified as a result of the effects of social investment. The dynamics in the distribution of households by poverty condition is a function of the average income for the last three periods, and of the extreme and relative poverty lines, which coincide with the annualized Cost of the basic and enlarged food basket.

Public investment in institutional management improves the efficiency of actual public revenue recovery, not only because it can allow better control of fraud; but in a positively or encourage way, because the society is more inclined to contribute when it participates in the decision-making processes. This is one of the reasons of why there is a link between the distribution of State/ regional investment mix according to functions and the productive efficiency of the regional economy.

Finally, this sub-model contains a very basic sub-block destined for modeling the tourism, for which the number of tourists is calculated through integration of annual variations of tourists. The total number of tourists has effects on water consumption, the use of land near the coast and the distribution of the GVA by sectors.

Public sector Sub-model (Investment Distribution)

This sub-model aims to simulate the evolution of the different capital endowments. Two types of expenditure are considered: infrastructure and complementary. Eleven functions are taken into account: management, social, education, health, tourism, energy, water, communications, transport, environment, production. This block contains one of the more substantial parts of the model in what refers to the regional planning: the decisions of how to allocate the public expenditure.

Sustainable Development Indexes

The Human Development Index (HDI) is defined as a geometric average of the Knowledge Index, the Longevity Index and the Standard of Living Index. The last UNDP methodology (2010) uses the following formulation:

$$\text{HDI} = (\text{Knowledge Index} * \text{Longevity Index} * \text{Standard of Living Index})^{1/3} \quad (1)$$

Each of the components is expressed with a value between 0 and 1, for which the following general formula is used:

$$\text{Index of the component} = \frac{real\ value - minimun\ value}{maximun\ value - minimun\ value} \quad (2)$$

- Knowledge Index = (Index of average time of schooling * Index of expected time of schooling)$^{1/2}$ /0.951).
- Longevity Index= (Life Expectancy at birth-20)/ (63,2).
- Standard of Living Index= [LN(GDP per capita in international dollars with an implicit rate of purchasing power parity) – LN(163)]/ [LN(108211)-LN(163)].

On the other hand a Governance Index is calculated which is a function of the public investment in management.

Environment, Hydric Resources and Climate Change Sub-model

This sub-model groups indicators that are calculated from other sub-models. For spatial reasons, basically these four are considered:

- Forest Cover (Ha)
- Protected Land (Ha)
- Index of coastal areas affected by tourism
- Index of Water Quality

The following are the main descriptions for the equations:

- The percentage of forest land is determined in the sub-model of land uses. The quality of the forest is determined, in part, by investments in environment.
- The quality of the water depends on the average pH in the water (function of mining activities) and on the population coverage of drinking water (function of infrastructure investments in sanitation, in charge of *Sedalib* Company).

- Variation of the protected area is the result of the manageable levers of the model: (a) the New Protected Surface and (b) the Fraction or rate of destruction, which ultimately has to do with the number of tourists. A standard index of its evolution is obtained from the extension of these areas.
- The Index of coastal areas affected by tourism has a behavior and an explanation similar to the protected area.
- Finally, the Index of Environmental Quality (IEQ), which is defined arbitrarily, is negatively affected by the index of affected coastline, while the rest of indexes affect it positively.

Land Uses Sub-model

This sub-model calculates the evolution of land by different types: crops, pastures, forest, protected and other uses. Actual or effective variation of surface from one type to another is subject to the following restrictions: 1) Only 7 flows are considered: gain / loss of crops, reforestation, deforestation, net change of pastures and protected areas (model levers, planned according to livestock and environmental strategic plans), and other land variation (difference between the extension of the region and surface of the rest of the land; 2) All net variations of a period are deducted from the Other surface (could be the case that the Other surface is not large enough so a fraction should be detracted also from other type of land as for example pastures or forest (in this version simplest the formulation is considered); 3) It is assumed that deforestation is equivalent to a loss of suitable forest surface (the land is no longer of forest type and passes to Other Land). The same logic applies to the reforestation and the rest of flows; 4) Protected areas may be composed of different types of land, but it is considered under this category.

The sub-model also considers that the gain rate of suitable land is a function of public investment in water, particularly in irrigation systems. The baseline scenario considers investment projects already planned as Chavimochic and Jequetepeque. For its part, the loss of suitable cropland is of exogenous and random nature, since it is caused by natural disasters like El Niño, as a consequence of Climate Change.

Reforestation depends of a fraction of public investment in environment. The average annual deforestation rate is estimated at 2.5%, according to the III national agricultural census of Peru. Finally, the model takes into account that the evolution of tourism is going to occupy a portion of coastline and will affect negatively the environmental indexes.

3. Baseline Scenario: External Conditions (Projected and Not Manageable)

Below are past and projected trends for the major external conditions which form the baseline scenario, pointing out when necessary, the main hypothesis assumed.

Demography Context

During the last decade the male and female birth rates have been falling towards some more than 2%, the female being slightly less than the male. Currently the rate of infant mortality in childbirth is still quite high, and public investments in health and maternity are projected, so birth rates again will increase slightly to levels around 3%.

Meanwhile, life expectancy has increased by more than 2 years in the last decade and it is estimated that will increase towards 78 years in 2025 (public investments in health will improve the treatment of patients, among other reasons). Mortality rates, that exclude the infant mortality in childbirth, are inversely related to life expectancy, so it is estimated a decrease (see figure 5).

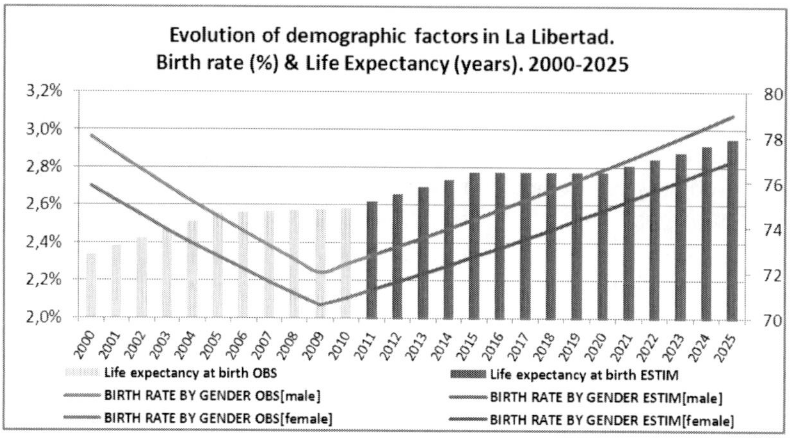

Source: Authors´ elaboration in base on INEI information.

Figure 5. Evolution of demographic factors in La Libertad Region, Peru.

The rates of Immigration according to gender and age groups (g1: less than 15 years; g2: between 15 and 65 years; g3: more than 65 years) are substantially higher in the Group g2, given that is the segment of the population of greater demographic dynamism, representing the labor force. Such dynamic is directly affected by the unemployment rate in the region, which attracts or repels more population according to its level. In the last decade the behavior of immigration in this population group has substantially differed between men and women; in the first case the immigration rate has risen from 2.8% to around 4%, while in the second case it has declined very slightly below 3.5%. Immigration rates are expected to be reduced, especially in the case of women, given the evolution of the unemployment rate, which will increase slightly. In the rest of population groups rates remain constant, and always below 1% (see figure 6).

Emigration rates are assumed constant and below 1%, except for men older than 65 years that is estimated above 10%, with a peak of more than 25% in 2009, and a gradual decline. Studies show that most of the emigration corresponds to retirees who return to their places of origin.

The baseline scenario considers a trending behavior for rates of potentially active population (PAP), in line with the increase in population with medium or high education, and with the decline in population without education or with primary school. In addition, it is expected a continuation of recent rates of public investment in education.

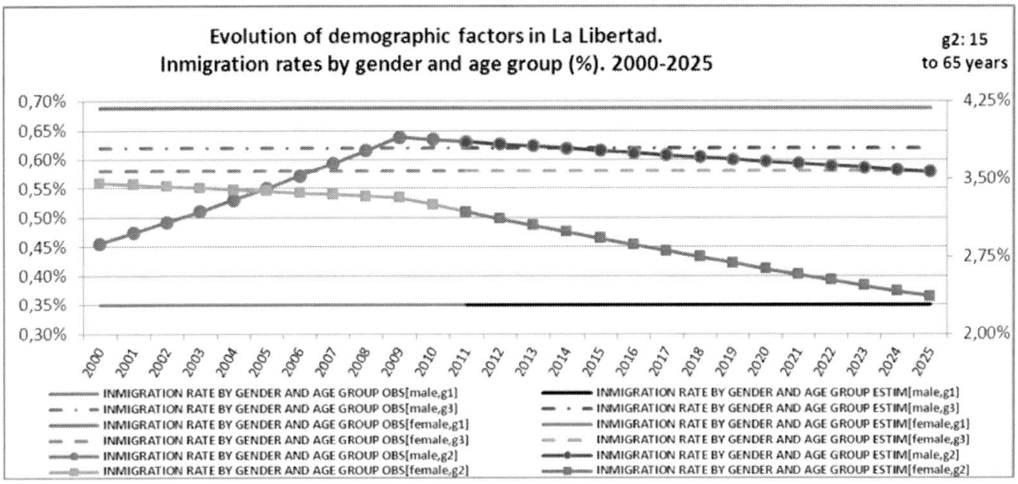

Source: Authors´ elaboration in base on INEI information.

Figure 6. Evolution of demographic factors of La Libertad Region, Peru: Immigration rates.

Labor Market and Sectorial Production Context

The higher increases of the active population occur in the female gender with medium or low education, that start with relatively low values in the year 2000 (below 45% for the population with fewer education) and above 55% in 2011. It is foresee activity rates higher than 60% by the year 2025 for all groups and genres except one.

During the last decade, the proportion of non-poor households has increased significantly while households in relative and extreme poverty have declined, having already complied, by the year 2011, the 2015 objectives of the Millennium on this issue (poverty less than 11.5% of the population). On the other hand, the baseline scenario assumes a declining evolution of the average number of members per household, in accordance with other Latin-American countries, around 3 persons per household. The number of income receivers per household is stable for each of the categories of poverty around 2 (see figure 7). The expected evolution of households by poverty condition is the consequence of various interactions between the sub-systems of the model, and is shown in the outputs section.

In the last 10 years most proportion of employees has corresponded to the segment of male population with medium levels of education (23 to 27%) or low levels (16 to 23%), followed by women with low levels of education (15 to 20%). It is estimated that the proportions of employees with medium levels of education will continue to rise until close to 32% in the case of men, and to 23% in women's case. The main reason for this is that the principal activities in the region of La Libertad belong to the agricultural sector and its related industry, mining and construction (gold, cement, etc.), and tourism to a lesser extent, that do not need much qualification on the employees (see figure 8). On the other hand, other sectors more needed of employees with high level of education, such as the academic, which is important in the region that host the second University complex of the country, do not have a very large demand for employment, at least in the considered baseline scenario (an alternative scenario could consider the creation of more technological or research centres).

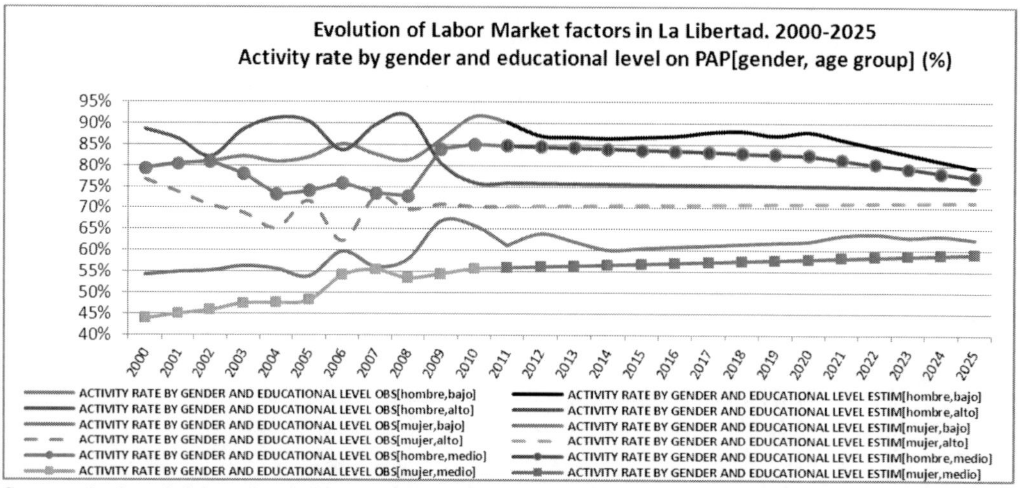

Source: Authors´ elaboration in base on INEI, MEF and MINTRA information.

Figure 7. Evolution of the Labor Market factors in La Libertad Region, Peru (2000-2025).

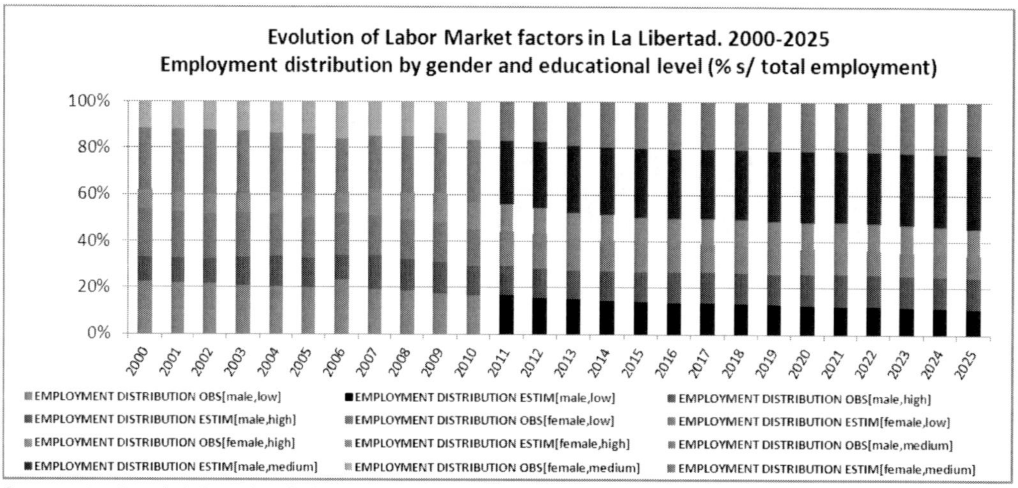

Source: Authors´ elaboration in base on INEI information.

Figure 8. Evolution of Labor Market factors in La Libertad Region (2000-2025): Employment.

In recent years, the productivity of all sectors has increased, especially in the industrial sector that has doubled in the last decade. For the baseline scenario it is assumed a rising trend, with moderated increases in the productivity of the sectors of construction, which returns to reach values close to the industrial sector towards the year 2025, and the sectors of services, logistics and government. The hypothesis considered is the expectation of a technological and infrastructure improvement of the region, as well as of the urbanization process that would generate significant induced effects in these sectors (see figure 9).

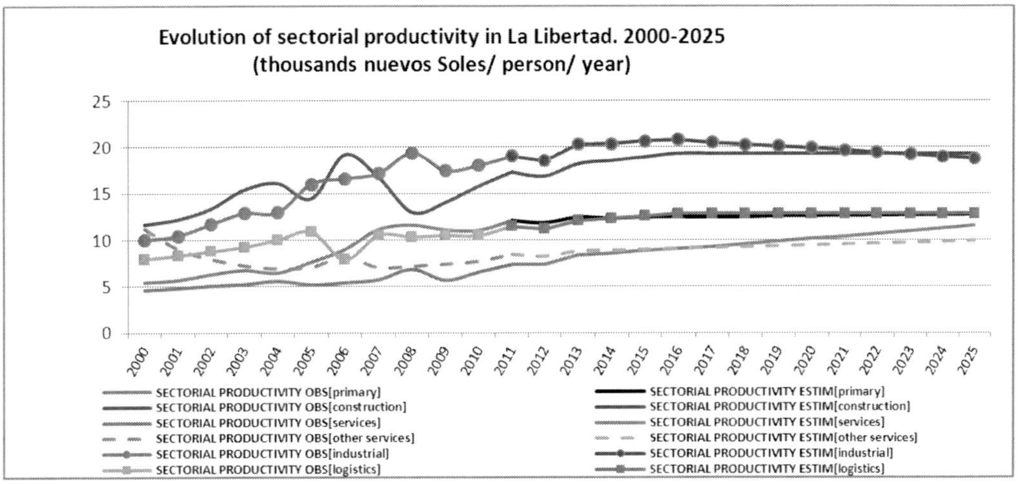

Source: Authors´ elaboration in base on INEI, MEF, Produce, La Libertad Region information.

Figure 9. Evolution of sectorial productivity in La Libertad Region (2000-2025).

Wage income data come from ENAHO surveys conducted by INEI, and have some important fluctuations, mainly in the sector of the construction for the years 2003 (>20%), 2005 (>33%), 2006 (>33%) and 2010 (>16%), in the logistics sector - transport and communications - for the year 2006 (>29%), and in the industrial sector for the year 2006 (24%). In the years 2000 and 2001 there were wages declines in the industrial sector (-10%), construction (-7%, -10% in 2004) and logistics (-1.5%).

The baseline scenario assumes higher growth rates of wages between 2011 and 2025 for the primary sector - agriculture, mining and fishing - and services (5%) because of the productive development planned in the region, the urbanization of rural areas and the promotion of tourism. The Other Services sector - public services, education, healthcare, Government, etc.- will present an annual wage increase of 3.5%, the industrial sector of 3%, the construction of 2.5%, and the logistics of 1% (see figure 10).

The disposable income of the household (of the income receivers) consists, in addition to the income from the work, of other revenues tax discounted - current transfers and remittances, self-employed income, subsidies to families, imputed rentals, donations and extraordinary income such as awards or inheritances-.

The evolution of non-labor income per capita is very different according to the condition of poverty; between 2000 and 2010 beneficiaries of non-poor households received on average 2.5 times of what the poor households did, which received on average less than 700 soles/ year. Base scenario assumes a relative increase in non-labor income per capita received by poor households (average of 1390 soles/ year for households in relative poverty, and 1290 soles/ year for households in extreme poverty) representing half of the received by the non-poor (see figure 11).

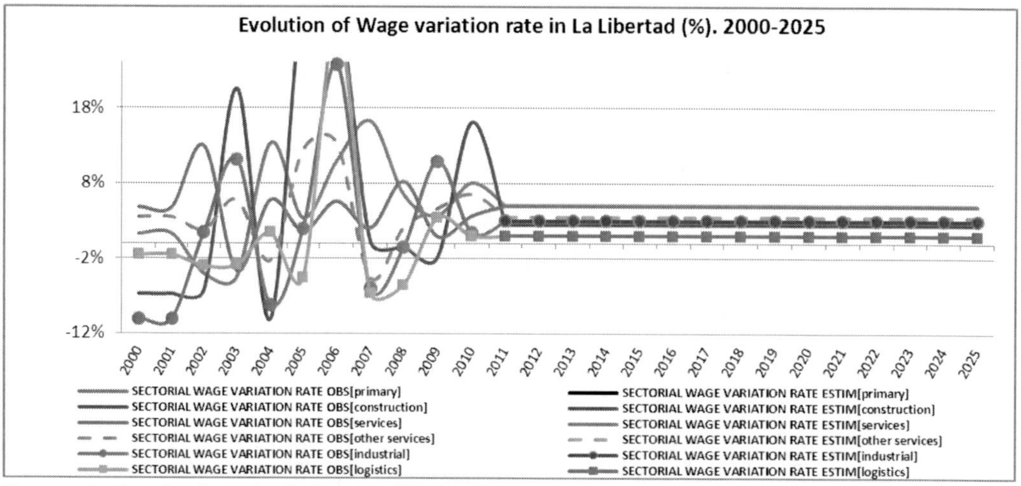

Source: Authors´ elaboration in base on INEI, MINTRA, Produce, MEF information.

Figure 10. Evolution of wage variation in La Libertad Region, Peru (2000-2025).

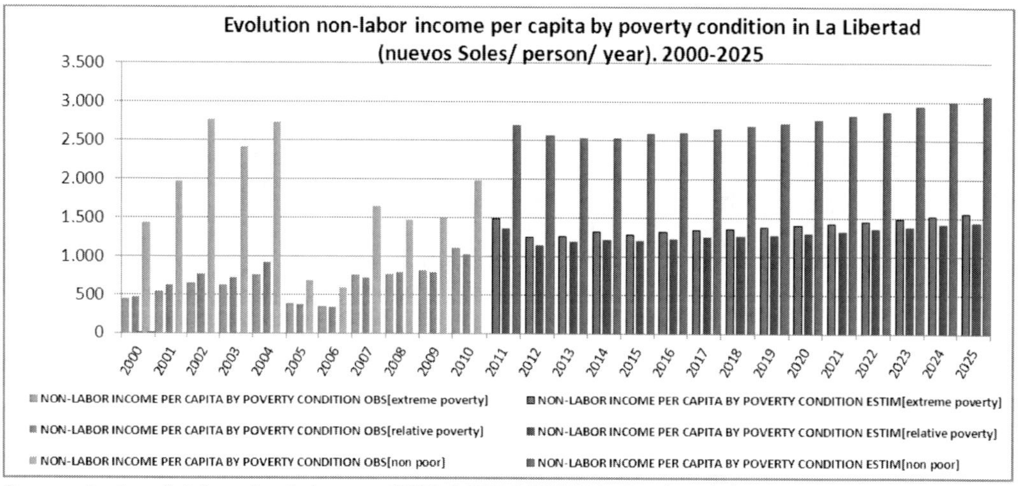

Source: Authors´ elaboration in base on INEI, MEF, MINTRA, Produce information.

Figure 11. Evolution of non-labor income per capita by poverty condition in La Libertad Región (2000-2025).

Socioeconomic Context

The average annual growth of real GDP in La Libertad during the first decade of the 21st century has been 3%. The global economic crisis of 2000-01 had little impact in the region (although the phenomenon of El Niño severely affected the region in 2001, which grew only 0.3%), while the current global economic crisis is only noticed in 2009 (-6%). The years 2006, 2007, 2010 and 2011 showed growth above 8%. Real GDP stood at 10882M soles/ year, 102% more than in the year 2000 (see figure 12).

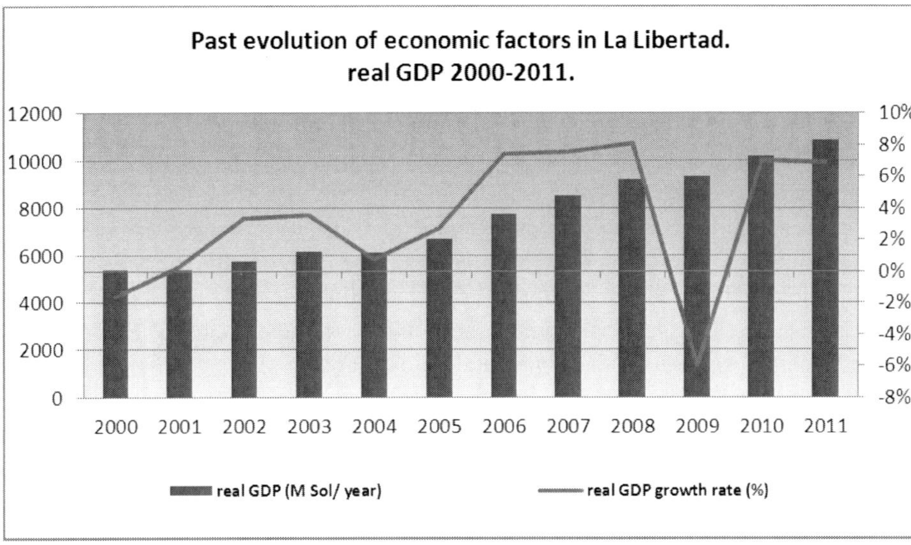

Source: Authors´ elaboration in base on INEI, MINTRA, MEF, Produce information.

Figure 12. Past evolution of economic factors in La Libertad Region: Real GDP 2000-2011.

The cost of the Basic Food Basket (BFB) or extreme poverty line, measure the monthly expenditure per capita necessary to acquire a standard-basket of food; on the other hand, the cost of the Expanded Food Basket (EFB) or (relative) poverty line extends the standard-basket of food with other commodities. Both indicators are a function of inflation. Between 2000 and 2011 the BFB increased an 84% and the EFB a 79% (see figure 13).

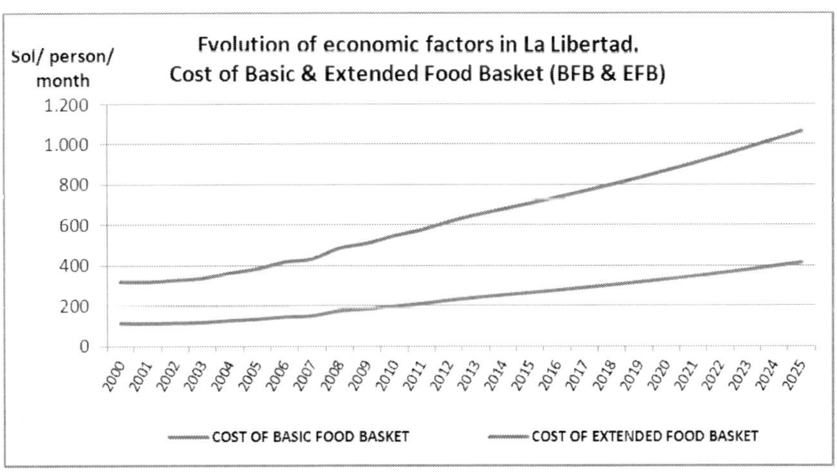

Source: Authors´ elaboration in base on INEI, MINTRA, MEF, Produce information.

Figure 13. Evolution of economic factors in La Libertad Region: Cost of basic and extended food basket.

Exchange rate of nuevos Soles per $ has been reduced from 3.5 in 2000 to less than 3 in 2011. The baseline scenario assumes its stabilization at 2.9 based on the IMF forecasts up to the year 2017. On the contrary, the deflator of the GDP, with base 1 in 1994, increases from

1.5 in 2000 to 2 in 2011. The baseline scenario maintains the trend with an average annual growth of 2%, reaching more than 2.5 in 2025. Average inflation in the period 2010 - 2010 was 2.5% per annum with various fluctuations in the years 2002 (almost 0%) and 2008 (5.8%). The baseline scenario assumes a stabilization of the inflation at 2 %.

The interest rate (annual average of the current effective lending rate for less than 1 year) decreased in the years 2000 and 2001 from 2% to 1%, and has remained stable since then. The scenario base assumes its stabilization at 1%.

The annual average variation of oil imports was close to 19% per year between 2000 and 2010, with wide fluctuations (see figure 14). The baseline scenario assumes a decrease in energy dependence, with the implementation of public policies, energy (hydro / electric plants, wind energy, solar) and environmental (bio-ethanol, palm / cane sugar cultivation, recycling).

The average annual growth in the number of tourists in the region of La Libertad was higher than 9% per year in the period 2000-2010. From the TSA (Tourism Satellite Account or CST in Spanish), the studies foresee an average growth of 13% per year in the total number of tourists received in the region for the coming years (includes internal tourism that overnight in rooms available by the hotel offer, mostly because of business).

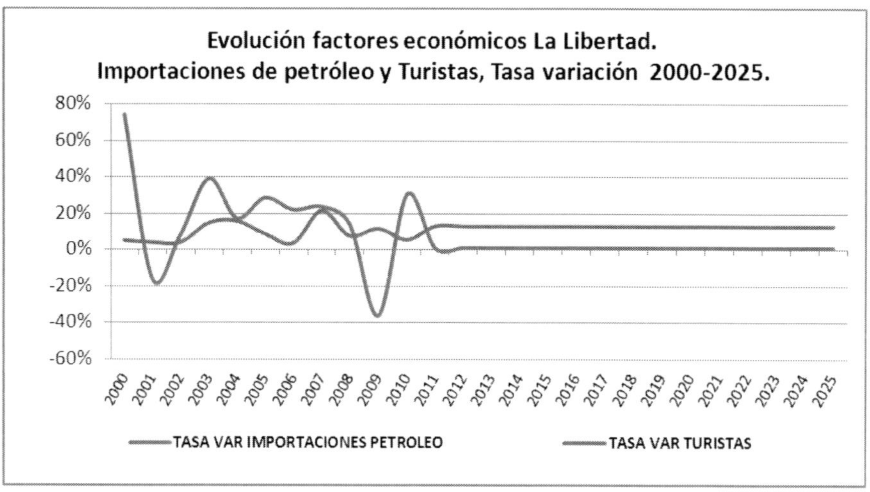

Source: Authors´ elaboration in base on INEI, MINTRA, MEF, Produce information.

Figure 14. Evolution of economic factors in La Libertad Region: Imports of petrol and tourists. Variation rate (2000-2025).

4. Scenario Planning for the Distribution of Public Investment in the Region of La Libertad: Base Scenario versus HDI Maximization Scenario

The source of information for the data between the period 2000 and 2012 is the national system of public investment (SNIP), in charge of the MEF (Economics and Finance Ministry). Planning is for the period 2013 to 2025, with five-year reviews of the goals and objectives of the Strategic Plan for the region.

Identifying the Most Important Sub-Groups of the Basic System

The model **subsystems** classify activities in La Libertad in 6 sectors: primary, industrial, construction, services, logistics, and other services. These sectors group the main different **branches of activity** used in the national accounts, namely: agriculture and fishing, mining, industry, electricity and water, construction, retail services, transport and communication, restaurants and hotels, government, and others.

The main target groups of public investment are families and businesses in the region of La Libertad. A portion of the budget for the investment projects comes from donations and transfers of international agencies, and they tend to be focused on support for the fulfillment of the objectives of the Millennium (UNDP), and for helping in emergencies constructions (e.g., floods of the El Niño phenomenon).

Identifying the Main Attributes of the Sub-Groups

Sources of Funds

There are three possible geographic segmentations that can be analyzed: State, regional and municipal. The decentralization Act enters into force as of 2004, and determines different budgetary allocations to these three levels. Given the purpose of the study, the model does not consider the municipal level, and their corresponding investments are allocated to the regional budget. Therefore two budgetary areas set out in the public investment in the region of La Libertad, which are: State and Regional.

Functions

This categorization of public investment corresponds to groups of the classification of the SNIP on the basis of programs. The model considers the following functions: management (administration, justice, defense, etc.), social (social assistance, employment benefits), education, health, tourism, energy, water (hydric resources and sanitation), communications, transport (aerial, terrestrial, metropolitan), environment and production (promotion of agricultural, livestock, fisheries, industry, or rural extension).

Typology

Two types of investment are differentiated depending on infrastructure or other additional investment (equipment, fixed assets, intangibles, services for third parties, studies, grants, etc.).

Public investment in **management** is the most relevant factor to increase the degree of implementation of the budget, both at the State and regional level; It also determines the Governance Index (GI). **Social** investment has effects on non-labor income of households; Public investment in **education** has effects on the rate of educational enrolment; Public investment in **health** has effects on the birth rate; Public investment in **tourism** has effects on the unitary GVA per tourist; Public investment in **energy** has effects on the rate of variation of oil imports; Public investment in **water resources** has effects on the growth rate of croplands and the coverage of drinking water for the population; Public investment in **communications and transport** has effects on Total Productivity Factor (TFP); Public investment in **environment and natural resources** has effects on the rate of reforestation.

Public investment in **production** has effects on sectorial productivity and the returns of GVA by branch.

Identifying the External Context

The variation in GDP will undoubtedly influence in the budgetary constraints, as well as in the public deficit (and debt). Certain budget items will depend on other internal factors such as the rate of unemployment, which has a direct influence on the volume of employment subsidies (supplementary type investment spending). On the other hand, the volume of trade (exports and imports) or indicators of tourism (especially those of foreigners) are dependent on the international economic situation and other factors as the price of oil and the exchange rate. All this can result in gaps or inefficiencies in the results obtained after the execution of the investment as a consequence of a reduction in expectations for demand, an increase in production costs, or a reduction in the productivity of the factors.

Internal Conditions or Manageable Levers

The planning proposed in the baseline scenario and the scenario for the maximization of the HDI is set out below, indicating the values of the main levers of management (managed by the Regional Government and the responsible) and pointing out the main hypothesis assumed when required. Planning is divided in two periods:

1) From 2011 to 2015: which is the year set for the first revision of the Millennium of the program of development goals of the United Nations in Peru (UNDP).
2) From 2016 to 2025. That completes the time scope in the actual case.

Taxes a Subsidies

The tax burden on families has placed at levels above 8% from 2006 on, with the exception of the years 2009 and 2010. The baseline scenario plans the maintenance of average tax burden at 8.5% (see figure 15 and 16).

On the other hand, the average subside rate for families (with respect to GDP) in the region has remained close to 5% until 2011, except in the years 2008 and 2009 due to the economic world crisis that generated more unemployment and hence more employment subsidies. The Base scenario plans to keep the rate at 5%.

Most significant subsidies to companies are in the sectors of electricity and water (average of 3% until 2011; in fact corresponds to a fraction of the taxes generated in this branch, to cover the costs of production), and agriculture and fisheries (average of 0.8% up to 2011). Mining, industry and tourism are significantly less subsidized (<0.3%) than the rest of sectors. The baseline scenario plans, an average rate of subsidies of 2.6% for electricity and water, of 0.5% for agriculture- fishing, of 0.06% for tourism, transport and industry, of 0.05% for mining, and of 0.02% for other services.

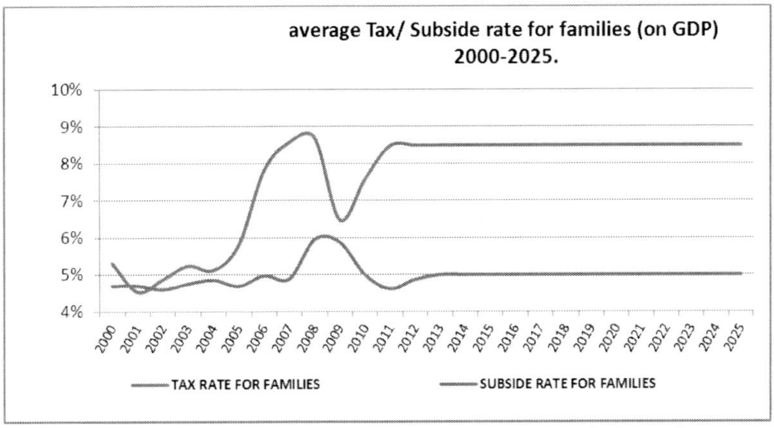

Source: Authors´ elaboration in base on INEI, MINTRA, MEF, Produce information.

Figure 15. Average tax / subside rate for families (on GDP).

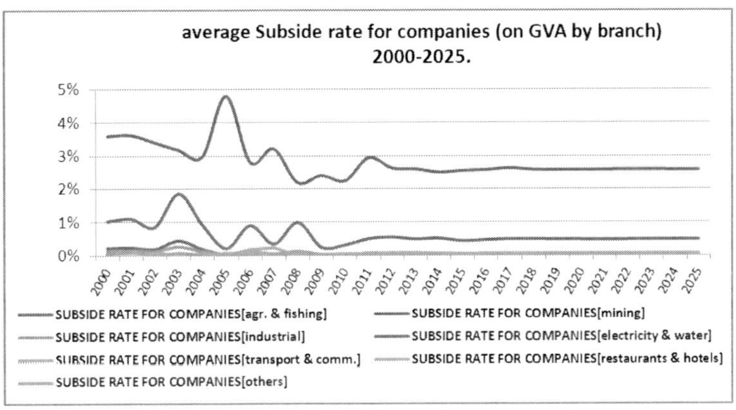

Source: Authors´ elaboration in base on INEI, MINTRA, MEF, Produce information.

Figure 16. Average subside rate for companies (on GVA by branch) (2000-2025).

The Base scenario plans the maintenance of tax rates for companies at these values (see figure 17): 13.2% for the branch of electricity and water, 11.1% for the branch agriculture and fishing, and 10.65% for the rest of branches (except for the government, which obviously does not pay taxes).

Public Investment

For the ***baseline scenario*** the planning / programming of State (left) and regional (right) public investment (left) from 2012 on is a moving average of the previous 7 years. Investment is differentiated between **infrastructure** (__) and **supplementary** (__) -equipment, fixed assets, intangibles, services for third parties, studies, grants, etc.-.

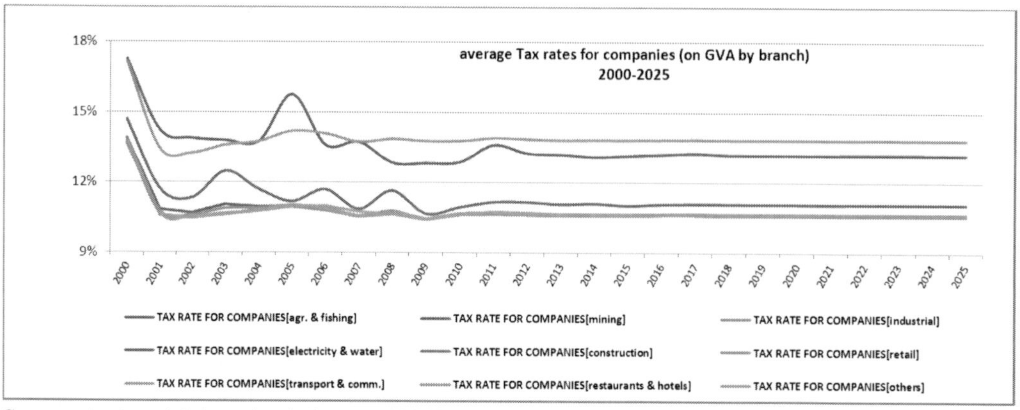

Source: Authors´ elaboration in base on INEI, MINTRA, MEF, Produce information.

Figure 17. Average tax for companies (on GVA by branch) (2000-2025).

HDI Maximization Scenario

The ***HDI maximization scenario*** optimizes the distributions of public investments (identified by a black line __) according to source, functions and types of investments and taking into account the following considerations: 1) the total State/ regional budget is equal to the baseline scenario, and 2) setting of minimum ranges in the values of investments by source, function and type, so no sudden breaks appear in projects and policies already budgeted in different strategic plans (see figure 18).

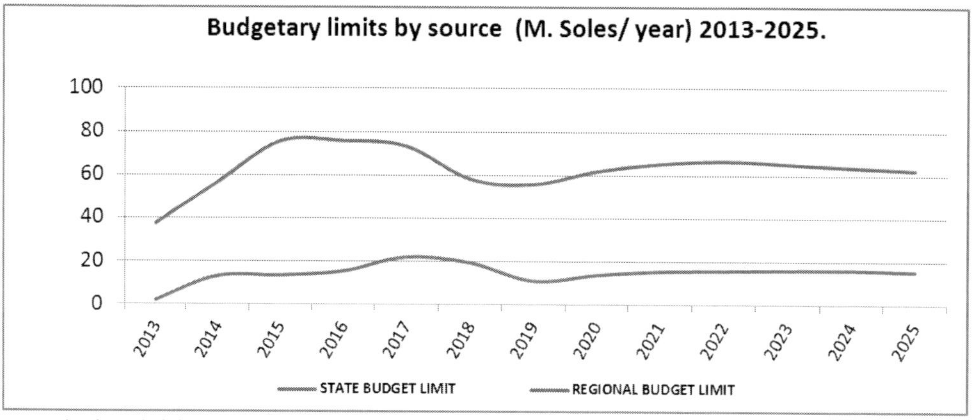

Source: Authors´ elaboration in base on INEI, MINTRA, MEF, Produce information.

Figure 18. Budgetary limits by source (2013-2025).

Management

Investment in management influences the degree of implementation of the programed investment. It includes activities as defense, justice, administration, etc. (see figure 19 and 20).

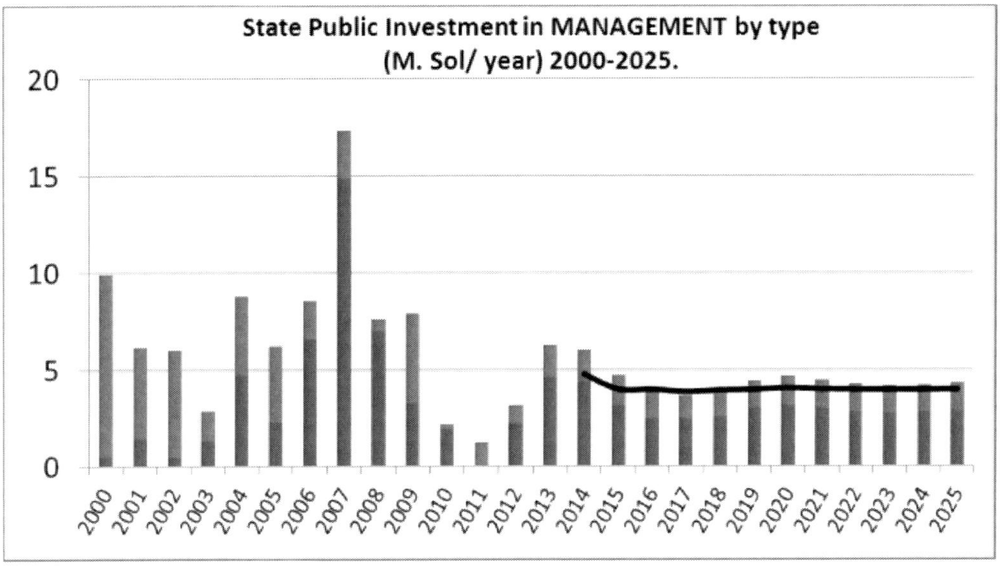

Source: Authors´ elaboration in base on INEI, MINTRA, MEF, Produce information.

Figure 19. State investment in management.

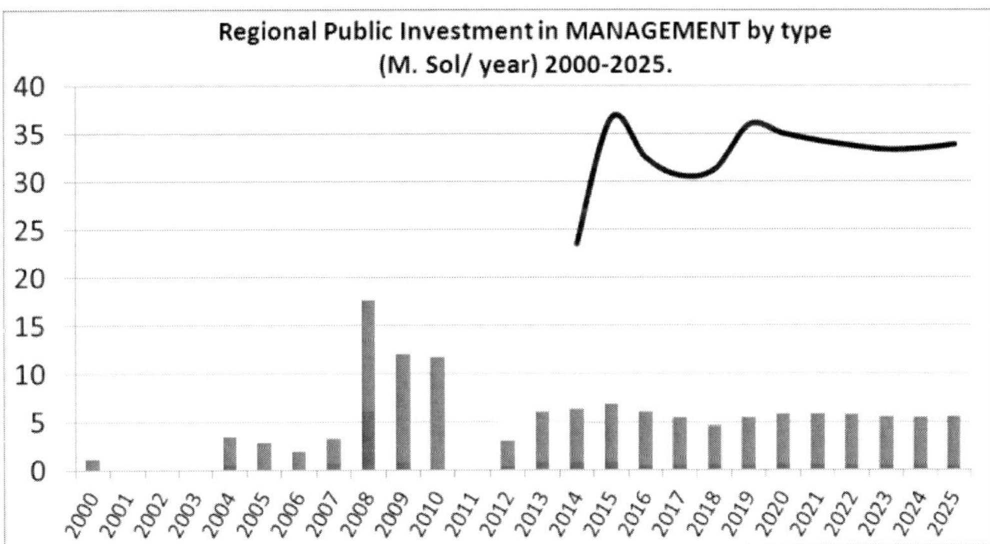

Source: Authors´ elaboration in base on INEI, MINTRA, MEF, Produce information.

Figure 20. Regional public investment in management by type.

Social

Social investment is composed of social assistance, pensions, rural development, employment subsidies, culture, sports, nursing homes, social or sports centres, etc. (see figure 21 and 22).

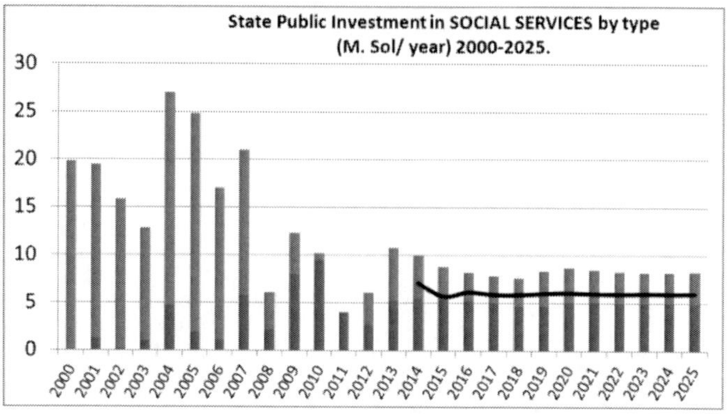

Source: Authors´ elaboration in base on INEI, MINTRA, MEF, Produce information.

Figure 21. State public investment in social services by type (2000-2025).

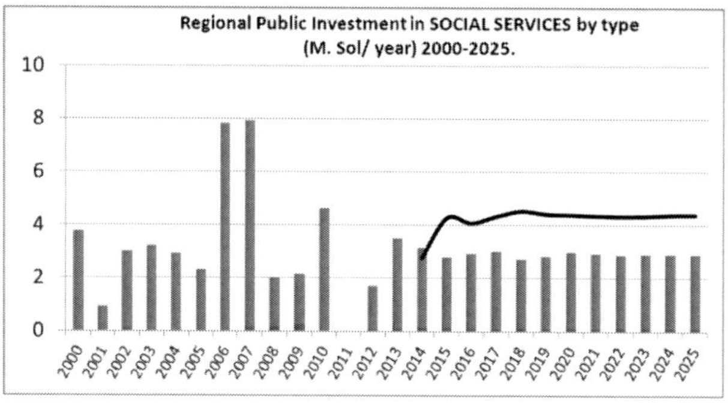

Source: Authors´ elaboration in base on INEI, MINTRA, MEF, Produce information.

Figure 22. Regional public investment in social services by type (2000-2025).

Education

La Libertad Region is the second University campus of the country with the National University of Trujillo and other universities. The best HDI scenario considers the expansion of programs of construction of educational and technological centres (see figure 23 and 24).

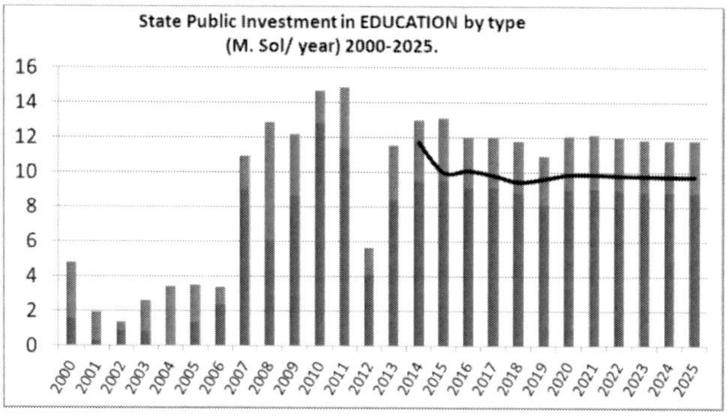

Source: Authors´ elaboration in base on INEI, MINTRA, MEF, Produce information.

Figure 23. State public investment in education by type (2000-2025).

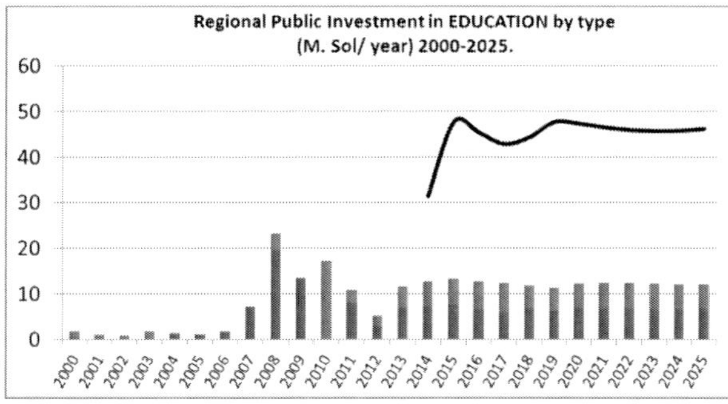

Source: Authors´ elaboration in base on INEI, MINTRA, MEF, Produce information.

Figure 24. Regional public investment in education by type (2000-2025).

Health

Investment in health has been transferred to the regional level from the year 2004 onwards (see figure 25 and 26). The baseline scenario continued with the construction of health centres, hospitals, laboratories, etc., with special emphasis on the specialty of maternity (program to reduce infant mortality).

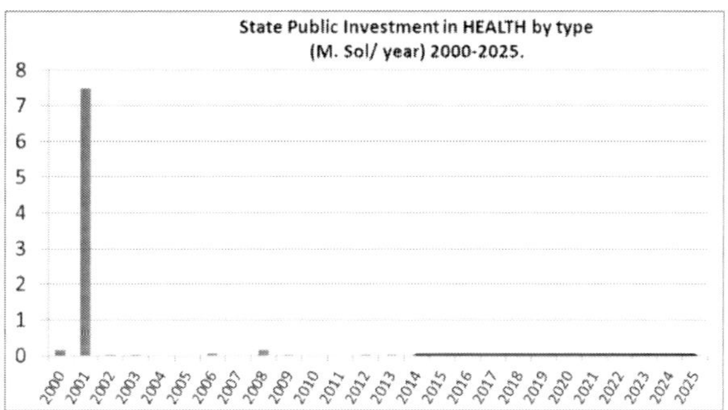

Source: Authors´ elaboration in base on INEI, MINTRA, MEF, Produce information.

Figure 25. State public investment in Health by type (2000-2025).

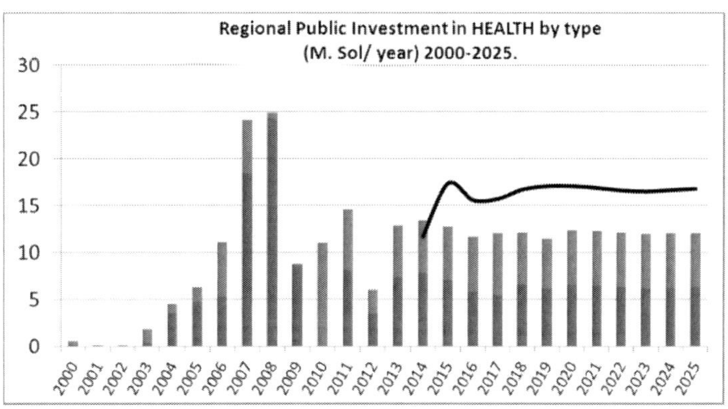

Source: Authors´ elaboration in base on INEI, MINTRA, MEF, Produce information.

Figure 26. Regional public investment in health by type (2000-2025).

Tourism

Public investments in tourism are very modest and most devoted to restoration of heritage and studies (see figure 27 and 28).

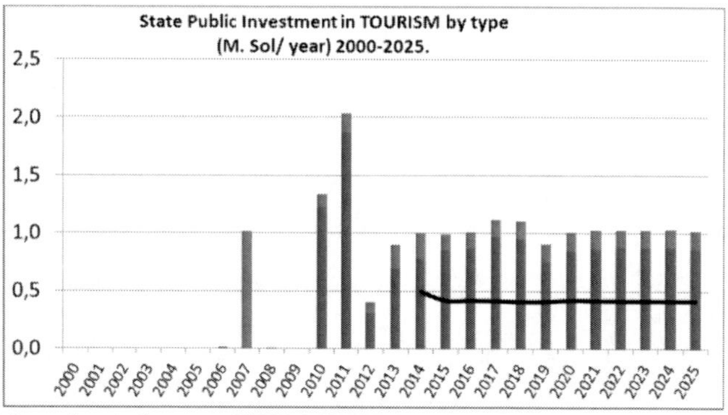

Source: Authors´ elaboration in base on INEI, MINTRA, MEF, Produce information.

Figure 27. State public invesment in tourism by type.

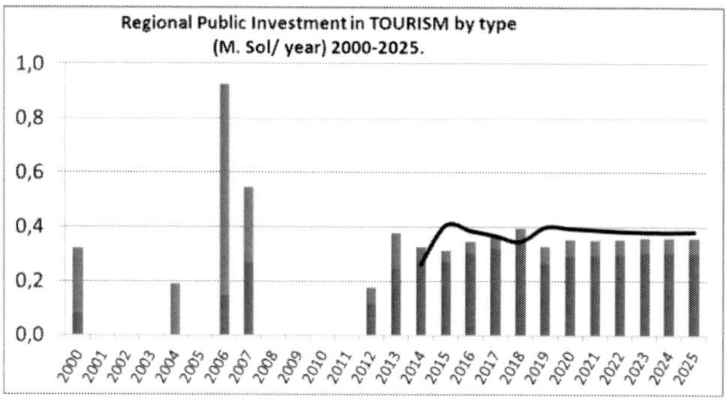

Source: Authors´ elaboration in base on INEI, MINTRA, MEF, Produce information.

Figure 28. Regional public investment in tourism by type (2000-2025).

Energy

The baseline scenario includes major State projects of construction of dams and power plants hydro/electricity, as well as regional projects of smaller scale such as the construction of electrical substations (see figure 29 and 30).

Water Resources

The baseline scenario takes into account the continuation of irrigation projects as the Chavimochic, which will begin Phase III, or the Jequetepeque-Zaña (located in the Department of Cajamarca, affecting other two departments such as La Libertad and Lambayeque). Projects of sanitation (sewerage, water purification, etc.) are also included (see figures 31and 32).

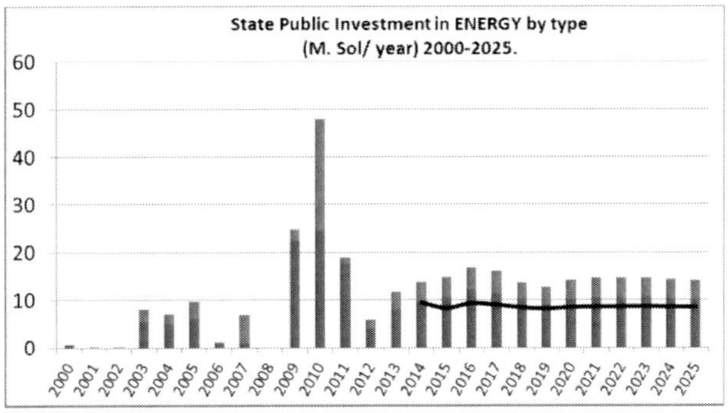

Source: Authors´ elaboration in base on INEI, MINTRA, MEF, Produce information.

Figure 29. State public investment in Energy by type (2000-2025).

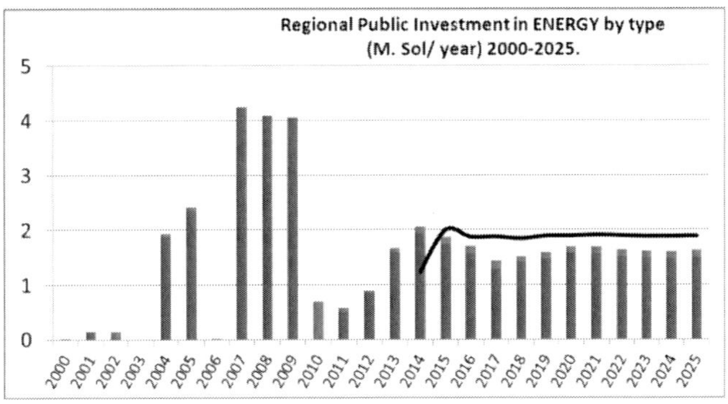

Source: Authors´ elaboration in base on INEI, MINTRA, MEF, Produce information.

Figure 30. Regional public investment in Energy by type (2000-2025).

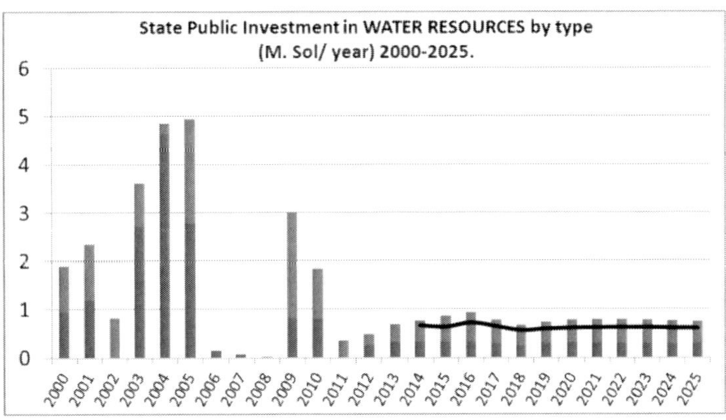

Source: Authors´ elaboration in base on INEI, MINTRA, MEF, Produce information.

Figure 31. State public investment in water resources by type (2000-2025).

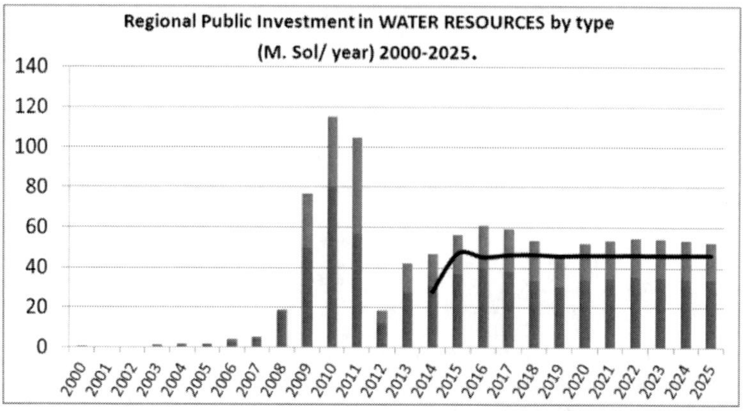

Source: Authors´ elaboration in base on INEI, MINTRA, MEF, Produce information.

Figure 32. Regional public investment in water resources by type (2000-2025).

Communication

Most State public investment is dedicated to the management of spectrum, and in some cases the installation of antennae and telecommunications stations (see figure 33).

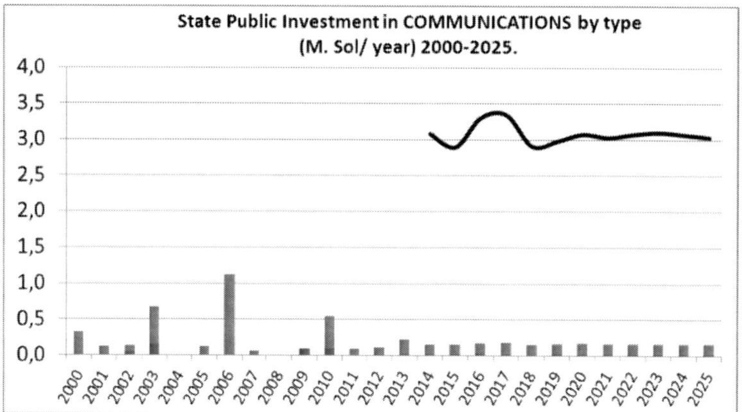

Source: Authors´ elaboration in base on INEI, MINTRA, MEF, Produce information.

Figure 33. State public investment in communications by type (2000-2025).

Transport

Most of the public investment focuses on the maintenance, rehabilitation and construction of roads; air transport has much lower budgeted investment, and even less the metropolitan transport (see figure 34 and 35).

Environment

Construction work due to disasters and emergencies (caused by unpredictable natural phenomenon such as El Niño) account for much of the environmental infrastructure investment. The Base scenario contemplates to follow programs of reforestation, recycling, cleaning and protection, and rural extension according to the strategic plans of the region (see figures 36 and 37).

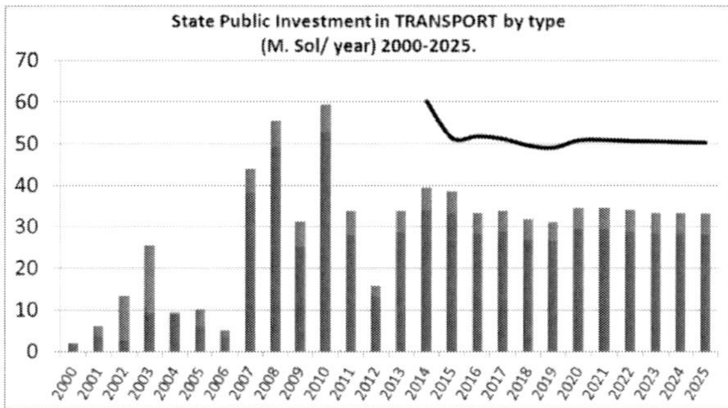

Source: Authors´ elaboration in base on INEI, MINTRA, MEF, Produce information.

Figure 34. State public investment in transport byt type (2000-2025).

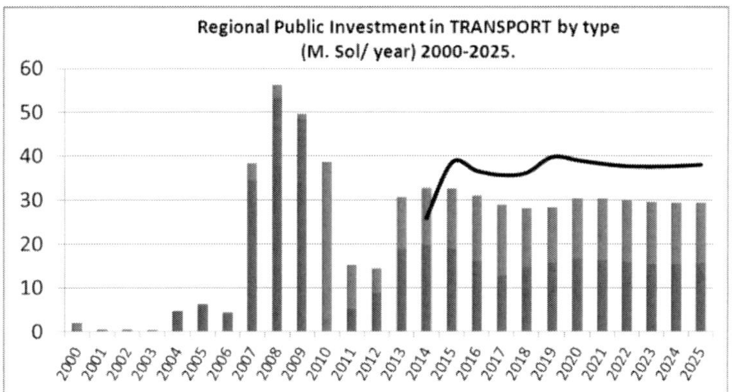

Source: Authors´ elaboration in base on INEI, MINTRA, MEF, Produce information.

Figure 35. Regional public investment in transport by type (2000 2025).

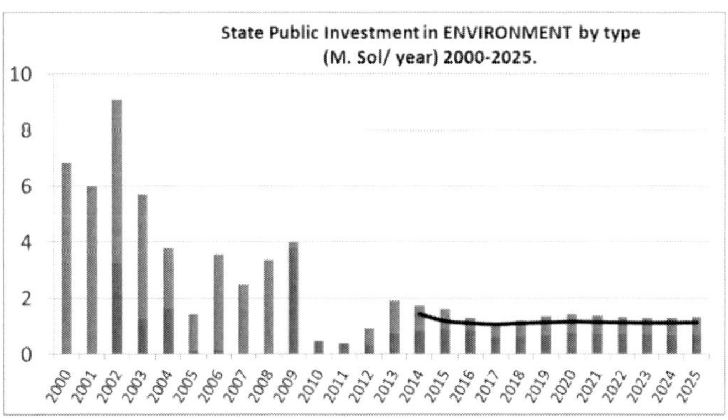

Source: Authors´ elaboration in base on INEI, MINTRA, MEF, Produce information.

Figure 36. State public investment in environment by type (2000-2025).

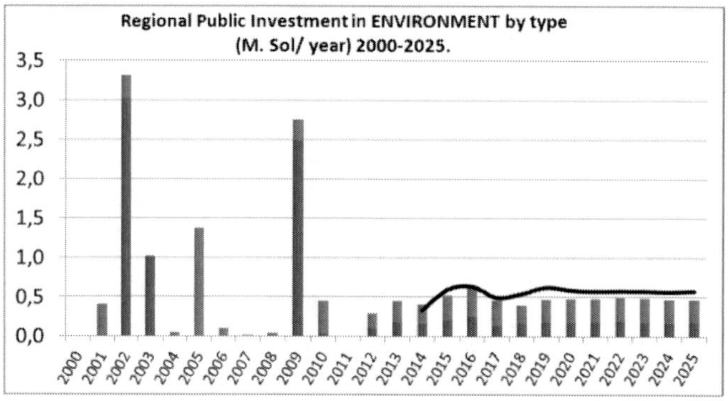

Source: Authors´ elaboration in base on INEI, MINTRA, MEF, Produce information.

Figure 37. Regional public investment in environment by type (2000-2025).

Production

It is planned to continue with programs of support, promotion, technological advancement and training in farming, fishing, mining, tourist activities and industrial activities (includes production subsidies) Figure 38 and 39 show the public investments.

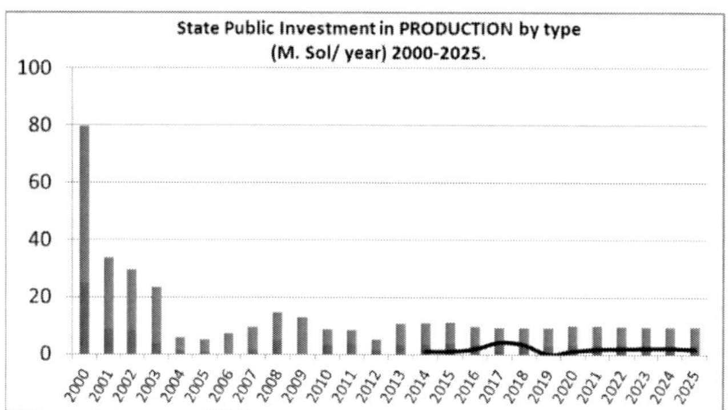

Source: Authors´ elaboration in base on INEI, MINTRA, MEF, Produce information.

Figure 38. State public investment in production by type (2000-2025).

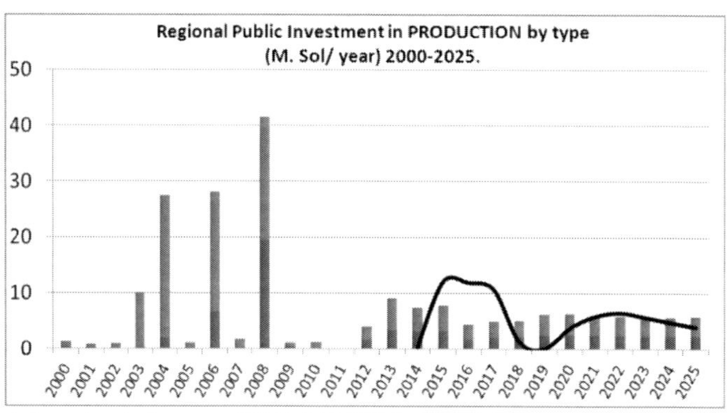

Source: Authors´ elaboration in base on INEI, MINTRA, MEF, Produce information.

Figure 39. Regional public investment in production by type (2000-2025).

Land Use and Environmental Policies

The territory of La Libertad has a total area of 2550 thousand hectares (Ha). Five types of surfaces are considered in the model according to the current use of the land, which are: crops, pastures, forest, protected, and other use. A simplified formulation of the dynamics of surface variation is used, reducing the number of flows.

The Base scenario estimates net gains of croplands and forest (surfaces of 591.4 Ha and 194.2 Ha at 2025, respectively), at the expense of Other land, due to programs of reforestation and to irrigation projects; the area of pasture remains unchanged, since the base scenario does not consider strategic plans of non-intensive cattle raising. The protected area also remains unchanged and has 152 thousands Ha (see figure 40).

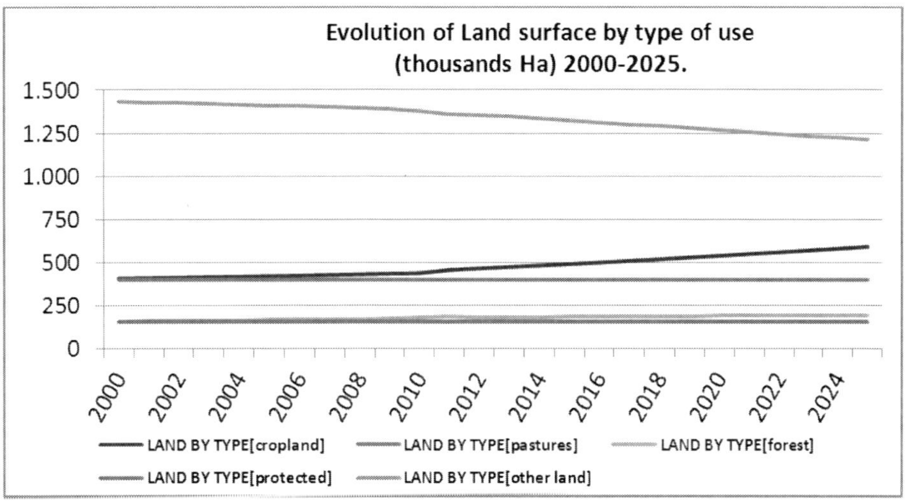

Source: Authors´ elaboration in base on INEI, MINTRA, MEF, Produce information.

Figure 40. Evolution of land surface by type of use (2000-2025).

5. Outputs of the Simulations: Base Scenario versus Optimum HDI Scenario

Demography

The simulation of the baseline scenario estimates an average annual population growth of 1.2% in the first five years (2010-2015) and of 1.5% in the next decade (2015-2025). The total population exceeds 1.85M by 2015 and 2.14M in 2025. The proportion of the population between 15 and 65 years old decreased from 63.8% in 2010 to 62.8% in 2025, while the population less than 15 years old decreased from 30.1% to 29.5%, and the proportion of the population older than 65 years increased from 6.2% to 7.7% (see figure 41 and 42).

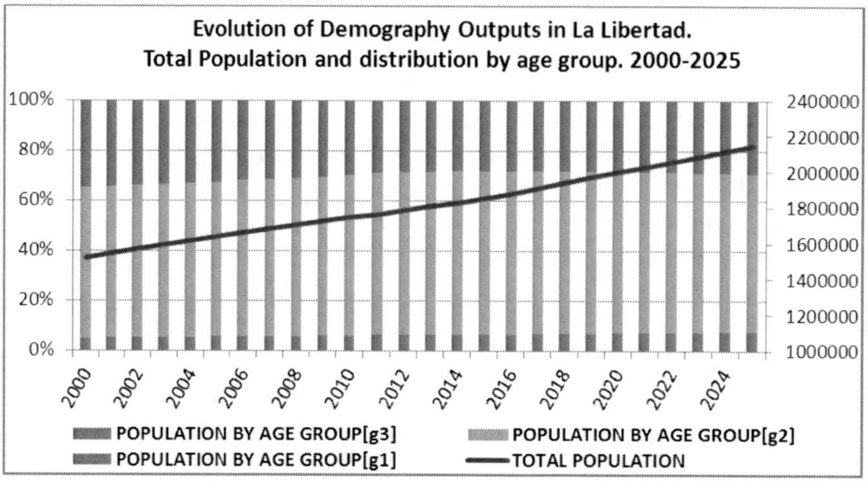

Source: Authors´ elaboration in base on INEI, MINTRA, MEF, Produce information.

Figure 41. Evolution of demography outputs in La Libertad Region, Peru.

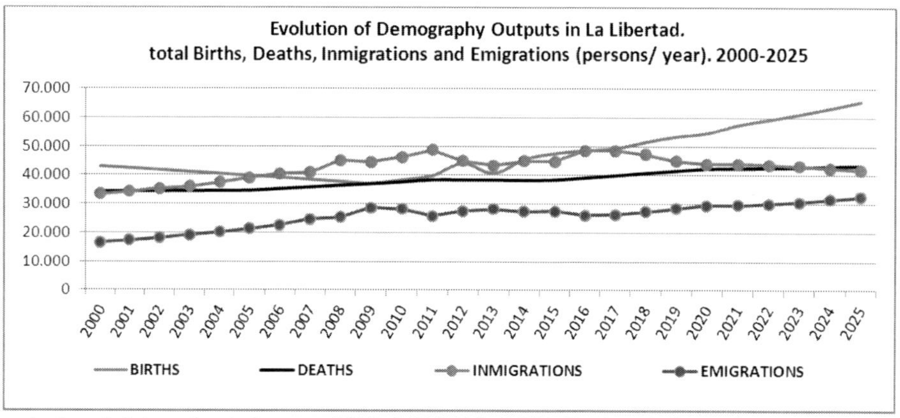

Source: Authors´ elaboration in base on INEI, MINTRA, MEF, Produce information.

Figure 42. Evolution of demography outputs in La Libertad Region, Peru: Total births, deaths, immigrations and emigrations (2000-2025).

The simulation of the baseline scenario has resulted in the following annual average growth of the flows that affect the level of population (see figure 43 and 44).

average annual Growth Rate (%)

Total Flows	2010-2015	2015-2025	2010-2025
BIRTHS	4.37%	3.27%	3.63%
DEATHS	0.42%	1.22%	0.96%
INMIGRATION	-0.64%	-0.70%	-0.68%
EMIGRATION	-0.55%	1.72%	0.96%

Source: Authors´ elaboration in base on INEI, MINTRA, MEF, Produce information

Figure 43. Average annual growth rate.

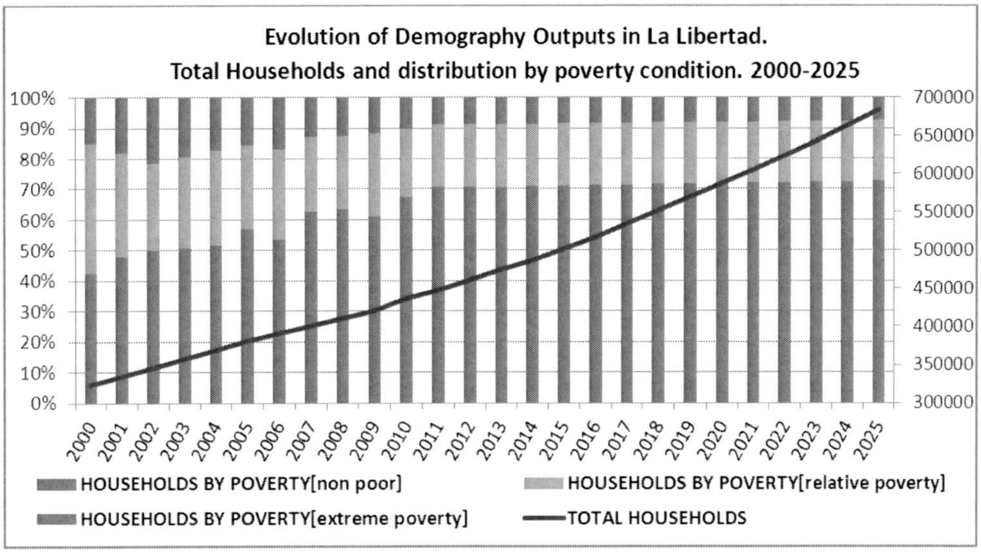

Source: Authors´ elaboration in base on INEI, MINTRA, MEF, Produce information.

Figure 44. Evolution of demography outputs in La Libertad Region, Peru: Total households and distribution by poverty condition (2000-2025).

Simulation of the baseline scenario has resulted in an average annual growth of the households of 3% in the first five years and in the following decade. Households exceed 501 thousands by 2015 and 683 thousands in 2025. The proportion of non-poor households increase of 67.4% in 2010 to 71% in 2015, and 72.6% in 2025; Meanwhile, households in relative poverty passed from 22.4% in 2010 to 20.5% in 2015, and 20% by 2025, and the proportion of households in poverty extreme is reduced from 10.2% in 2010 to 8.4% in 2015, and 7.4% in 2025. This means that results successfully overpass the Millennium poverty goal of 11.5% by 2015.

Labor Market and Production

The simulation of the baseline scenario estimates an average annual growth of the active population of 1.27% in the first five years, and of 1.94% over the next decade. The total active population exceeds the 985 thousands in 2015 and the 1.19 million in 2025. The proportion of work force according to educational level rises at 2% per year for the high educated, at 3.3% for medium educated, and falls -1.5% for low educated between 2010 and 2025.

Total employment is growing at an average annual rate of 1.22% during the first five years, and 2.88% over the next decade. The unemployment rate will gradually increase reaching 8% by the year 2025.(see figure 45)

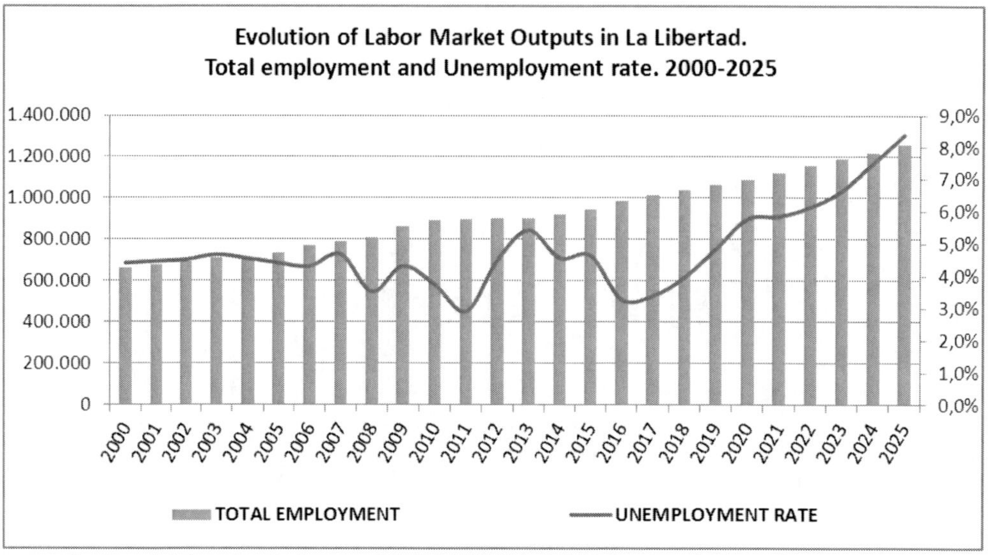

Source: Authors´ elaboration in base on INEI, MINTRA, MEF, Produce information.

Figure 45. Evolution of labor market outputs in La Libertad Region, Peru: Total employment and unemployment rate (2000-2025).

Between 2010 and 2025 the growth of employment is higher when higher is the degree of education; employees with a high level of education are growing at an average annual rate of 6%, while employees with a medium level of education grows at 4.5%; finally those with low level of education decreases at -0.2%.

The average annual growth of employment between 2010 and 2025 according to sectors are: 2.85% for services, 2.75% for the industrial, 2.22% for the logistics of 2.12% for primary, 1.87% for construction, and 1.48% for the government and other services (see figure 46).

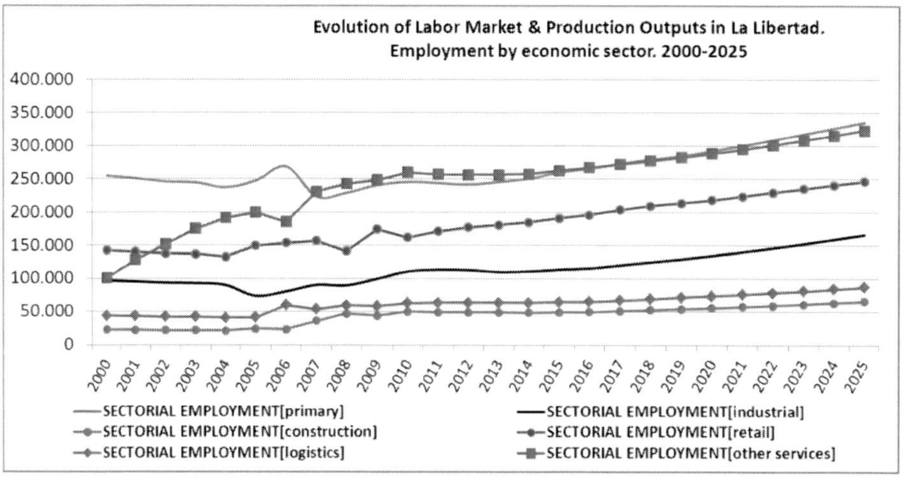

Source: Authors´ elaboration in base on INEI, MINTRA, MEF, Produce information.

Figure 46. Evolution of labor market and production output in La Libertad Region, Peru: Employment by economic sector (2000-2025).

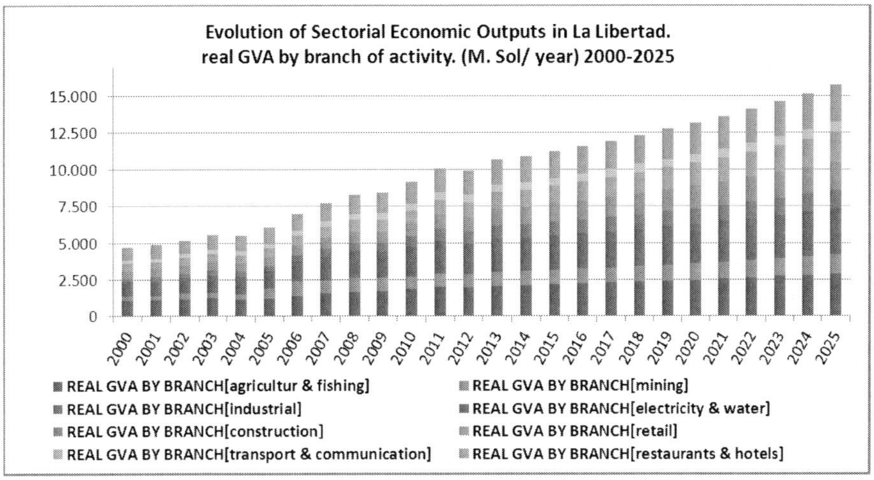

Source: Authors´ elaboration in base on INEI, MINTRA, MEF, Produce information.

Figure 47. Evolution of sectorial economic output in La Libertad Region, Perú: Real GVA by branch of activity (2000-2025).

The average annual growth of real GVA between 2010 and 2025 according to branches of activity are: 9.2% for restaurants and hotels, 5.8% for retail, 4.4% for electricity and water, 3.6% for transport and communication, 3.3% for other services and construction, 3.1% for agriculture and fisheries, 2.9% for industry, 2.8% for the government, and 2.7% for mining. The proportion of touristic GVA passes from representing 3% in 2010 to 8.6% in 2025 (see figure 47).

In the baseline scenario average annual growth of wages according to sectors are: rises of 1% and 5% for primary and retail services, 3.5% for the government sector and other services, 3% for industry, 2.5% for construction, and 1% for logistics (see figure 48).

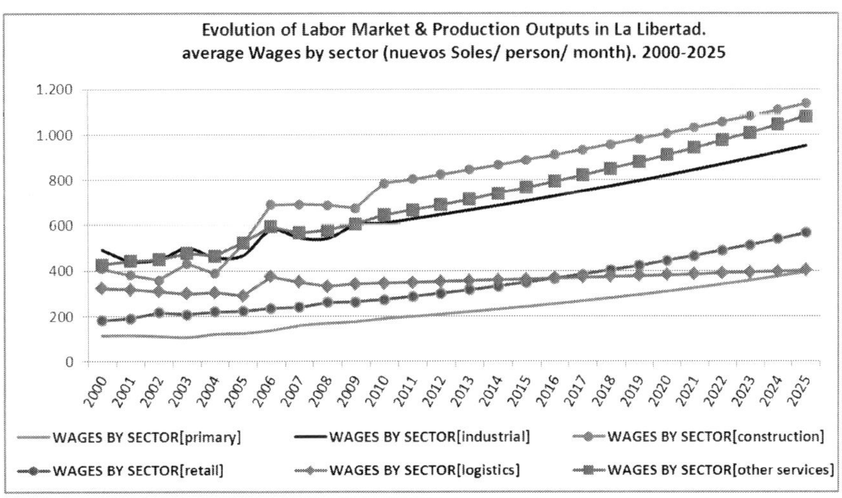

Source: Authors´ elaboration in base on INEI, MINTRA, MEF, Produce information.

Figure 48. Evolution of labor market & production outputs in La Libertad Region, Peru: Average wages by sector (2000-2025).

Socio-Economics and Households Income

The growth of real GDP in the region is stable with an annual average rate above 3% (see figure 49).

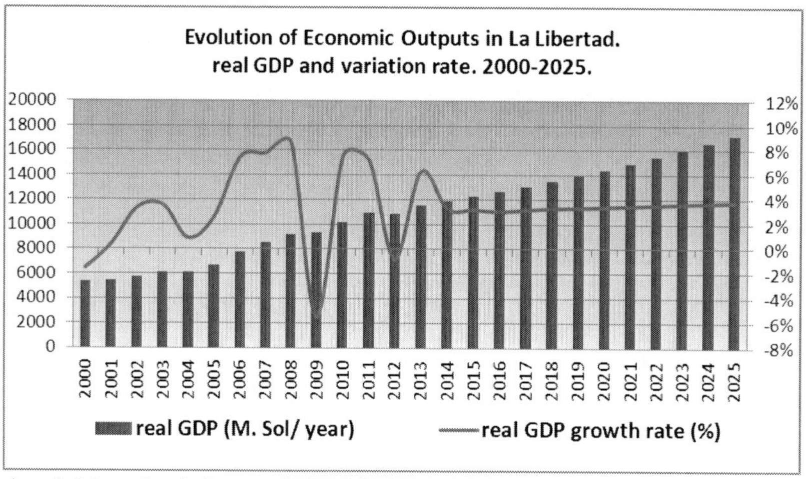

Source: Authors´ elaboration in base on INEI, MINTRA, MEF, Produce information.

Figure 49. Evolution of economic output in La Libertad Region, Peru: Real GDP and variation rate (2000-2025).

Real GDP per capita of the region passes from 6200 new Soles in 2010 to more than 8200 by the year 2025, which represents an accumulated increase of 41%; the distribution of income per household by poverty condition tends to improve the indexes of equity like the Gini coefficient or the Lorentz curve, so that the average income for households in extreme poverty increases by 6.9%, for households in relative poverty increases by 5.6%, and for non poor households by 1.9% (see figure 50).

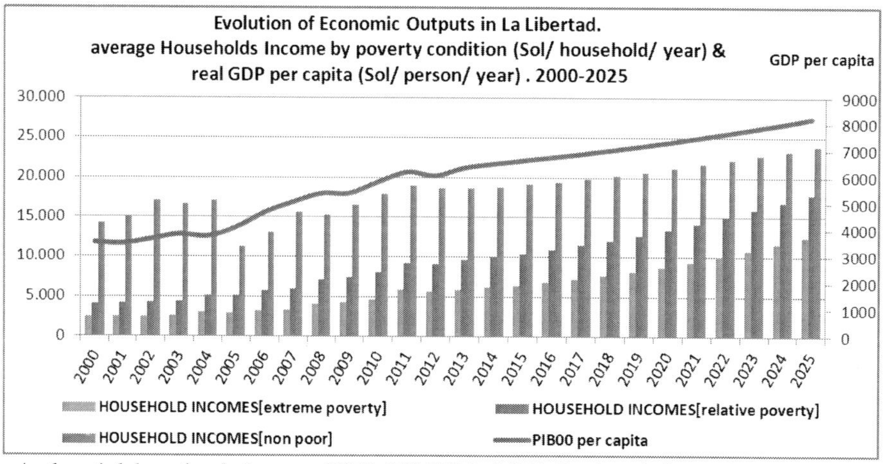

Source: Authors´ elaboration in base on INEI, MINTRA, MEF, Produce information.

Figure 50. Evolution of economic output in La Libertad Region, Peru: Average households income by poverty condition & real GDP per capita (2000-20025).

Total investment in the region, in current terms, passes from 2950M nuevos Soles/ year in 2010 to 6450M nuevos Soles/ year by the year 2025, representing a cumulative increase of 119% in 15 years; the proportion of Foreign Direct Investment (FDI) increases 9 percentage points reaching 26% by the year 2025 and representing more than 2750M nuevos Soles/ year. Meanwhile, private investment passes from 2600M nuevos Soles/ year to close to 6300M nuevos Soles/ year (increase of 142% in 15 years), while public investment decreases by 50% (see figure 51 and 52).

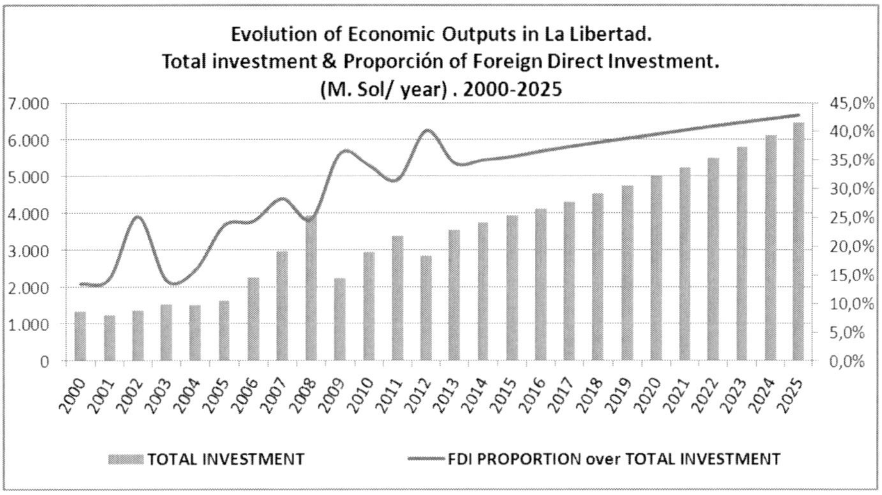

Source: Authors´ elaboration in base on INEI, MINTRA, MEF, Produce information

Figure 51. Evolution of economic outputs in La Libertad Region, Peru: Total investment & Portion of foreign direct investment (2000-2025).

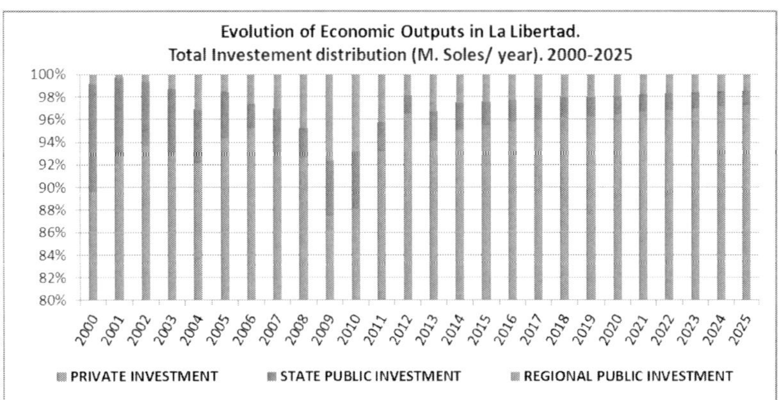

Source: Authors´ elaboration in base on INEI, MINTRA, MEF, Produce information.

Figure 52. Evolution of economic outputs in La Libertad Region, Peru: Total investment distribution (2000-2025).

Disposable income in the region, in current terms, goes from 16700M news Soles/ year in 2010 to close to 37500M by the year 2025, representing a cumulative increase of 124% in 15 years; from the year 2013 private savings increased by 2.8% per annum (see figure 53).

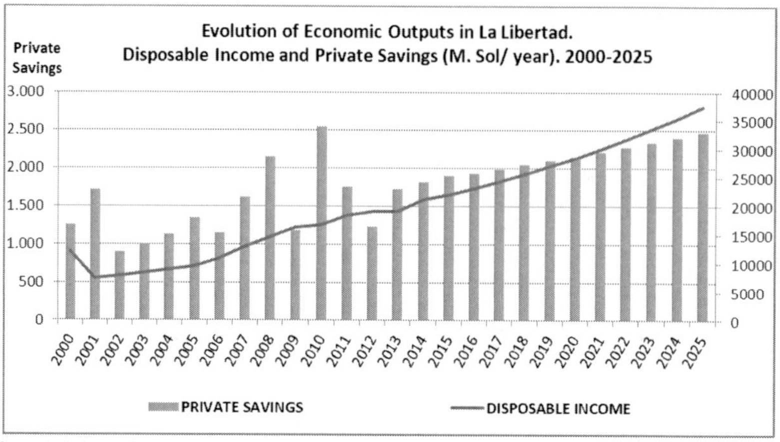

Source: Authors´ elaboration in base on INEI, MINTRA, MEF, Produce information.

Figure 53. Evolution of economic outputs in La Libertad Region, Perú: Disposable income and private savings (2000-2025).

Other Indicators

The forecast of the number of tourists visiting the region take into account what is planned in the baseline scenario (13% annual variation rate); without a doubt, hotels will increase in parallel to the expected demand, reflected in the strong variation of the GVA of the branch of activity of hotels and restaurants. The Governance Index remains above a value of 120, while the Water Quality Index suffers a sharp decline in the year 2007, and returns to grow to a value of 101.7 in the year 2025 (see figure 54).

The difference in HDI values between the baseline scenario and the optimum is 1.2 percentage points in the year 2025, reaching a value close to 0.74 in the optimal scenario; the main reason is the increase in the Knowledge Index, caused by an optimized distribution of public investment. The Standard of Living Index in the optimal scenario is barely increased compared with the Base scenario (see figure 55).

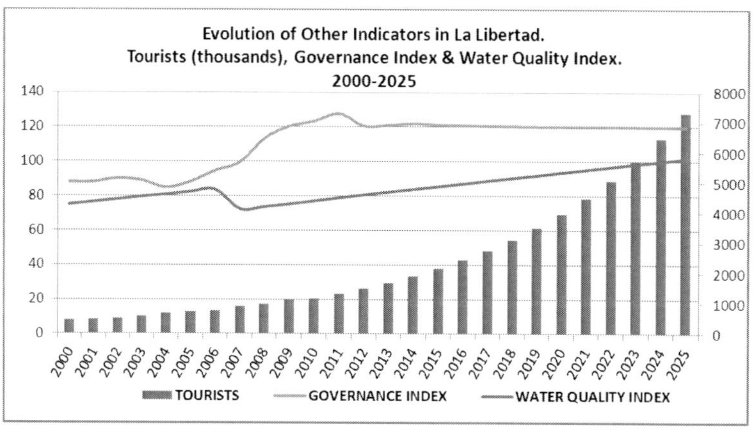

Source: Authors´ elaboration in base on INEI, MINTRA, MEF, Produce information.

Figure 54. Evolution of other indicators in La Libertad Region, Peru: Tourists (thousands), governance index & water quality index (2000-2025).

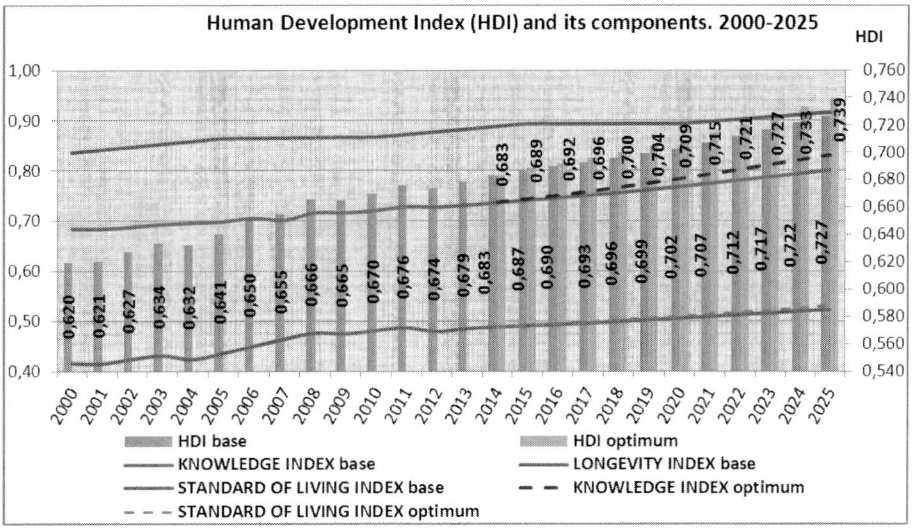

Source: Authors´ elaboration in base on INEI, MINTRA, MEF, Produce information.

Figure 55. Human development index (HDI) and its components (2000-2025).

CONCLUSION

The present paper has shown how important it is to have a dynamic integrated view of issues as the ecological, economic and social ones and how they interplay in between them, affecting the sustainability of La Libertad Región, Peru.

With a model built as the one shown in the present chapter, it is possible to test diverse kind of scenarios which could serve to the Peruvian govermment to learn on how to manage a region like La Libertad Region in search for its sustainable development. In this case, for brevity, only two scenarios are compared, one is the Base Scenario which is compared with the HDI maximization scenario. From this kind of comparisons, state policies can be given with more capacity of reflection and viewing their consequences.

One final reflection is that this analysis can be done at low cost, compared with the traditional way of working in our countries, where strategic decisions are taking without deep analysis of their consequences.

REFERENCES

Fernández-Arias, E., Manuelli, R. et al. (2005) Sources of growth in Latin America: What is missing?. Inter-American Development Bank, Washington.

Meadows, D.H., Meadows, D.L., Randers, J., y Behrens, W. (1972) The Limits to Growth. New York: Universe Books.

Paredes, C. E. (2009) Crecimiento, productividad y eficiencia de la inversión en el Perú. USMP.

PROINVERSIÓN, Inversión Extranjera en el Perú.

Robinson, J. y Tinker, J. (1996) Reconciling ecological, economic and social imperatives: towards an analytical framework. International Development Research Centre.

Seminario, B., Rodríguez, M., et al. (2007) Métodos alternativos para la estimación del PBI potencial 1950-2007. Universidad del Pacífico, Perú.

In: Health, Violence, Environment and Human Development ... ISBN: 978-1-62948-038-1
Editors: A. Cotte Poveda and C. I. Pardo Martínez

Chapter 11

MODELING FOR SUSTAINABLE DEVELOPMENT OF A PERUVIAN RIVER BASIN: A SYSTEM DYNAMICS APPROACH

Ricardo A. Rodríguez-Ulloa*
CENTRUM Católica Business School,
Pontificia Universidad Católica del Perú, Perú

ABSTRACT

The present paper has as an aim to model the sustainable development of a Peruvian river basin. For doing this, a system dynamic approach was used, following its diverse steps as a methodology, in order to develop a robust model that could allow test diverse scenarios of sustainable development for that river basin. The river basin analyzed in this occasion is the one named Chira-Piura, which is located at the North West zone of Peru. Diverse variables intervene in the sustainable development of a river basin however there are some ones which are of main importance as the water management of the river basin, the population evolution, the climate change, the agro industrial and agricultural development, the flora and fauna among the main ones. Aspects like supply, demand, use, quality of water, land use and so on, are important variables that this study covers. The aim of this paper is to see the advantages and disadvantages of using the System Dynamics Approach for understanding and modeling the sustainable development of Chira – Piura river basin, analyzing diverse scenarios, as well as to develop and propose some policies in order to improve its sustainable development.

Keywords: System dynamics methodology, water management, sustainable development, Peruvian river basin

* Email: rrodriguezu@pucp.pe.

1. Introduction

This article shows the application of the System Dynamics Methodology for the study of the sustainable development of the Peruvian basin, the Chira – Piura river basin (Peru). The article begins with a description of Chira-Piura basin, its extension, the kind of mineral resources it has, the flora and fauna existing in it, the hydrographic sources that provide water for the basin, the agriculture activities existing there as well as the tourism activities developed there. All of these issues turn around the main issue of a river basin which is water. Then this paper examines the water supply, water demand and water quality under a system dynamics view and its impact in the sustainability of the Chira – Piura river basin. Then it describes the system dynamics methodology, its phases and its application in the study of the mentioned river basin. Finally, the article gives a reflection on the System Dynamics Methodology, its advantages and disadvantages and conclusions for further research concerning both the river basin study and the system dynamics methodology.

To apply a system dynamics approach for the study of Chira-Piura river basin means a new approach in studying Peruvian river basins with several distinctions which could be worth to be mentioned:

1) First of all the usual kind of study of river basins nowadays around the world are still mainly descriptive, showing qualitative and numeric information of diverse issues existing in a specific river basin as a static description of what is happening there. Examples of this kind of approach can be found in the works as the one done by UNESCO (2009)[1], In Peru, government institutions like the Environment Ministy[2], Agriculture Ministry[3], the Water National Authority (ANA)[4] or SENAMIH[5] provide mainly descriptive and statistical information on the behavior of important issues to be considered in the management of a river basin. However the weakness of all of this approach is the lack of an integrative (systemic or transdisciplinary) view that results of linking the diverse information these organizations provide. This could be obtained, if instead of managing disseminated information that leads to isolated and biased decision making, the information to collect should be defined after a systemic view of a river basin could be obtained. This could leads to define properly the required information needed to be collected for an integrative study of a river basin.
2) The second weakness of this approach is the static view of the situation of a river basin. This static view is usually presented through statistics of the situation or even in forecasts of isolated variables. The lack of an integrative and dynamic view, through the time, of the behavior of strategic variables does not contribute to the understanding of diverse interlinked phenomena that really occurs in a river basin.
3) In that sense, proposing a system dynamics perspective for the study the Chira-Piura river basin means a different view of approaching it. The main contribution of the system dynamics approach in studying the river basin are twofold: a). Apply a systemic view for the study of the river basin linking qualitative and quantitative

[1] Facing the Challenges, Case Studies Volume, UNESCO, 2009, Paris
[2] http://www.minam.gob.pe/
[3] http://www.minag.gob.pe/portal/
[4] http://www.ana.gob.pe/
[5] http://www.senamhi.gob.pe/

variables in a closed loop causal manner. b). The systemic interaction of these closed loop causal diagrams allows the understanding of diverse kind of behaviours that the traditional thinking can not provide. If additionally this analysis is done with the use of the computer to simulate the behavior of key variables along time, then the richness of the analysis and learning about how the real world phenomena behave is greatly improved.

4) Concerning the application of system dynamics to the study of a river basin, it is necessary to mention that although this approach to river basins is relatively new, there have been some researchers around the world that are working in the field. Thus it could be mention the work conducted by Karamouz, Akhabari, Moridi & Kerachian (2006) on conflict resolution in the management of river water quality based on a system dynamics modeling. Another similar study is the one done by Yu, Chen, Lin & Liaw (2003) revels how the system dynamics approach can be a useful tool for planning sustainable development. Another study which shows how system dynamics is used in environmental issues is the one conducted by Stave (2002), in which she proposes using system dynamics to improve public participation in environmental decisions related to air quality problems.

Finally, the reason to do a system dynamics study for the Chira – Piura river basin is because, thought there are some studies around the world using system dynamics for studying the sustainable development of a river basin, there is a lack of these kind of studies en Peru. Concerning this, the idea of this study is to contribute to create a system dynamics theory for the sustainable management of river basins in general and especially the ones located to the Pacific Ocean side.

2. The Chira Piura- River Basin (Peru)

The Chira – Piura river basin, located north-west of Lima (Peru), about 850 km from Lima, is one of the most important watersheds existing in Peru, hence the importance of its study. Table 1 shows some facts about Chira-Piura river basin.

Table 1. General data Basin Chira-Piura (Peru)

Chira Basin (In Purple) - Piura Basin (In Dark Green)
Geography: Located in the dept. Piura
Area: 29852.86 km2
Climate: Coastal Zone: Little rain, high temperatures.
Highland area: Presence of rain.
Flora and Fauna: Coconut, custard, lucuma, lemon, mango, orange, coffee, deer, goats, reptiles, birds, fish
Population: 1981: 1'030, 335 inhabitants; 1993: 1'300, 000 inhabitants; 2007: 1'600, 000 inhabitants

Source: Adapted from the Peruvian National Water Authority (ANA).
Access to internet: http://www.ana.gob.pe:8088/media/9920/exptecnico.pdf.

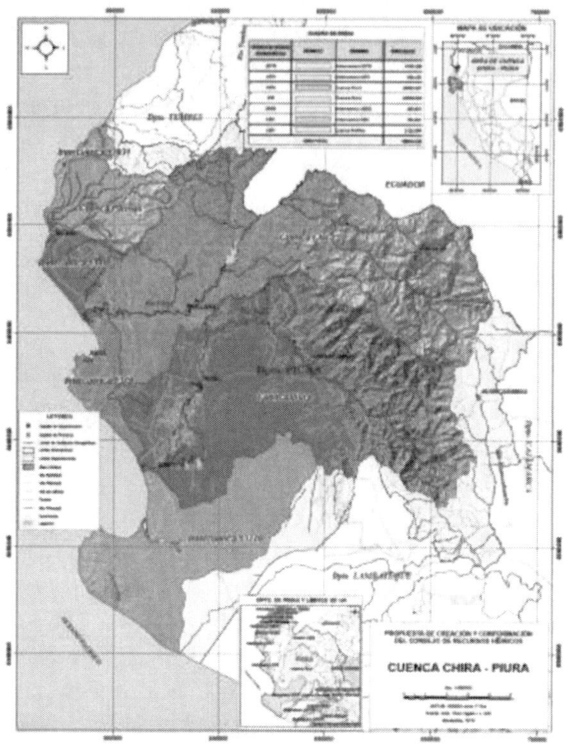

Source: Peruvian National Water Authority (ANA).
Access to internet: http://www.ana.gob.pe:8088/media/9920/exptecnico.pdf

Figure 1. Map of River Basin Chira – Piura (Perú).

3. Application of System Dynamics Methodology

System dynamics (SD) was developed by Prof. Jay W. Forrester (Forrester, 1965) from the Massachusetts Institute of Technology (MIT), USA. The aim of SD is to simulate the possible behaviors (scenarios) of variables of interest for the analyst, conforming them an interrelated system of variables interlinked by closed loop causal relationships.

Applying the system dynamics methodology (see Figure 2) (Richardson and Pugh III, 1981), the existing dynamic problem is defined, showing the reference mode of the mentioned problem and from there the dynamics hypothesis is established, which could attempts to explain the dynamic behavior of the reference mode of the defined dynamic problem.

The dynamic problem is defined as the growth in demand for water by different users of the river basin, in relation to the amount of water supply that the river basin can provide. Then the Dynamic Analysis phase is done, considering the available data that allows confirm or not the behavior considered in the reference mode and the causality explained in the dynamic hypothesis. At this part of the study, the causal diagram is developed to express the dynamic hypothesis of the dynamic problem. Then this causal diagram is converted into a system dynamic model, using the Stella software.

Having done the Dynamic Analysis, a set of scenarios to determine diverse kind of behaviors of relevant variables of the problem is done, and finally some policies concerning the sustainable management of the river basin are tested. Among the policies that arise is to build dams to store the unused water, instead that it goes to sea. Another policy that can be simulated is to improve the rate of water consumption in the production of a metric ton of agricultural products to improve the agricultural management of the river basin.

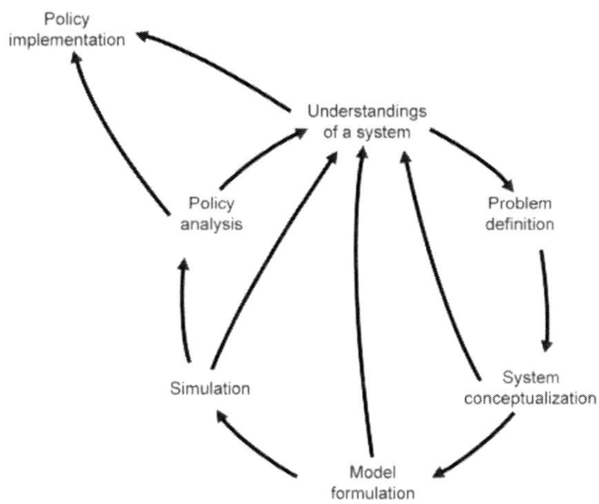

Source: After Richardson and Pugh III, 1981.

Figure 2. System Dynamics Methdology (SDM).

In both policies are seen the impact of agricultural growth over the flora and fauna of the river basin and their levels of attractiveness, because it is what moves tourism activities in the river basin. From all of this, some convenient policies are expressed and recommended to implant in the river basin, at the end of the article. Finally the paper reflects on the advantages and limitations of the system dynamics methodology in the study of the problem of a sustainable river basin management.

3.1. Defining the Dynamic Problem

Figure 3 shows a long view of the "reference mode" till year 2060, showing the dynamic problem. As it can be seen, there is a significant water demand. On the other hand, there will be water supply that will be affected by several factors, being the main, the climate change, which will cause to be overtaken by the demand for water due to diverse factors as: population growth, the increment of tourism activities to the river basin, the growth of the agricultural industry and agriculture activities and the negative impact of the increase in the previous factors in the flora and fauna of the river basin, as well.

3.2. Dynamic Approach Assumptions

The dynamic hypothesis defined in this study is expressed in Figure 3, where the demand for water will exceed water supply. This demand for water will increase, due mainly to the increase in agriculture, agribusiness and tourism in the to Chira Piura river basin. The central question is: *"Is it possible a sustainable development of the Chira – Piura river basin, given the conditions of growth and development that has been generated in this area?"*

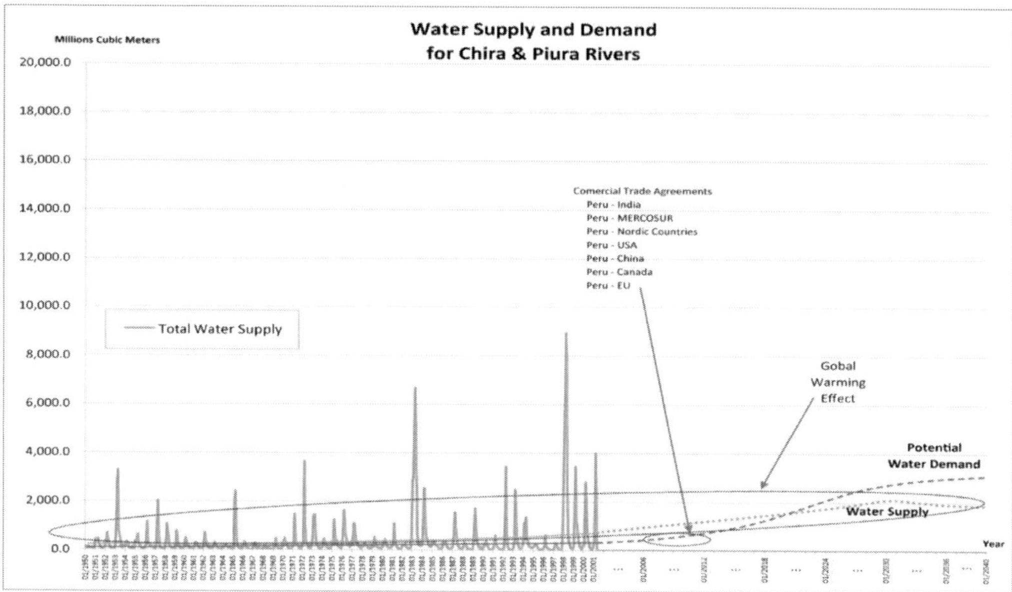

Source: Author´s elaboration in base of information provided by the Peruvian National Water Authority (ANA).

Figure 3. The Dynamic Problem: Water Demand greater than Water Supply in a long view of the Chira-Piura River Basin.

3.3. Dynamic Analysis

The Dynamic Model considered in Figure 4, covers the diverse aspects of the dynamic problem. It is shown below, as a Causal Diagram. For a better understanding of the overall causal diagram, what follows shows the sequence of modules compounding the overall causal diagram (see figure 4).

It can be seen in Figure 5, the population dynamics of the people living in the Chira-Piura river basin. It is very important to visualize its growth, because it will demand for more water in the future.

Figure 6 shows that if the population growth, the anti-ecological practices of the population will increase. These anti-ecological practices will affect the wildlife stock (flora and fauna) and therefore will have an impact on the attractiveness of the river basin, since it is based on the stock of flora and fauna.

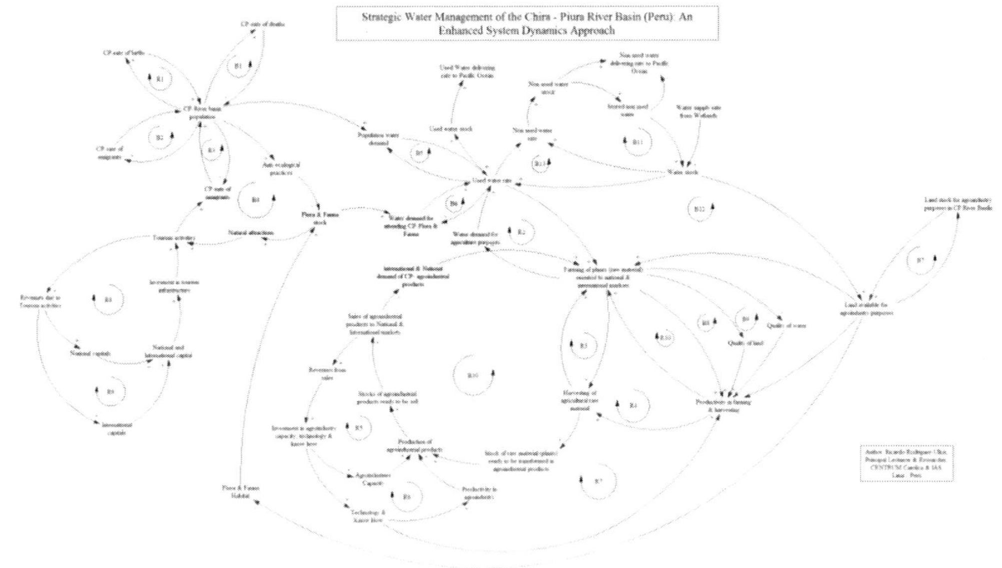

Source: Author´s elaboration.

Figure 4. Overview of the Causal Diagram about the Dynamic Problem of the Chira – Piura river basin, Peru.

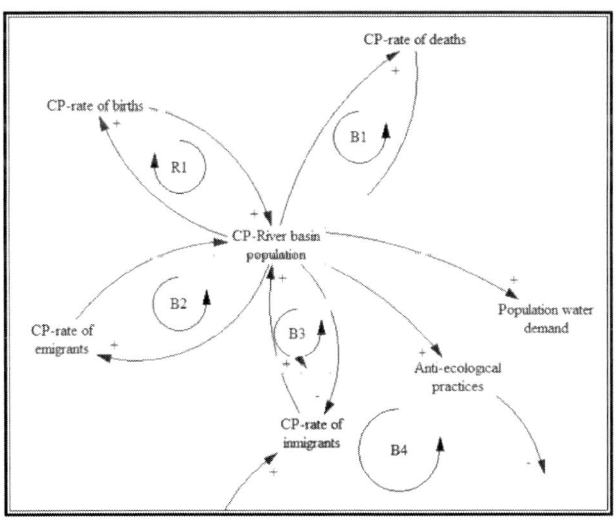

Source: Author´s elaboration.

Figure 5. Population Dynamics in the Chira-Piura river basin, Peru.

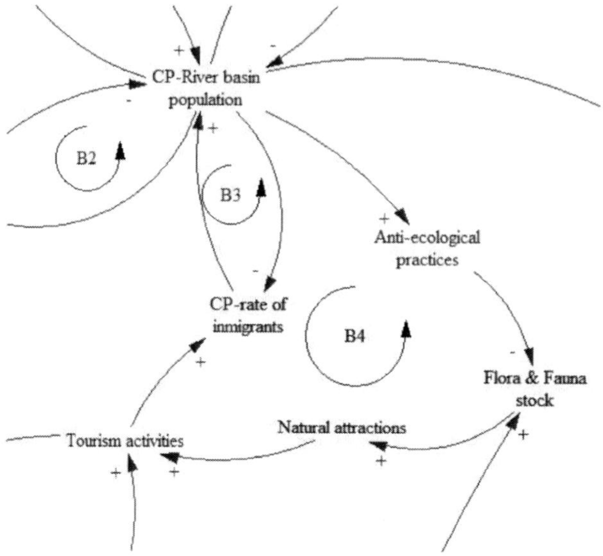

Source: Author´s elaboration.

Figure 6. Dynamics of the population´s growth impact in the flora and fauna of the Chira-Piura river basin and its consequences in the tourism attractiveness of the river basin.

Figure 7 shows the stock of water that will be used by the various stakeholders in the Chira-Piura river basin.

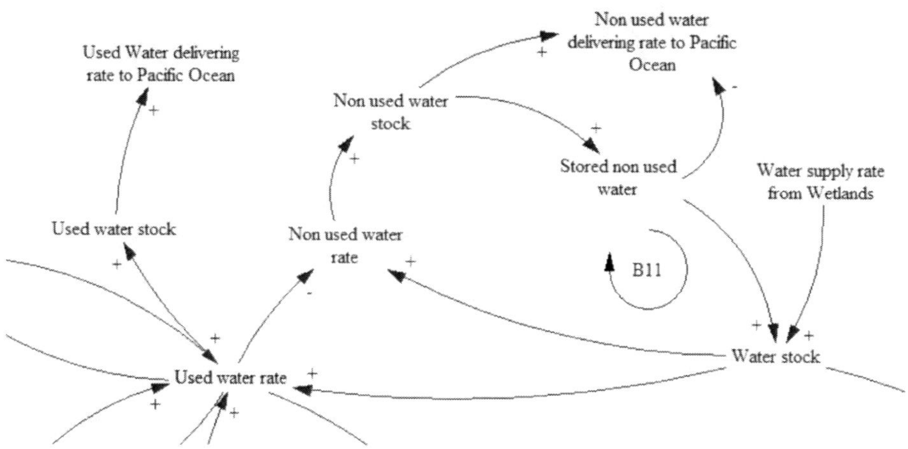

Source: Author´s elaboration.

Figure 7. Stock of Water for the use of different stakeholders of the Chira-Piura river basin, Peru.

Figure 8 shows the flows of water that diverse stakeholders are using, which in this preliminary model are considered that are basically: the population of the river basin, the agriculture and agro-industry activities as well as the wildlife (flora and fauna). In a more detailed model to be developed in the future, it will be taken into account the use of water by the industry in general, mining and services activities in general, more than only tourism.

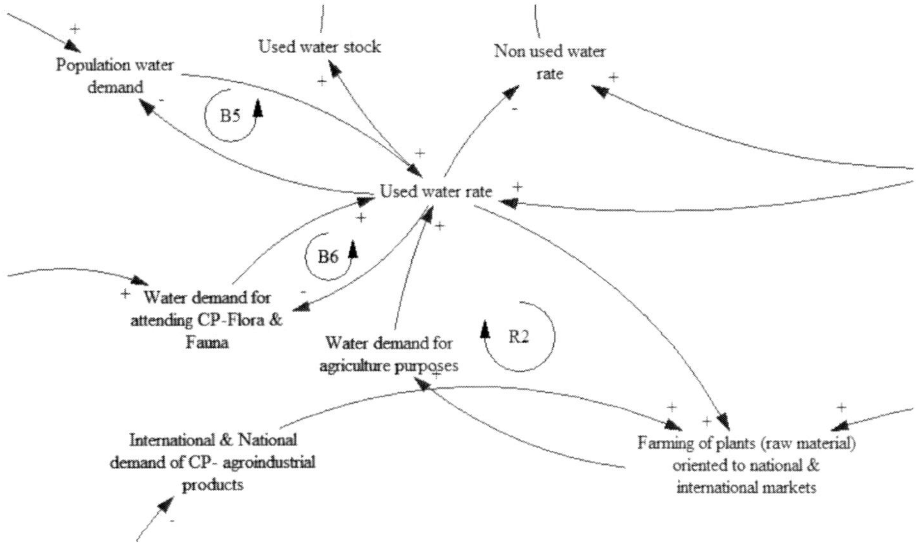

Source: Author´s elaboration.

Figure 8. Flow Basin Water use according to the needs of users.

One thing to be considered of great importance in the study of the demand of water is the consideration assigned to the agriculture activities that is developed in the river basin, considering that this sector is the largest consumer of water.

Figure 9 shows the diverse closed loops generated by the agricultural activities being done in the Chira-Piura river basin. Factors such as water quality, soil quality, land availability for cultivation, contrasted with the amounts of farming is performed in the basin, for determining the productivity of agriculture and also crop volumes along time. These harvest volumes serve as raw material to develop agro-industrial activities (see Figure 9).

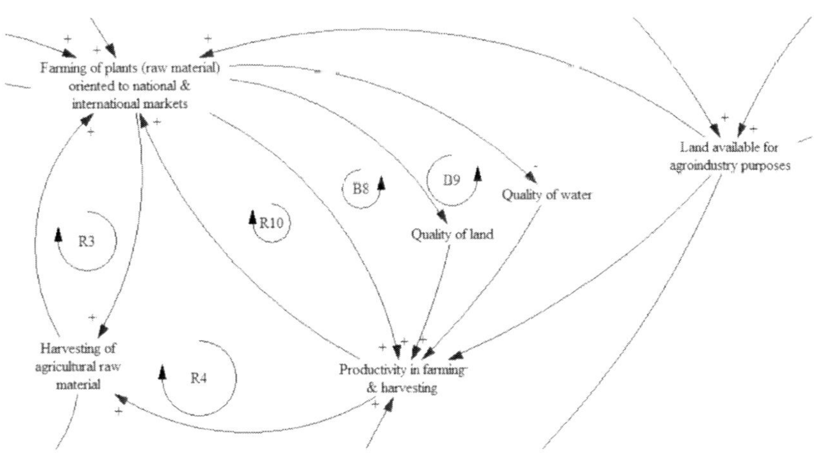

Source: Author´s elaboration.

Figure 9. Causal Diagram showing the dynamics of water consuming by the agriculture sector in Chira – Piura river basin.

Figure 10 shows the causal diagram indicating how the production process from the raw material (eg crops) become agro industrial products ready to be placed in national and international markets.

Figure 11 shows the causal diagram of the revenues generated by sales of main products and from there, the necessary investments in production capacity, technology and know-how.

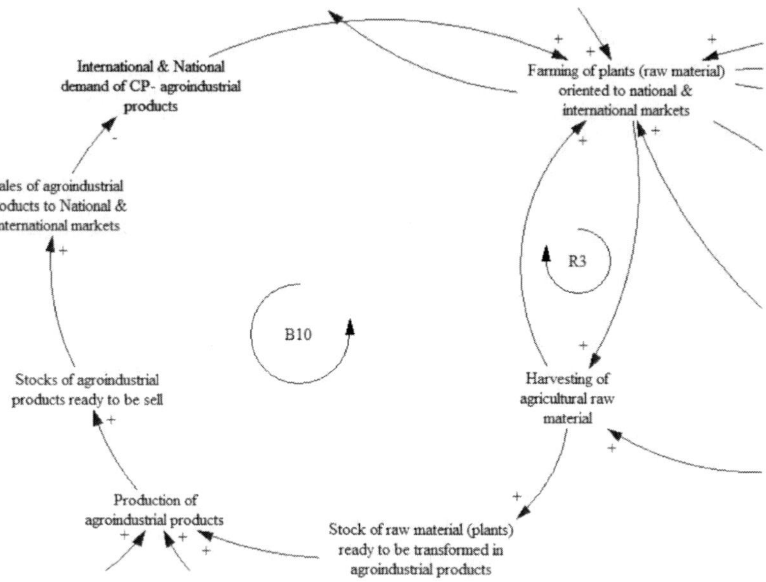

Source: Author´s elaboration.

Figure 10. Relationship between harvest volume, stock of agro - industrial products and sales in domestic and international markets.

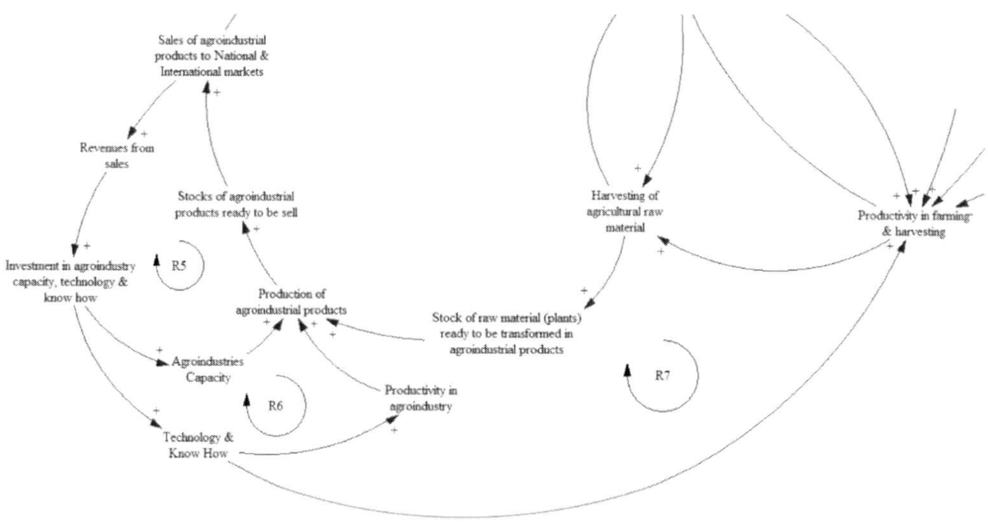

Source: Author´s elaboration.

Figure 11. Revenue generated from sales of products and Investment Agroindustrial Production Capacity, Technology and Know-how.

Figure 12 shows the impact of investments in tourism in the Chira Piura river basin, which will impact on the development and growth of the population.

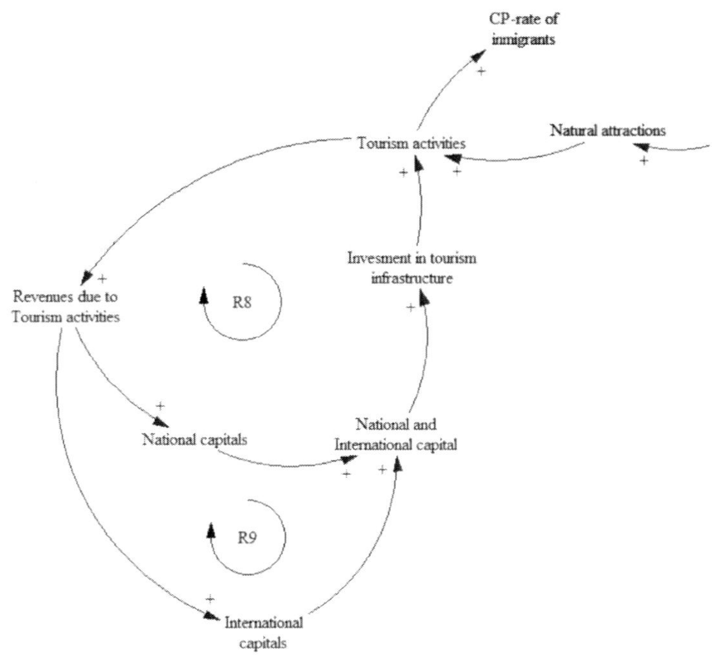

Source: Author´s elaboration.

Figure 12. Impact of investment in tourism in the Chira-Piura river basin.

From causal diagrams shown in the previous figures, it was possible to build a Forrester model and simulate in the computer to test the behavior along time of various variables to observe the state of development of the problematic variables and think from there on possible policies to adopt in the future. This led to the development of a system dynamics model developed with Stella, with which it was possible to begin to understand the different behaviors of the study variables.

A serious difficulty encountered at this stage of the application of the System Dynamics Methodology was the data needed to simulate the diverse variables. For example a variable extremely important for the evaluation of sustainable development of the river basin is the right valuation of the flora and fauna existing therein. Unfortunately there is not much theoretical and practical work on the subject and therefore it was necessary to work with estimated percentages and in a globally manner.

Another variable has been difficult to obtain is the projected demand for agro industrial products, with a long-term perspective (2060), and this has been this way, because still now, Peruvian state entities, responsible for managing the development of agro- industry, do not have the analytical tools to perform long-term planning of the production supply, in this case, of the Chira-Piura river basin.

This issue is not as easy as it would be needed to have models on global market´s demand for agribusiness products from this geographic zone in order to feed with this information to the system dynamics model, and on this basis, estimated the amount of water demanded yearly till 2060 year.

Another variable highly unpredictable is climate change, which has an effect on rainfall along the territory of the iver basin, and in the case of the Chira-Piura basin, it has a significant impact due to the fact that this river basin is located at the north west of the country, zone which is usually affected by the El Niño sea water current phenomenon characterized by its warm water.

As part of the analysis phase, it was developed the system dynamics model in the computer, based on previously reported causal diagrams. Thus in this stage of the System Dynamics Methodology some modules of the System Dynamics computer model developed using Stella are shown, in order to visualize both the problems and possible courses of action in the future, from the study of scenarios and related policy approaches that could be taken looking for sustainable growth and development of the river basin. Thus, we show an overview of the population module of the river basin, as an overview (see figure 13).

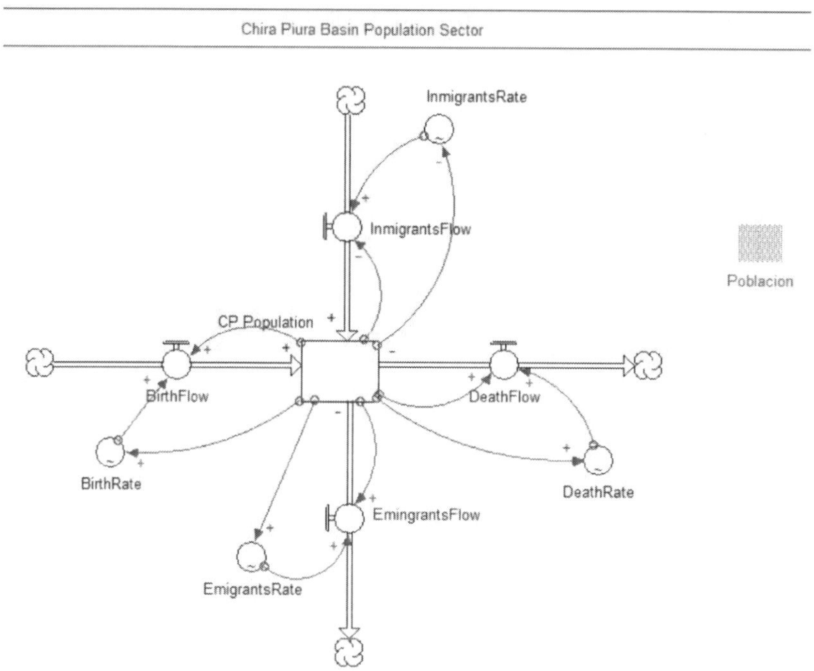

Source: Author´s elaboration.

Figure 13. System Dynamics Model Population Basin.

Also it was modeled the system dynamics attractiveness module of the flora and fauna of the river basin, as shown in the figure 14.

Also it is shown in Figure 15, the DS module for agriculture, agroindusrty as well as marketing in domestic and foreign markets for the products offered by the basin.

As shown in Figure 15, the chain of agricultural crop is affected by water quality and land productivity affect agricultural production, and anything that happens in the agriculture sector will affect the agro industrial production to accomplish the national and international demand of agriculture and agro industrial products.

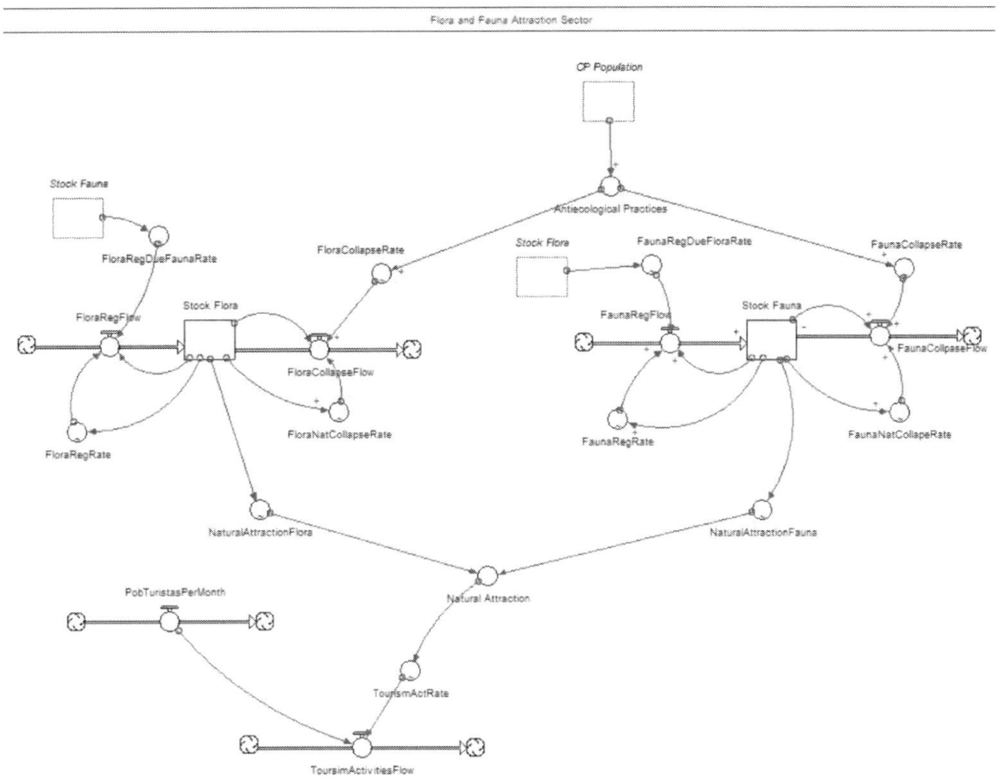

Source: Author´s elaboration.

Figure 14. Module of the system dynamics attractiveness module of the flora and fauna of the Chira-Piura river basin.

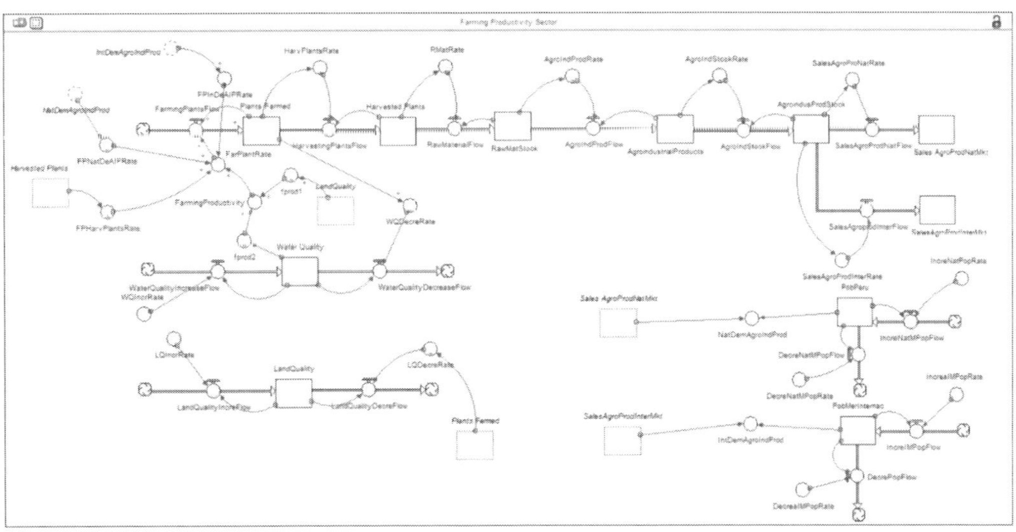

Source: Author´s ellaboration

Figure 15. Module Agricultural and Agroindustrial Production Basin.

Also this module shows sales generated by the action of the marketing activities of agricultural and agro industry products in domestic and international markets and, estimating the monthly demand of them in domestic and foreign markets, having on this a long view till 2060. The SD model is being developed in their other modules, being needed to validate the information used by them in order to have a right calibrated model.

5. Design Policy

The development of System Dynamics Methodology (SDM) has allowed to run the model and to find many scenarios that are likely to occur, according to existing situations. So if you look at the population module, for example, you can see the behavior of the population dynamics of the river basin (see figure 16).

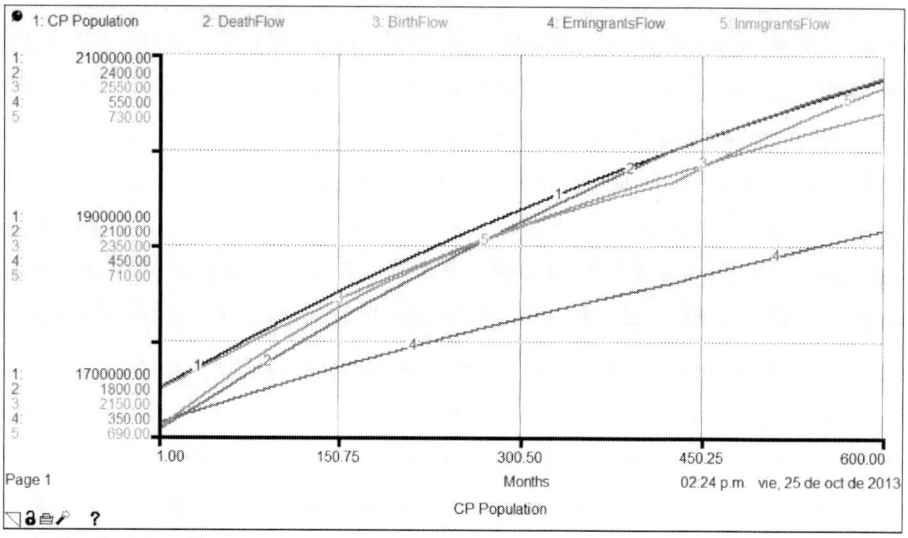

Source: Author´s elaboration.

Figure 16. Behavior of population dynamics in the Chira-Piura river basin, towards year 2060.

As a further aspect, one can see in Figure 15, than while the human population is increasing throughout the time, this will affect the flora and fauna of the river basin, as it will be seen in the following figures. A major government policy could be to stabilize population growth, and even lower it, aspect that is directly related to the need for a coherent strategic national development plan.

Figure 17 shows how the growing flow rates of flora and fauna are depleted, basically because anti-ecological practices done by the population of Chira-Piura river basin, if they were no trained in the practice of ecological attitude in their relationship with the flora y fauna of the river basin.

To prevent this occurring, an important policy which will be needed to implement would be to develop a process of ecological education for the population of the Chira-Piura basin. This is corroborated by the graph of Figure 18 that shows how the increase in population will increase anti-ecological practices making them to increase the flow rate of the collapse of the flora and fauna of the river basin (monthly) in a horizon to year 2060.

Figure 19 also shows how with the growth of a not educated population in environmental issues (likely scenario) impacts negatively on wildlife (flora and fauna) stocks seriously endangering their existence in a relatively short term.

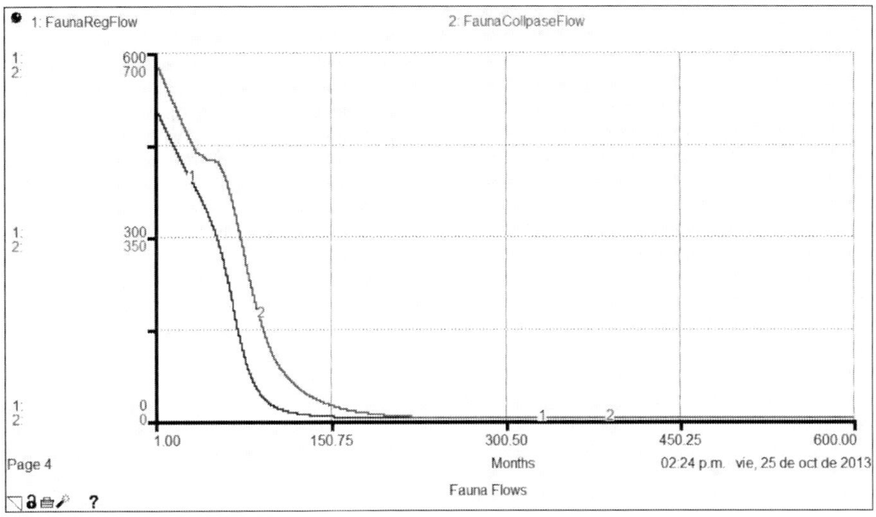

Source: Author´s elaboration.

Figure 17. Behavior of flora and fauna under a current conditions scenario projected to 2060 year.

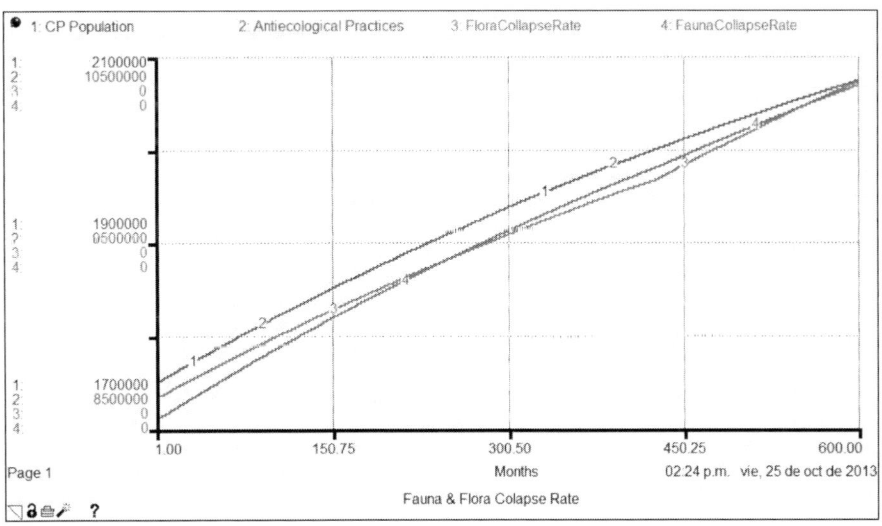

Source: Author´s elaboration.

Figure 18. Probable scenario of population dynamics, the growing of anti-ecological practices and the growth of collapse flow rate of the flora and fauna of the river basin (monthly) towards year 2060.

On the other hand, having exhausted the flora and fauna (likely scenario), with the increase of a non-educated population in ecological issues, it can be seen as well how the lack of flora and fauna stocks will impact in the level of attractiveness of the river basin, for tourism purposes (see Figure 20).

A policy necessary to prevent this happens to the flora and fauna and likewise, is to plan the developing of an ecological education for the Chira – Piura river basin population, and likewise, the tourists who visit the river basin meet a set of standards, practices and policies established to protect it.This should be extended to agriculture, agro-industry and tourism activities in general, because only doing this it can be possible to preserve the flora and fauna of the basin.

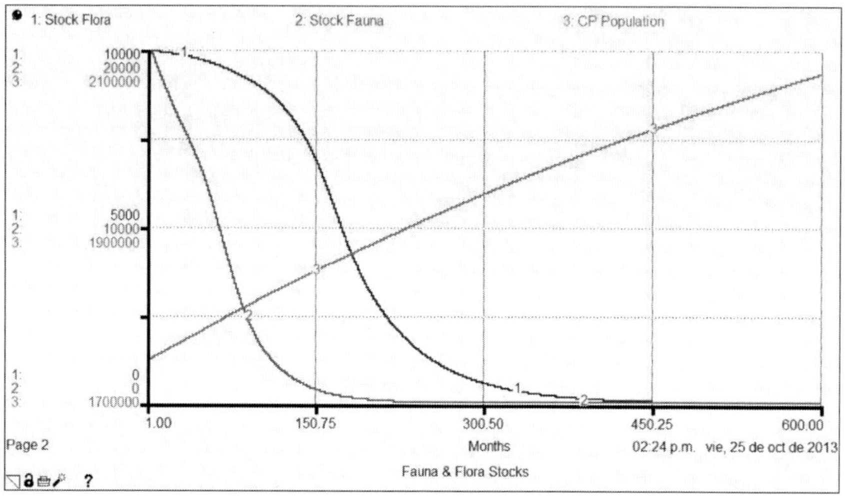

Source: Author´s elaboration.

Figure 19. Probable scenario of flora´s, fauna´s and human´s stocks and population behavior in Chira-Piura river basin.

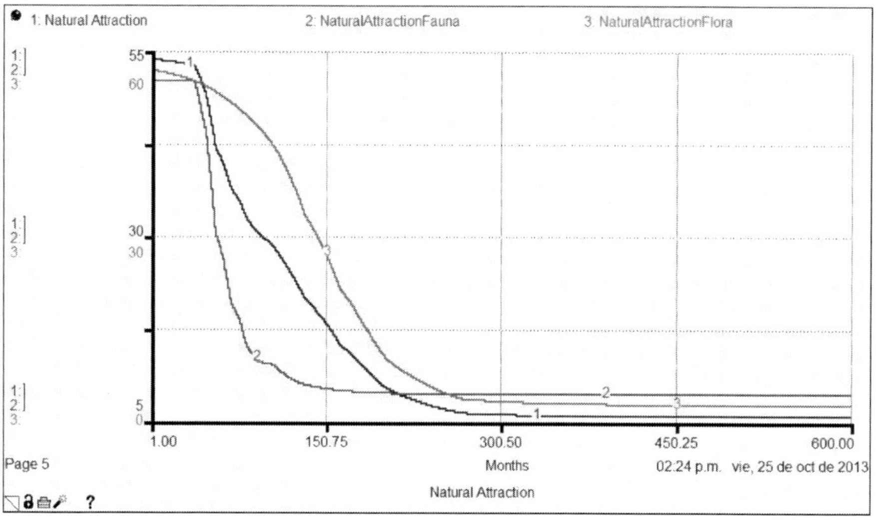

Source: Author´s elaboration.

Figure 20. Probable scenario for 2060: Impact in the attractiveness of the river basin due to flora and fauna serious deterioration.

In Figure 21 you can see the evolution of agriculture (likely scenario). It shows the crop flow of the basin, depending on the demand for domestic and foreign markets. It is also considered the quality of water and land, which depend on the level of use of land and the levels of quality of use of water sources.

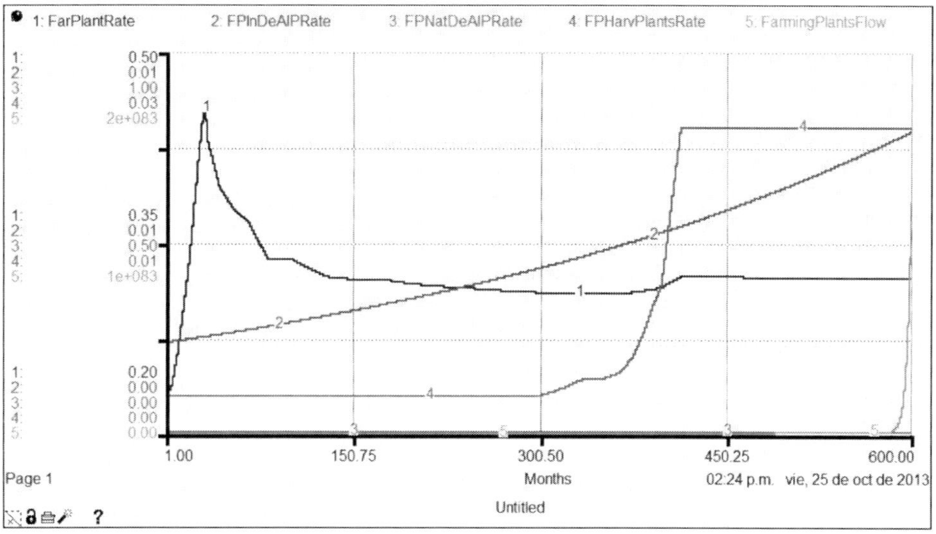

Figure 21. Probable scenario of the behavior of agricultural crop and agro industry production towards year 2060.

From the study of the likely scenarios and having properly calibrated the model, it is possible to design policies for strategic management of the river basin, for which the model presented here can serve as a decision making instrument to determine which are the variables needed to work, to improve the sustainable management of the river basin.

For the sake of brevity, we do not indicate more information examined in the basin, which have to do with strategic water management and tourism, considering the impact of three scenarios of the impact of the phenomenon of climate change (i.e pessimistic, likely, optimistic).

It is also important to mention that having considered diverse policies to be adopted, considering the scenarios that arise due to climate change (pessimistic, likely, optimistic), it is necessary to do an evaluation of these policies, usually following the cost-benefit criterion. The benefit may even be qualitative.

Evaluated these policies, the next stage of the System Dynamics methodology needs to be done, which is explained in the following pages (policy implementation). The policies recommended by this study are:

- Educate the public and employers on an ecological culture.
- Manage the agriculture sector in a sustainable manner in order to manage the quantity and quality of water adequately taking into account that agriculture is the largest user and consume of water in the river basin.

- Preserve the flora and fauna of the river basin, in order to not lose its attractiveness, because it would affect tourism activities as well as the proper future of the population living in the Chira – Piura river basin
- Control the growth of the population of the basin in order to maintain an ecological balance. This should include appropriate coordination with the strategic plan of Piura Region and the national strategic plan in charge of the Peruvian National Center for Strategic Planning (CEPLAN).
- Manage the supply and demand of water properly, storing water in reservoirs, in order to have water supply in drought periods, which can greatly improve the yield of agriculture and agribusiness of the river basin.
- Establish clear marketing plans of agricultural products produced in the river basin, from the estimation of the national and international demands for these products. This will serve to make an appropriate plan to manage water supply and quality of it in order to alleviate the demand for it, in terms of agricultural production to meet the demand of agricultural products nationally and internationally. The same can be said for other sectors, as mining, tourism as well as the water services to be provided to the human population living in the river basin as well as the flora and fauna conservation along the time till 2060.

6. Policy Implementation

Done the study of possible policies to be implemented in the real world, its implementation must be required, for which this will entail project management for policies implementation.

Entering into this issue involves project management and for doing this following guidelines of the Project Management Institute (PMI) would be recommended in order to carry out the policies proposed in the previous section.

Finally, for the management of the river basin and in order that environment policy solutions can be simulated previously to the decisions for its implementation, a Simulated Learning Environment (SLE) was developed, The SLE is described below. Thus, Figure 22 shows the main menu to enter to the SLE.

The main menu of the SLE for sustainable strategic management of the Basin Chira - Piura (Peru) shows a number of options to manage and navigate within this dynamic learning environment. Figure 23 shows the water supply (in iron) provided by the Chira river and its use (in clear blue). As shown, there is a large non used water amount.

Figure 24 shows the water supply (in iron) of Piura river and its use (in clear blue). Also this figure shows that the supply of water is not efficiently used by users.

Figure 25 shows overall supply and water use in the Chira – Piura river basin, which as it can be seen, it involves a significant amount of water that is not used and much of it goes to the Pacific Ocean without being used.

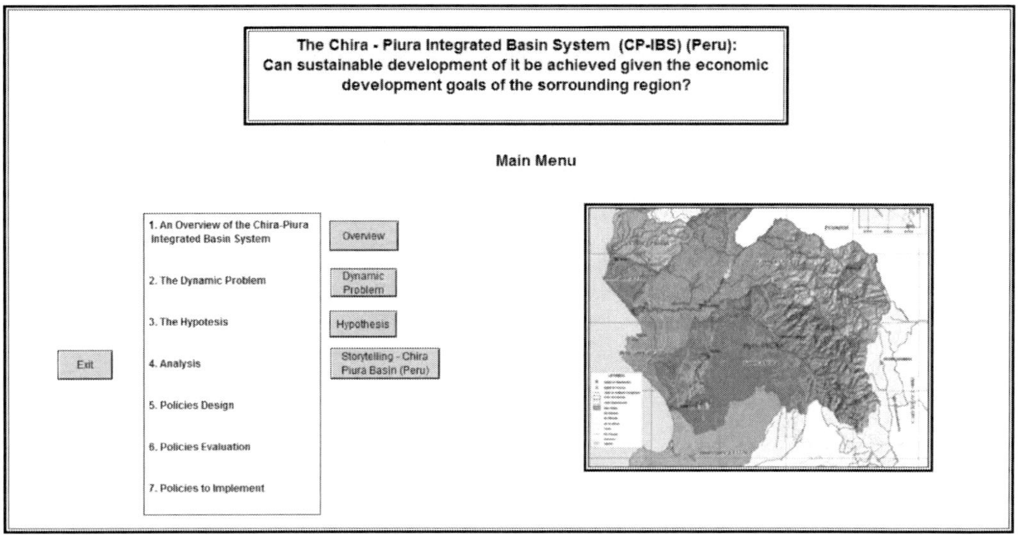

Source: Author´s elaboration.

Figure 22. Initial Screen of the SLE for learning the dynamic sustainable management of the Chira-Piura River Basin, Peru.

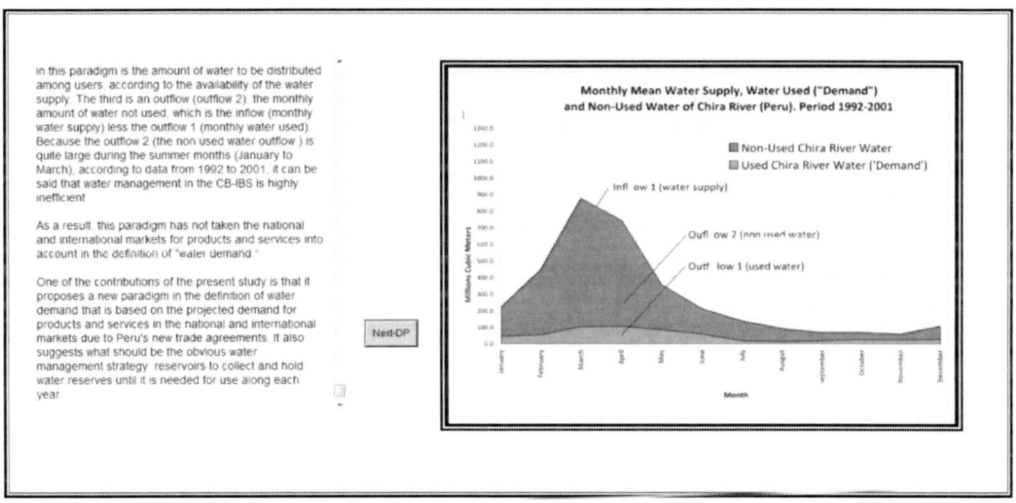

Source: Author´s elaboration based on information provided by the Peruvian National Water Authority (ANA).

Figure 23. Supply and Chira River water use.

The idea is to establish and simulate government policies to implement investments in building reservories to store water, allowing to change the patterns of water use throughout the year in a steady manner over a determined amount of water supply rather than focusing, as now, in the early months of each year (January-March), decreasing water supply significantly in the following months.

Figure 26 shows, as an example the problem of water management in the basin, in order to show the users of the SLE, which is the dynamic problem.

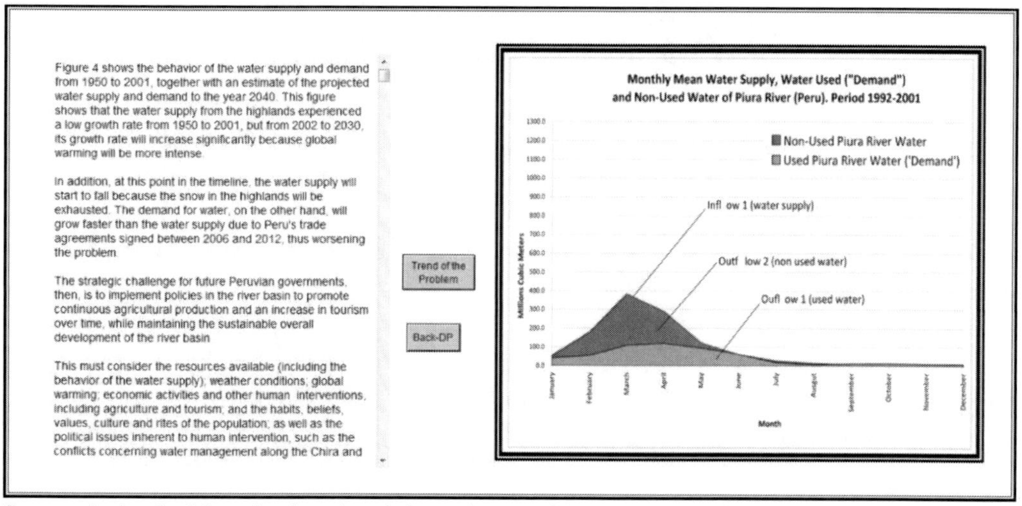

Source: Author´s elaboration based on information provided by the Peruvian National Water Authority (ANA).

Figure 24. Dynamics of Piura river water supply and its use.

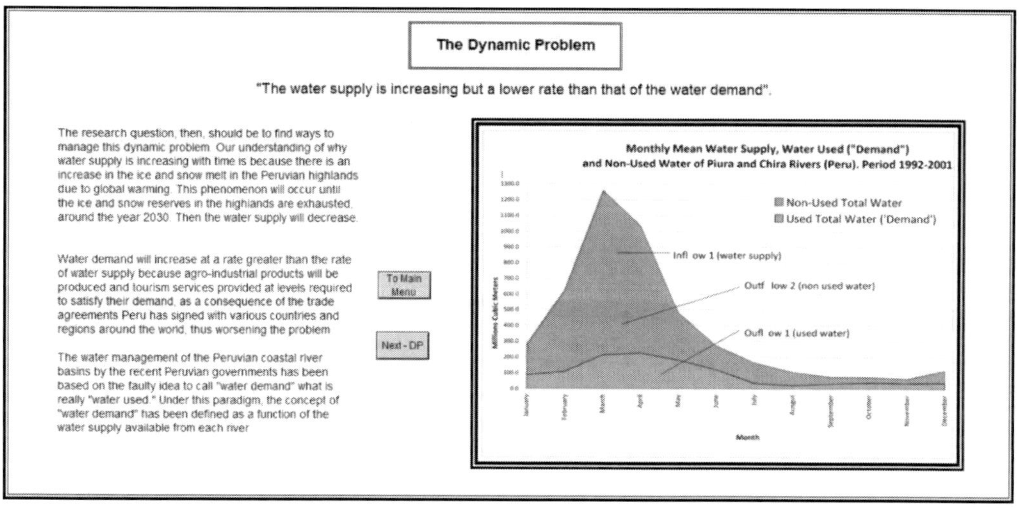

Source: Author´s elaboration based on the information provided by the Peruvian National Water Authority (ANA).

Figure 25. Total monthly average of water supply and use of Chira-Piura river basin (Peru).

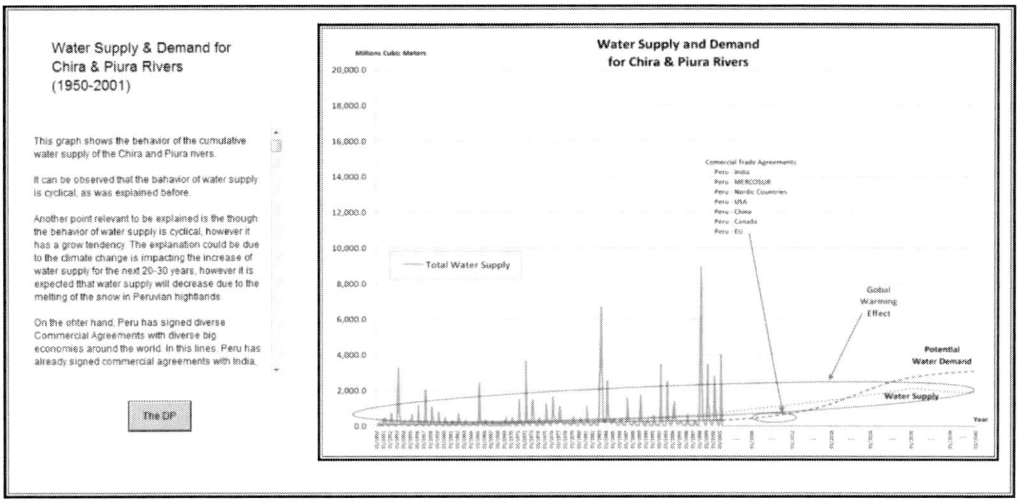

Source: Author´s elaboration based on the information provided by the Peruvian National Water Authority (ANA).

Figure 26. Trend of Water Supply and Demand Basin Chira-Piura (1950-2050).

Figure 27 shows the whole causal diagram that allows an integrated system dynamics management of the Chira – Piura river basin.

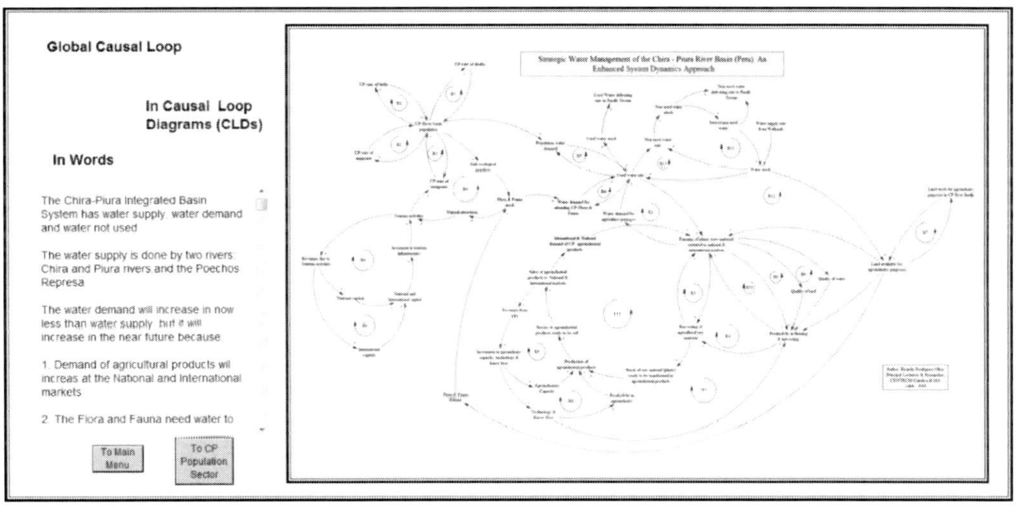

Source: Author´s elaboration.

Figure 27. Integral causal diagram for the system dynamics sustainable management model of the Chira Piura river basin.

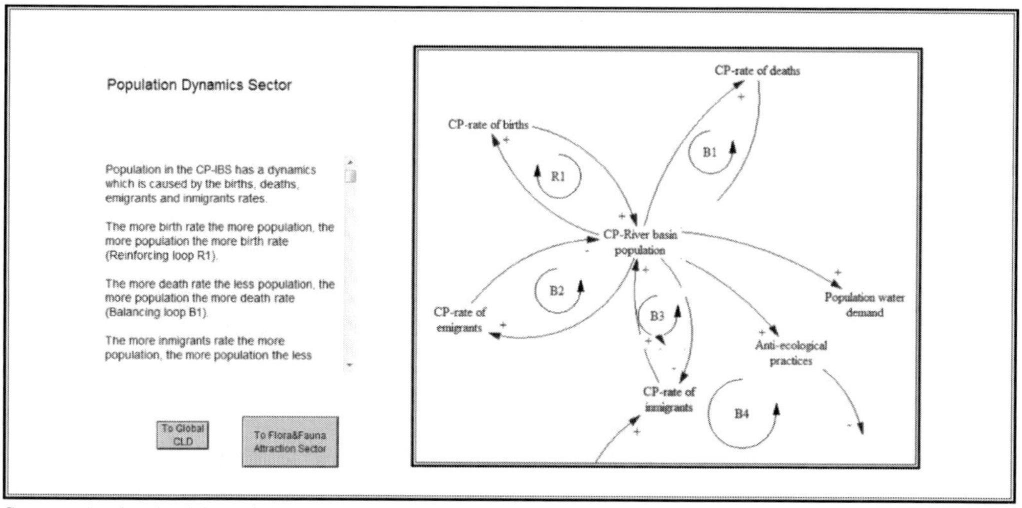

Source: Author´s elaboration.

Figure 28. Module of the population dynamics in the basin.

Figure 28 shows in detail the dynamics of the population of the river basin. Operating the SLE is possible to access to the graphics displayed in the previous figures 21 to 27.

7. Reflections on the System Dynamics Methodology

The development of System Dynamics Methodology (SDM) allowed us to see what are the advantages and disadvantages of using it in the study of sustainable development of the river basin.

7.1. Advantages

a) The SDM is a methodology to see dynamically over time the behavior of various strategic variables of the problem under study.
b) The system dynamics vision gives a global view of the impact of diverse variables over time and how they are related causally.
c) It also allows to simulate scenarios of the river basin development and see the consequences of that scenarios. In this case, three kinds of scenarios: pessimistic, probable and optimistic scenarios were planned to consider.
d) It allows to test and establish policies and strategies for improving the situation under study after doing diverse simulations considering different conditions.
e) It is not expensive compared with the option to try to implant those policies in the real world with consequent social, political and economic costs as usually occurs in the management of state issues of Latin American social realities.
f) System dynamics is one of the most powerful methodologies to analyze complex situations that human beings face. Its approach allows, with the support of computer simulations, to understand the dynamics through the time of the behavior of diverse

variables in the real situation, that without this way of approach it could be impossible for human beings to devise the consequences of interlinked closed loop relationships of variables conforming the situation being under study.

7.2. Disadvantages

a) Traditional SDM does not consider the diverse worldviews of the existing stakeholders in a complex situation such as the sustainable management of a river basin. However it is important to mention that an area of work within SD tradition is what is known as Group Model Building (GMB) (Vennix, 1999), where there exists a general tested framework in order to construct consensual system dynamics models.
b) Does not consider those soft kind of variables that usually exist in complex situations as the management of water in a river basin (i.e. power and interest of diverse stakeholders, conflicts among stakeholders, alliances among interest groups, cultural beliefs, rituals, habits, ways of being of people, customs practiced by people, among them.
c) Assumes that the expert SD modeler´s perception of the problem or that of the client for whom the model is being done are the ones most important in the process of constructing the system dynamics model of the problem situation, however other systems thinking approaches (Checkland, 1981, Wilson, 2000, Rosenhead and Mingesr, 2001), claim to consider more than one or two view points when analyzing a problematic situation and aspire to get viable solutions for the stakeholders intervening in it..
d) Define just one problem, as the central problem to be analyzed, leaving other ones as secondary issues to be considered around the one considered as the main problem. In this case, the problem of water supply and demand in the river basin is considered the main problem and all issues and themes on the analysis of the river basin go around this, when, in reality, the real world contains a network of interconnected problematic issues which conforms complex messes of issues conforming what are called wicked problems (Conklin, 2005) and which are detected only if we look at the situation, since diverse worldviews. This kind of interconnected issues conforms what is known as "problematic situation" (Checkland, 1981; Checkland and Scholes, 1990; Checkland and Holwell, 1998; Checkland and Poulter, 2006).
e) The fact of not considering the worldviews of diverse stakeholders creates the problem of not knowing whether the policy proposals to be implemented in the real world are systemically desirable and culturally feasible.

CONCLUSION

Some conclusions can be mentioned concerning the present issue. These conclusions can be from the point of view of issues concerning the Chira-Piura river basin as well as from the point of view of the Systems Dynamics Methodology (SDM).

Concerning the Chira-Piura river basin, it is clear that a more detailed and accurate information is needed in order to obtain a more reliable system dynamics model. The important point which comes as an outcome of the present study, is that it has been detected which is the information needed in order to understand the complexity encountered in this river basin.

An additional point that arises from the study, concerning the Chira-Piura river basin, is that not only there exists important quantitative information that needs to be feed up into the model, but there also exists important qualitative variables which need to be taken into account in order to consider strategic issues concerning the sustainable management of the river basin. Among these issues are: the divers points of view of stakeholders living and concerned with the Chira-Piura river basin. This issue is also correlated with another soft issue which is the power, in its diverse facets, that is being exerted by stakeholders, in order to implant their interests and worldviews over the other ones in the river basin. In that sense is very important to study the conflicting views and alliances among stakeholders that exists in the river basin.

Another topic which is very important to consider, is that there are silent stakeholders which have to do with the future of the river basin and which their "worldviews" should be taken into account. They are the natural resources as water, the flora and fauna, speaking in a general manner. Further research is aiming to consider those issues in search for the sustainable development of this river basin.

Concerning the SDM, it has proven that is a powerful instrument to analyse through time the behaviour of strategic variables of interest for the analysts and potential interested people like clients or other stakeholders.

However the study is telling us that for an adequate use of SD, it is needed a more accurate information which can leads to build good calibrated models. However, as a learning point, it can be said that this study conducted a more deep understanding of the interlinked relationships existing between soft and hard variables in this complex portion of the real world.

An additional and final reflection concerning the present study is that further research could be needed in the side of SDM in order to combine it with other systemic approaches, methodologies and philosophies, in order to consider not only a system dynamics problem but a set of system dynamics problems that conforms a interlinked problematic situation which needs to be study dynamically and with the precision of the system dynamics approach along time.

REFERENCES

Conklin, J.; 2005: Dialogue Mapping: Building shared understanding of wicked problems, John Wiley & Sons, Chichester.

Checkland, P., B., 1981: Systems Thinking, Systems Practice, John Wiley & Sons, Chichester

Checkland P., B. and Scholes, J., 1990: Soft Systems Methodology in Action, John Wiley & Sons, Chichester

Chekcland, P., B. and Holwell., S., 1998: Information, Systems and Information Systems: Making Sense of the field, John Wiley & Sons, Chichester.

Checkland, P., B. and Poulter., J., 2006: Learning for Action: A short definitive account of Soft Systems Methodology and its use for Practitioners, Teachers and Students, John Wiley & Sons, Chichester.

Forrester, J. W., 1965: Industrial Dynamics, The MIT Press, Cambridge.

Karamouz, M.; Akhbari, M.; Moridi, A.; Kerachian, R.; 2006. A system dynamics based conflict resolution model for river water quality management, *Iranian Journal of Environmental Health Science Engineering*, Vol. 3, No. 3. pp. 147-160.

Morecrof, J., 2007: Strategic Modelling and Business Dynamics, John Wiley & Sons, Chichester.

Richardson R, Pugh L III (1981) Introduction to system dynamics modeling with dynamo. MIT Press, Cambridge.

Rosenhead, J. and Mingers, J.; 2001: Rational Analysis for a Problematic World, Problem Structuring Methods for Complexity, Uncertainty and Conflict, John Wiley & Sons, Chichester.

Stave, K.A.; 2002. Using system dynamics to improve public participation in environmental decisions, *System Dynamics Review*, Vol. 18, No. 2.

Sterman, J., 2000: Business Dynamics, Prentice Hall.

Vennix, J.; 1999. Group Model Building: Facilitating Team Learning using System Dynamics, John Wiley and Sons, Chichester.

Wilson, B.; 2000. Soft Systems Methodology, John Wiley & Sons, Chichester.

Yu, C.H.; Lin C.F.; Liaw, S.L.; 2003. Development of a system dynamics model for sustainable land use management, *Journal fo the Chinese Institute of Engineers*, Vol. 26, No. 5, pp. 607-618.

INDEX

#

A

B

D

E

F

G

H

I

J

K

N

O

P

Q

R

S

T

U

V

W

X

Y

Z